CABINET GOVERNMENT
IN AUSTRALIA

S. ENCEL

Cabinet Government in Australia

MELBOURNE UNIVERSITY PRESS

First published 1962

Printed and bound in Australia by
Melbourne University Press, Parkville N.2, Victoria

Registered in Australia for transmission
by post as a book

London and New York: Cambridge University Press

TO OUR PARENTS

PREFACE

THE GENERAL PROPOSITION on which this book is based is that political institutions should be studied as elements in a political system, which is in its turn the outcome of a social system. In such a study, the character of the institutions should be related to the political and social aspirations embodied in them, to the actual process of government, and to the nature of the social relationships found in the particular society. More briefly, a political institution should be treated as a sociological, and not only as a political, phenomenon.

In endeavouring to achieve this, I have preferred to disregard the orthodox constitutional divisions imposed by a federal constitution. In so far as cabinet government in Australia is an expression of a single political system (or 'political culture', to use Gabriel Almond's term), I have regarded federal and state cabinets as related aspects of the same situation. This has undoubtedly made the study longer, but I hope more valuable. For the convenience of the reader, detailed accounts of matters pertaining to either level are separated in the text and indicated in the contents table.

The book would have been impossible without the encouragement and assistance of a large number of people, all of whom cannot be thanked individually. I should like to acknowledge the large amount of 'inside information' given to me by ministers and ex-ministers, by serving and retired officials, by journalists, clerks of parliament, and the like. Mr Allan McKnight, at that time Assistant Secretary in the Prime Minister's Department, Canberra, inspired my original interest in the subject. To Professor L. F. Crisp, who has helped me at every stage and in numerous ways, I owe a special debt of gratitude. Professor Geoffrey Sawer kindly read and criticized Parts II and III in their draft form. Mrs Joyce Hodgson typed some of the early drafts, but the main burden of typing was borne by Mrs R. M. Evans, whose co-operation was indefatigable and invaluable.

To Sir Allen Brown, former Secretary of the Prime Minister's Department, I am indebted for access to the archives of the Department for the period 1901-35. I should like to thank the staff of the Commonwealth National Library and of the Mitchell Library for their assistance. Miss Lilian Gardiner, of Sydney, kindly allowed me to read and quote the minutes of federal Labour caucus, 1901-23, of which a copy had been retained by her father, the late Senator Albert Gardiner. Unfortunately, two collections of papers, those of Alfred Deakin and W. M. Hughes, were not available to me, but Professor R. M. Crawford permitted me to examine Deakin's cabinet diary.

In its original form, the work was submitted as a thesis for the degree of Ph.D. at the University of Melbourne. Considerable revision has been made for the purposes of publication, and suggestions in this regard were made by Professor K. C. Wheare, Professor R. N. Spann, and Mr Alan Davies. Miss B. M. Ramsden and Miss Betty Roberts, of the Melbourne University Press, patiently led me through the mazes of the editorial process and suggested improvements to the text. Any remaining errors of fact, defects of presentation, and, of course, all statements of opinion, are my own responsibility.

S.E.

Australian National University
February 1961

CONTENTS

ABBREVIATIONS

Cmd	Command Papers
C.L.R.	Commonwealth Law Reports
C.P.	Commonwealth Papers
L.J.K.B.	Law Journal King's Bench
L.R.A.C.	Law Reports Appeal Cases
ML	Mitchell Library, Sydney
Parl. Deb. (C. of A.)	*Parliamentary Debates,* Commonwealth of Australia
Parl. Deb. (N.S.W.)	*Parliamentary Debates,* New South Wales
Parl. Deb. (W.A.)	*Parliamentary Debates,* Western Australia
P.P. (C. of A.)	*Parliamentary Papers,* Commonwealth of Australia
P.P. (N.S.W.)	*Parliamentary Papers,* New South Wales
S.M.H.	*Sydney Morning Herald*
V.L.R.	Victorian Law Reports

Part 1

INTRODUCTION

1

AN ESSAY IN INTERPRETATION

Cabinet and the British Political System

A CONTINENTAL HUMORIST once wrote that to Continentals, life is a game; to the English, cricket is a game. Alternatively, one might observe that to the British, life is a serious business and politics a game not unlike cricket. It is more than a coincidence that cricket and cabinet government were invented on the same soil, and no one familiar with the conventions that govern Lord's need be puzzled by those which operate at Westminster and in Whitehall.

Jennings[1] has noted that British politics depend less on representative than on responsible government—the control of affairs by ministers responsible to an elected legislature. Parliamentary *government,* in the full sense, was no more successful in seventeenth-century Britain than it has recently been in a number of other countries, and it took a century of conflict and violence before the parliamentary executive, in the form of a committee of the majority party, emerged under the guidance of that arch-fixer, Sir Robert Walpole. The evolution of the system since then constitutes the real history of British politics, whose characteristic form has remained that of responsible government, rather than democracy as defined in the Gettysburg address. Other constitutional systems provide for a parliamentary executive, but in Britain it is, as Jennings says, the core of the system.

The British cabinet is not only a constitutional device but the keystone of a political arch, whose structure depends on a uniquely interlocked set of factors—cultural, economic, sociological. Jennings' now classic study takes for granted alike the existence and the uniqueness of this complex setting, and it remains a work of constitutional law rather than an analysis of political processes. This constitutional emphasis (though balanced by Jennings' more

[1] *The British Constitution* (1st ed., Cambridge, 1941), p.142.

I

recent studies of party politics) is of limited value in a study of the workings of the executive government in a country such as Australia, where the important relationships that determine the fate of ministries are not, to any great extent, 'constitutional' in the accepted sense. The parliamentary executive, as embodied in the seven written constitutions of Australia, is little more than a simulacrum of cabinet government. Political institutions cannot be transplanted — a truth whose painful consequences become more evident every day.

Responsible government in Australia rests on social and political foundations quite other than those which make cabinet government such a distinctively British phenomenon. It is important to make the differences explicit, because the workings of the Australian political system are understandable only if one asks: what are the processes characteristic of it, and to what extent is it possible to apply to them the concepts and the forms derived from British experience? It has been more usual to ask, rather, to what extent the forms of political activity developed in Britain have taken root or been modified in Australia. The difference between these two questions, slight at first glance, has important consequences. The latter approach, which is traditional, takes the British pattern for granted, as a norm from which Australia deviates in observable ways. Comparisons are then made which may be both pointless and invidious. Lord Attlee, in his autobiography, is quite sure that the Australian Labor Party's rule of electing ministers by ballot of the parliamentary party is wrong,[2] by which he apparently means inconceivable in Britain. It is not only inconceivable but irrelevant. Caucus selection of cabinet is explicable only if it is viewed in the Australian political context, and not as a departure from British principles, to be mentioned in rather pained tones.

A more adequate understanding is likely to emerge if British institutions are taken not for granted, but as the outgrowth of a unique social configuration. If Australia is similarly treated, the reasons for the adoption of what is, superficially, the same form of government will become clearer, as will the true nature of both the differences and the similarities to the original model. Bagehot perceived, nearly a century ago, that the English constitution presupposes a 'deferential' society, where the many are content to be ruled by the select few, and the select few, for their part, recognize their obligations towards the many. The result is a unitary government, whose powers are defined by convention rather than by law, with a minimum of institutional checks on its authority, with its

2 *As it Happened*, p.156.

personnel drawn largely from the educated classes, and linked in numerous ways, obvious and less obvious, with the rest of the 'Establishment'. The intricate web of rules governing the operation of this unique institution defies definition. It was Lord Eustace Percy who once described British politics as a game played by two teams each taking turns at the wicket. The behaviour of Labour governments between 1945 and 1951 has, in most respects, only confirmed the accuracy of this interpretation.

Bagehot's great merit was to point out that a body unknown to the constitution was actually the most important part of the governmental structure, so anticipating by two generations the now familiar emphasis on the 'informal' organs of politics and administration. The limits within which this informal body must function are defined by the conventions whose evolution since 1832 has been so illuminatingly explored by Jennings, whose example suggests that a study of similar informal processes at work in Australia will provide a similar clue to the evolution of political relationships in this country. But it must be added immediately that by emphasizing the 'informal' rather than the 'formal' characteristics of Australian government, we are led towards the conclusion that the use of the term 'cabinet government' in Australia does more to cloak differences than to establish similarities with Britain. The informalities with which British writers are concerned are not the same as those that dominate the Australian political scene, where appeals to accepted convention do not fall on receptive ears. If it is agreed that conventional rules are to operate, departures from the rules can be stigmatized as bad form and can be the subject of appeal — as in cricket. Jennings and Laski, in their attacks on the bodyline tactics of the Conservatives in 1909-11 and in 1931, are appealing to the spirit of good form as well as condemning the political objectives of Balfour and Baldwin. Although the processes of political decision-making in the two countries are in many ways similar, little is gained by assuming that the apparatus of convention which enshrines these processes in Britain can readily be applied to judge the situation in Australia, and judgments made in these terms can be merely exasperating without being illuminating — except about the mind of the critic. If any game expresses the spirit of politics in Australia, it is the schoolboy one called 'keepings-off', whose rules are made largely *in situ*.

Cabinet, in Australia as well as in Britain, is the supreme decision-making body, but its decision-making functions may be viewed as part of any one of four distinct though related systems. As a piece of constitutional machinery, it may be seen in its relation to other parts of the constitutional system — in particular, the Crown and parliament. It is also the apex of the party system — the object and focus of the party struggle. Thirdly, it constitutes the highest organ of administration, and its relations with the administrative system are of the greatest importance. Finally, it is a body of political leaders, an *élite* group, whose individual personalities, social origins, and routes to power merit study in themselves. It is remarkable that both Laski and Jennings, to quote them again, between them deal with three of these aspects, but hardly at all with the second one mentioned — the relation between cabinet and the party system.[3] Of Jennings' fifteen chapters, eight are concerned with the constitutional evolution towards fully responsible government, and the party system is barely referred to. In Laski's case, the prime interest is in the use of cabinet as an instrument of social change, and beyond remarking that the party system is the root of collective responsibility, he has little else to say about it. The role of the majority party is to provide a field from which its ruling committee can be chosen, and to map the general course of government policy. Its function is not to rule; that is the prerogative of cabinet.

Perhaps the most eloquent indication of the difference between the two countries lies in the fact that no discussion of cabinet government in Australia would be satisfactory without placing the main emphasis on the relations between cabinet and the government party (or parties). More than that: it would be inconceivable. The prevailing Australian conception of the state requires that cabinet be regarded as an instrument of the popular will, expressed through the demands of organized interest groups and of political parties. Recognition of this widely-held assumption is crucial to an understanding of the role of cabinet in the political system, and we may pause to examine it.

The Australian Concept of the State

Thirty years ago, a distinguished historian described the Australian view of the state as 'a vast public utility, whose duty it is to provide the greatest happiness for the greatest number'.[4] This view, individualistic in origin, regards the state as collective power at the service of individual rights, and is confined to no particular class. Hancock and his contemporary Eggleston[5] paint a picture of

[3] W. Ivor Jennings, *Cabinet Government;* H. J. Laski, *Parliamentary Government in England* and *Reflections on the Constitution* (Manchester, 1951).

[4] W. K. Hancock, *Australia*, p.61.

[5] F. W. Eggleston, *State Socialism in Victoria,* esp. chs. 1 and 3.

governments, operating enterprises like the railways, that are unable to withstand the 'destructive vandalism' of special interest groups, so that the 'public utility' becomes the public trough.

Since the railways are under no necessity to square their ledger, they become an instrument in the hands of politicians for squaring the electors . . . a government is particularly slow to confess that it has got into a bad business, for its mere entry into it has created vested interests which express themselves immediately in politics . . . losses accumulate in a lump, and the crisis, when it comes, is likely to be prolonged and severe. The wretched government has so many scraggy chickens, and when they come home to roost they all seem to come at the same time.[6]

The situation arises because, ever since the grant of responsible government in the 1850s, Australian governments have been deeply involved in the economic growth of the country, either through providing public utilities like transport, electric power, water and sewerage, through the active provision of capital for investment, or through regulatory activities. It was this predominantly economic function of governments that laid the basis for the emergence, in the 1880s and 1890s, of a view of the state as a vehicle for implementing the specific objectives of a series of organized interest groups, whose well-being depended obviously and greatly on state action.[7] At the same time, Australian governments could ignore such traditional preoccupations of government as defence and foreign affairs, which tend to emphasize the independent role of the machinery of state. These could safely be left to Great Britain. Contemporary observers, especially visitors from Europe, were struck by the narrowly limited character of political disputes, which did not resemble the broad areas of disagreement between class-based European parties. 'In appearance', wrote Albert Métin, the Labour movement was 'what we call a *class party,* carrying on a struggle against the bourgeoisie. In reality, they include employers and salaried workers and are concerned simply with obtaining good working conditions in the world as it is.'[8] Theoretical arguments, he goes on, are at a discount in such circumstances. 'On either side, the poverty of ideas astonishes those who are accustomed to European polemics. The employers express an intransigent opposition based on the defence of their profits; there are no arguments, but only a declaration of war.' The working classes,

[6] Hancock, op. cit., pp.120-1.
[7] For a fuller discussion see S. Encel, 'The Concept of the State in Australian Politics', *Australian Journal of Politics and History,* 1960, vol. 6, no. 1.   [8] *Le socialisme sans doctrines,* p.74.

similarly, eschew general questions: 'Socialism, whose philosophy appeals to many European reformers, does not attract the Australasian workers and actually disturbs them by the very breadth of its ideas. When I asked a Labour man to outline his programme, he replied: "My programme? Ten Bob a Day!" '[9] On another occasion, a party leader to whom Métin addressed the same question pointed to the Treasury benches, remarking: 'My programme is to get those fellows out.'

André Siegfried, observing a similar situation in New Zealand, was struck by the primitive conception of political problems displayed by colonial politicians. 'Their strength makes them unconscious of obstacles, and they attack the most delicate questions much as one opens a path through a virgin forest with an axe . . . At heart they are probably convinced that politics are not as complicated as they have been made out to be.' The government, moreover, is close at hand, a fit object for manipulation.

> With us the State is always a distant and rather mysterious institution, which excludes all idea of personality. We laugh at the story which tells of the misadventures of the citizen who wanted to see the State. In New Zealand, nothing is easier. It is enough to find the Prime Minister. If you are an influential elector he can refuse you nothing.[10]

A striking expression of such sentiments was given by W. A. Holman, later Labour Premier of New South Wales, in a famous public debate with the conservative Prime Minister of Australia, George Reid, when he said:

> We regard the State not as some malign power hostile and foreign to ourselves, outside our control and no part of our organized existence, but we recognize in the State, we recognize in the Government merely a committee to which is delegated the powers of the community . . . only by the powers of the State can the workers hope to work out their emancipation from the bonds which private property is able to impose on them today.[11]

Holman, moreover, was expressing sentiments largely shared by his opponent, who took pride during the debate in pointing out how he himself, as Premier of New South Wales some years earlier, had used state activity to benefit the community. They would both have agreed with the view of William Pember Reeves in New

9 Ibid., pp.255-6.
10 *Democracy in New Zealand*, pp.53-7.
11 *Socialism* (the Reid-Holman debate), Sydney, 1906, pp.62-3.

Zealand that 'true democracy consists in the extension of state activity'.[12]

This philosophy of government owes little to Burke, Mill, or Marx, but a great deal to Bentham, or rather to a simplified version of utilitarianism (Disraeli's 'screw-and-lever philosophy'), which had to struggle much harder for success in the complex society of Britain and Europe. That reformed utilitarian, Mill, wrote that on this view forms of government

> are regarded as wholly an affair of invention and contrivance
> . . . Government, on this conception, is a problem, to be worked
> like any other question of business . . . the minds of those who
> adopt this view of political philosophy look upon a constitution in
> the same light (difference of scale being allowed for) as they
> would upon a steam-plough, or a thrashing-machine.[13]

We may now attempt to reduce these views to a more precise formulation. The 'operative concept'[14] of the state that emerges from the foregoing discussion is of a body which, to paraphrase one of the most famous of all definitions, acts as the administrative agency of the masses. That is to say, it is a body where the organs of government and their concomitant institutions, like the party system, exist not to frame national policy but to execute the expressed demands of the community as formulated in practice by organized bodies claiming to interpret the general interest correctly. It exists in a social context where group conflicts are only to a limited extent the result of clashes between social classes, so that party conflicts are less important than disagreements between extra-party interest groups. This concept regards the state as committed rather than neutral. To mitigate the effects of commitment, state intervention, whether of a regulatory or operating character, tends to be detached as much as possible from the traditional state machine and dealt with in either a quasi-judicial or 'non-political' manner, or to be diffused among a number of organs with claims to sovereignty in their own sphere. J. D. B. Miller describes the situation in terms of the unrelenting pressures of 'syndicates' — 'organizations of people whose economic and vocational interests have induced them to band together for action to their common advantage . . . which exercise continual influence over party policy'.[15] As a result, government becomes decentralized to allow

12 Quoted, Métin, op. cit., p.229.
13 *Representative Government* (Everyman ed.), p.175.
14 Cf. A. D. Lindsay's discussion of 'operative ideals' in *The Modern Democratic State* (London, 1943), ch. 1.
15 *Australian Government and Politics*, p.54. Miller's term, employed as

the development of 'organs of syndical satisfaction' which can adjust competing interests. By the same token, parliament becomes primarily an organ of adjustment between conflicting 'syndicates': 'party leaders do not say this on public platforms, but they find themselves compelled to do it when in office'.[16]

Under such conditions, the widespread network of state action — public corporations, marketing boards, industrial tribunals, and the rest—becomes itself one of the active elements of the social pattern. This is true above all of the machinery of industrial arbitration, which began as a means of settling specific disputes but soon became a device for fixing wages and salaries on a national scale with the full authority of the law behind its awards. 'A new province for law and order' was the description given to the system by one of its earliest and greatest figures, Mr Justice Higgins, who fixed the first national basic wage in 1907, and the effective occupation of this province by an arm of the state has had the profoundest political and social consequences. It is impossible to think of the state as an 'epiphenomenon', as it is both in liberal-democratic and in Marxist political theory, and the acceptance of the social role of the state dominates Australian political practice. The political parties are sometimes described as 'irrational'[17] in their policies and attitudes, but this is to fail in recognizing the intimate links between interest group, party, administrative agency and cabinet. At both federal and state levels, but especially the latter, large-scale government intervention has given rise to a collection of more or less self-contained administrative satrapies whose internecine conflicts are often demonstrably 'irrational'. These segmented governmental machines are themselves part of a segmented society, where Miller's 'syndicates' are of such importance. In the sense that these competing groups perceive their own particular interests and pursue them with gusto, their actions are quite rational; 'irrationality' can arise inside the parties or within the administration because all these pressures cannot easily be reconciled in a rational manner, especially where resources are limited. Perhaps the acuteness of the problem accounts for the quite unparalleled use of Royal Commissions in Australia as a method of canalizing these pressures and thereby reducing them below the threshold of discomfort.[18]

---

an alternative to the more usual 'interest group', is not altogether felicitous. The original French 'syndicat' is not easy to domesticate in English, where syndicate usually suggests lotteries or other financial games of chance.

16 Ibid., p.55.   17 e.g. A. F. Davies, *Australian Democracy*, esp. ch. 1.
18 A. H. Cole, *A Finding List of Royal Commission Reports in the British Dominions* (Harvard, 1939), lists 194 for Canada, 157 for New

One of the most important features of state intervention in this form has been the growth of machine politics on the American rather than the British model. During the nineteenth century, colonial ministries came and went with kaleidoscopic rapidity, reflecting on the parliamentary scene the shifting patterns of interest-group alignments. The intrusion of the state machine as a major political force in the late years of the nineteenth century led to a comparative stabilization of these relationships, and consequently to stable ministries which have remained in office sometimes for decades at a time, with changes of personnel occurring largely by co-option following death or retirement.[19] In several notable cases, such long-lived governments have fallen when they could no longer mediate the 'irrational' conflicts between their supporting interest groups and the requirements of efficient administration.

Most of these long-lived governments have been Labour, and this may be interpreted partly in terms of Labour's greater readiness to exploit the situation on a comprehensive scale, and partly to the homogeneity of the trade union movement as compared with the diversity of interest groups on the non-Labour side, particularly where there is a conflict between city and country interests. The successful welding of these groups in South Australia has enabled an unbroken Liberal ascendancy since 1934, at the cost of making the Liberals an interventionist party. In Victoria, which alone has not experienced the long-lived governments of other states, the relative weakness of Labour has been counter-balanced by splits between and within the non-Labour parties; periods of comparatively stable government since 1910 have usually required the existence of an interventionist alliance, as between the Country Party and Labour from 1935 to 1942. On the other hand, the success of Labour in the states is one of the prime causes of interstate clashes within the national party, where the state branches may act as competing political machines.

The total picture is not one which can readily accommodate the conventions of cabinet and ministerial responsibility that have evolved in Britain, especially when we find Labour spokesmen insisting that a Labour government is only a 'reflex' of the industrial movement. Nor is Labour the only party to adopt this

Zealand, 139 for South Africa, as against 710 (!) for Australia. At an average of eight per year Royal Commissions have a strong claim to be included as 'organs of syndical satisfaction'.

[19] e.g. South Australia, 1934 to date; Tasmania, 1934 to date; Western Australia, 1934 to 1947; Queensland, 1932 to 1957; New South Wales, 1941 to date.

viewpoint; it is explicitly embodied in the rules of the Country
Party and the Liberals practise it with the minimum of preaching.
The results are obvious not only to students of politics. D. H.
Lawrence, visiting Australia *en route* to New Mexico at a time of
acute factional strife between the New South Wales Labour government and the trade unions, wrote in *Kangaroo* that it was
absurd to talk of 'responsible government', because in Australia
governments were responsible only in the same sense as domestic
servants. 'The proletariat appoints men to administer the law, not
to rule. These ministers are not really responsible any more than
the housemaid is responsible. The proletariat is all the time responsible, the only source of authority.'

The Characteristics of Cabinet Government

We began by arguing that cabinet government in Britain operates
through 'conventions' for which there are few strict counterparts
in Australia. This is not, of course, true inasmuch as there are
certain norms or regularities in both cases which can be observed
and formulated, but true inasmuch as 'conventions' mean something like the rules of cricket. The purpose of this introductory
chapter has been to point out the influences which determine the
norms that apply under Australian conditions. But it may also be
useful to look at the corresponding influences at the back of the
apparatus of political convention and administrative organization
that makes up the British cabinet system.

Cabinet office represents, in the first place, the top of the ladder
of power and prestige. In 1834, Lord Melbourne's secretary could
overcome his master's feeling that the Prime Ministership would
be a 'damned bore' by protesting that 'such a position never was
occupied by any Greek or Roman, and if it only lasts two months,
it is well worth while to have been Prime Minister of England'.
According to Greville, Melbourne replied, 'By God, that's true —
I'll go.' In 1957, Philip Toynbee could write that, while Britain
still had a governing class, membership of the cabinet remained
the greatest prize open to an ambitious man.[20] Cabinet remains,
in fact, the heart of the 'Establishment', and the nature of the
Establishment remains a key to the understanding not only of
cabinet but of the process by which important political decisions
continue to be made. Kinship and descent are almost as important
in these circumstances as they were in the days of Disraeli's
'phalanx of great families', as the Bank Rate Inquiry of 1958

[20] 'Who Governs Britain?', *Twentieth Century,* October 1957.

disclosed,[21] or as the London Press discovered in 1957 when it traced the family tree of Cecils and Cavendishes in the Macmillan government. Nor is it only under a Conservative administration that the governors are so different from the governed. The original character of the British Labour Party as a movement of social protest was reflected in the social heterogeneity of its early ministries. Now that Labour governments are an accepted part of the scheme of things, their membership differs from their Tory counterparts only in that the upper-middle class lump is leavened by proletarian rather than aristocratic elements.[22]

The importance of the aristocratic principle — or of a 'vocation of leadership'—lies partly in the general recognition that the function of the British government is to govern. The working of British politics reflects the belief that governments can be trusted with power, a belief inseparable from the remarkably unitary character of the constitution. There is neither a written basic law that binds the legislature and the executive, nor are the legislative and executive arms constitutionally separated. The strength of cabinet depends on the constitutional supremacy of parliament. Joseph Chamberlain may have been politically incautious, even in 1886, when he declared that no government should 'truckle to the multitude', but he was expressing a principle that remains influential to the present day. The parliamentary leaders of the Labour Party, Attlee and Greenwood, sought the approval of the party conference, then meeting at Bournemouth, before accepting Churchill's invitation to join a national government in 1940, but from 1945 the Attlee government made it clear that it did not regard the National Executive Committee of the party as having any right to guide its policies. Lord Attlee recalls the proposals made in 1931, after the MacDonald debacle, to restrict the powers of a future Labour Prime Minister. 'Further experience,' he observes with his usual restraint, 'has led to these proposals being dropped.' He adds, waspishly, that the position of chairman of the N.E.C. 'is not always well understood'.[23]

The strength of a British cabinet rests also on the relations between ministers and civil servants, and the evolution of the administrative class, in particular, has been of tremendous import-

21 For an analysis see T. Lupton and C. S. Wilson, 'The Social Background and Connections of Top Decision Makers', *Manchester School,* 1959, vol. 27, no. 1.

22 Jean Bonnor, "The Four Labor Cabinets', *Sociological Review,* 1958, vol. 6, no. 1.

23 Attlee, op. cit., pp.138 and 156. The distressing lack of understanding to which Lord Attlee refers was displayed by a professor of political science, Harold Laski, chairman in 1945.

ance. The importance of this link depends partly on the fact that the functions of the administrative class are to give disinterested advice on policy to ministers, but also on the social linkages between politicians and officials. The significance of the administrative class as a source of strength to the government has never been better put than in the words of its own members:

> The business of government . . . calls for the application of wide and long views to complex problems, for the pursuit, as regards each and every subject-matter, of definite lines of action, mutually consistent, conformed to public opinion and capable of being followed continuously while conditions permit . . . it is the special duty of the administrative class of the civil service to set these wider and more enduring considerations against the exigencies of the moment.[24]

The other important characteristic of the administrative class — its social affinities with the circles from which the great bulk of ministers in all but the early Labour governments were drawn— was a matter for criticism and apprehension by many students of the civil service before 1945. As W. A. Robson wrote in 1937, the system

> produced men at the top of the administrative machine whose educational and social background was similar to that of the Ministers and Councillors whom they served. The Foreign Secretary and the Permanent Under-Secretary of State could spend a week-end together on terms of essential equality . . . All this has made for that tacit understanding based on common feelings which is far more valuable than verbal explanations as an aid to co-operation.[25]

Apprehensions about what might happen when a Labour government came to power proved largely unjustified, which is a comment not only on the strength and flexibility of the cabinet-civil service relationship, but also on the extent to which the Labour government of 1945-51 differed in composition from its predecessors.

The dependence of cabinet government on a stable two-party system is, of course, recognized in Britain, but to an outside observer the party system appears to be taken too much for granted. It is often true that those phenomena which are most characteristic are also those most taken for granted, as this one was

---

[24] *Memorandum by Association of First Division Civil Servants*, presented to the Royal (Tomlin) Commission on the Civil Service, 1929-31. Cf. Jennings, op. cit., ch. 5.
[25] *The British Civil Servant* (London, 1937), p.17.

in W. S. Gilbert's famous verse. From the remarkable stability and continuity of the two-party system stems a great deal that is typical of British politics, from the belief in government by discussion and compromise to the cricket-pitch conventions of cabinet government. To paraphrase Laski, it is the British party system that makes cabinet responsibility possible, and, at least as important, it accounts largely for the predominant role of the Prime Minister.[26]

Two other points may be mentioned briefly. Strong central government is an historic consequence of the need for defence, and defence requires the pursuit of foreign policy, which, *pace* Clausewitz, is largely an extension of defence by peaceful methods. The Cabal of Charles II's reign was, it will be recalled, the Privy Council committee on foreign affairs. Colonial governments, including that of the United States, have developed their distinctive features while acting as junior partners of European powers in defence and foreign policy, and their structure has been determined only to a very minor extent by such preoccupations. The process of remedying such egocentricity is a painful one, if the vicissitudes of United States government in the last two decades are any indication.

There remains the standard of behaviour to be expected from ministers of the Crown. In this respect, also, much is taken for granted, yet it should not be in the face of evidence from lesser breeds like the French, the Americans — or the Australians. Asquith's principle that 'ministers ought not to enter into any transaction whereby their private pecuniary interest might, even conceivably, come into conflict with their public duty' may seem elementary, but even lip-service to the principle may be difficult to obtain in a country where the state is regarded as an organ to be manipulated for the benefit of individuals or groups. 'It is a mistake,' said Mr Attlee in the debate on the Lynskey Report in 1949, 'for Ministers or senior officials to deal with individual cases other than through the regular machinery of the department.'[27] No cheers would greet this statement in Australia.

*

Seven characteristics have been mentioned which are associated with the working of cabinet government in Britain. Others of a

---

26 Cf. J. Barents, 'The Dutch Cabinet System', *Public Administration* (London), 1952, vol. 30, no. 1. Professor Barents shows how the prevalence of coalition ministries renders collective responsibility virtually impossible, and how the position of Prime Minister has emerged only very gradually.

27 *Debates* (H.C.), 5th ser., 3 February 1949. Cf. M. R. Robinton, 'The Lynskey Tribunal', *Political Science Quarterly*, 1953, vol. 68, no. 1.

constitutional nature could be added, such as the personal role of the monarch, but those just detailed are, in this context, the most significant ones. A number of the chapters that follow will be devoted to a demonstration that, in Australia, each of these seven characteristics is either absent or replaced by its antithesis. That these different or antithetical features are linked with the conception of the state described earlier in this chapter will be seen if they are now briefly mentioned.

To begin with, cabinet office does not enjoy the prestige, nor politicians the status, that is their share in Britain. D. H. Lawrence did not see that 'distinction in the very being' between the proletariat and the ruling classes which was the case in England. 'In Australia nobody is supposed to rule, and nobody does rule, so the distinction falls to the ground.' The social composition of cabinets lends no colour to any notion of a governing class. The composition of governments varies so much that a glance at the careers and occupations of the members of a ministry will at once identify the party or parties from which it is drawn. Secondly, although the precise extent to which any government acts as the instrument of influential groups anxious to extract advantages from government policy is always doubtful, there is no doubt that its role is seen as one of 'delivering the goods', and this view, whether spoken or unspoken, is usually present in the political struggles described in succeeding chapters. Party leaders attack the dominance of 'outside interests' or 'party juntas' only when they have broken with them.

The relation between ministers and officials is different, partly because there is no administrative class. The idea of such a *corps d'élite,* let alone its existence, would be difficult to imagine. But it is also important that a high proportion of senior government officials are professional men, experts in a particular field, whose talents are not, except in the odd case, valuable to the government in the same way as are those of the four hundred or so members of the 'higher civil service' in Britain. Moreover, they are split up among departments and public corporations in a way that obstructs, where it does not positively prevent, the growth of *esprit de corps.* Lastly, their social contacts with ministers are of importance only in occasional instances.

The fourth point — the role of the party system — is in some ways the most important. Australia has never, except for brief intervals, possessed a two-party system which is 'genuine' in the British sense. Although the assertion requires some caution, it is possible to argue that cabinet emerged in Britain as a consequence of the division of parliament into Whig and Tory groups. No such argument is possible in Australia, where it can be held with considerable plausibility that the existence of cabinet government is the chief *raison d'être* of the party system. The history of parties is marked by continuous struggles for power, or rather for access to material advantage, which suggests that the existence of these main parties only masks a much greater diversity, restrained from breaking forth by the exigencies of capturing office. Collective responsibility, as a result, becomes modified until it is sometimes unrecognizable.

Fifth, the relative unimportance of defence and foreign affairs — matters to be left, except in certain special cases, to the British government — has meant that even the national government existing since 1901 has had only very limited opportunities to acquire the stature of a decision-making organ which must operate in terms of some concept of the 'national interest' or the 'international situation' involving more than the material interests or prejudices of influential pressure groups. Sixth, the question of the probity of ministers, and of the legitimacy of private interests that may conflict with the public interest, is a matter that assumes a different light in a country where there is no vocation of leadership, no governing class whose position requires it to have the reputation of Caesar's wife. The long list of ministers who have been charged with corruption, and the repeated refusal of governments to lay down rules about the private interests of their members, reflect a basic difference of outlook about the standards appropriate to public life, and, by implication, about the proper functions of government. Finally, a written federal constitution, and the pervasive influence of federalism throughout politics, add a dimension whose importance will appear again and again.

Conclusion

The argument of the preceding pages has been conducted in contrapuntal form, the better to emphasize the contrast between the political institution which is the theme of this study — Cabinet in Australia—and the British institution of the same name on which it is putatively modelled. The outcome of the discussion appears to be a denial that the expression 'cabinet government' should validly be applied to the Australian system, if by that expression is meant an institution working on similar lines to its prototype. This would be to exaggerate the iconoclastic tendencies — if any — of this study. The *institutional* similarities between the two countries are considerable and deliberate. 'Cabinet government' remains an accurate label for the formal structure and the functioning of executive authority in Australia, and there is little point in seeking an alternative term. The important point is whether the divergences that do indisputably occur are to be regarded as (regrettable) lapses from the British norm, or whether they are to be interpreted as the outcome of a political system which, though derived from Britain, has its own inner logic. An analogous problem may be found in the world of gastronomy. Australian wines are made from European grape varieties, and the best of them can compare with European vintages, but it is pointless to describe them as 'claret' or 'hock', and Australian vintners are at last beginning to depart from this irritating practice. Although Australian politics depend on the same forces as politics everywhere, they must be interpreted according to local realities.

Part II

THE CONSTITUTIONAL BACKGROUND

2

CABINET IN THE COLONIES AND STATES

Origins

CABINET GOVERNMENT in Australia has gone through a process of evolution reflecting the gradual development of Australia from a penal colony into a sovereign state. After the personal autocracy exercised by the early Governors, the first step towards responsible government was contained in the instructions to Governor Darling in 1825, requiring him to establish an Executive Council consisting of his senior officials, on whose advice he was to act. The establishment of the Executive Council was a further step in the growth of constitutional government in Australia, which had commenced in 1823 when the British parliament passed the New South Wales Judicature Act, setting up a nominated Legislative Council and a Supreme Court. By the year 1834, similar Executive Councils had been set up in the other colonies (South Australia, Van Diemen's Land and Western Australia). The Council usually comprised the Governor, the Colonial Secretary, the Colonial Treasurer, the Surveyor-General, the officer commanding the military forces of the colony, and the head of the Anglican church. For a short time the Chief Justice of the Supreme Court was also a member. This composition recalls the early days of the Privy Council in England.

Agitation for responsible government, which had begun almost with the establishment of the first Legislative Council, was reinforced by the Durham Report of 1839, advocating the grant of self-government to the Canadian provinces, in which the distinction between representative and responsible government was vigorously expounded. Subsequent British legislation, especially the Australian Colonies Government Act of 1850, went a long way towards granting representative institutions, but the colonists continued to press for what they regarded as the full British system of ministers sitting in and responsible to parliament. As a result of their controversy with the Colonial Office, the words 'responsible government', which at that time were virtually synonymous with 'independence', acquired a double-barrelled significance. Self-government, in the colonial view,

> could never be obtained while the Governor had command of a revenue which was free from legislative supervision and while he consulted none but permanent officials who were appointed by the Secretary of State . . . The term responsible government . . . came to mean government by the advice of ministers chosen from and responsible to the Legislature. In other words, it came to be applied to the form of government which had existed for many years in the United Kingdom, although without specific recognition and without a distinctive name.[1]

In 1852, Sir John Pakington, soon after succeeding Lord John Russell as Secretary of State for the Colonies, agreed to these demands, and asked the legislatures of New South Wales, Victoria, South Australia, and Tasmania to draft constitutions for submission to the Colonial Office. In all the drafts submitted there was remarkably little reference to ministerial responsibility, perhaps because of a deliberate intention to follow British usage by allowing cabinet's existence and powers to rest largely on convention. The more likely explanation is that the colonists were concerned, above all, to secure control over their own domestic affairs, against a British refusal to endorse any rigid distinction between domestic and external questions, which were to remain in the hands of the Colonial Office. In the end, both parties came to an understanding that domestic affairs would be in the hands of responsible ministers who were members of the colonial legislatures, and the understanding was reached partly by agreement to avoid contention over the exact phraseology of the colonial Constitution Acts. Nevertheless, as we shall see later, the existence of written provisions, no matter how slender, regarding a cabinet system, has led to political and legal disputes about its true status.

Constitutional Provisions in the Colonies

In Australia, as in Britain, cabinet conforms to Maitland's description of it as an 'extra-legal organisation'.[2] Although the original colonial constitutions contained various provisions which might be construed as establishing a cabinet system, Harrison Moore was generally correct in observing that cabinet government is 'fore-

[1] A. C. V. Melbourne, in *Cambridge History of the British Empire*, vol. 7, pt. I, p.276.
[2] *The Constitutional History of England*, p.387.

shadowed rather than established in the Constitutions . . . in spite of expressions in the Constitutions, which assume the existence in fact of the system, the cabinet system rests to this day [1919] in Australia mainly, as it does in England, wholly upon conventional understandings and practices rather than upon positive law'.[3]

On the other hand, despite some ambiguity in the constitutional provisions, there was a general understanding that the Governor would govern only on the advice of his cabinet. K. R. Cramp remarks about New South Wales that its constitution 'does not expressly state that parliament is to control the Executive; neither does it in any way imply the term "responsible government". Yet it was distinctly understood that the passing of the Act would involve the establishment of such a system.' The Secretary of State for the Colonies made this quite clear in a dispatch to the Governor directing that responsible government was now operative in New South Wales.[4]

Some examples, both of the constitutional provisions and of their omissions, may now be given. In Victoria the 1855 Constitution Act provided, under Section 17, that ministers were exempt from the general disqualification preventing the holder of an office of profit under the Crown from sitting in parliament. Section 18 provided that of the officials named in schedule D, at least four must be members of the Legislature. Section 37 stated that appointments to public office were to be made by the Governor on the advice of the Executive Council, except 'officers liable to retire from office on political grounds, which appointments shall be vested in the Governor alone'. By this discreet means was it provided that the Governor exercised the royal prerogative of commissioning his cabinet. Section 48 permitted the Governor to abolish certain political offices (thus allowing changes in the constitution of the cabinet); Sections 50 and 51 provided pensions for retired ministers.

To correspond with the constitutional arrangements, the Governor's commission and instructions were changed, empowering him to appoint the Executive Council himself instead of making temporary appointments pending Colonial Office approval. These alterations, observes Jenks, were 'almost the only changes in the commission, and though they are really important, it requires a trained eye to see why they are important'.[5] Moreover, the term 'responsible ministers' was used only once in the Constitution Act

3 M. Atkinson (ed.), *Australia: Economic and Political Studies*, p.82.
4 K. R. Cramp, *State and Federal Constitutions of Australia*, pp.58-9.
5 E. Jenks, *The Government of Victoria*, p.208.

—in schedule D, listing the offices whose holders were not subject to disqualification. It also occurs in the margin of two other sections of the Constitution Act. Keith differs somewhat from the two writers already quoted, arguing that the provision for an Executive Council, on whose advice alone the Governor was to act, constitutes a 'legal compulsion' towards responsible government 'as compared with Canada and New Zealand, where it rested from the beginning on usage alone'.[6]

There are, in fact, four provisions which occur in all colonial constitutions that may be said effectively to establish the basis of cabinet government. These relate to the Executive Council, to Ministers of State (often called 'officers liable to retire on political grounds'), the exemption from disqualification for parliamentary membership for the holders of certain offices, and the provisions either permitting or insisting that ministers sit in parliament.

The New South Wales Constitution of 1856 made a similar distinction between ministers (appointed by the Governor) and other officials (appointed by the Governor-in-Council). The holders of an office of profit were forbidden to sit in the Legislative Assembly, unless these offices were included among five posts listed in the schedule to the Act, or other posts not exceeding five. Until 1902, the Constitution Act gave no overt recognition of the fact that ministers were the effective members of the Executive Council. 'Strictly speaking,' says Keith, 'there is no legal necessity for a single minister to be in Parliament.'[7]

In Victoria, the original provision was that four out of seven ministers listed in schedule D must be in parliament. The Officials in Parliament Act of 1883 provided for not more than ten ministers who might sit in parliament, 'provided always that such officers shall be responsible ministers of the Crown and members of the Executive Council'. In 1903, this was altered to provide that no minister could retain office for more than three months without becoming a member of parliament. The Executive Council, however, could still contain members who were not ministers, or ministers without portfolio (i.e., not listed in the schedule). Of the eight ministers provided by the 1903 Act, only four were required to be in parliament at any one time. The practical significance of this curious amalgam of provisions is nil, as there have never been any ministers who were not members of parliament.

6 A. B. Keith, *Responsible Government in the Dominions,* p.50.
7 Ibid., p.55.   At the federal convention of 1897, a delegate from New South Wales maintained that one of the members of the first (Herbert) ministry in Queensland had not been a member of parliament.   (Federal Convention Debates, p.796.)

Queensland followed the New South Wales example almost literally; in 1897, however, the Act was amended to authorize ministers to sit in parliament. Tasmania also made little specific provision, ministerial appointments not even being distinguished from others made by the Governor or the Governor-in-Council. In 1872, however, the Chief Secretary, Treasurer, Attorney-General, and Minister of Lands and Works were required to sit in parliament. No connection is established between tenure of ministerial office and membership of the Executive Council.

Western Australia provided in 1890 that the Executive Council should consist of Ministers of State, who must obtain a seat in parliament within three months of their appointment.

The case of South Australia stands out from the rest as one of particular interest, because it represents the only occasion where an attempt was made to entrench the principles of responsible government in the language of the constitution. This arose from a dispute between the Legislative Council and the Governor, who attempted to insist on his discretion being incorporated in the draft constitution. Sections 32, 33 and 39 of the Constitution Act provided that all ministers must become, within three months, members of parliament. All ministers were to be *ex officio* members of the Executive Council. Ministers were to lose office if they lost their seats in parliament or 'by reason of inability . . . to command the support of a majority'.[8] Section 33 reads:

No officer of the government shall be bound to obey any order of the Governor involving any expenditure of public money, nor shall any warrant for the payment of money or appointment to or dismissal from office be valid except as herein provided, unless such order, warrant, appointment, or dismissal be signed by the Governor and countersigned by the Chief Secretary.

A further unusual feature of the South Australian Constitution Act was that, alone among the colonial constitutions, it did not require ministers to be re-elected to parliament after being appointed to ministerial office.

While the provisions just outlined provide the essential framework of responsible government, a number of other matters differ as between the states. Most of these date from the early years of responsible government in the colonies; others are matters of practice. In New South Wales, South Australia and Western Australia, ministers resign their membership of the Executive Council

8 Section 39 was also intended to compensate officials who would lose their positions after the transfer of power.

when they lose office. In Victoria and Tasmania, ex-ministers retain their membership.[9] The distinction is drawn by describing those actually occupying ministerial office as being 'under summons'. A question regarding membership arose in the early years of responsible government, when some ministers, apparently assuming that they should follow the example of Privy Councillors, refused to resign from the Council when they gave up their portfolios. Royal instructions issued in 1859 permitted the Governor to deal with such problems by granting the power to remove members from the Executive Council. This power was not, of course, exercised in Victoria and Tasmania. Victoria is the only case where the distinction between members under summons and those not under summons is formally recognized in the Governor's instructions. In Victoria also, the officer commanding the military forces was originally a member of the Executive Council, because he acted as deputy to the Governor. The practice disappeared when the Chief Justice was given a commission as Lieutenant-Governor.

In Queensland, the procedure of Executive Council meetings is laid down in great detail by the letters patent and instructions to the Governor. Section 4 of a new set of letters patent constituting the office of Governor, issued in 1925, states that the Executive Council is to contain all those who were councillors before the new letters patent were issued and anyone else whom the Governor may appoint. This appears to mean that anyone can be a member who belongs by virtue of a Queensland statute as well as through gubernatorial appointment. Even at this late date, it was not expressly provided that ministers should be members.

The practice grew up in some colonies of appointing one minister as Vice-President of the Executive Council, with the function of deputizing for the Governor at meetings of the council. In New South Wales, a deputy is provided in the constitution; in practice, he has always been the government leader in the Legislative Council. The title of Vice-President was first used in the Martin ministry of 1866. The Vice-President usually has another portfolio, most frequently that of Attorney-General or Minister of Justice. The office was first paid in 1907, and in 1932 was added to the schedule of ministers exempted from disqualification for membership of parliament. In Queensland, the post was established by the Officials in Parliament Act of 1874, with an extra salary of £300 over and above the ministerial salary. This was confirmed by a further Act in 1884. The Premier has for many years occupied the post by statute.

9 In Queensland, no special provision exists.

No other state has established this office. In Victoria, the post of unofficial government leader in the Legislative Council became a paid and therefore constitutionally recognized office in 1940.

Some of the Acts provide for a statutory number of ministers in the upper house. The Victorian Constitution Act of 1903 laid down that of eight ministers, not more than two should be in the Council and not more than six in the Assembly. Later amendments have increased the number of ministers but have not enlarged the statutory minimum required to sit in the upper house. In South Australia, it was provided in 1908 that of the six ministers, not more than four should be in the Assembly; the Constitution Act of 1953 changed the number to five. In Western Australia, the Constitution Amendment Act of 1899 specified that at least one minister should be in the upper house. Both Victoria and New South Wales have provisions permitting ministers who are not members of the Legislative Council to appear there in order to speak on government Bills. The opportunity has been utilized only in Victoria, and that not since 1905.

All the colonial constitutions except that of South Australia originally provided that ministers, on being appointed to office, should vacate their seats in parliament and offer themselves for re-election. The significance of this provision seems to be historical, for it was evidently regarded by the British authorities as a limitation on party manoeuvres in the colonial parliaments. However, in most cases the provision was abolished before fifty years had passed: in Queensland in 1884 (although the fact seems to have gone unnoticed until 1897, when it was pointed out during a parliamentary debate on a further amendment to the constitution); Tasmania in 1900; New South Wales in 1906; Victoria in 1914. Western Australia, which inserted the provision for re-election in its Constitution Act of 1889 despite the fact that it had already been abolished in two colonies, retained it until 1947.

Queensland has recently added a new variation to the provisions regarding disqualification from parliamentary membership on the grounds of holding an office of profit. The Officials in Parliament Act of 1945 states that the holder of an office of profit, when elected to parliament, automatically vacates the office of profit. Apparently the Queensland government wished to lessen the difficulties in the way of public servants standing for parliamentary seats.

The office of Premier has almost no legal status. As in Britain, there is an official table of precedence which lays down the respective positions to be occupied by the Prime Minister of the Commonwealth and the Premiers of the states. Until recently, however, there did not exist such further statutory recognition as provided in Britain by the Chequers Estate Act of 1918 and the successive Ministers of the Crown Acts passed since 1937. Even the use of the title has been slow to emerge. Colonial constitutions imply that the chief minister will be the Colonial Secretary (or Chief Secretary, as he became). Governors' instructions issued at the outset of responsible government gave precedence to this office over the other ministerial posts. New South Wales was the only colony to use the more sonorous title of Prime Minister consistently, although it was also used in Tasmania, where it was common in the nineteenth century to assume that office without any other portfolio.

Membership of the Executive Council has rarely possessed any honorific or other significance of the kind attached, for example, to membership of the Privy Council. During the struggle between the two houses of the Victorian parliament that dragged on from 1865 to 1869, a group of twenty-two members of the Executive Council of Victoria addressed a petition to the Queen, asking her to intervene to prevent the McCulloch government from acting unconstitutionally. The petition was ignored. Tasmania, on the other hand, has sometimes followed the practice of appointing judges of the Supreme Court to membership of the Executive Council, but no other state has followed suit.

One case is on record, however, where membership of the corresponding body in another dominion has been bestowed on an Australian politician as an honorific gesture. This was the occasion in 1916 when W. M. Hughes, on his way from Australia to Great Britain, was appointed a member of the Canadian Privy Council.

The ambiguity and cautious wording of the colonial constitutions led to disputes about the precise constitutional status of cabinet government in Australia. The principal figure associated with this controversy was George Higinbotham, who, as Attorney-General, figured prominently in the Victorian constitutional deadlocks of the 1860s, and later, as Chief Justice, reasserted his views on the matter. Higinbotham held, with all the stubbornness of a powerful personality, that responsible government was established by the constitution alone, and consequently any provisions in the royal instructions which purported to confer certain powers upon the Governor were invalid. In 1888, for example, a case came before the Supreme Court of Victoria involving the power to exclude 'undesirable' immigrants (Chinese in this case). Beyond vesting the executive authority in the Governor, the colonial constitutions said little or nothing on the subject, although, of course, they conferred full legislative power on the colonial legislatures. Some doubts were raised because the Privy Council had already decided in several cases that a governor was not a viceroy with general powers, but could exercise only those powers granted in the prerogative instruments of appointment. In the particular case, the majority of the Supreme Court held that the government of Victoria had no power to exclude aliens under its executive authority because the power was not specifically granted to the Governor. Higinbotham dissented, holding that the Governor had power to do anything 'necessary or expedient for the reasonable and proper administration of law and the conduct of public affairs'.[10] Although this view would be generally accepted in the twentieth century, Higinbotham's reasons for holding it have long ceased to be of any significance. He maintained throughout his life that the Constitution Act provided all the authority needed for government action on internal matters, and the Governor's instructions were therefore irrelevant or illegal, or both.

The intensity with which Higinbotham held these views was reflected in his own actions. In 1864, when he was Attorney-General, a Victorian judge[11] took a holiday in Queensland and wrote a letter to the Governor informing him that he would be absent from the colony for several weeks. A dispute arose over the rights of judges to take leave at their own pleasure, and the Governor wrote back, on Higinbotham's advice, that no judge had the right to leave the colony without permission or to communicate with the Governor other than through the medium of the Attorney-General. Unfortunately for Higinbotham, his attitude rebounded on him years later when, as a judge, he had to report on a capital case for the Executive Council. He wrote to the Attorney-General asking that a request for a report on the case should come from a minister and not from the Governor. He also wished to know whether the report was required because of a provision in the Governor's instructions, pointing out that if this was the case, he would refuse to make the report. The Attorney-General wrote back in terms very similar to those Higinbotham had used twenty years earlier, telling him in effect to mind his own business.

A further instance of confusion about the status of colonial cabinets arose in Queensland in 1874 during a case before the

10 Toy v. Musgrove (1888), 14 V.L.R. 349.
11 The famous Sir Redmond Barry.

Supreme Court involving the cancellation of some Crown leases, when evidence was introduced of a decision in the matter made at a cabinet meeting. The Crown objected that evidence given by former ministers of discussions in cabinet was not admissible as proof of a government decision, because legally only the Executive Council could make decisions. Lutwyche J. upheld the objection, pointing out that the cabinet was not a constitutional body, and that its decisions were only 'binding and effectual if they . . . are ratified by the action of the Executive Council'.[12]

However, the Privy Council reversed this decision and ruled that reports of discussions held in cabinet could be admitted as evidence.[13] Their Lordships apparently did not place cabinet government in the colonies on a footing with its parent institution, especially as it could legitimately be contended that the colonial cabinets were 'established' by written constitutions in Higinbotham's sense, and were therefore not unknown to the law. Confusion over this point has persisted until the present day.[14]

[12] *R.* v. *Davenport* (1874), 4 Q.S.R. 99.
[13] *Davenport* v. *Reg.* (1877), 3 L.R.A.C. 115.
[14] See ch. 4; cf. also Sawer, 'Councils, Ministers and Cabinets in Australia', *Public Law*, 1956, vol. 1, no. 1.

3

FEDERAL CABINET AND THE CONSTITUTION

WHEN CLAUSES defining the structure of the executive government were drawn up at the various federal conventions of the 1890s, they followed the pattern of many other pieces of Commonwealth legislation — i.e., a composite or synthesis of provisions already existing in the colonies or states. The provisions of Section 61 to 65 of the Commonwealth Constitution Act may generally be traced to identical provisions in already existing colonial Constitution Acts. There was, moreover, no doubt in the minds of the draftsmen about the intent to establish cabinet government. Quick and Garran's commentary on the new constitution declares that there is a great difference between the traditional conception of the British constitution embodied in Section 61, vesting executive power in the Queen, and the 'modern practice of the Constitution as crystallized in the polite language of Section 62'.[1] Out of the Executive Council created by the Act 'will spring a body, in Bagehot's words, "by and through whose agency a close union, if not a complete fusion, is established between the executive and legislative powers — THE CABINET" '.[2] The great ambition of the framers of the constitutions of 1855-6, to 'acclimatize' responsible government, was clearly realized in the federal constitution.

The constitutional framework of federal cabinet offers two points of peculiar interest, one of which is the result of the special problems of federalism. The federal issue is now of historical interest only, but the other provision, laying down that all ministers shall be members of the federal Executive Council, has caused repeated difficulties in modifying the structure of cabinet.

At the first series of federal conventions in 1891, comparatively little attention was paid to the federal problem, although some attempts were made to entrench the principles of responsible government in the constitution. The original draft presented to the convention was fairly definite on the necessity for ministers to sit in parliament, but during the debate in committee there was a tendency to deprecate the rigidity of this requirement. Griffith thought that instead of specifying that Ministers of State must

1 John Quick and Robert R. Garran, *The Annotated Constitution of the Australian Commonwealth*, p. 703.   2 Ibid., p.382.

become members of parliament within three months of obtaining office, the example of some colonies should be followed in providing that ministers 'may' sit in parliament. Parkes, on the other hand, attempted to insist on the supremacy of the lower house, and suggested that ministers should sit in parliament and should hold office subject to the confidence of the House of Representatives. In the end the convention took a middle course, and provided that there should be a federal Executive Council, the members of which should be the heads of departments, that they should hold office during the Governor-General's pleasure and that they should be capable of sitting in either house.

When the debate moved from committee to the full convention, Wrixon made yet another attempt to introduce a reference to responsible government and proposed that in addition to being members of the Executive Council, the political heads of departments should be called 'responsible Ministers of the Crown'. The vagueness of the term 'responsible' did not commend it to the convention. In an attempt to compromise, Griffith suggested that the heads of departments should be called 'the Queen's Ministers of State for the Commonwealth'. This was accepted.[3]

The peculiar wording of Section 64 of the Commonwealth Constitution is the result, therefore, of the attempt to ensure that the federal cabinet should abide by the same principles of responsible government already embodied in colonial constitutions. In the event, there was never any attempt to make the system work otherwise, but the clause has led to practical difficulties discussed in a later chapter.

Elective Cabinets

Between 1891 and 1897, when the second series of Federal Conventions took place, disquiet grew among conservative politicians that a federal cabinet, responsible to the lower house, and made up principally of representatives from the larger states, would adversely affect the position of the smaller states. An attempt was therefore made to introduce a system which would safeguard 'States' rights' in the same way as it was hoped the Senate would do. The principal supporters of such a scheme were Griffith (now Sir Samuel Griffith and Chief Justice of Queensland), Sir Richard Baker, President of the South Australian Legislative Council, and Andrew Inglis Clark, at that time Attorney-General of Tasmania. The only politician of radical temper among this group was Cockburn of South Australia.

3 Ibid., pp.128-39.

Their argument was chiefly designed to give the Senate, as the States' House, equal status with the popular house in everything, including control over cabinet. It was argued that this was the essential principle of federation, and weighty precedents were cited following the examples of Switzerland, the French Senate and the United States Senate (although the latter could only be quoted indirectly). Griffith and Baker argued that responsible government would mean the dominance of the lower house, whereas the balance of federation demanded that the Senate, like the House of Representatives, should be able to make and unmake cabinets and to influence cabinet policy. Two main proposals were put forward. The first was that, following the American pattern, ministers should need the approval of Senate on their appointment. Once approved, however, only the confidence of the lower house would be required. The second and more drastic proposal, modelled on the Swiss Federal Council, was that ministers should be elected for a fixed term at a joint sitting of both houses.

The controversy led to a considerable amount of pamphleteering between 1896 and 1898, obviously designed to carry the convention debates before a wider public. In response to a request by the Queensland parliament, Griffith published a booklet in 1896 in which he argued in favour of an elective system. He repudiated the precedent of Canada, which had been cited against the supporters of elected ministries, by arguing that Canada was not a 'true' federation because of the predominance of the dominion government. He pointed out that 'responsible government' had never yet existed in a true federation. To preserve the character of this ideal, it was necessary to modify the principles of responsible government.

> In a Federal Legislature the position and power of the Senate would be very different from that of any of the existing Australian Second Chambers. If it is accepted as a fundamental rule of the Federation that laws shall not be altered without the consent of the majority of the people and also the majority of the States . . . why should not the same principle be applied to the no less important branch of State authority — the Executive Government?[4]

The ministry, he argued, should be obliged to resign if the Senate were to withhold supply or pass a motion of no confidence. Consequently, some special provisions about the term of office of ministers would be required. Ministers should first be approved

4 Sir Samuel Griffith, *Notes on Australian Federation*, p.3.

by the Senate (which could not, however, subsequently withdraw its approval). The House of Representatives would, of course, have co-ordinate powers. He also made the curious prediction that under a federal constitution a government could not simply dissolve the lower house if it had lost the confidence of parliament, a prediction that has been falsified on numerous occasions.

Nevertheless Griffith, despite his quite firm views on the matter, did not advocate that they should be entrenched in the constitution, because his conclusion was simply to recommend that ministers be appointed by the Governor-General.

Sir Richard Baker was altogether more vigorous and extreme in his advocacy. Having had his view turned down by the 1897 convention at its Adelaide session, he proceeded to restate his views in the form of a pamphlet. Cabinet government, he argued, was a very recent growth, unknown to the theory of the British Constitution, not sanctioned by law and usurping the powers of parliament. The existence of cabinets in a federation as a committee of the lower house 'must be a standing menace to the States' House'. What was needed was a hybrid embodying the virtues of cabinet but also possessing 'such qualities as will render it consistent with, if not an absolute equality, at all events an approximate equality in power between the two Federal Houses'. The best model for this purpose was Switzerland. He argued that

> the best test of any republican form of government is the security offered to minorities; that majorities will always look after themselves; that Federation is a compromise between the desire to unite and the desire not to unite; that the Senate should be the expression of that desire; and that unless we have a real live Senate, no matter what its theoretical powers may be, it will soon cease to express the Federal idea [i.e., if the cabinet system were introduced].

And he quoted his ringing peroration before the convention: 'If we adopt this cabinet system it will either kill Federation or Federation will kill it.'[5]

The clue to Baker's resistance is to be found in a revealing statement that cabinet government would result in 'amalgamation' rather than federation.[6] In pursuit of his aim he went to considerable

[5] Sir Richard Baker, *The Executive in a Federation*, p.6. This slogan was a variant of the more famous sentence uttered by Hackett of Western Australia at the 1891 convention: 'Either responsible government will kill federation, or federation . . . will kill responsible government'. (Federal Convention Debates, p.280.) Hackett also spoke of the failure of responsible government in Britain and Canada, but like Baker and Griffith, he did not advocate a presidential type of executive, which was fairly generally opposed.   [6] Federal Convention Debates, 1897-8, p.784.

lengths in an attempt to modify the accepted conventions of cabinet government. For example, he opposed collective responsibility, on the somewhat curious ground that it was the reason for the conversion of politics into a struggle between 'ins' and 'outs'. Ministers should be independent officers in the administration of their departments, and it should be parliament rather than cabinet which adjudicated on financial matters. His view was the most extreme one, but it found a sympathetic echo both in the other small states and in other upper houses. For example, the President of the Victorian Legislative Council, Sir William Zeal, moved that the constitution should provide for two of the Ministers of State mentioned in Section 64 to be Senators. There was general opposition to this on the grounds that it was overloading the constitution with detail, but members of other colonial upper houses whose interests were safeguarded by similar provisions in their own constitutions supported the amendment. Zeal's motion was effectively squashed by George Reid, who opposed it on the grounds that ability should be the only criterion of selection, and observed: 'Take my honourable friend himself. If he were sent up to represent a government in the Senate you could not find another like him to begin with. He is so good that no one would ever think of anyone else after him.'[7]

The simple answer to Baker was given in a speech by Henry Bournes Higgins, who observed that given Baker's premises, his conclusions were irresistible. If the actions of the federal government were to require the assent of the states as well as that of the electors, responsible government would be impossible. He compared responsible government favourably with the American system, which was what Baker's scheme would amount to. The broad reasons in favour of it were that it worked and people were accustomed to it. The American Civil War, he asserted, could hardly have broken out if there had been strong and undivided control by the central government.[8]

Even stronger opposition to Baker and Griffith was voiced by A. B. Piddington, another member of the convention, in a pamphlet published in 1898, which attacked the excessive powers given to the Senate by the federal constitution. The framers of the constitution, he argued, expected that the weight of precedent would bring about the operation of responsible government, and so they had merely specified that ministers were to sit in parliament. This reasoning would break down because of the powers given to the Senate, whose 'novel basis of authority and function' would pro-

7 Ibid., p.801.   8 Ibid., p.792.

vide 'the rock upon which Responsible Government would split'. Canada had avoided this danger by making the Senate subordinate to the House of Commons, and had not made the mistake of 'giving their solar system two suns'.

His forebodings about the Senate sound positively comical to a twentieth century observer. He wrote:

> The Senator of Australia would be a man wearing the star and garter of his constituency whenever he rose to speak; and how would such a magnifico compare in his own estimate or that of his province or of the nation or of the outside world, with the inferior creature who is returned to Parliament by a fraction of his own electorate — the whole colony?

Could it be supposed that this chamber, 'comprising the strongest and most ambitious politicians of the continent, and animated by an *esprit de corps* of unusual intensity, would be content to be ignored for long in the formation and control of the cabinet?' With this overweening influence it could, even without taking the final drastic step of refusing supply, be the dominant partner in the legislature, making and unmaking ministries at its whim.[9]

These arguments are only understandable in the context of a situation where party government was in its infancy. At the time of these debates, the Labour Party had just been formed and was not to wield effective power in either state or Commonwealth until more than a decade had passed. Even in Britain there was hardly yet the understanding that the working of cabinet government in a parliamentary democracy depends upon the character of its party system. Just as the conservatives who attempted to entrench the position of the states against the future Commonwealth failed to foresee the way in which a comparatively stable party system would frustrate their efforts, so the radicals greatly exaggerated the potential threat to popular government lurking in the powers of the Senate.

A more temperate view was put by Robert Garran, in a book published during the course of this controversy. He remarked that federalism did not, in fact, demand the existence of any one kind of executive authority. The real lesson to be learned from the American presidency and from the elective Swiss Federal Council was the fact that such institutions had deep roots in local politics and social history. 'Our home growth is the cabinet system; its applicability to federalism is proved by the example of Canada.' It was also important, he urged, to allow scope for change. Respon-

9 A. B. Piddington, *Popular Government and Federation*, p.5.

sible government was a new thing and subject to evolution. 'It depends largely upon rules which are constantly varying, growing, developing, and the precise direction of whose development it is impossible to forecast . . . we must be careful to lay down only the essential principles of popular government, leaving the details of form as elastic as possible.' He went on to enunciate three principles suggested by the history of cabinet government in Britain. These were, firstly, appointment of ministers by the Crown during pleasure; secondly, the right of a minister to sit in either house; and thirdly, that revenue could be raised or spent only with the consent of parliament.[10]

Garran, too, made predictions which have not been entirely borne out. Possibly influenced by his opponents, he thought that the ministry might need the confidence of both houses. A somewhat more accurate prediction was that 'Premature dissolutions of the Federal Parliament with the consequent expense of national re-elections, would prove inconvenient and . . . will be allowed to fall into disuse. This, again, may tend towards the permanence of the Ministry during the life of a Parliament.'

[10] R. R. Garran, *The Coming Commonwealth,* pp.148-50.

4

CABINET AND THE HIGH COURT

IT HAS SOMETIMES been contended that the written character of the seven Australian constitutions renders the status of cabinet government in Australia rather different from that of the British prototype. This view has, on the whole, been rejected by Australian constitutional authorities, on the grounds that a study of the actual provisions shows them to be permissive rather than mandatory. The judgment of the Privy Council, reversing Lutwyche J.'s decision in 1874, is an example of the confusion exhibited even by their Lordships at a time when Bagehot's writings were still novel.

The real differences between Britain and Australia are political rather than constitutional. Even the position of the Crown, which until 1926 was formally different in Britain and Australia, has differed for political rather than for constitutional reasons. The survival of some of the royal prerogatives in Australia has been the result of party relationships in Australian parliaments, rather than of any fancied difference between the status of a colonial Governor and the British monarch in regard to their right of independent action.

Nevertheless, the existence of a written constitution, and of a written federal constitution in particular, has to some extent borne out Dicey's maxim that federalism means conservatism and legalism. Questions of interpretation arise over the existence of specified legislative powers which have sometimes appeared to limit the executive authority of governments in Australia, or could be argued by interested parties to limit the freedom of action of a minister or of a government. Although the case of *Toy* v. *Musgrove* raised the same question twelve years before federation, all the cases cited in this chapter involve only the Commonwealth, whose position has been complicated because its powers are all enumerated, and sometimes doubtful in extent. Partly as a result, a number of cases have been heard in the High Court involving challenges to Commonwealth executive acts.

The main problems arise over the power of a minister to take executive action without specific parliamentary endorsement or delegation. The basic view of the Court in this matter, at any rate, was stated in the famous *Engineers' Case*. The majority judgment, delivered by Isaacs J. on behalf of himself and Knox C.J., Starke and Rich JJ., emphasized the principle of responsible government embodied in the Commonwealth Constitution and warned against the danger of citing American parallels. The important argument was that where legislative authority is given, the corresponding executive power is necessarily implied.[1]

The leading case in this sphere is the *Wooltops Case* of 1922.[2] On this occasion, the Court considered the implications of several sections of the constitution dealing with the executive power, and distinguished three aspects of the vesting of executive authority in the Governor-General by Section 61. Firstly, Section 61 places the Commonwealth's executive power in the Crown; secondly, it enables the Governor-General to exercise this power; and thirdly, it defines its operation by stating that it 'extends to the execution and maintenance of the Constitution and the laws of the Commonwealth'. In this passage the terms 'execution and maintenance' refer to 'the doing of something immediately prescribed or authorized by the Constitution', while 'laws of the Commonwealth' refers to acts of the federal parliament.[3]

Dealing with the third aspect, Isaacs J. pointed out that the validity of executive acts had still to be determined, because the section only distinguishes between the Commonwealth and the states, but does not cover the legality of a particular executive act within its own sphere. Sources of authority for any act must, therefore, be examined, and of these he distinguished three. The first is British law where no Commonwealth legislation exists; secondly, there are the powers which derive simply from the existence of executive authority and are recognized by the courts, e.g., the protection of executive officials in the course of their duty; finally, there are Acts of the Commonwealth parliament. Where the Commonwealth is exercising power concurrently with the states, it must legislate before its executive functions can be exercised.[4]

Finally, the Court went on to point out that Commonwealth executive power was not specifically defined by constitutional provisos as in the United States (the most famous being the approval of the Senate in treaty-making). As a result, the Commonwealth could not impose taxes unless the particular tax had been specifically legislated for. On this basis, the Court ruled against the Commonwealth in the particular case, because it held that the Com-

[1] *Amalgamated Society of Engineers* v. *Adelaide Steamship Co. and Others* (1920), 28 C.L.R. 129.
[2] *The Commonwealth* v. *Colonial Combing Spinning and Weaving Co. Ltd,* 31 C.L.R. 421.   [3] Ibid., p.431.   [4] Ibid., p.439.

monwealth government could not, without parliamentary sanction, enter into agreements concerning the production of wooltops which involved payments to or by the Commonwealth. Isaacs, Higgins and Starke JJ. held in a joint decision that such agreements involved either taxation or the appropriation of public moneys, and were therefore void.[5]

In several other cases, the Court has upheld the view stated in the *Wooltops Case* that the executive power is implied in the legislative power. In the case of *Walsh and Johnson,* Starke J. ruled that a minister's power to do things exists because parliament is authorized to legislate on the matter. If parliament is not authorized to legislate or has not legislated, the minister cannot simply act on the grounds that his action is incidental to the execution and maintenance of the constitution.[6] However, in the *Clothing Factory Case,* where Victorian clothing manufacturers objected to the fact that the Commonwealth government's clothing factory was supplying uniforms to state government departments and other public and private concerns, the Court ruled in favour of the Commonwealth. In this case, the Court held that the action was incidental to the defence power. The internal organization of a clothing factory was 'largely a matter for determination by those to whom is entrusted the sole responsibility for the conduct of naval and military defence . . . in such a matter, much must be left to the discretion of the Governor-General and the responsible ministers'.[7]

These cases imply the view that parliament can delegate legislative power to the minister. Other cases where a similar view has been expressed were those of the *Welsbach Light Company* in 1916; *Roche* v. *Kronheimer* in 1921; the *Transport Workers' Case* in 1931; and the *Uniform Tax Case* in 1942.[8]

Another group of cases has turned on the minister's power to bind the Crown by his actions. The Court's views on this matter have not been entirely consistent. In the *Bread Case*[9] in 1916, which established the fact that the Commonwealth could do many

---

5 Following two British decisions in the same year: see *Attorney-General* v. *Wilts United Dairies Ltd,* 91 L.J.K.B. 897, and *Mackay* v. *Attorney-General for British Columbia,* 1 L.R.A.C. 457.

6 *Ex parte Walsh and Johnson, in re Yates* (1925), 37 C.L.R. 138.

7 *Attorney-General for Victoria* v. *The Commonwealth* (1935), 52 C.L.R. 559.

8 *Welsbach Light Co. of Australasia* v. *The Commonwealth* (1916), 22 C.L.R. 268; *Roche* v. *Kronheimer* (1921), 29 C.L.R. 329; *Victorian Stevedoring and General Contracting Pty Ltd and Meakes* v. *Dignan* (1931), 46 C.L.R. 73; *South Australia* v. *The Commonwealth* (1942), 65 C.L.R. 373.

9 *Farey* v. *Burvett* (1916), 21 C.L.R. 433.

things in prosecuting a war which were not obviously related to its defence power, a separate judgment by Isaacs J. argued that the minister could make regulations of far-reaching import because the defence power carried with it the royal war prerogative. This argument, which was obviously intended to buttress the widest possible interpretation of the defence power, might not, of course, appeal equally to the Court in peace time.

A more recent case has defined the relationship between a minister as head of a department and as a member of the Executive Council. In the case of *Radio Corporation Pty. Ltd.* v. *the Commonwealth*[10] Evatt and Dixon JJ. argued that the minister was not merely a member of the Executive Council on whose advice the Governor-General acts; he is also the member through whom the executive government acts in the particular matter, and has the authority to make a particular order or direction in an individual case.

The outcome of these decisions and of more recent challenges to particular administrative acts has been to establish the fact that the freedom of action of a minister in an Australian cabinet is limited only by a certain waywardness in the disposition of the High Court to interpret some actions as being 'incidental' to the power exercised. In general, the similarity in the constitutional status of cabinet government in Australia to its counterpart in Britain has been underlined by the Court's decisions.

[10] (1938), 59 C.L.R. 192.

Part III

CABINET AND THE CROWN

5

THE CONSTITUTIONAL FRAMEWORK

IN THEORY, the powers of the Governor-General of Australia and of the state Governors are very great. Like the royal prerogative from which they emanated, however, their retention depends on their non-employment. In practice, there have been few examples of Governors attempting to exercise their prerogatives directly since about 1880, with the important exception of the dissolution of parliament. Some miscellaneous uses of the prerogative are mentioned in succeeding chapters.

To some extent, the constitutional provisions, and those in the letters patent, commission, and instructions, represent an anachronism in that they confer powers on the Governor or Governor-General which he never exercises. These powers are better understood as being conferred on the executive authority as such, and since official recognition that the Governor acts only on the advice of his responsible ministers was incorporated in revised instructions in 1892, the sting has been taken out of the possibility of independent action, which aroused a good deal of real or artificial indignation during the first generation of responsible government.

The fact remains that Australian Governors have been able to exercise independent discretion far more frequently than the British monarch. This is not a reflection of a different constitutional situation, as is sometimes argued, but of a party system and an electoral system in some states which periodically leads to crises that provoke the exercise of gubernatorial discretion. Unstable party alliances and deadlocks between the two houses of parliament have, in particular, led to frequent requests and almost equally frequent refusals of dissolution.

The offices of Governor and of Governor-General are established by a few sections in each Australian constitution, of which the Commonwealth Constitution may be taken as a representative example. Section 2 creates the office; Section 3 assigns a salary of £10,000 and makes a permanent appropriation for it; Section

4 provides for powers to be exercised by an administrator if necessary. Section 126 provides for the appointment of deputies to act for the Governor-General anywhere in the Commonwealth.[1]

The powers of the Governor or Governor-General are, of course, conferred by those sections of the constitution dealing with the executive government (see chapter 1). In addition, three documents issued by the Crown confer certain powers and functions. These are the letters patent constituting the office of Governor, the Governor's commission, and the royal instructions. Until 1879 the appointment of colonial Governor was always accompanied by a set of separate letters patent; but, following representations from the Canadian Attorney-General, the practice was introduced, in the Australian colonies as elsewhere in the Empire, of a permanent set of letters patent establishing the office of Governor. The letters patent give Governors power to make grants of Crown land, to appoint judges and other officials, to grant pardons, to suspend or remove Crown officials (a power granted expressly in the case of ministers by instructions under the sign manual in 1859, following an attempt by a defeated ministry to stay in office), the summoning, prorogation, and dissolution of parliament, and the appointment of a deputy. Duties enumerated include the care and use of the public seal and the appointment of an Executive Council.

These powers and duties were further elaborated by permanent instructions given under the sign manual, including the power to summon the Executive Council, which cannot proceed with business until it is summoned; the appointment of a president for the Executive Council in the Governor's absence; and the right to act in opposition to the Executive Council in cases of imperative necessity, provided the circumstances are immediately reported to the Crown.

On the establishment of the office of Governor-General following the passage of the Australian Constitution Act through the British parliament, letters patent were issued on 29 October 1900. At the same time new letters patent were issued to all state Governors, which have since been amended several times. The New South Wales letters patent and instructions may be taken as an example of the present provisions in these documents. They describe the boundaries of the state, the Governor's powers and authorities, the oaths which he must take, the use of the public

[1] Used in the early days to enable state Governors to sign warrants for expenditure, and occasionally when federal ministers have been sworn in by a state Governor.

seal, the constitution of the Executive Council, the grant of lands, the appointment of judges, the granting of pardons, the remission of fines, the suspension or removal of officers, the summoning, dissolution, and prorogation of parliament, and the appointment of deputies for the Governor. The provision regarding the dissolution of parliament is of interest. It states: 'The Governor may exercise all powers lawfully belonging to Us in respect of the summoning proroguing or dissolving any legislative body, which now is or hereafter may be established within Our said State.' This provision was last amended in 1935 and contains an implied reference to possible changes in the character of the Legislative Council (the abolition of which was an important issue in New South Wales politics in the 1920s).

The Governor's instructions correspond largely to the powers given by letters patent. They include the following:

In the execution of the powers and authorities vested in him, the Governor shall be guided by the advice of the Executive Council, but if in any case he shall see sufficient cause to dissent from the opinion of the said Council, he may act in the exercise of his said powers and authorities in opposition to the opinion of the Council, reporting the matter to Us without delay with the reasons for his so acting.

In any such case it shall be competent to any member of the said Council to require that there be recorded upon the minutes of the council the grounds of any advice or opinion that he may give upon the question.

The instructions also contain a list of certain Bills of the state parliament which must be reserved for the assent of the British monarch. The topics covered are divorce; grants of land or money to the Governor; laws affecting the currency of the state; laws inconsistent with treaty obligations; Bills of 'extraordinary nature and importance' which may prejudice the royal prerogative, the rights of non-resident British subjects, or the trade and shipping of the Empire; and finally, Bills containing previously vetoed or disallowed provisions. In the latter case, reservation is subject to the dispatch of instructions from the Secretary of State, or to a clause in the Bill which may require it to obtain prior royal assent, or to the necessity of meeting an emergency, except where the legislation may be repugnant to the laws of England.

The provisions regarding reservation and disallowance of Bills indicate most clearly the archaic character of the instructions. Since federation, functions relating to currency, external affairs, and external trade have been exercised by the Commonwealth government. The instructions also reflect the results of conflict over the right of the Governor to grant pardons. In 1900 they were revised to provide that the grant of a pardon or a reprieve should not be exercised except upon the advice of the Executive Council in capital cases or of a minister in other cases. The Governor is also instructed to consider the effects of likely repercussions outside the state.

Ever since Higinbotham's day, conflicts, not to say confusion, have prevailed over the relationship between the constitutional clauses regulating the powers of the Governor and the Executive Council, and the nature of the instructions and powers given to the Governor in documents under the royal sign manual. A number of aspects may be considered briefly.

The Scope of the Royal Prerogative

The exercise of a general prerogative by Governors was explicitly denied by a High Court judgment in 1922. In the *Wooltops Case,* Higgins J. declared that 'the Governor-General is not a general agent of His Majesty with power to exercise all His Majesty's prerogatives; he is a special agent with power to carry out the Constitution and the laws, and such powers and functions as the King may assign to him'.[2] This proposition that a Governor or Governor-General did not have the status of a Viceroy had already been enunciated by the Privy Council some years earlier in the case of *Commercial Cable Company* v. *Governor of Newfoundland,*[3] a judgment which Higgins J. cited with approval.

Although this point is now quite clear, the exercise of particular powers may still be open to doubt. An example of such confusion was provided in the debates over the Acts Interpretation Bill introduced in the Commonwealth parliament during the first few months after federation. This measure was modelled on existing colonial and British legislation and contained a clause providing that the Act would bind the Crown. Deakin, the Attorney-General, stated that the intention of this phrase was to ensure that in any future Acts, 'affecting . . . the prerogative of the Crown, we shall be able to apply without question to the words of that measure the definitions which are contained in this Bill'.[4] A lengthy debate followed, and the clause was recommitted for further consideration. It was pointed out during the debate that although the Bill was modelled on the British Interpretation Act of 1889, the British

[2] *The Commonwealth* v. *Colonial Combing Spinning and Weaving Co. Ltd,* 31 C.L.R. 453-4. [3] (1916), 2 L.R.A.C. 616.
[4] *Parl. Deb.* (C. of A.), 1901, 1: 789.

authorities had objected to the particular phrase, because they feared its possible implications in certain crucial matters such as appeals to the Privy Council and legislation on foreign affairs. Answering these objections, Deakin pointed out that use of the phrase relieved the government of interpreting the same question every time a Commonwealth Act was challenged. 'It might be submitted by some refined argument that, as this act did not bind the Crown, its interpretation of these particular words in an act which did bind the Crown would not be binding.'[5] As the British Act obviously had the same intention, he therefore proposed that the language implied in it should be embodied in the Commonwealth Act. This meant the substitution of the words 'shall be binding on the Crown' for the earlier version. In this form the clause was passed.

The Governor and the Executive Council

Legalistic confusion has also surrounded the definition of the relations between the Governor and the Executive Council. State and Commonwealth constitutions refer sometimes to the 'Governor' or 'Governor-General' and sometimes to the 'Governor-in-Council' or 'Governor-General in Council'. The latter phrase means the Governor or Governor-General acting on the advice of the Executive Council, which he does in all cases except those of appointing ministers and summoning or dissolving parliament. At times, however, attempts have been made to entrench the principle of responsible government in this part of the various Constitution Acts, by providing that the term 'Governor-in-Council' be used almost to the exclusion of the single word 'Governor'.

The colonial politicians who took part in the federal convention debates obviously had in mind their own experiences or those of their predecessors with strong-minded Governors and attempted to limit the powers of the future Governor-General in this way. In 1891, for instance, Reid and Carruthers of New South Wales proposed that the wording of Section 61 should refer to the vesting of the executive power in the 'Governor-General-in-Council' rather than the 'Governor-General'. Reid argued that the prerogative in the colonies was limited to the right of summoning, proroguing and dissolving parliament, of issuing proclamations, of pardoning offenders, and so forth. Executive acts, on the contrary, were done only on the advice of the Executive Council. Barton, later Prime Minister, lulled these fears by pointing out that the accepted constitutional practice was that prerogative acts were only done on

5 Ibid., 1901, 1: 832-3.

ministerial advice, so that the amendment was unnecessary, and the movers did not press the matter to a division.[6]

However, the issue was reopened at the convention of 1898, where Deakin introduced an amendment to Section 68 of the constitution, in which control of the armed forces was vested in the Governor-General as the Queen's representative. He proposed to delete the references to the Queen and after the word Governor-General to insert the statement, 'acting under the advice of the Executive Council'. Deakin referred, in his argument, to papers recently tabled in the New South Wales parliament dealing with disputes in that colony over the relative authority of the Governor and the ministry over the armed forces, and quoted the opinion of Todd that the royal prerogative in military matters could be exercised only on advice. Two cases were in point in New South Wales. During the Parkes ministry in 1881, the commandant of the New South Wales forces offered the British government an artillery battery for service in South Africa during the first Boer War, without previously informing the government. During the Dibbs ministry in 1890, the officer commanding the New South Wales forces was given the right to consult the Governor directly on matters of discipline. Further examples were cited from Victoria in the 1860s, as well as the dismissal of the Molteno government in Cape Colony by Sir Bartle Frere in 1878.

The amendment was opposed by Barton, who argued that such prescriptions were unnecessary. The 1881 case was exceptional and should not be treated as an example of what was likely to happen in most circumstances. He quoted the minute written to the Governor by Parkes at the time: 'The military forces have been called into existence by the Parliament, and are paid out of the revenue of the colony and they are as much subject to the control of the responsible government existing in this colony as any other branch of the public service.' As long as it was generally agreed that the prerogative was granted on the understanding that it was to be exercised on advice, the use of the words 'Governor-General-in-Council' rather than 'Governor-General' would make no difference. To insert them would only make the constitution-framers ridiculous for their lack of understanding of constitutional law. A division was taken and despite the support given to Deakin by several other radicals, notably Kingston, Cockburn and Isaacs, his amendment was defeated.[7]

A recent constitutional writer observes that the legal reason

6 Federal Convention Debates, 1891, pp.765-6.
7 Ibid., 1898, pp.2249-64.

for the Governor's inability to act independently, except on the so-called 'personal' prerogatives, is the refusal of the courts to recognize any exercise of Crown authority unless the order is sealed or counter-signed by a minister of the Crown. Following Dicey, he says, 'There must be somebody else to accept responsibility for any act done by the King, or by the Governor-General or by a State Governor in his name; because the King, Governor-General, or State Governor cannot be held personally responsible.'[8] Even in the case of the personal prerogatives, such as the dissolution of parliament and the appointment of ministers, advice must normally be taken, because unless the Governor can find a different Executive Council to give different advice, the most fundamental convention of all comes into play — namely, that the ministry must have the confidence of the lower house of parliament. If a Governor were to refuse the advice of a ministry, and then were forced to reappoint it, still giving the same advice, because he could not find an alternative ministry with support in the lower house, his position would become untenable.

The Appointment of Ministers

In the early years of responsible government, there seems to have been some confusion in the minds of Governors about their right to scrutinize the membership of a ministry. A particularly curious example occurred in Victoria, which was, in 1855, the first colony to introduce responsible government. Governor Hotham received the constitution, as passed by the British parliament, in October of that year. With it came the instructions that it must be proclaimed within one month after receipt. The Colonial Secretary, Haines, was commissioned to form a government in November, but his commission was accompanied by a minute from the Governor insisting on his right to veto the appointment of any minister, and to consent to any measure before it was introduced into parliament. His misunderstanding of the nature of cabinet government was indicated in the statement that he did not 'wish to attend cabinet meetings'.

This particular incident had an ironic sequel. The four members of Hotham's Executive Council agreed to join the first administration under responsible government at his wish, but were afraid of losing their pensions if they were defeated at an election. The constitution only provided that they would receive them if they were 'compelled to retire on political grounds', a phrase whose meaning was clear to nobody. By a subterfuge, Haines and the

8 T. P. Fry, *The Crown, Cabinets, and Parliaments in Australia*, p.29.

Attorney-General, Stawell, persuaded the Governor to release them from office on 'political grounds'; he then re-appointed them to the seats they had vacated in the Legislative Council, with their old positions. In the meantime they had been able to claim their pensions.[9]

Although no similar incidents occurred elsewhere, Jenks, evidently still imagining himself in Hotham's day, could write in 1891 that the Governor could make changes in the proposed cabinet if the list contained 'the name of anyone against whom very serious objections exist, or proposes a new and revolutionary arrangement'.[10]

The Governor and Cabinet

Throughout the nineteenth century, the fear that Governors could refuse to take the advice of their responsible ministers, or could be instructed by the Colonial Office to refuse advice, continued to haunt the minds of colonial politicians. Wheare suggests that despite the granting of responsible government, the obscurity of the term and the repeated refusal of British governments to distinguish clearly between 'domestic' and 'external' affairs, made the colonies effectively subordinate to the United Kingdom government, despite the existence of a general convention of equality. Apart from the fact that the Governor might legally act, even in domestic affairs, on the advice of Her Majesty's ministers rather than his own, 'it was not laid down anywhere in legal or non-legal rules that the Governor, as the representative of Her Majesty, would be required to act in accordance with the rules which Her Majesty obeyed in similar circumstances'.[11]

The accepted convention at this time was that the Governor could refuse advice in extreme cases, so long as he was able to find other ministers who would accept responsibility *post factum* for his actions. The matter was raised at the Colonial Conference in 1887, where Deakin attacked the prevailing view, but could not obtain the support even of his own fellow-Australians. It was clear, says Keith, that many colonial politicians still believed in the exercise of a wide discretion by the British Crown.[12]

In the twentieth century, of course, this position has been greatly modified, culminating in the decisions of the Imperial

9 The incident is described in H. G. Turner, *A History of the Colony of Victoria*, vol. 2, ch. 3. One of the four, Childers, Collector of Customs, subsequently became British Chancellor of the Exchequer.

10 Jenks, *The Government of Victoria*, p.273.

11 K. C. Wheare, *The Statute of Westminster and Dominion Status*, pp.54-5.   12 Keith, *Responsible Government in the Dominions*, pt. 2, ch. 3.

Conferences of 1926 and 1930. Nevertheless, Keith suggests, the extent of the Governor's prerogative rights remains difficult to define. 'It is possible only when the Privy Council has definitely decided an issue, and few of these have arisen.'[13] The position was, however, eased by a decision of the Privy Council in 1920 that any prerogative power could be suspended by legislation.[14]

Keith's own view on the relations between the Governor and the ministry fluctuated considerably during his own lifetime. On many occasions he reaffirmed his view that the Governor could act only on advice, and that his disapproval of any advice given to him by the ministry could only be manifested indirectly. Nevertheless, in 1928 he wrote, 'normally the Governor has merely the power of resistance; he can refuse to accept advice and the ministry must then either withdraw the advice—appealing, if necessary, to the Secretary of State to over-rule the Governor—or resign'.[15] And again, 'He [the Governor] may not act without advice, but he can always refuse to act, and his refusal, whatever its constitutional result, is clearly legal. Similarly, he can dismiss a Minister who insists on acting, even within his own sphere of authority, contrary to the wishes of the Governor.'[16]

This statement is all the more remarkable when one considers that in the same work he takes every opportunity to condemn the action of the former Governor-General of Canada, Lord Byng, in refusing a dissolution to Mackenzie King in 1926, and to criticize various Australian Governors for similar actions. Keith's partisanship was, of course, well known, but he was dealing with a confused problem. Some attempt to straighten out the confusion was made by the Imperial Conferences of 1926 and 1930.

The Statute of Westminster

At the Imperial War Conference of 1918, two Dominion Prime Ministers attempted to do away with the function of the Governor-General as intermediary between the British and Dominion governments. W. M. Hughes, of Australia, was the prime mover, and he was supported by Sir Robert Borden, of Canada. At their instance, the conference adopted a resolution reading:

This Conference is of the opinion that the development which has taken place in the relations between the United Kingdom and the Dominions necessitates such a change in administrative arrangements and in the channels of communication between

13 Ibid., p.85.
14 *Attorney-General* v. *de Keyser's Royal Hotel* (1920), 1 L.R.A.C. 508.
15 Keith, op. cit., p.153.   16 Ibid., p.108.

their governments as will bring them more directly in touch with each other.[17]

To bring this about, Hughes and Borden proposed the introduction of direct communication between the British and Dominion Prime Ministers, and the abolition of Colonial Office intermediacy. The Colonial Secretary, Walter Long, and most of the Governors-General opposed this move, and its implementation was delayed until 1926. The so-called Balfour Report issued by the Imperial Conference of that year declared that 'The Governor-General of a Dominion is the representative of the Crown, holding in all essential respects the same position in relation to the administration of public affairs in the Dominion as is held by His Majesty the King in Great Britain.' The Governor-General, moreover, was not 'the representative or agent of His Majesty's Government in Great Britain or of any Department of that Government'.[18] The 1930 Imperial Conference took this further by resolving that the constitutional status of the Governor-General had been altered by the 1926 declaration, and from now on 'the constitutional practice that His Majesty acts on the advice of responsible ministers applied also in this instance'.[19]

Since 1927, the Australian Governor-General has ceased to act as the channel of communication with the British government. The Statute of Westminster, passed as a consequence of the Imperial Conference of 1930, removed restrictions on the legislative competence of dominion parliaments apart from those laid down in their own constitutions. The failure of the Commonwealth to adopt sections 2-6 of the Statute before 1939 meant that when the war broke out uncertainty continued over the scope of the legislative competence of the Commonwealth parliament (and by implication, the executive authority of the Commonwealth government). The Attorney-General, Dr H. V. Evatt, stated during the debate on the adoption of the Statute of Westminster in 1942 that the necessity for reserving Bills passed by the Commonwealth parliament had sometimes led to delays of up to four months, a situation which was intolerable in wartime.[20]

The declaration of 1926, and the Statute of Westminster itself, still leave untouched the question of the relationship between state Governors and their ministries. As a result, the states remain subject to disallowance, reservation, and lack of extra-territorial legislative power. The situation has not been eased by the adoption of

[17] Ernest Scott, *Australia During the War*, pp.184-8.
[18] Cmd. 2768, 1926.   [19] Cmd. 3717, 1930.   [20] Wheare, op. cit., ch. 8.

any convention to regulate the relation between state Governors and their ministers (although the government of Canada has overcome this by agreement with the provincial governments). Despite this uncertainty, decisions of the High Court and the Privy Council since 1926 suggest that there is little doubt in practice that the relationship of the Governor to his ministers is in all important respects the same as that of the Governor-General to the federal ministry. Forsey[21] and Evatt hold that this applies both in Canada and in Australia.

Evatt lists a number of unsolved problems which have not been settled by the adoption of these conventions:

(1) the extent of the Governor's reserve power in refusing advice or acting on his own initiative;

(2) although it is clear that in appointing a new Governor-General the British monarch now acts on advice, it is not clear what would happen if this advice were immediately followed by a general election and a new ministry were to come to power;

(3) as the relation of 'agency' has been formally abandoned, has a Dominion government any redress against a Governor who acts in a way of which it disapproves? 'The Imperial Conference's adoption of the Balfour Report did not make any provision for solving *bona fide* disputes between Governor and Ministers where the former insisted upon his possession of some real discretionary authority.'[22]

In company with Harrison Moore, he rejects Keith's criticism of the suggestion in the 1926 report that in a matter concerning a dominion the British monarch should act on the advice of dominion ministers. An English constitutional writer has taken a similar view against Keith, arguing that 'just as the King, in matters affecting the United Kingdom, takes the advice of his Prime Minister in London, so in matters affecting Canada he will take the advice of his Prime Minister in the Dominion, and in the case of Australia, that of his Prime Minister in the Commonwealth of Australia, and so forth'. It was not to be supposed that Lord Stamfordham (King George V's private secretary) would 'run the Empire'.[23]

The Royal Visit, 1954

An odd complication arose in the relationship between the British

21 *The Royal Power of Dissolution in the British Commonwealth.*
22 *The King and His Dominion Governors,* p.195.
23 E. Jenks, 'The Imperial Conference and the Constitution', *Cambridge Law Journal,* 1927, vol. 3, no. 1.

monarch and the Australian Governor-General (and also the New Zealand Governor-General) as a result of the visit of Queen Elizabeth to these two countries in the summer of 1953-4. Doubts concerning the relation between the prerogative and delegated functions made it necessary to pass, in both countries, special Acts to define the situation. The Royal Powers Act of 1953 enabled the Queen, when in Australia, to perform in person any statutory powers exercisable by the Governor-General (with a saving clause respecting the Governor-General's powers). The Act provided, moreover, that these powers were to be exercised on the advice of the Executive Council. A Canadian writer observes that 'in the absence of special legislation forcing the Queen to share in their performance, there are certain Head of State functions which are delegated by Parliament to the Governor-General exclusively'.[24]

An earlier example of the same problem had in fact almost arisen at the very outset of federation. The first Governor-General, Lord Hopetoun, in a letter to the first Commonwealth Prime Minister, Edmund Barton, questioned the constitutionality of the opening of the federal parliament by the Duke of York (later King George V). Hopetoun pointed out that he had been told by the Colonial Secretary, Joseph Chamberlain, that His Royal Highness would bring a message from the Queen, but that the actual opening of parliament would be by the Governor-General.[25]

The Federal Problem

The existence of seven representatives of the British Crown in Australia has occasionally raised the difficult question of the 'divisibility' of the Crown, to which no answer seems likely.

The general position of the Crown in Australia, as laid down by the High Court, is that it cannot be eliminated from any Australian constitution except by an Act of the British parliament.[26] This seems to imply that the Crown is indivisible, but in a later judgment, Latham C.J. remarked that although the indivisibility of the Crown was politically important, it tended 'to dissolve into verbally impressive mysticism. It is of little assistance where the Commonwealth can sue a State.'[27] He repudiated the suggestion of an earlier Chief Justice, Sir Samuel Griffith, that the Crown should be regarded as several legal persons to get over this difficulty.

[24] Thomas Franck, 'The Governor-General and the Head of State Functions', *Canadian Bar Review*, 1954, vol. 32, no. 3, p.1092.
[25] Letter dated 21 February 1901 (Barton Papers, Commonwealth National Library, Canberra).
[26] Isaacs J. in *Taylor* v. *Attorney-General for Queensland* (1917), 23 C.L.R. 474.   [27] In *Minister for Works* v. *Gulson* (1944), 69 C.L.R. 38.

The matter was complicated in the earlier period of High Court interpretation of the Commonwealth Constitution (i.e., before 1920) by the doctrine of 'immunity of instrumentalities'. The case of *d'Emden* v. *Pedder*[28] established that state Acts of Parliament do not bind the Commonwealth executive. The principle of indivisibility enunciated by Isaacs J. as early as 1908[29] was, however, complicated by introducing the notion of 'agents', meaning that disputes could arise over the limits of the powers of the agents through the division of the powers of the Crown between Commonwealth and states. A recent writer suggests, instead, that the correct principle is to assert the indivisibility of the Crown with the accompanying proviso that it acts in different localities depending on local legislation which binds the Crown in various ways. This formulation makes allowance for the existence of responsible government, and also for federalism.[30]

28 (1903), 1 C.L.R. 91.
29 *R.* v. *Sutton* (1908), 5 C.L.R. 789.
30 W. A. Wynes, *Legislative, Executive, and Judicial Powers in Australia,* ch. 12.

6

THE POWERS OF A GOVERNOR

THE DECISIONS of the 1926 and 1930 Imperial Conferences, although removing any fancied stigma of constitutional inferiority from the countries of the British Commonwealth, did not really ease the problems of deciding what are the powers and functions of a Governor. For one thing, the assimilation of the status of the Governor-General to that of the British monarch implies that a settled situation does exist in the United Kingdom, a proposition which rests, as Evatt rather tartly remarks, only on assertion. In fact, whenever there has been a problem regarding the choice of the next Prime Minister, the right of the monarch to act on personal discretion has become a matter of controversy, as it did over the commissioning of Baldwin in 1924, of Ramsay MacDonald as head of a National government in 1931, and of Harold Macmillan in 1957. Even the prerogative of dissolution came perilously close to public discussion during the Asquith government's struggle to curb the House of Lords fifty years ago.

What is clear is the patent fact that the British political system works remarkably well, and that only in exceptional cases does the question of the monarch's right to select the new Prime Minister, to dissolve the House of Commons, or to refuse advice, ever arise. In a situation where the important differences are political ones, constitutional definitions can do little to alleviate controversies that arise over the actions of a Governor.

It should also be remembered that the 1926 and 1930 decisions refer only to the Commonwealth government, and make no mention whatever of the six state Governors. In practice, the margin of uncertainty is small, but it is real enough to produce a situation like that which occurred in New South Wales in 1932. The problem of the Governor's power is further aggravated by his transitoriness. On the one hand, as Bagehot wrote many years ago, the fact that Governors are not there for life has its advantages.

They are always intelligent, for they have to live by a difficult trade; they are nearly sure to be impartial, for they come from the ends of the earth; they are sure not to participate in the selfish desires of any colonial class or body, for long before these desires can have attained fruition, they will have passed to the other side of the world, be busy with other faces and other minds, be almost out of hearing what happens in a region they have half forgotten.

The price of these advantages may sometimes be too high, notwithstanding, for a colonial Governor is a man with no permanent interest in the colony. Because of the time it takes for him to understand its politics he is 'apt to be a slave to the prejudices of local people near him', and governs not 'in the interest of the colony, which he may mistake, but in his own interest, which he sees and is sure of. The first desire of a colonial Governor is not to get into a "scrape", not to do anything which may give trouble to his superiors—the Colonial Office—at home, that might cause an untimely and dubious recall.'[1]

Throughout the nineteenth century, there was a conflict of opinion between politicians, who maintained that a Governor could act only on the advice of responsible ministers, and the Colonial Office, which though reluctant to interfere in specific cases, wished the Governors to retain some discretion. In 1892, the royal instructions to Governors were revised, directing them to take ministerial advice in all cases, and to use their discretion only where imperial or other external interests were involved. This step had been preceded by a long series of incidents where Governors had attempted to intervene in the interests of what they conceived to be constitutional propriety.

Sir George Bowen, who held office both in Queensland and Victoria, was emphatic about the importance of the Governor's role. He wrote of the 'great and pervasive influence' of a conscientious Governor, of 'delicate crises to be smoothed away, and how serious the constitutional and imperial interests to be guarded —always, however, with the gloved hand and the sheathed sword— by the Queen's representative'.[2] Bowen quite soon had a chance to assert his discretion; in 1866, the Macalister government in Queensland was in debt, and proposed to issue government banknotes to solve its difficulties. The Governor's reaction to this was to withdraw his sword a little too openly from its sheath. His instructions laid down that he must reserve Bills affecting the currency, and he informed Macalister that he would 'under no circumstances' assent to the proposed measure. Before parliament could meet, he made a public statement giving his opinion that it would be wrong to bring down the Bill, as it could not become law. 'Precious time,' he said, should not be occupied 'which could

1 Walter Bagehot, *The English Constitution*, p.207.
2 S. Lane-Poole, *Thirty Years of Colonial Government*, vol. 1, p.80.

be employed in discussing and maturing measures which *can* be brought into immediate operation.' These measures, he believed, were the issue of Treasury Bills and an increase in taxation. Although Bowen was undoubtedly exasperated by the shifty tactics of Macalister (known to the public as 'Slippery Mac'), his action in trying to force the issue was misguided and led to a remarkable political crisis. Macalister resigned, and refused to withdraw his resignation at Bowen's request. The Governor then called upon Herbert and Raff, leaders of the opposition party, who agreed to put through more palatable legislation. They did not accept office, as this would have necessitated re-election to parliament, but asked to be sworn in as Executive Councillors without portfolio.

Macalister, not surprisingly, objected, claiming that a money Bill which was not introduced by responsible Ministers of the Crown would be unconstitutional. His party withdrew from the Legislative Assembly; Herbert and Raff managed to scrape together a quorum, standing orders were suspended, and a Bill authorizing an issue of Treasury bonds was rushed through both houses and received immediate assent. Next morning the new ministry was gazetted in the regular way. Public feeling was now at boiling point, and Herbert was surrounded in the streets of Brisbane by an angry crowd, his hat was knocked over his eyes, and he was pelted with stones and mud. The Governor was publicly denounced for his partiality, and a petition was sent to the Colonial Office for his removal, which was ignored.[3]

At a somewhat later date, one of the most notable of Australian Governors-General, Sir Ronald Munro-Ferguson, opposed the suggestion made at the Imperial War Conference in 1918 for direct contact between the governments of the British Commonwealth, on the grounds that the Governor-General represented an indispensable part of the Commonwealth structure. He argued that if the Governor-General were no longer the channel of communication between the British government and the dominion government, he would lose much of his prestige and would not know what was happening in the relations between the two countries. He would not be able to advise the Crown on public affairs or to give an impartial opinion on the views of the various political parties.

As the Crown represents the chief link between the United Kingdom and the dominions, and presents the only kind of

[3] Cf. T. A. Coghlan, *Labor and Industry in Australia,* vol. 3, pp.1177-9. Herbert, who had been first Premier of Queensland, later became permanent head of the Colonial Office, where his experiences in Queensland and elsewhere evidently disposed him to caution in dealing with self-governing colonies. (See Hall, *Australia and England.*)

security under the British constitution for that continuous
national policy on which so much depends, it does seem unfortunate that, at this juncture, the status of a Governor-General
should be reduced to that of a British resident attached to a
Dominion Government and with less real power than a
Dominion Minister attached to the Imperial Cabinet.[4]

One more example of the 'broad' view of the Governor's position may be quoted from the Commonwealth Year Book. This
statement lays down that

> a Governor is entitled to the fullest confidence of his Ministers,
> to be informed at once of any important decision taken by his
> Cabinet and to discuss them with the utmost freedom. He can
> point out objections, give advice, deprecate measures, and urge
> alterations, subject, however, to his remaining always behind
> the scenes . . . even in the case of a ministerial act he can forbid
> a Minister to take any action on pain of dismissal.

The somewhat startling assertion is also made that the Governor
is not bound to be satisfied with the legal correctness of ministerial
advice and 'in matters of law he must exercise his own judgment
if he is in doubt'.[5]

Professor Keith, in spite of his frequent lapses, appears on the
whole to have taken the view that the Governor's discretion should
be minimal. He quotes an article by the radical publicist, Goldwin
Smith, written in the 1890s: 'A Governor is now politically a
cipher; he holds a petty court and makes champagne flow under
his roof, receives civic addresses and makes flattering replies, but
he has lost the power not only of initiation but of salutary control.'
Keith suggests that this picture is more accurate than the older
view held by Todd, who regarded a Governor as a kind of pre-
siding genius, watching over and checking the excesses of colonial
politicians. Keith qualifies his remarks by observing that a man
with the right personal qualities may do much. 'If he has tact and
ability there is opened a wide field of influence . . . he can point
out objections, he can criticize, suggest, and obtain alterations even
in purely local policy, apart altogether from his function of dealing
with Imperial interests.' His conclusion, however, is that it is fatal
for a Governor to be thought to have discretion concerning such
an important matter as the dissolution of parliament: 'A Prime
Minister will hesitate to unburden himself freely to a Governor

4 Scott, *Australia during the War*, p.186.
5 *Commonwealth Year Book*, 1925, no. 18, pp.78-80.

who may remember afterwards his confidences and feel bound to take them into account when later he would come to him . . . for a dissolution.'[6]

Dr Evatt, who is in general inclined to stress the need for reducing the discretion of Governors to a minimum, feels none the less that this limitation should be achieved by defining quite clearly what a Governor can or cannot do. He complains of the absence of any general rule as to the extent of the Governor's discretion to refuse to act on ministerial advice. In each case, the Crown representative must decide for himself what is just and expedient. The ideal situation would be one where the 'exercise of great prerogative powers is controlled and regulated by general principles openly stated and applied with complete indifference to the welfare or detriment of particular parties or interests'.[7]

Action at the Governor's Discretion

The difficulties of discretionary action, already great enough in constitutional principle, are further enhanced by the sometimes intolerable conditions in which a decision must be made. One of these arises from the dual allegiance owed by a Governor to the local population and to the British Crown through the relevant department (since 1947, the Commonwealth Relations Office). There have been numerous occasions when actions taken on the advice of local ministers incurred the displeasure of the Secretary of State for the Colonies (who was the minister concerned until 1925). Colonial Office displeasure does not always work in the same direction; for instance, an attempt by a Governor to behave constitutionally and resist advice by his ministers which he thinks to be illegal may be politically embarrassing for the British government.

In the first generation after the grant of responsible government, the attitude of the Colonial Office was sometimes a source of great discomfort for Australian Governors. The most famous picture of an interfering Colonial Office is given in Buller's description of 'Mr Mother-Country', a fussy and nervous busybody who had to be consulted on every trifle of administration.[8] After the grant of responsible government, Colonial Office caution in not putting forth ideas unless they were clearly desired by colonial opinion

6 Keith, *Responsible Government in the Dominions,* pp.105-7.
7 H. V. Evatt, *The King and His Dominion Governors,* pp.144-5.
8 That this was an unjustified caricature of Sir James Stephen is now generally agreed. Cf. Bell and Morrell, *Select Documents on British Colonial Policy 1830-60;* Hall, *Australia and England,* pp.45-63; Paul Knaplund, *James Stephen and the British Colonial System 1813-1847.*

was just as marked. 'Thirty years earlier Downing Street had been subject to reproach for its jealous restriction of colonial rights and its minute supervision over colonial affairs; now it was so shy of Imperial responsibilities that . . . it waited for popular feeling in the colonies to give the lead.'[9]

There was, indeed, a case in the early history of New South Wales that caused a public outcry about interference from Whitehall. A certain ex-convict named Tawell, who had returned to England where he was hanged for murder in 1845, had left property in Sydney to trustees in order to evade the law that the property of a convicted felon was forfeit to the Crown. A dispute arose between the law officers of the British government and the New South Wales law officers whether the transaction was legal and the trustees could continue to administer the property. The argument dragged on over a number of years; in the meantime, responsible government had been granted, and the elected Attorney-General of New South Wales continued to take the same view as his predecessors. Finally, a completed deed of grant arrived from Britain, but the Prime Minister of New South Wales (who held the portfolio then known as Colonial Secretary) refused to affix the official seal. The Governor, on instructions from the Secretary of State, went to the Colonial Secretary's office and applied the seal to the document himself. Cowper, the Colonial Secretary, then tendered his resignation but the Governor, Denison, declined to accept it on the grounds that this case dated from the period before responsible government and such events were not likely to recur.

In the twentieth century the reluctance of the British authorities to intervene in domestic politics has been evident in one or two cases. A notable instance was their attitude during the struggle to abolish the upper house of the Queensland parliament which ended in 1922. A Bill to this effect was originally introduced in 1915. The Legislative Council promptly amended it, and sent a memorial to the Governor giving reasons why the Bill should not be passed, with the request that this be transmitted to the Secretary of State for the Colonies. Neither the Governor nor the Secretary of State took much heed of this approach. After a further series of attempts, a Labour government secured a majority in the Legislative Council in 1921. The Bill was then passed by both houses and reserved for the King's assent, as required by the Constitution. In November of that year, a further memorial was sent to the Governor by nine members of the Legislative Council, giving reasons

9 Bell and Morrell, op. cit., p.6.

why it should not be abolished, and a petition to the King was signed by six former ministers. The Secretary of State, having received the memorial and the petition, cabled to the Governor, stating that His Majesty could not be advised to accede to the demands contained in them: 'After careful consideration of all the circumstances, I cannot but regard the matter with which the Bill deals as essentially one for local determination.' A contemporary writer observes that these remarks were 'a distinct and possibly a final asseveration of refusal to interfere in the domestic politics of the dominions'.[10]

H. L. Hall, after a careful study, is inclined to blame the 'excessive touchiness' of Australians for exacerbating a naturally difficult situation. He remarks:

> Australian nationalism was bred of ignorance both of Britain and of the outside world, and helped by her pride in the White Australia policy and the mass of social legislation; it was fostered by pungent criticism, and hammered into shape in the conflicts with the Colonial Office. Through it all runs intense suspicion of Imperialism in any shape or form.[11]

He goes on to point out that in any domestic crisis there was so much propaganda value in alleging colonial interference that it was fatally easy to do so. A South Australian newspaper once admitted this frankly when it wrote: 'A collision with the Secretary of State would doubtless be a capital advertisement for an ambitious minister.'[12] As against this, Hall quotes case after case of the care and patience exercised by the Colonial Office to get a true picture of the situation in the colonies, without relying exclusively on the 'man on the spot', as it was continually urged to do. Sir Henry Taylor, who became a high official of the Colonial Office, wrote in his autobiography of the trials of dealing with 'furious assemblies and foolish governors'.

In this relation a curious part was played by the Agents-General, who were sometimes responsible for aggravating tensions that already existed between the Governor and the colonial ministry. On occasion, the ministry would receive information from the Agent-General before the official dispatch arrived for the Governor; and, equally, the ministry would communicate with the Agent-General without informing the Governor, asking him to make representations to the Colonial Office. The Agent-General, for his

---

10 C. A. Bernays, *Queensland—Our Seventh Political Decade,* p.78.
11 Hall, op. cit., p.39.
12 *South Australian Register,* 18 April 1894; quoted, Hall, op. cit., p.62.

part, though it was his duty to transmit all such messages, might sometimes add a private note to soften their impact.[13]

The probability of being attacked by local politicians, no matter what action was taken, made life hard for Governors. Governor Denison very narrowly escaped a vote of censure from the New South Wales parliament over his action in the Tawell case, because, his term having just expired, he sailed out of Sydney Heads while the motion was still being debated. One of his successors, Sir Hercules Robinson, was censured by parliament in 1875 for approving the dismissal of a volunteer officer from the colonial militia, after he had previously been attacked in the press in 1872 concerning a reprieve for a noted bushranger. In 1914, the House of Assembly in Tasmania passed a resolution criticizing the Governor for his insistence that parliament should be dissolved before he would commission a new ministry.

In all these cases, the Governor received no support from the Colonial Office: and in the Tasmanian incident he was actually reprimanded. An exception was in 1877 when Governor Weld, also in Tasmania, was censured by the House of Assembly for granting a dissolution but upheld by the Colonial Office.

The isolation and embarrassment of a Governor's position in the face of local criticism were expressed most poignantly by the Governor-General of Canada, Lord Byng, in a letter to King George V during the constitutional crisis of 1926. Byng explained that as only nine months had passed since the previous election, he had appealed to the Prime Minister, Mackenzie King, 'not to put the King's representative in a position of appearing unconstitutional'. Byng went on to explain why he had rejected this request, dangerous though it was to refuse. Although his refusal embodied 'the rejection of the advice of an accredited Minister, which is the bedrock of constitutional government', he considered that the advice offered was 'wrong and unfair, and not for the welfare of the people'. He revealed that King had asked him to consult the British government, but he adhered rigidly to the constitutional proprieties by pointing out that Britain should not appear to be meddling in Canada's domestic politics. 'The relationship of the Dominion to the Old Country would be liable to be seriously jeopardised . . . whereas the incompetent or unwise action of the Governor-General can only involve himself.' Lord Byng foresaw, sadly, that his position would be made impossible, commenting that King would 'take a very vitriolic line against himself, in spite of his protestations of friendship'.[14] His case makes it only too

13 Cf. Hall, op. cit., pp.61-2.   14 Harold Nicolson, *King George V*, ch. 28.

painfully clear that conscientious adherence to constitutional principles will not save a Governor or Governor-General from embarrassment. If anything, it may aggravate his position, especially when his critics have the fortune to be returned to office, as King's Liberal Party was in the election that followed.

Even comparatively innocent statements made by a Governor interested in public affairs may make him the subject of public attack by interested groups. In 1953, the president of the New South Wales branch of the Returned Servicemen's League criticized a reference to pensions by the Governor-General at the annual congress of the R.S.L. The gentleman in question, Mr Yeo, observed that the opening address delivered by the Governor-General, Sir William Slim,

> seemed like a request not to embarrass the Federal Government too much. No doubt the Governor-General was advised by the government on what to say. If that is so, I claim he was wrongly advised. I think the government may be trading on the fact that the Governor-General is an ex-serviceman to resist pressure from the R.S.L.[15]

Both the nineteenth and twentieth centuries offer a number of illustrations of these difficulties. In the case of the prerogative of pardon, the accepted position until 1872 was that the Governor could exercise this in person. In that year, however, a notorious bushranger, Frank Gardiner, who had given up his earlier career and become a peaceful resident of Queensland, was arrested, extradited to New South Wales, and sentenced to life imprisonment for his earlier activities in that colony. A petition for his release was sent to the Governor, Sir Hercules Robinson, favourably endorsed by Henry Parkes, then Premier of New South Wales. Instead of accepting the petition, Robinson decided that Gardiner must serve ten years of his term before he was released. A public outcry was raised, and as a result, Parkes proposed that all petitions for pardon or reprieve should be accompanied by a minute from the Minister for Justice. Robinson approved of this and the Secretary

15 *Age*, Melbourne, 29 October 1953. There has been no parallel to the Queensland incidents of 1919-20, when the Theodore Labour government appointed one of its ministers, Lennon, as Lieutenant-Governor, and used him not only to swamp the upper house, but also as a mouthpiece. In the address from the throne in 1920, Lennon attacked the 'overseas financiers' who had refused to grant a loan to the state government. The speech was reprinted as an election pamphlet. Later, because of the refusal of the Chief Justice to act, Lennon was placed in the embarrassing position of appointing himself President of the Legislative Council. (Bernays, op. cit., pp.5-6.)

of State for the Colonies, Lord Carnarvon, endorsed his decision
in a dispatch in 1875.[16] An amusing illustration of the confusion
surrounding the exercise of such personal prerogatives, even as late
as 1910, occurred after the advent to power of the McGowen
Labour government in New South Wales. A miners' leader, Bowling, who had been sentenced to prison under the previous (Wade)
ministry, was pardoned in one of the first acts of the new government. The case had been the subject of great public controversy,
and the government was unsure of its position. Accordingly, a
meeting of the full Executive Council was called to present the
minute to the Governor recommending pardon, in order to impress
him with the gravity of the matter should he choose to exercise his
discretion. The Governor, Lord Chelmsford, signed without hesitation, cutting short the eloquent speech that McGowen had prepared
to convince him that Bowling should be pardoned. 'Gentlemen',
he remarked, 'the recent elections decided this.'[17]

One of the most frequent causes of political crises in Australia
has been deadlock between the two houses of parliament, and
Governors have regularly been embarrassed in these cases by advice intended to browbeat the upper house. Some governments,
confronted with a nominated Legislative Council, have tried to
swamp it with their own nominees, and New South Wales in
particular has a long history of such crises. In 1925, the Premier,
J. T. Lang, advised the Governor, Sir Dudley de Chair, to appoint twenty-five new Legislative Councillors. He agreed, but
only after insisting on a written statement of advice from the
Attorney-General, E. A. McTiernan. The government now attempted to abolish the Council, but some of its new nominees
'ratted' on their 'suicide pact', and the Council rejected the
motion for its own abolition. In 1926, Lang asked the Governor
to appoint further nominees, but Sir Dudley refused and asserted
his right to use his discretion. The New South Wales government
appealed to the Colonial Secretary, Mr L. S. Amery, who refused to interfere, and in a letter dated 14 July 1926, stated
that the British government would not issue instructions to a state
Governor. In the opinion of Dr Evatt, this was an application of
the Balfour declaration to the position of a state Governor.[18]

The most famous case of deadlock occurred in Victoria in

16 Cf. Hall, op. cit., pp.202-3.
17 H. V. Evatt, *Australian Labor Leader*, pp.258-9. The Clerk of the
Executive Council observed that the Governor knew the constitutional
position, even if the ministry did not.
18 Evatt, *The King and his Dominion Governors*, ch. 14. This view was
not shared by Keith.

1865-9, with Higinbotham as the leading figure.[19] A Bill providing for a protective tariff was introduced by the McCulloch ministry, in which Higinbotham was Attorney-General, and thrown out by the Legislative Council, which also refused to grant supply to the government. The Governor, Sir Charles Darling, signed warrants for expenditure on ministerial advice; the administration, having no money through the normal channels, borrowed from the banks and used customs revenue. The Governor was censured by Cardwell, Colonial Secretary in the Russell ministry, who also criticized him for condoning the abandonment of free trade. Parliament was then dissolved, but in the meantime a petition had been addressed to Cardwell by twenty-two former Executive Councillors, asking him to intervene. Darling forwarded the petition with a note that he would not be able to trust the advice of any of the petitioners should they hold ministerial office in the future. (The note was probably drafted by Higinbotham.)

The ministry was returned at the elections, and after a further deadlock a joint sitting of parliament passed a compromise tariff Bill. However, Darling was recalled, and the government of Victoria, at Higinbotham's instigation, decided to show its disapproval of this action by voting a gift of £20,000 to Lady Darling, as Sir Charles, being a British official, could not accept it. The Council refused to approve the 'Darling Grant' and the new Governor, Manners-Sutton, was instructed not to agree to the inclusion of the grant in an appropriation Bill. Higinbotham made a violent attack on these proceedings, in which he denounced the then Secretary of State, the Duke of Buckingham, as 'a foreign nobleman', and denied his right to 'pronounce, in terms of authority, by virtue of his office, on the legality or illegality of the advice which the advisers of a Responsible Government tender to the Governor'.[20] In 1869, this stormy petrel resigned, and as a private member introduced a set of five resolutions in the Assembly condemning Whitehall interference in Victoria's internal affairs, which had made self-government a myth. 'The million and a half of Englishmen who inhabit these colonies and who during the last fifteen years have believed they possessed self-government, have been really governed during the whole of that period by a person named Rogers!'[21]

Higinbotham retired from politics several years later, and became Chief Justice of Victoria, continuing to hold unwaveringly

---

19 E. E. Morris, *Memoir of George Higinbotham*, pp.162-89.
20 Ibid., p.170.
21 Frederic Rogers (Lord Blachford) was Permanent Under-Secretary at the Colonial Office from 1860 to 1871.

to the belief that responsible government did not admit of any intervention in domestic affairs by the Colonial Office. His prickly personality and his exaggerated suspicion of Whitehall were demonstrated on a well-known occasion in 1885, when he was asked by the Colonial Secretary to advise on the revision of the royal instructions (which was accomplished in 1892). His reaction was hostile and suspicious, and in his reply he condemned the 'sinister and clandestine' policy of the Colonial Office.

Manners-Sutton (later Lord Canterbury) inherited the deadlock, and despite strenuous attempts to maintain constitutional propriety he became the target of bitter personal attacks. In a dispatch, he wrote of a small clique which 'bitterly resented his refusal to enlist himself blindly as a member of their party . . . the interposition by the Governor of his authority in opposition to his ministers would be the signal for an overpowering manifestation of popular feeling in favour of those ministers'. The only choice he could make depended 'not on the abstract merits of the course adopted by me, but on the preponderance of the evils attendant on any other course'.[22] These words were recalled some years later by Sir George Bowen, now Governor of Victoria, when the Council in 1877 refused supply because the Berry ministry proposed to introduce payment of members. The ministry's riposte was to dismiss several thousand government officials on the famous 'Black Thursday', on the grounds that the exchequer was empty. On Colonial Office advice, Bowen did not interfere, and was at once attacked and abused by the conservative majority in the Council and its press supporters. In a dispatch to the Colonial Secretary, Hicks-Beach, he recalled mournfully that his predecessors, 'Mr La Trobe, Sir Charles Hotham, Sir Henry Barkly, Sir Charles Darling and Lord Canterbury . . . have been pursued both in the Colony and in England, if they merely tried to preserve their constitutional neutrality and do their constitutional duty'. Lord Dufferin, when Governor-General of Canada, had declared that it was better for a Governor to be 'too tardy in relinquishing this palladium of Colonial liberty than too rash in resorting to acts of personal interference'. It would, he concluded, now be 'an act of perilous infatuation in an Australian Governor to cause the removal of a ministry by his own individual act and on account of proceedings of purely colonial concern'.[23]

Bowen was, in fact, pursued by his critics in London, for a

22 Dispatch to the Secretary of State, 4 February 1868.   The events of these years are discussed by Hall, op. cit., pp.183-95.
23 Lane-Poole, op. cit., pp.113-14.

group of expatriate Victorians asked Hicks-Beach to interfere, and the latter actually sent a reprimand to Bowen. The latter's action was, however, supported in the House of Commons by Gladstone and Childers (once Attorney-General of Victoria), and when Berry and one of his ministers, C. H. Pearson, went to London to persuade the Colonial Office to intervene,[24] Hicks-Beach refused, contenting himself with a letter to the Legislative Council asking its members to follow the practice of the House of Lords.

It will be evident from these cases that the constitutional status of a Governor in Australia, at least in the nineteenth century, depended not only on the difference between the status of a monarch, 'in for life', and a transient Governor, but also on the disposition of colonial politicians openly to regard the formal machinery of the Crown as a proper object for manipulation in their own immediate interests. The position of the Governor, in other words, is a result of the prevalent attitude towards the state discussed in the first chapter. It is doubtful whether British politicians have been any more scrupulous than their counterparts in Australia or Canada in their use of power to gain material advantage, but their actions have normally been calculated to avoid the imputation that the monarch can be regarded as their supporter. Conservative politicians have evidently felt that the monarch should, in a political crisis, act as a Conservative, even when the Conservative party is in opposition, but they have stopped short of publicly suggesting that the monarch should disregard the advice of his ministers. Again, though the suggestion is not infrequently made that the monarch has some right to weigh advice given by responsible ministers, this view is unlikely to take the form of public advocacy that he should reject it. Once the monarch's decision is announced, moreover, controversy is most unlikely. All these unlikely things have occurred with some frequency in Australia, as in other Commonwealth countries, and although the greater stability of governments in the twentieth century has made these events much less common, the same attitudes may be found whenever a crisis does erupt. Some latter-day cases may be cited in this connection.

In 1924, the Lyons government in Tasmania advised the Administrator (i.e., the Chief Justice acting in the absence of a Governor) to assent to an Appropriation Bill which had been amended by the upper house. After consulting the Colonial Office, the Administrator gave assent, having received a written statement from the

[24] So much for opposition to 'Whitehall interference'.

Attorney-General that the upper house had no constitutional right to amend a money Bill.[25] Shortly afterwards, the Legislative Council repeated its action, and on this occasion the new Governor, Sir James O'Grady, again gave his assent at the request of the ministry.

An even more determined attempt by an upper house to interpose its authority between the ministry and the representative of the Crown occurred in 1931, when the Scullin Labour government was in a minority in the Commonwealth Senate. Under the Transport Workers' Act, certain regulations had been promulgated which were opposed by the anti-Labour majority in the Senate, and a motion of disallowance was passed. However, owing to the parliamentary procedure by which the Senate met on Wednesday and adjourned early on Friday, the House of Representatives, which assembled on Tuesdays and adjourned later on Fridays, was able to keep the regulations in force for five days in every week. When this game of point-counter-point had gone on for some little time, the Senate addressed a petition to the Governor-General asking him to refuse assent to the offending regulations. The Governor-General of the day was Sir Isaac Isaacs, formerly Chief Justice and a member of the High Court bench for twenty-three years. He replied that he was bound to act on ministerial advice, but added that he had himself examined the situation and could not find any illegality in the actions of the government. He went on to observe that even apart from the legal position, any action other than that advised by ministers would lay him open to a charge of partisanship through accepting irresponsible advice. If there was a legal question, it could be taken to the High Court. (In the *Transport Workers' Case*,[26] the High Court in fact upheld Isaacs' view.)

Evatt, commenting on Isaacs' action, remarks that the position of any Governor would be much easier if he were to follow this example. Even in cases where he is convinced that the action is illegal, his position would be 'enormously strengthened if, even in such cases, he limits his intervention to persuading or even compelling Ministers to have the legality of the challenged action tested before the Courts of the land'.[27]

An outstanding instance of a Governor who ran into trouble by endeavouring to act otherwise was that of Sir Gerald Strickland,

25 The Tasmanian constitution does not provide for the supremacy of the lower house in regard to money Bills, except that they must originate there. The Attorney-General relied on a Privy Council decision of 1886 which affirmed that colonial lower houses were supreme in respect of money Bills.
26 (1931), 46 C.L.R. 73.
27 Evatt, *The King and his Dominion Governors*, p.191.

Governor of New South Wales, in 1916. Late in 1916, the Australian Labor Party was split asunder by the issue of conscription for military service, which resulted in the exodus from the party of its ablest leaders, including the Commonwealth Prime Minister, W. M. Hughes, and the New South Wales Premier, W. A. Holman. An election was due in New South Wales in December, 1916. Holman, who had formed a minority 'National Labor' government with the rump of his supporters, was anxious to avoid an election at this moment, and with the support of the Opposition, pushed through a Bill to extend parliament's life for one year. Strickland refused to assent to this measure on the grounds that Holman did not have the confidence of the Assembly, and therefore he could not accept his advice on any but routine matters.[28] Holman regarded this as a demand for his resignation and appealed to the Colonial Office. He attacked the Governor for taking notice of parliamentary proceedings, of which he should be informed only through official channels. The Lloyd George government recalled Strickland, who had in the meantime consented to the Act lengthening the life of parliament, presumably on Colonial Office instructions.

A controversy in *The Times*, London, took place some time later in which the principal figures were Professor Keith and C. G. Wade, who had been Leader of the Opposition at the time of Strickland's removal and was now New South Wales Agent-General in London. Keith and Wade both argued that the only solution in such cases was the universal rule that a Governor must act on the advice of his ministers. Writing some years later, Keith suggested that Strickland had been recalled because his attitude was politically embarrassing to the British government, in view of the opposition of the Labour Party to conscription and the possibility of a Labour win if an election had been held in New South Wales at the time. 'The episode', he remarked, 'proves clearly that a Governor cannot rely on much moral support in any dispute with a Ministry.'[29]

The Dismissal of the Lang Ministry

The case which, above all others, raised all these issues in their

[28] Strickland, a Catholic, was evidently hostile to the conscription policy, which was opposed by a large section of the Catholic community. A contemporary doggerel verse ran:
'The political split in the Labor arena
Was delicatessen to della Catena.'
(Strickland had the papal title of Count della Catena.) Quoted, Evatt, *Australian Labor Leader*, p.423. [29] Keith, op. cit., p.121.

most acute form was the dismissal of the Lang ministry in New South Wales in 1932 by the then Governor, Sir Philip Game. As the facts of this case have frequently been rehearsed, only a brief summary need be given here. The incident arose out of a dispute between the federal government, then headed by J. A. Lyons, which, in common with five of the six state governments, had implemented a set of measures collectively described as the 'Premiers' Plan' to combat the depression. The Lang government had alone refused to enact similar measures, and had repudiated interest payments due on state debts. In April 1932, the Commonwealth parliament passed the Financial Agreement Enforcement Act requiring all state moneys to be paid to the Commonwealth, in conformity with the financial agreement between the states and the Commonwealth which had been inserted in the Commonwealth Constitution in 1928. The Lang government's response was to issue a circular to all New South Wales government departments instructing them to cease operating government bank accounts and to pay all receipts to the Treasury. By this means it was hoped to frustrate the provisions of the Act passed by the Commonwealth. The Governor requested the withdrawal of the circular, on the grounds that it placed the Crown in the position of breaking the law. Lang refused to withdraw it; the Governor then asked for his resignation; after this had been refused, the Governor sent Lang a letter informing him that he had been dismissed.

The possibility of the Lang government being dismissed had already been canvassed. In a series of letters to the press exchanged between Professor Harrison Moore and Keith early in 1932, Moore invoked the doctrine of the 'mandate' to urge the dismissal of the Lang government (on the grounds that a Labour government had been defeated in the federal election at the end of 1931, and that voting in New South Wales had been against the Labour Party). The use of such an argument is so dubious that it hardly needs to be considered. More significant are the two points in Keith's correspondence. While observing that the Constitution provides for judicial action to be taken against the activities of the New South Wales government, Keith added the politically tendentious remark that it was right for the Governor to take action if he could be sure of the consequences. Keith later made use of this escape clause when he supported Governor Game's action in dismissing Lang.

The Governor himself did not rely on any such argument. He merely based himself on the illegality of the Lang government's circular, which undoubtedly infringed the State Audit Act (although, as both Keith and Evatt agree, this required testing in Court). What is even more interesting is the use by Governor Game of a phrase employed by Todd to justify a similar dismissal in Canada in 1878, when M. Luc Letellier, Lieutenant-Governor of Quebec, dismissed the provincial government. Todd had remarked that it was 'the bounden duty of a governor to dismiss his ministers if he believes their policy to be injurious to the public interest'. Evatt observes that the frequent use by Sir Philip Game of the term 'bounden duty' in his correspondence with Lang suggests he shared Todd's viewpoint.

The sacking of the Lang government is the only case of its kind in Australian history, which does not offer any parallel to the eight instances of dismissal of provincial governments that occurred in Canada between 1856 and 1915. Moreover, the incident represents a climax which can probably never be repeated. Not only have the relations between state and federal governments changed radically since 1932, but the observance of constitutional proprieties has become wellnigh universal.

Before the dismissal took place, the suggestions already made that the Lang government ought to be dismissed by the Governor had been the subject of some public discussion. This required the supporters of dismissal to hold that the position of the Governor *vis-à-vis* his ministers was different from the accepted position in Great Britain, which implies a denial that the Balfour Report could be applied to the position of state Governors. One contemporary writer argued that a state Governor was subject to the authority of the Secretary of State for the Colonies in a way not applicable to the Governor-General since 1926. He added that 'the increasing tendency of twentieth century British Secretaries of State to stand aloof and thrust responsibility upon local Ministers in Australian States no less than in Dominion governments has not carried them so far as to deny all discretionary power to Colonial Governors'. Moreover, the fact that a state Governor was only a bird of passage provided grounds for giving him greater powers than the British monarch, who could not be recalled or dismissed. 'A Governor-General may err and be recalled without his office necessarily disappearing or falling into disrepute; not so the monarch whom he represents.'[30]

An ironic footnote to the story was written in 1935, when Sir Philip Game was succeeded by Sir Alexander Hore-Ruthven (later, as Lord Gowrie, Governor-General), who made a statement

[30] F. Alexander, 'The State Governor and his Powers', *Australian Quarterly*, 1931, no. 10, pp.79-81.

on his arrival in Sydney confirming the duty of the Governor to act on ministerial advice whatever his personal convictions. The *Labor Daily,* controlled by Lang, commented that 'Downing Street' had now apparently recognized the enormity of its error in 1932 when 'the Dominions Office, by its silence, acquiesced in this repudiation of the State's charter of responsible government'.[31] From such a statement, let any one who desires extract a constitutional principle if he can.

The Power of Veto

Power to withhold assent from Bills was conferred on Governors from the outset, despite attempts to do away with it. In 1855, Lord John Russell explained why the British government had rejected the proposal of the New South Wales Legislative Council to override the power of veto conferred on the Governor by his instructions, through the insertion of appropriate clauses in the new constitution of the colony. The instructions, he pointed out,

> however binding on the Governor's discretion, are not in the nature of legal conditions, the non-observance of which in any way affects the validity of colonial Acts. The clauses in question would not, therefore, have removed any substantial legal impediment, while they would have fettered the supreme executive authority in a manner wholly inconsistent with the preservation of the general interests and unity of the Empire.[32]

Under the original Constitution Acts, the Governor was empowered to withhold assent or to reserve Bills for the assent of the British sovereign. A reserved Bill would not become law until notice of assent had been given by the Governor, and might be disallowed within two years after its passage. The Australian States Constitution Act, 1907, laid down three classes of Bills which might be reserved: (a) those altering the constitution of the legislature or of either house of the legislature, (b) those affecting the salary of the Governor, (c) Bills which must be reserved under the provisions of any subsequent State Act, or which contained a provision requiring their reservation. Provisions in the Governor's instructions concerning reservation remained unaffected. Bills passed under emergency conditions do not require reservation; in other cases, the Governor may declare that assent is withheld. Bills dealing with the electoral machinery were exempted from reservation, thus overriding provisions in some individual state constitutions.

31 Quoted by Evatt, *The King and his Dominion Governors,* p.152.
32 Quoted, Bell and Morrell, op. cit., p.166.

The power of reservation or disallowance became almost entirely formal within twenty years of the initial grant of responsible government, and only five Acts were disallowed in the period 1856-73. Altogether, assent was withheld from forty Bills in the colonial period, but most of them were ultimately passed, sometimes without the amendments requested by the British government. Most of these were concerned with 'imperial interests'. By the time of federation, the veto had become little more than a method of securing consultation and delay. Moreover, despite the reluctance of the United Kingdom government to allow the growth of immigration restrictions and protective tariffs, it gradually gave way on these and other questions. Three Acts of the British parliament still require the reservation of state Acts. These are the Colonial Courts of Admiralty Act, 1890; the Merchant Shipping Act, 1894; and the Colonial Stock Act, 1900. The latter provides that laws affecting colonial securities recognized in Britain as trustee stocks may be disallowed if they are repugnant to British law.

The Imperial Conference of 1926 altered the veto power by laying down that apart from constitutional or statutory provisions dealing with dominion affairs, the dominions alone had the right to advise the British monarch on their own affairs, and the British government should not, therefore, give contrary advice. In 1929, the matter was considered by the conference on the Operation of Dominion Legislation and Merchant Shipping Legislation (O.D.L.), whose proposals were accepted by the Imperial Conference of 1930. Disallowance was to end and the Governor's powers on reservation to be modified. The British government was to cease giving advice to Governors on discretionary reservation; compulsory reservation was to be governed by statute alone; and both discretionary and compulsory reservation could be abolished by a constitutional amendment. The Statute of Westminster, enacted in 1931, made it possible for the dominions to remove those forms of obligatory reservation required since the passage of the Colonial Laws Validity Act in 1865.

In the present century, the reservation of state laws has been purely formal in character, although it is applied to a fairly large number of measures. Between 1900 and 1950, thirty-two Bills were reserved in South Australia, twenty-one in Tasmania, twenty in Victoria, and fifteen in Queensland. The only case where the British government attempted to veto a substantive policy matter occurred in Tasmania in 1907. In that year parliament passed a law called the Mining Companies (Foreign) Act, which was reserved by the Governor for the royal assent. The assent was refused, on the grounds that it might make English creditors suffer because of the neglect of local officials over whom the creditors could have no control. On 4 February 1908, the Secretary of State, Lord Elgin, pointed this out in a cable to the Tasmanian government, and asked whether the latter would be prepared to amend the terms of their Bill so as to impose penalties on officials of companies who neglected to register the mortgages and debentures held by English owners. However, the matter seems to have lapsed after some further correspondence.[33]

Reservation in the Commonwealth

The application of the veto to Commonwealth Acts has always been much more limited. Section 59 of the Commonwealth Constitution provides for disallowance but there is only one specific provision concerning the reservation of Acts. Quick and Garran observe that 'this method of conserving imperial interests is more satisfactory and more in harmony with the larger measure of self-government granted by the Constitution than the old system of instructing the Governor not to assent to certain classes of Bills'.

Section 58 also provides that the Governor-General has discretionary power to withhold assent from Bills or to recommend amendment to parliament. On this point, however, Quick and Garran remark that on a strict interpretation of the constitution

> it would not be legal for Her Majesty, through the Secretary of State for the Colonies to fetter the discretion of the Governor-General by instructions . . . the Governor-General will be entitled to receive from the law officers of the Commonwealth a report in reference to each bill, specifying whether there is any legal objection to assent to it . . . as a general rule, the Governor would be justified in accepting and acting upon statements of such functionaries in local matters.[34]

The only detailed provisions concerning reservation are to be found not in any royal instructions, but in Section 74 of the constitution, designating laws that limit the matters on which appeals may be made to the Privy Council. Apart from this, however, there have been one or two cases where the British government has attempted to influence the policy of the Commonwealth by use of the reservation power. In 1901, for instance, the Governor-General, Lord Hopetoun, wrote to the Prime Minister, Barton, that he would not give his assent to the Kanaka Exclusion Bill and the

---

[33] Information kindly supplied by Mr C. K. Murphy, Clerk of the House of Assembly and Librarian to Parliament.
[34] *The Annotated Constitution of the Australian Commonwealth,* pp.691-2.

Alien Immigration Restriction Bill until they had been referred to the British government.[35] In this case, and later in 1905-6, the British government did attempt, with only minor success, to persuade the Commonwealth government not to discriminate against non-white residents of the British Empire. In 1901, for example, the Foreign Office advised that the Immigration Bill should be disallowed, but it was passed despite this protest. In 1905, the Secretary of State cabled to the Governor-General requesting that Bills discriminating against Asiatics should be reserved. In March 1906, Deakin protested against this instruction and in May the Secretary of State withdrew it.[36]

Three other cases may be mentioned for the sake of completeness. The Customs Tariff Bill of 1906 and the Judiciary Act of 1914 were reserved, the latter because of its clauses dealing with Admiralty jurisdiction. This requirement, and the related one of Acts dealing with merchant shipping, were removed when the Commonwealth parliament adopted Sections 2-6 of the Statute of Westminster in 1942. Finally, the Australian Flag Act, 1953, was reserved for the personal assent of the Queen during the royal visit to Australia in 1954, and was formally assented to at a special meeting of the Privy Council attended by its Australian members.

The Governor-General and State Governors

In the early years of federation, controversies arose repeatedly over the respective functions of the Governor-General and the state Governors. An enormous amount of confusion and misunderstanding contributed to various squabbles over status and procedure, squabbles which reflected the reluctance of the states to recognize that federation meant the effective loss of powers they had previously exercised as colonies.

At the outset, there was some feeling that the existence of a Governor-General had rendered obsolete the office of state Governor. A curious example of this is to be found in a cable sent by the man who almost became the first Prime Minister of the Commonwealth, Sir William Lyne, then Premier of New South Wales, to the New South Wales Agent-General in London in 1900. Lyne apparently felt that his own colony would desire to abolish the

[35] Letter dated 11 December 1901 (Barton Papers, National Library Canberra).
[36] I am indebted to Mr D. C. S. Sissons for bringing these two cases to my attention. The correspondence is contained on two files originally marked EAO4/7831 and PMO6/679 (C-A).

office of state Governor, or at least materially reduce its importance and its emoluments upon the arrival of the first Governor-General, Lord Hopetoun. His cable read:

> Inform Mr Chamberlain personally that Parliament will undoubtedly in this colony, and, I believe, in Victoria and South Australia, considerably reduce the salary of State Governors. Press him to appoint Lord Hopetoun State Governor of New South Wales in addition to Governor-General of the Commonwealth; in that case, I can induce our Parliament not to reduce salary and allowances. It is very generally admitted that present Governors cannot remain long after arrival of Governor-General . . . dual nomination proposed would give great satisfaction to mother colony.[37]

Although Lyne's proposal came to nothing, the Labour Party has long advocated the abolition of the office of state Governor, and a specific recommendation to this effect was made by the New South Wales state conference of the party only a few years ago.[38]

There is no parallel in Australia with the theoretical subordination of Lieutenant-Governors in the Canadian provinces to the Governor-General, and it has never been suggested that state Acts of parliament should be subject to disallowance by the Governor-General. The main source of dispute was a comparatively trivial matter, that of the 'channel of communication' with the British government. Before federation, colonial Governors were the official channel for correspondence with Whitehall. Shortly before the proclamation of the Commonwealth, the Colonial Secretary, Joseph Chamberlain, wrote to the six colonial Governors that this practice would continue, 'except insofar as communications of general Australian interest or on subjects reserved to the Commonwealth are concerned, with regard to which the Secretary of State will naturally correspond with the Governor-General'. He would himself send the Governor-General copies of all dispatches to the states, and requested the Governors to act similarly.[39]

In 1906, the Prime Minister, Alfred Deakin, wrote to the Governor-General reviewing the failure of the states to follow Chamberlain's request. After the original rule had been modified to apply only to copies of dispatches considered by a Governor to have a federal bearing, the then Governor-General, Lord Northcote, had pointed out in 1904 that it was being ignored. After a

37 MS. in the Mitchell Library, Sydney. Lyne's suggestion harks back to the commissions issued to Governors Fitzroy and Denison as 'Governor-General and Governor of N.S.W.'
38 *S.M.H.*, 10 June 1957.
39 Dispatch from Secretary of State, 2 November 1900.

further complaint in 1905, Chamberlain's successor, Lord Elgin, reminded the states of their obligations, and Deakin then suggested a compromise by which copies of all dispatches should be sent to the Governor-General, who would himself decide whether there was anything of federal importance in them to be communicated to Commonwealth ministers. Deakin had little hope that his proposal would be accepted, concluding that it was 'hopeless to expect that unanimity can be obtained in any change which in the opinion of state ministers would depreciate the dignity of the state in comparison with the Commonwealth'.[40] The federal government apparently gave up further attempts to have Chamberlain's ruling enforced, and with the ending of correspondence through the Governor-General in 1927 the formal basis of the dispute has largely disappeared.

It only remains to note that the 'channel of communication' dispute was used in several cases between 1901 and 1907 by the states to try to assert that they still retained some control over external affairs, which had become a Commonwealth responsibility after federation.[41]

40 *C.P.* 103, ser. 4, vol. 1, 23 October 1906 (C-A).
41 These were the 'Vondel' case (South Australia), the Weigall case (New South Wales), and the Benjamin case (Queensland). The 'Vondel' incident is discussed by Sawer, *Australian Federal Politics and Law 1901-1929*, pp.31-2.

7

THE PREROGATIVE OF DISSOLUTION

OF ALL the powers allotted to a Governor or Governor-General, the right to dissolve parliament is undoubtedly the most important, and its importance has lasted to the present day, unlike most of the other powers which now exist only on paper.

Its political significance is obvious. The freedom of a Premier to obtain a dissolution at his discretion gives him a potent weapon both against dissidents in his own party and against a recalcitrant opposition in parliament. Its importance, however, is enhanced by the persistence of some degree of discretion on the part of the Governor. Cases still occur where the element of uncertainty about the Governor's acceptance of advice to dissolve is of the greatest political importance. As a result, more has been written on this point than on any other single aspect of the gubernatorial office. We shall be concerned here only with the main arguments that have been used in cases where a dissolution crisis has arisen, to demonstrate the evolution of the Governor's discretion in the matter, and, most importantly, how its exercise is bound up with certain characteristic features of Australian politics.

The constitutional and political aspects of discretionary power have passed through fairly definite historical phases. The year 1914, which marked a turning point also in graver things, may rank as a watershed in constitutional development. Before 1914 it could be said that professions of discretionary power on the part of the Governor corresponded to reality; since that date discretion has been asserted, but probably not exercised to any significant extent. The year was marked by two important dissolution crises, and although in each case the Crown representative insisted on his right to decide for himself, public and political opinion seems to have regarded the events as demonstrating the fact that in this case, as in others, the Governor or Governor-General must act on advice. The Balfour Report of 1926 may be regarded as merely an endorsement of a position reached twelve years before.

Political developments, by a coincidence, also reached a climax at about this time. From the beginnings of responsible government until the early years of federation, Australian politics were characterized by a 'French situation'—frequent elections, brief tenure of office, shifting coalitions, deadlocks between the two houses of parliament, and frequent requests to dissolve parliament. This kaleidoscope reflected the absence of a genuine party system as well as the absence of a 'limited oligarchy agreed on essentials'. From the 1890s onwards, the emergence of the Labour Party provided a new twist to the situation, and the early years of federation were characterized by three or even four-cornered party conflicts in the Commonwealth and the states. Practically all the dissolution crises between 1904 and 1914 were the result of this situation. However, by 1914 the outlines of a two-party system—Labour and anti-Labour—had emerged in the Commonwealth and in every state except Victoria, where Labour did not succeed in forming a majority government until 1945.

Since World War I, crises have arisen for rather different reasons. The first major political crisis after 1914—the conscription split in the Labour Party in 1916—was to be the first of a series of internecine battles within the Labour movement. After 1919, the emergence of the Country Party led to a stable three-party system in the Commonwealth and several of the states. Crises arose because of quarrels between the Country Party and its conservative allies, except in Victoria where, between 1935 and 1942, and again between 1950 and 1952, Country Party governments ruled with the support of Labour. In other cases, the character of state politics has changed to one of monolithic or near-monolithic party dictatorship, as in Queensland, South Australia, Tasmania, and New South Wales. Only where basic instabilities exist, as in Victoria and Tasmania, do crises still occur with any frequency.[1]

During the early phase from 1856 to 1914, the general rule was insistence by the Governor on his discretion, against attempts by politicians to assert that advice to dissolve must automatically be accepted. At the same time, Governors normally attempted to exhaust the possibilities of forming an alternative government before granting a dissolution. In South Australia, for example, whose governmental instability was notorious even in an unstable age, a dissolution was granted in 1871, after the ministry had been defeated by the casting vote of the Speaker, on the explicit grounds that no alternative government was possible. Lord Normanby, then Governor of Victoria, pointed out in 1881 that automatic dissolution would be a threat to the independence of parliament. The views expressed by Governors were shared by a number of constitutional authorities and by some politicians, especially when they

---

[1] In Victoria, electoral gerrymandering was the cause until 1952; in Tasmania, a small parliament and proportional representation lead to tiny majorities which may disappear overnight.

were in opposition. Professor W. E. Hearn, author of *The Government of England*, criticized 'the exaggerative doctrine that the Crown can do no act without some responsible adviser . . . a dissolution ought never to be tried until every other means of carrying on the Government has been exercised'.[2] At a somewhat later date, the Governor of Victoria was criticized by the Legislative Assembly for granting a dissolution to the Bent ministry in 1908. In his reply, giving a detailed analysis of the parliamentary situation at the time, he pointed out that no stable alternative government was in view, rejected the notion that a Premier had an absolute right to a dissolution, and concluded by declaring that his duty was 'to take the course which I thought most likely to meet with the approval of the constituencies'.[3]

A former Premier of New South Wales and Prime Minister of the Commonwealth, Sir George Reid, referred in a similar strain to his own experiences. 'The practice in the Dominions is quite different from that in Great Britain. His Majesty's Ministers in England have their own way in such matters. It is not so in the Dominions.'[4]

Professor Keith, despite frequent oscillations, seems to have reached a mean position with the statement that the Governor must possess *some* discretion in the matter. 'It is obvious,' he wrote, 'that a Ministry which has obtained a dissolution is not entitled, if it is barely sustained in office, to ask for one again at an early date, and if a Ministry neglects its duty, it may be the obligation as well as the right of the Crown to decline to accept advice.' Keith probably had one or two Australian cases in mind when he added that 'it might be necessary for the Crown to dismiss a Ministry which defied the will of parliament and would not advise a dissolution'.[5]

The question of the Governor's discretion in dissolutions was discussed at the Colonial Conference in 1887. Bell and Fitzherbert of New Zealand, and Berry of Victoria, supported the abolition of discretion and the assimilation of colonial to British practice. They were opposed, however, by Downer of South Australia, Griffith of Queensland and Service of Victoria, as well as by Shea of Newfoundland, and in the face of this disagreement the British government conveniently decided to do nothing.

Keith is critical of what he describes as the tendency of the Colonial Office to encourage governors in the colonies and domi-

---

[2] Letter to Henry Parkes in 1872; quoted, Parkes, *Fifty Years in the Making of Australian History*, pp.249-50.
[3] Quoted by Evatt, *The King and his Dominion Governors*, p.230.
[4] *My Reminiscences*, p.246.
[5] *Responsible Government in the Dominions*, p.156.

nions to act on British practice and to accept advice wherever
offered. In 1879, for instance, the Canadian government advised
Lord Dufferin, the Governor-General, to dismiss the Lieutenant-
Governor of Quebec, M. Letellier, after he had intervened directly
in provincial politics. Dufferin was hesitant to act, but was advised
by the Colonial Secretary to accept the advice of his government.
In 1892, during a struggle between the two houses of the New
Zealand parliament, the Ballance ministry asked the Governor-
General, Lord Glasgow, to swamp the upper house. He was re-
luctant to do so, but again the Colonial Office advised him to accept
the advice of his ministers.

A more recent constitutional writer, Dr Forsey, affirms the view
that the frequency both of grants and refusals of dissolution in
the colonies and dominions as compared with Britain is the result
of differences in political character rather than of constitutional
status. 'The existence of a multiple party system, or the presence
of Independents in sufficient numbers to hold the balance of
power, or the looseness of party organisation, and the fact that all
alternatives had already been tried, gave reasonable grounds for
belief that an alternative government could carry on.'[6] On the
other hand, a convention of self-denial has operated in Britain to
an extent hardly conceivable in Australia. The prevailing view,
which Forsey calls the 'Peel-Russell-Gladstone doctrine', is that a
dissolution should not be asked for unless a major question of
policy is at stake. This principle has been frequently invoked in
the dominions and the colonies, both by ministries and by governors, on the one side to justify grants and on the other to support
refusals. Perhaps it should also be mentioned that colonial governors have not been entirely free of a certain attitude of disdain
towards the politicians with whom they had to deal. Keith suggests
that the action of the Tasmanian Governor in 1914 in endeavouring to insist on a dissolution was probably justified politically although not constitutionally. 'The episode . . . simply represented
the drastic attitude adopted by noble Lords to petty Colonial
Premiers in the days of the beginnings of responsible government.'[7]

Whether Keith was right on this point, it is certain that most
Governors were well aware that colonial politicians were in the
habit of asking for a dissolution to extricate themselves from a
difficult situation. In 1886, the Robertson ministry in New South
Wales was defeated on a no-confidence motion, and promptly

6 E. A. Forsey, *The Royal Power of Dissolution in the British Commonwealth*, pp.69-70.   7 Keith, op. cit., p.171.

asked for a dissolution. The Governor, Lord Carrington, refused, and asked Robertson whether, had their positions been reversed, Robertson would have granted him a dissolution. The Premier is said to have replied, 'I'd see you damned first.' A similar attitude was taken by the Governor of Victoria, Lord Canterbury, in 1872, but he received rather different treatment from the disgruntled Premier.

In 1871, the McCulloch ministry secured a dissolution of the Victorian parliament in ordinary circumstances, and resigned after being defeated in the Legislative Assembly. The Duffy ministry then took office, and after a defeat on a motion of no confidence, asked for a dissolution. In a memorandum to the Governor, the ministry argued that a British government had 'absolute discretion', and pointed to its support in the country. The Governor dismissed the British analogy, and added that he would refuse a dissolution to any other government in similar circumstances. Duffy accused him of taking a personal interest in the matter, alleging that he had come to Victoria 'to increase his balance at the banker's', which he had done by marrying into a squatter's family. According to Duffy, the Governor had 'betrayed the interests of the community to the opulent minority'.[8] The Melbourne correspondent of *The Times* also accused Canterbury of personal and political prejudice against Duffy, who was an Irish rebel and a Catholic. Whatever the substance of these accusations, it remains true that the Governor's actions were constitutionally proper by the standard of the time, and that he had been selected for his post with some care by Disraeli after the Darling grant affair had shown the need for a firm and capable governor.

The advent of the Labour Party, and the consequent recrystal- lization of political forces, led to a series of dissolution crises in the ten years preceding the outbreak of World War I. In 1904, the Philp ministry in Queensland resigned after its budget had been passed by only one vote. The crisis was precipitated by the secession of a group of Liberal members who supported the formation of a ministry under the Speaker, Morgan. The new government, formed in coalition with the Labour Party, had a very narrow majority and was soon defeated. A request for a dissolution was refused. The Governor then commissioned the opposition leader, Rutledge, to form a government, and it was not until this proved impossible that Morgan was recalled and granted a dissolution, which resulted in the return of the Liberal-Labour coalition by a comfortable majority.

[8] C. Gavan Duffy, *My Life in Two Hemispheres,* vol. 2, pp.341-2.

The Labour Party was again involved in a crisis in South Australia in 1906. On this occasion it was the Labour leader, Price, who was Premier in a coalition government of which Peake, the Liberal leader, was Treasurer. The government was defeated in the upper house and requested a dissolution. The Governor refused because the ministry had only a small majority in the House of Assembly, and parliament was less than two years old. He insisted that the Opposition leader, Butler, must be asked to form an alternative government. When Butler failed, the Governor granted Price a dissolution on the understanding that the election would be held on the issue of the franchise for the upper house, a Bill to enlarge which had been the occasion for the government's defeat in the Legislative Council.

We now return to Queensland, where the same coalition (now headed by the Labour leader, Kidston, after the resignation of Morgan) was still in office. Kidston, and the majority of Labour members of parliament, had refused to accept the instructions of the Labour convention, but the Labour Party continued to support the Kidston government in parliament. After a defeat in the Legislative Council, Kidston asked the Governor, Lord Chelmsford, to swamp the upper house. When he refused, Kidston resigned. The Governor then summoned the Leader of the Opposition, Philp, who undertook to form a ministry. When the Legislative Assembly met, Philp introduced a motion for the adjournment of the house, which was defeated. Instead, the Assembly passed a resolution disapproving of the change of government. The Governor then sent for Kidston and asked him to support a motion for the adjournment in order to enable Philp to form a ministry. This was done, and a week later, the new ministry met the Assembly, which then refused to pass supply.

In spite of these repeated defeats, Philp did not resign and tried to carry on. The Assembly now adopted a memorandum to the Governor asking him not to grant a dissolution to the Philp government, pointing out that it was only six months since the previous election. In his reply, Lord Chelmsford argued that the deadlock between the houses could only be resolved by a mandate from the electors, and granted Philp a dissolution.

Evatt argues that Chelmsford's action was wrong, in that he should not have assisted Philp to defy a parliament which had only recently been elected. He admits that the motive, which was to make certain that the ministry enjoyed popular as well as parliamentary support, was perfectly proper. Nevertheless, 'actual intervention by the granting of a dissolution early in the life of a parliament is almost bound to cause a grave constitutional crisis'.[9] This view is challenged by Forsey, who suggests that if the Governor had the right to dismiss Kidston, then he also had the right to grant Philp a dissolution. The dismissal of Kidston clearly indicated the view of the Governor that the support of the Assembly was not a sufficient index of popular support on the major question at issue, i.e., the relations between the two houses.[10] (It is, of course, very probable that Lord Chelmsford had in mind the equivocal position of Kidston as a result of his conflict with the Labour Party outside parliament.)

Shortly afterwards the Lieutenant-Governor of New South Wales was also compelled to choose between two party leaders. In 1911, a squabble in the parliamentary Labour Party led to two members resigning their seats. The Acting Premier, Holman, by diversionary tactics in parliament, gained time to see the Lieutenant-Governor, Sir William Cullen, and asked that parliament be prorogued while by-elections were held. When Holman resigned after this request was refused, Cullen also refused to grant Wade, the Opposition leader, a dissolution as a condition of taking office. Holman then withdrew his resignation and parliament was prorogued.

In a number of these cases, attempts were made to insist that the granting of a commission to form a ministry should involve an undertaking to dissolve parliament immediately afterwards. In 1914, the Liberal government of Tasmania resigned after a split among its supporters had brought about its defeat on a no-confidence motion. Governor Macartney sent for Earle, leader of the Labour Opposition, but tried to insist that he ask for a dissolution as soon as he had taken office. Earle, having been commissioned, refused to request a dissolution, and the Colonial Secretary, Harcourt, reprimanded the Governor for his action. His dispatch laid down that the Governor cannot dissolve the legislature except on advice, that a dissolution cannot be imposed as a condition of the issue of a commission to form a government, and that Earle must be regarded as having accepted responsibility for the Governor's action in insisting on a dissolution and equally for having changed his mind about requesting one.

Although insistence by the Governor on attempting to find an alternative ministry has been the commonest reason for refusing a dissolution, the necessity of obtaining supply has always been an added consideration. In 1877, the Governor of New South Wales,

9 Evatt, op. cit., p.139.
10 Forsey, op. cit., pp.129-30.

Sir Hercules Robinson, found himself involved in a game of musical chairs as a result of this insistence. He refused a dissolution to the Robertson ministry, which had been defeated in the Legislative Assembly, because supply had not been granted. Parkes then assumed office, and after being defeated, was refused a dissolution on the same grounds; Robertson accordingly formed a second ministry, was again defeated, and was refused a dissolution as supply had still not been passed. The Governor's action aroused much criticism, but he was upheld not only by the Colonial Office but by the Speaker of the House of Commons and by Sir Erskine May.

Another case where the Governor based his action on the necessities of good government was that of Western Australia in 1907, where the Legislative Council threw out a Bill providing for a land tax. The Premier tendered his resignation, but the Governor, Sir Frederick Bedford, refused to accept it on the grounds that the government still possessed the confidence of the Assembly. He did not, he declared,

> feel justified in taking such action as would undoubtedly result in a serious dislocation of the business of the country, and there appeared to be a reasonable expectancy that the Legislative Council would accept the expressed wishes of the Legislative Assembly if again submitted to them.[11]

He granted a prorogation of parliament for three weeks, during which the Premier was able to arrange a compromise with the upper house.

Dissolutions in the States since 1914

The last forty years of Australian state politics are distinguished both by the comparative infrequency of dissolution crises, and by the relative absence of controversy over the conventions to be applied in the granting or refusal of a dissolution. With the two important exceptions of Victoria and Tasmania, whose politics have been marked for a long period by what may be called 'built-in' types of instability, there have been no refusals of dissolution since 1921. Moreover, although Governors have usually taken every opportunity of asserting the reality of their discretion to grant a dissolution, their role has in fact changed to that of the honest broker, ensuring only that essential services are maintained while contending political groups fight out their quarrels. A particularly odd case of this behaviour occurred in New South Wales in 1927.

11 *Parl. Deb.* (W.A.), new ser., 1907, vol. 31, p.1504.

To understand the situation it is necessary to retrace some of the political history of the era. J. T. Lang had become Labour Premier in 1925, with the support of a large group of militant trade unions, and had promptly been involved in a series of struggles within his cabinet and the parliamentary party. The Easter conference of the state A.L.P. in 1927 adopted the so-called 'Red Rules', which gave the unions supporting Lang a dominant voice within the party, and also gave Lang complete authority in the political sphere in a manner granted to no Labour leader before or since. The only two ministers who had attended this conference were Lang himself and his only reliable supporter in cabinet, Willis, Vice-President of the Executive Council.

Lang's opponents within the parliamentary party retorted by re-pudiating the decisions of the Easter conference, by a majority of twenty-five to eighteen. A government official described in the Press as 'an authority on the constitution' was quoted as observing that 'the Governor probably would not ask the Premier to return his commission, simply because a meeting of caucus had expressed the view that Mr Lang no longer held their confidence'. The Governor could not ask for Lang's resignation unless he were defeated in parliament, and if the parliamentary party were to send a delegation asking for Lang's dismissal, the Governor would probably not recognize it.[12]

At this stage, Lang decided to force a showdown. On the 26 May, he asked the Governor to convene a meeting of the entire Executive Council—i.e., the whole ministry with the Governor in the chair. At the meeting, he produced a minute providing for a prorogation of parliament in preparation for a dissolution. The Governor then asked each minister in turn whether he supported this request, and it was found that only Willis did so. According to a press report of this meeting, the Governor remarked that the government had become a laughing stock and the situation could not be allowed to continue, but when he was asked to stay and discuss the matter with ministers, he refused and adjourned the meeting.

Lang then followed Sir Dudley de Chair to Government House, and was granted a long interview, after which three letters were exchanged: one, from Lang, handing in his resignation, and one from the Governor accepting the resignation and that of his cabi-net. This was followed by a further letter commissioning him to

12 *S.M.H.*, 25 April 1927. The Governor was Sir Dudley de Chair, who had refused Lang's advice in 1926.

form a new government, on the understanding that parliament would be dissolved at the earliest possible date.

Later in the same day an official statement was issued from Government House to the effect that Mr Lang

had advised His Excellency to dissolve the present parliament. His Excellency was prepared to accept this advice, but Mr. Lang found himself at variance with the majority of ministers . . . after consideration His Excellency decided to recommission Mr. Lang to form a new administration, on condition that a dissolution should be held [sic] at the earliest possible time after the completion of the electoral rolls, and that in the meantime, ministers should confine themselves exclusively to routine matters of administration.[13]

On three occasions since 1920, a crisis has been caused through the defeat of a government dependent upon the vote of the Speaker. The New South Wales Labour government which took office in 1920 depended on the fact that a member of the Nationalist Party had accepted the Speakership, giving the government a majority of one. Shortly before the Christmas recess in 1921, the Speaker resigned, and the government was then defeated on the adjournment. The Premier, Dooley, was refused a dissolution and a Nationalist government under Sir George Fuller took office. A new Speaker was then elected on the understanding that he would support the dissolution of parliament by the Fuller ministry. Having been elected, however, he refused to do so, and Fuller, after fully seven hours in office, requested a dissolution, was refused and resigned. Dooley was recalled, finished the business of the session, and secured a dissolution in the following February.

Two similar crises have occurred in Tasmania during recent years. Tasmania, which operates under a system of proportional representation, is perpetually confronted with a situation where no party has a majority of seats, and a government can only take office through acceptance of the Speakership by a member of the opposition party. In 1934, the state constitution was amended to provide for deadlocks resulting from this stage of affairs; a party with a majority of primary votes is entitled to form a government if both parties gain an equal number of seats. Since that year, the Labour Party has always had a majority of primary votes and consequently has governed continuously. In 1948, the Cosgrove Lab-

---

[13] *Daily Telegraph,* 27 May 1927. The gaps in this story—especially what went on at the interview between Lang and the Governor—are even more fascinating than the story itself.

our government was returned with a majority of one over the Liberal Party and several Independents, so that when the Speaker had been appointed, the government was forced to rely on him for its majority. In 1949, an independent member accepted the Speakership, but resigned in the following year as a protest against one of the appointments made by the government. The Premier then asked the Governor, Sir Hugh Binney, for a dissolution. He claimed that the government was frustrated by the parliamentary situation, and asserted that since the Balfour Report of 1926 governments had an automatic right to a dissolution. The Governor refused to accept this advice and summoned the Leader of the Opposition, who declined to form a government. Sir Hugh Binney then recalled Cosgrove and informed him that, having satisfied himself that no alternative government was possible, he would agree to a dissolution.[14]

A similar situation arose in 1956, when the Minister for Housing in the Cosgrove government crossed the floor and voted against the government, having already resigned from the Labour Party. This action gave the Opposition a majority, and it was widely believed that the Administrator, Chief Justice Burbury, who was acting in the absence overseas of the Governor, Sir Ronald Cross, would commission the Leader of the Opposition to form a government.

The Premier, however, cabled to the Governor, who was then sailing back to Tasmania after a holiday in the United Kingdom, asking him to fly home. Sir Ronald Cross reciprocated this somewhat flamboyant gesture and boarded a plane in Ceylon. On his arrival he was presented with two memoranda, one from the Opposition leader, pointing out that he could form a government, and the other from the Attorney-General asking for a dissolution. According to the press report, the latter memorandum argued once again that the Governor must always act on advice, and that the deadlock provision of the constitution meant that the Labour Party should be given the chance to determine whether it still possessed the confidence of the electorate. (At this time parliament still had eighteen months of its life to run.)

The dissolution was granted. An accompanying official statement pointed out that (a) supply was available until the end of the following month; (b) the Opposition leader's request had been rejected; (c) the decision to grant dissolution did not imply the acceptance of the argument that the Governor could refuse a dissolution only in extreme circumstances, nor did it imply agreement

14 F. C. Green (ed.), *A Century of Responsible Government*, pp.258-9.

with the Attorney-General's submission on the effect of the dead-lock provision of the constitution.[15]

In Victoria, a consistent pattern was repeated four times between 1924 and 1952. In each case, a quarrel took place over electoral redistribution, and in each case a short-lived minority government was formed as a result. In three of these instances, the minority government was refused a dissolution after being defeated in parliament. In 1924, after the Nationalist and Country Parties had fallen out, a Labour ministry under Prendergast held office for four months with Country Party support. When the ministry was defeated after a rapprochement between the two other parties, Prendergast was refused a dissolution by the Governor, Lord Stradbroke. In 1943, the Dunstan (Country Party) government was defeated by a combination of the Labour and United Australia Parties, after it had depended for support on each in turn. A Labour government under Cain then held office for five days, and was refused a dissolution after its defeat in parliament.

In 1945, a composite ministry under Dunstan was defeated by a combination of Labour and some dissident Liberals, and resigned. After Cain, the Labour leader, and Hollway, the Liberal leader, had both failed to form a ministry, the leader of the dissident Liberals, Macfarlan, formed a caretaker administration, which obtained supply and was granted a dissolution.

In 1952, the McDonald (Country Party) government was defeated by a combination of Labour and a group of dissident Liberals, led this time by Hollway. Supply was refused by the Legislative Council, and McDonald asked for a dissolution. After interviewing all the party leaders, the Governor refused McDonald's request for a dissolution and commissioned Hollway, presumably to ensure the passage of supply. After only seventy hours in office, the Hollway government was defeated on a motion of no-confidence and was refused a dissolution. The Governor then recalled McDonald, commissioned him to form a government, and granted him a dissolution which resulted in the return of Labour. Hollway requested that the papers concerning his request for dissolution should be published, but he was refused because of the privileged character of the documents. Like his long line of predecessors, Hollway did not let the refusal pass without comment; he alleged that the Governor's action had 'no precedent', and 'made constitutional history which would have very serious repercussions'.[16]

[15] Hobart *Mercury,* 12-21 September 1956. The Governor's statement makes it difficult to conceive *any* reason for the grant of a dissolution.
[16] *Age,* 31 October 1952.

Refusal of Dissolution in the Commonwealth[17]

In the case of the Commonwealth, 1914 stands out as the critical year. On that occasion, after a series of refusals in 1904-09, Sir Ronald Munro-Ferguson granted a double dissolution on somewhat controversial grounds. Since that time, Governors-General appear to have been guided fairly strictly by the advice tendered to them; their main concern has been to ensure the continuity of administration. The 1926 Report seems to have induced successive Commonwealth governments to follow the British practice to the extent of refraining from placing the Governor-General in an embarrassing situation.

In 1904, the first Commonwealth Labour government, a minority one headed by J. C. Watson, asked for a dissolution after being defeated on the Arbitration Bill. The Governor-General, Lord Northcote, refused without giving any reasons. His motives were nevertheless fairly plain, because the general election had taken place only eight months previously and the Free Trade party under Reid was willing to form a government. In 1905, this government was defeated during the debate on the Address-in-Reply by a combination of Protectionists and Labour. Reid's request for a dissolution was again refused. Similar considerations evidently prevailed in this case, as parliament still had eighteen months to run and the Protectionist leader, Deakin, was assured of Labour support.

In 1909, a minority Labour government led by Andrew Fisher was again defeated by a combination of the two other groups, this time in the form of a unified party which took office under the name of the Fusion ministry. Fisher's request for a dissolution followed very closely the text of the statement made by the Duffy government in Victoria in 1872, and for good measure added that the fusion was unlikely to remain united and would not receive popular support.

The views of Keith and Evatt on this case are, as usual, in conflict. The former regarded the refusal as being against constitutional usage; the latter as being according to precedent. One suspects that Keith was influenced by his disapproval of the fusion between the two non-Labour parties. The Governor-General, Lord Dudley, seems to have acted on the established principle that an alternative government was possible.

The 1914 double dissolution was, after the fusion of 1909, the

17 Cf. the account given by Crisp, *The Parliamentary Government of the Commonwealth of Australia,* ch. 9.

most significant political event since federation. Joseph Cook, having replaced Deakin as leader of the Fusion (Liberal) Party, took office in 1913 with a majority of only one in the House of Representatives, and a hostile majority in the Senate. In 1914, the government decided to provoke a dissolution and introduced a Bill doing away with preference to unionists in the Commonwealth Public Service. The Senate rejected the Bill twice, and the deadlock provision of Section 57 of the constitution was invoked. It has been suggested by one writer, who was at the time private secretary to the Leader of the Opposition in the Senate, that Labour was also prepared to force a dissolution; if they had wanted to avoid one, they could have used a number of stalling devices which could not indisputably be classified as 'failing to pass' the Bill, as required under Section 57.[18]

Cook requested a dissolution, pointing out that the provisions of Section 57 had been fulfilled and stressing that the discretionary power to grant a double dissolution could be exercised only on the advice of ministers with a majority in the House of Representatives. The Governor-General asked Cook whether he would object to an opinion from the Chief Justice on the matter. Cook indicated that he had no objection, and the Chief Justice, Sir Samuel Griffith, accordingly prepared a memorandum which emphasized that the Governor-General must be 'personally satisfied, after independent consideration of the case' that a double dissolution was warranted. He also stated that although the Governor-General 'cannot act except upon the advice of Ministers, he is not bound to follow their advice, but is in the position of independent arbiter'.[19]

After considering this memorandum, Munro-Ferguson granted a double dissolution which resulted in a sweeping victory for the Labour Party. The Governor-General's action was disputed at the time by Labour and later by Professor Keith. W. M. Hughes, who had been Attorney-General in the Labour government of 1910-13, asserted that the Governor-General's action was against the precedents set by Lord Northcote and Lord Dudley. He argued that the possibility of an alternative ministry was not exhausted, as the government had only a majority of one in the lower house and was in a minority of seven to twenty-nine in the upper house. Keith supported this point of view, suggesting that Munro-Ferguson

[18] J. E. Edwards, 'The Double Dissolution as a Political Weapon', *Parliamentary Affairs*, 1950, vol. 4, no. 1, pp.92-100.

[19] Quoted by Scott, *Australia During the War*, pp.17-19. Whether Munro-Ferguson acted properly in asking for advice from someone other than a responsible minister is open to doubt. Cf. Sawer, *Australian Federal Politics and Law 1901-1929*, pp.121-4.

should have given Labour a chance to form a government and then have granted a dissolution had it failed. As in the 1909 case, Keith was confusing the issue through hindsight, as Labour had won the election in both cases. He regarded Munro-Ferguson's decision as a watershed in the history of gubernatorial discretion, and built up an elaborate apparatus of speculation on the premise that because Munro-Ferguson had been a fairly prominent Liberal M.P. during the struggle with the Lords from 1909-11, he had decided to apply the newly-reaffirmed British principle to Australian conditions. He was, says Keith, 'accustomed to the doctrine of the duty of the Crown to act on ministerial advice, lately vindicated so signally by the passing of the Parliament Act . . . if this had been realized, the attacks made on his impartiality and capacity would have been avoided'.[20]

Keith's view is sharply controverted by several other writers. The official war historian, Scott, asserts that 'it is quite certain that the Governor-General had arrived independently at the conclusion that a double dissolution was the only solution of the parliamentary deadlock, and exercised the discretion which he maintained that he possessed'. Scott was in the fortunate position of being able to quote documentary evidence from the Novar papers. Evatt takes the same view, pointing out that the reference to precedents is misleading because, in fact, Munro-Ferguson referred to the parliamentary situation as his predecessors had done. According to Evatt, Munro-Ferguson's decision establishes the fact that so long as the formal conditions laid down in Section 57 are complied with, it is of no consequence whether the actual dispute has been deliberately manufactured, as the 1914 affair undoubtedly was.

Since 1914, two dissolutions have been the subject of controversy. In 1929, the Bruce-Page Government was defeated on a proposal to amend the arbitration system, when several members of the government parties crossed the floor during the committee stage and voted with the Opposition. Bruce immediately declared that this meant parliament must be dissolved. He was attacked for this statement by E. G. Theodore, deputy leader of the Labour

[20] Keith, op. cit., pp.137-8. Munro-Ferguson, M.P. for Leith from 1886 to 1914, was for a time parliamentary private secretary to Lord Rosebery. He was a member of the group of Liberal Imperialists ('Limps'), including Asquith, Haldane and Grey, who were an important ginger group in the Liberal Party before the great victory of 1905, and were friendly with Sidney and Beatrice Webb. The latter dismisses him in her diary as 'merely a pleasant young aristocrat'. (*Our Partnership*, p.228.) As Lord Novar, he became Secretary of State for Scotland from 1922- to 1924.

Party, who argued that 'the registering of any opinion by this Committee cannot be taken as an instruction to the Governor-General to dissolve the Parliament'. The Governor-General's discretion, he said, was free and unfettered, and although the government had decided to make the matter one of confidence, it could not simply tell the Governor-General that the vote meant an instruction to him to dissolve parliament.[21] When Bruce asked the Governor-General, Lord Stonehaven, for a dissolution, the leader of the dissidents, W. M. Hughes, declared that the request should have been refused and an alternative government attempted (presumably with himself as leader). The memorandum addressed to the Governor-General by Bruce and the Attorney-General, J. G. Latham, pointed out that no alternative government was possible, and asserted the existence of an automatic right to dissolution since the Balfour Report of 1926. Both the views expressed by Hughes and by the government were criticized at the time. F. W. Eggleston dismissed the objectors with the remark that the incidents showed 'how ignorant about constitutional doctrines are some of those whose business is to know better'. On the other hand, he denied that the 1926 Report had altered the necessity for the Governor-General to exercise his discretion, but 'it may be that Mr. Latham, whose legalism is exuberant and redundant, added this as a makeweight'. He laid down two principles—namely, that a government defeated on a no-confidence motion was not *automatically* entitled to a dissolution, but that when it was defeated on an important measure it was so entitled, especially when, as in this case, the resolution on which it was defeated explicitly challenged it to go to the country.[22] A similar view was taken by Alexander, who stressed that precedents from other Commonwealth countries must be treated with reserve. 'The position of the Governor-General with respect to the granting of dissolution must be investigated in direct relationship to the political background in which he is called upon to function as His Majesty's representative.' He observed, moreover, that neither the 1914 nor the 1929 case could be used as support for the view that usage in the dominions had been assimilated to that in the United Kingdom (whatever the Balfour Report might have said to the contrary). In the 1929 incident, no alternative government was really possible and there was no reason to suppose that the Governor-General accepted

---

21 *Parl. Deb.* (C. of A.), 1929, 121: 849. The vote had been taken on an amendment, moved in committee, to put the controversial Bill to a referendum.
22 'Australian Politics', *Stead's Review*, 1929, vol. 66, no. 10.

the view that he must automatically grant a dissolution on request. (Alexander did, however, raise a point which will be considered below—namely, the problem that might be raised by the appointment of an Australian with known political sympathies as Governor-General.)[23]

Another contemporary writer in the *Round Table* reiterated that comparisons between Britain and the dominions must be treated carefully because of the difference between the position of a British monarch and a dominion governor. He suggested that one of the important reasons for the continued use of discretionary power was the existence of a multi-party system. Only in a two-party system, where clear majorities might normally be expected, would there be a case for the principle of automatic dissolution on request, but in a three-party system, where minority governments were feasible, the exercise of discretion was right and proper.[24]

The 1951 Double Dissolution

The constitutional crisis of 1950-1, which was marked by a protracted deadlock between the non-Labour government and the Labour majority in the Senate, probably demonstrates the fact that although no Governor-General would now be willing to emphasize his discretionary authority, Commonwealth governments are likely to go to considerable pains to avoid presenting him with an awkward choice. This fact emerges from a statement made by the Prime Minister that he had informed the Governor-General 'he was not bound to follow my advice in respect of the existence of the conditions of fact set out in Section 57, but that he had to be himself satisfied that those conditions of fact were established'.[25]

The crisis arose over a Bill to amend the structure of the Commonwealth Bank. The Senate passed the Bill with amendments which were unacceptable to the House of Representatives, and persisted in them even after the lower house returned the Bill stating its disagreement with the amendments. Nearly five months later, the Bill was again passed by the House of Representatives and sent to the upper house. On this occasion the Senate passed the second reading, but instead of proceeding to the committee stage, referred the Bill to a Select Committee. In his letter requesting a dissolution, the Prime Minister quoted the considerations urged in 1914 that

23 'The Governor-General and Dissolutions', *Australian Quarterly,* 1930, no. 7, p.29.
24 'The Prerogative of Dissolution', *Round Table,* 1929, vol. 20, no. 1.
25 Documents Relating to the Simultaneous Dissolution of the Senate and the House of Representatives . . . on 19/3/51; foreword by the Prime Minister, Rt Hon. R. G. Menzies, p.4.

parliament was unworkable in its existing state, and added that if this were regarded as significant, then evidence could also be adduced of deadlocks on other Bills dealing with national service, with the dissolution of the Communist Party, and with social services.

The real controversy in this case arose over the phrase in Section 57 providing that the deadlock provision may be invoked if the Senate 'fails to pass' a Bill. The Governor-General was furnished with legal opinions, including one from the Solicitor-General, Professor K. H. Bailey, who quoted opinions by Harrison Moore and by Sir Robert Garran on the subject and concluded with the significant sentence that the decision was 'a matter rather of political interpretation or elucidation than a mere establishment of acts and events'.[26] The Labour Party at the time apparently took the same view, as Labour spokesmen queried the constitutional propriety of the Governor-General's decision, and there were rumours of a court case. The attitude of the Labour Party must be considered in relation to events inside the Labour movement at the time. The party was already torn by the conflict between the 'industrial group' wing and its opponents which culminated in an open breach early in 1955 and led to the establishment of the Democratic Labor Party in 1957. The split, intensified by a struggle over the party's attitude to the government's Bill to outlaw the Communist Party, had made Labour reluctant to provoke an election, and consequently a technique of delay had been adopted. However, the federal conference of the A.L.P. met in Canberra in March 1951 and instructed the party to oppose the Bank Bill.

It is against this background that one should interpret the comment made in the *Round Table* that a challenge in the High Court might result in a decision upsetting the validity of a double dissolution, because of the restrictions on evidence which would be applicable before the court. 'From the legalistic point of view, therefore, the Labour party's objections may have been valid, but once the political details are considered, such as the decision of the A.L.P. conference and public statements by Labour leaders, there can be little doubt of the existence of a deadlock.'[27]

The suggestion made by Dr Evatt, who was at this time Deputy-Leader of the Opposition, that the case should be taken to court, was in line with a point made frequently in his writings. In 1940,

---

26 Ibid., p.11.
27 *Round Table,* 1951, vol. 41, pp.286-7. The government also seems to have regarded the affair as politically touchy, since it delayed the publication of the documents for more than five years.

for example, he wrote that the obscurity surrounding the exercise of the prerogative of dissolution should be remedied by laying down firm principles in an Act of Parliament, which would also provide for court jurisdiction to deal with disputes and for prerogative remedies such as *mandamus*. It was 'pernicious', he went on, to assert that 'under modern constitutional practice, the Prime Minister for the time being "always has a dissolution in his pocket" '.[28]

The fears expressed by Evatt, and even more emphatically by Forsey, about the complete disappearance of the discretion of a Governor or Governor-General do not seem to be exemplified by recent examples of dissolution in Australia. There seems little sign that Forsey's fear of 'unscrupulous demagogues playing fast and loose with the constitution'[29] has been realized. In fact, the conditions he regards as desirable have in most recent cases been observed with considerable scrupulousness. These amount, in practice, to two—that the Crown should be guided by the parliamentary situation, and that it is entitled to insist on supply being obtained. The observance of the parliamentary situation implies that the government must have a majority, that it is not the subject of a censure motion, and that the cabinet is united in its request for a dissolution.[30] It also implies a negative criterion—that the likelihood of the government being returned must not be considered. There can be little doubt that these principles have been followed fairly closely in both the states and the Commonwealth since 1914.

[28] 'The Discretionary Authority of Dominion Governors', *Canadian Bar Review*, 1940, vol. 18, p.8.

[29] *The Royal Power of Dissolution in the British Commonwealth*, p.7.

[30] The latter point is based on the split in the South African government in 1939. General Hertzog's request for a dissolution was refused because he was supported by only a minority of his cabinet. Forsey also adduced the case of Lang in 1927, following Keith, who states incorrectly (*Responsible Government in the Dominions*, p.107) that a dissolution was refused. The account given above shows that no *refusal* actually occurred, Lang being evidently a more agile intriguer than Hertzog.

8

THE CHOICE OF A GOVERNOR-GENERAL

DESPITE the virtual disappearance of the discretionary powers of the Governor or Governor-General, the tradition that these powers *should* exist has never entirely vanished, and it comes to life particularly when there is a prospect of an Australian being chosen for gubernatorial office. An outstanding occasion was the appointment of Sir Isaac Isaacs, then Chief Justice, in 1930. Most of the press, and a variety of 'patriotic' organizations, indulged in what a critic called 'a mass of frothy invective' when the announcement was made, alleging that the bonds of Empire were being severed and that the Labour government was inserting 'the thin end of the wedge of republicanism'. The same writer observed sharply that if the ties of empire were so tenuous 'that a change of this kind could seriously endanger them, then they are not sufficiently substantial for the purposes they are supposed to serve'. It was most unlikely that the Governor-General would be biased simply because he was an Australian, partly because of the strong tradition that he must act only on advice, and partly because he would have to be all the more careful precisely because he was an Australian. In fact, such an appointment might actually impair the strength of the Governor-General's position. 'To appoint an Australian . . . [would be] to stereotype the existing impotence of the "Crown" in our political machinery.'[1]

Another writer complained that the position of Governor-General was being 'subjected to all the incidents of party politics', and went on to argue that the appointment went much further than the intention of the Balfour Report. 'It was certainly not intended, when the Imperial Conference declared in 1926 that the Governor-General is not to be regarded as a representative of the British ministry, that he should become the representative of a Dominion ministry.'[2]

Though the appointment of Sir Isaac Isaacs provided the greatest single occasion for controversy, the problem has a much longer history. It was already an article of faith among nineteenth century Australian nationalists that native sons should be appointed

1 *Stead's Review,* 1930, vol. 67, no. 6.
2 *Round Table,* 1931, vol. 21, no. 2.

to gubernatorial and military positions.[3] This attitude was in-herited by the Labour Party, which during most of its career has been the hierophant of Australian nationalism. The views of the Labour Party were stated at length during a parliamentary debate soon after federation. Senator Higgs asserted:

An Australian who has lived at least some ten years amongst us knows more about our habits and customs—knows the people and their ways—better than a stranger. He would not be likely to pander to class prejudices and would, I think, fill the position of Governor-General in a more satisfactory way than any gentleman imported. An Australian citizen in the position of the Governor-General would never make the mistakes that some Governors have made. He would not be likely, for ex-ample, to fall into the error made by some Governors I know of —half-pay officers—who have come out here and after being able to get in their wines free of duty, they sent them down to the auction room and secured the benefit of the increased price which had accrued. Nor would such a Governor-General be likely to make the mistake of paying English rates of wages to his servants. And, further, an Australian would not, I think, fall into the mistake made by a very popular Governor-General some time ago, who—seeing the unemployed in distress—distri-buted one hundred bottles of champagne among them.[4]

The policy of appointing Australian Governors-General was formally endorsed by the federal conference of the A.L.P. in 1919. The attitude of the Labour movement has several sources. It arises partly from fairly crude nationalist sentiments, partly from a reaction against the Imperial Federation propaganda of an earlier generation and partly as an expression of the general egalitarian temper of the movement. On the other hand, the preference of the non-Labour parties for appointing Britishers to gubernatorial posts arises partly from a crudely sentimental patriotism, fostered by such bodies as the Royal Empire (now Commonwealth) Society, the Victoria League, and ex-servicemen's organizations, and also as a simple reaction to Labour views.[5]

Apart from the selection of Australians, there have been fre-

---

[3] In the novel *Longleat of Kooralbyn* (1887) the authoress, Mrs Campbell Praed, made her hero, a fictional Premier of Queensland, declare his advo-cacy of Australians for these posts. The novel, first published in 1881 under the title of *Policy and Passion,* takes its political content from the career of the Palmer ministry (1870-4).

[4] *Parl. Deb.* (C. of A.), 1903, 15: 3413-14.

[5] Opposing party viewpoints on this matter were expressed at some length during the Budget debate in the House of Representatives in 1935. (*Parl. Deb.* (C. of A.), 1935, 147: 293-300.)

quent assertions of the right of Australian governments to select their own candidates for appointment to gubernatorial posts. In 1887, the Queensland government, under pressure from Irish Catholics, objected to the appointment of Sir Henry Blake, who had been a special magistrate in Ireland. The government also claimed the right to scrutinize all proposed appointments in future. At the colonial conference which was held later in the same year, South Australia and New South Wales backed up the claim, but Victoria dissented. Faced with this convenient lack of unity, the British government announced that it would not alter the procedure unless a united request came from the colonies. Although Blake resigned his position,[6] the British government refused to accept any suggestion that the names of future appointees would be submitted to colonial governments beforehand. The constitutional procedure for the appointment of a state Governor therefore remains that the appointment is made 'by the King on the advice of the Imperial government in consultation with the State government concerned. He is not appointed by the King automatically on the advice of such a State government.'[7] This arrangement was complicated whenever a Labour state government insisted on nominating an Australian candidate. 'As a State government was not recognized by the Imperial government as having any constitutional right to nominate anybody, and as the names of non-Australians only were submitted to it for comment, deadlocks sometimes occurred.'[8] In some cases, a state has been without a Governor for a considerable period; instead the Lieutenant-Governor, who is of course a local man, has administered the state. In Western Australia, a disagreement of this kind occurred in 1917. In 1933, a former Premier of Western Australia, Sir James Mitchell, was appointed and served as Lieutenant-Governor from 1933 to 1948. It was only in the latter year that a non-Labour government was instrumental in having him appointed Governor. He was then eighty-two.

An even more picturesque deadlock occurred in Queensland in 1920. The Governor, Sir Hamilton Goold-Adams, retired at the beginning of 1920. The Theodore Labour government appointed William Lennon, who had been a minister in the previous

6 Blake was appointed Governor of Jamaica, but his peregrinations did not end there. Still in the same year, the strongly Protestant population of Newfoundland refused to accept a Catholic, Shea, as Governor, and in consequence Shea was sent to Jamaica and Blake to Newfoundland. Cf. Hall, *Australia and England*, p.203.
7 *The Crown, Cabinets, and Parliaments in Australia*, p.14.
8 Ibid., p.16.

Ryan government, and later Speaker, as Lieutenant-Governor. Lennon's actions in his post were most disquieting to the more conservative sections of the community and at a meeting of representatives of pastoral and commercial interests a committee of three, headed by Sir Robert Philp, was appointed to go to London with a petition asking for the appointment of a Governor. This delegation arrived in England at about the same time as Theodore, who had gone in the attempt to raise a loan for state works. The Colonial Secretary, Lord Milner, met both Theodore and the opposition delegation, and subsequently three different versions of the event were given by the parties concerned. According to Philp and his followers, Theodore had not intended to ask for the appointment of a Governor, and the Opposition had won a victory by inducing the British government to make an appointment. According to Theodore, Milner had refused to meet the Philp delegation until he had discussed the matter with the Premier, to whom the name of the new Governor, Sir Matthew Nathan, was submitted. Milner himself said that the British government had made the decision to appoint Nathan before seeing either Theodore or the delegation.[9]

The Appointment of Sir Isaac Isaacs[10]

The Balfour Report of 1926 left vague the relationship between the governments of the dominions and the United Kingdom in relation to the appointment of future Governors-General. The report seemed to establish the principle that British ministers could not give advice to the King on dominion affairs, but on the other hand an Australian minister could not give advice directly to the King either (constitutionally, this would probably be *ultra vires*). In the absence of firm principles, a suitably tactful procedure had been worked out. The British government would dispatch some names, in a quasi-official manner, to the dominion government; the latter would reply with its own comments, counter-suggestions, and indications of preference; in the meanwhile, the King would be kept informed. When agreement was reached, the nominee would be approached by the British Prime Minister or the Dominions Secretary. If he accepted, the name would be formally presented to the King by the British government. This procedure had been developed in accordance with the generally approved statement made

---

[9] The varying accounts of this episode are critically examined by E. M. Higgins, 'The Queensland Labor Governments 1915-1929' (unpublished M.A. thesis, 1954), pp.40-1.

[10] The following account is based partly on private information and partly on the version given by Nicolson, *King George V*, ch. 28.

by Mr L. S. Amery, then Dominions Secretary, that he thought it in everybody's interest for the British government to be a party to any negotiations.

In 1929, however, the Scullin Labour government came to office with the firm intention of appointing an Australian, and without any experience of the niceties of procedure that had been developed in the thirteen years since Labour was last in office. The appointment of the Governor-General, Lord Stonehaven, was due to expire at the end of 1930, and the Scullin government submitted the name of Sir Isaac Isaacs, who had recently been appointed Chief Justice of the High Court. In response to the objections raised by the British government, Scullin pointed out that the Irish Free State and South Africa had already insisted on naming their own Governors-General.

To avert the difficulties of discussion by cable, the British Prime Minister, Ramsay MacDonald, asked Scullin to wait until he came to London at the end of the year for the Imperial Conference. Lord Stonehaven also urged Scullin to wait, stressing that the King liked to make these appointments personally. The government was not deterred, but argued that the 1926 Report made it clear that advice on the appointment of a Governor-General was a matter for the dominion government. At this point, the government's hand was forced by a leak which appeared in *The Times* of 23 April 1930, regarding the possibility of Isaacs' appointment. This was immediately taken up by the Australian Press, which waxed indignant, and by a number of patriotic groups and political organizations on the non-Labour side, who sent cables of protest to Lord Passfield, then Colonial Secretary.[11] Stonehaven and MacDonald again urged Scullin to wait until he arrived in London, and at the end of June the Prime Minister yielded.

In October, Scullin arrived in London, and entered into a series of discussions. The King's private secretary, Lord Stamfordham, indicated that the King was opposed to the appointment of Isaacs. In reply to Scullin's observation that the South African government had already been responsible for the direct nomination of Lord Clarendon in 1929, Stamfordham informed him that the King did not wish to strengthen this precedent, as it would undoubtedly buttress the demand for native Governors-General in other dominions, for example Canada. Such appointments were likely to be unfortunate because of the racial cleavages in these countries. It is

---

[11] The *Bulletin,* long an apostle of Australian nationalism, rejoiced at the fact that the appointment of an Australian would reduce the snob value of Government House social engagements (30 April 1930).

interesting, however, that the King was not opposed to the possibility that Governors and Governors-General should come from dominions other than the one to which they were appointed.

Scullin protested, emphasizing his belief that the real objection to Isaacs was only that he was an Australian. Lord Stamfordham continued to deny this and quoted the evidence that the appointment would not be favourably received in Australia. Disagreeing, Scullin said that he would be prepared to risk an election on the issue, but deprecated such a possibility, adding that if the King refused to make the appointment his government would be unable to prevent the outbreak of political controversy which until then it had been careful not to provoke. Finally, Scullin was summoned to a personal interview with the King which lasted three-quarters of an hour. At this conversation, the King made his objections clear. He pointed out that Scullin had not followed the usual practice of an exchange of formal suggestions and that this was the first time the wishes of the King in such cases had been ignored. When Scullin referred to the case of the Irish Free State, the King retorted that he hoped Australia would not wish to compare her relation to Britain with that of Ireland.

In the end, of course, the King gave way and signified that he would accept Scullin's advice. On the receipt of a formal submission from Scullin, the official statement was issued to the effect that 'His Majesty the King, on the recommendation of the Rt. Honourable J. H. Scullin, Prime Minister of Australia, has appointed the Rt. Honourable Sir Isaac Alfred Isaacs, KCMG, Chief Justice of Australia, to the office of Governor-General . . . .' The wording of this statement was unusual in two ways.[12] It underlined the fact that the recommendation had been made on the recommendation of a dominion Prime Minister, and it omitted the usual formula that the King had been 'pleased to appoint' the person in question. Lord Stamfordham's evidence indicates that the King was seriously perturbed by the whole incident. In a letter to MacDonald after the interview, Stamfordham said that the King had regarded himself as entitled to refuse Scullin but he was aware 'how easy it is to light and fan the flame of agitation by an ill-disposed minority—especially when, as in this case, constituted of trade unions, Communists, and Irish, not of the highest class'.[13]

[12] A question was actually raised about the legality of the appointment because of this wording.

[13] Nicolson, op. cit., p.482. Stamfordham had second thoughts about this explosive statement, for he wrote again on the same day emphasizing that while the King had told Scullin he would not give him the chance to start any minority agitation, the 'probable composition of the minority' had

This series of events took place at the same time as the sittings of the Imperial Conference, and as a result of the dispute over Isaacs, the conference issued a statement setting out the procedure to be followed in future appointments. The statement referred to the implications of the Balfour Report and went on to say that appointments were a matter between the King and the dominion government, that the responsible ministers giving the advice were the dominion ministers, that informal consultation was to take place, and that the dominion government itself was to be responsible for choosing a channel of communication with the monarch and for the wording of the instrument of appointment. Thus, just as the refusal of dissolution by Lord Byng in 1926 was the immediate occasion for the Balfour Report, the Isaacs case provided a similar occasion for a new declaration of imperial relations.

*

Since 1945, most of the fire has gone out of this dispute with the appointment of a second Australian Governor-General and the extension of his appointment by a non-Labour government, and with the appointment of distinguished Australian soldiers to the office of state Governor.[14] Nevertheless, a certain amount of controversy did occur over the appointment of W. J. McKell in 1947.

During the later years of the war, the Labour Prime Minister, Mr Curtin, decided to ask for the appointment of a member of the Royal Family as Governor-General. The motives for this were undoubtedly political, stemming from the outcry over Curtin's speech welcoming the close ties between Australia and the United States after the outbreak of the war with Japan in December 1941. The Duke of Gloucester was appointed, and took up his post at the beginning of 1945.[15] He held the office, however, for only two years, and late in 1946 the Prime Minister, J. B. Chifley, recommended the appointment of McKell, who was then Premier of New South

been Stamfordham's own suggestion. The Scullin government's persistence was partly due to its eagerness to score a psychological victory over the New South Wales Labor government of Mr Lang, with whom it was at loggerheads throughout its career.

[14] Lt-General (later Sir John) Northcott in New South Wales in 1946; Lt-General Sir John Lavarack in Queensland in 1947; Lt-General Sir Eric Woodward in New South Wales in 1958.

[15] The story told by Don Whitington (*The House Will Divide*, p.114) that Winston Churchill insisted on a royal appointment may be dismissed as lobby gossip. The political advantage to the Labour Party was sufficiently great to explain this choice. Nevertheless, Curtin was aware that there would be considerable opposition even in cabinet to the appointment, and he consulted only one or two of his closest associates before he made the recommendation.

Wales. There is a story that King George VI, like his father, opposed the appointment of an Australian, and after the compromise proposal of Earl Mountbatten had not proved acceptable to the King, Chifley then insisted on an Australian.[16]

McKell's appointment revived some of the acrimony which had surrounded the appointment of Sir Isaac Isaacs sixteen years earlier. One or two of the hotter heads among the Opposition announced that they would refuse invitations to Government House. Their objections to McKell, who was knighted in 1952, were apparently soothed by office. This did not, however, apply to the Speaker, A. G. Cameron, an irascible character who had been a minister in the Menzies government of 1939-41. Although Cameron had held the rank of major during World War I, his temperament was more like a sergeant-major's. Early in 1950, soon after he had been elected Speaker, a Press article alleged that he had 'slighted' the Governor-General by not remaining for the customary refreshments after the presentation of the Address-in-Reply. The matter was then raised in parliament, and Cameron justified his action by recalling some political history. In 1940 McKell, then Opposition leader in the New South Wales parliament, had made a personal attack on him.

> Among the terms which were used in regard to myself were . . . 'intemperate', 'blackmailing', 'bushranging', . . . 'an irresponsible, headstrong, egotistical man able to hinder the efficiency of our war effort' . . . The Government at that time was described as the 'vilest of vile coalitions' . . . On assuming the Speakership of this House, I took a calculated risk. I met the Governor-General for the second time in my life, and I trust that my conduct on that day was no disgrace to this House . . . On the 27th February last, in reply to an invitation, I called the attention of the Governor-General to his past attitudes to me. I informed His Excellency that I had no desire to accept the hospitality of those who spoke of me in the terms employed by him. To that letter, I have received neither an acknowledgment nor a reply . . . I, for my part, could do nothing other than what I did on the 22nd March, and that was to treat His Excellency with the strict formality and respect due to his high office, and remove myself from his presence as soon as my duties had been discharged.[17]

Opposition members then reminded Cameron of his own ruling

16 Whitington, op. cit., p.156. This tale should also be treated with reserve. What is more readily believable is the suggestion that one reason which influenced Chifley was that the appointment would profoundly anger J. T. Lang (whom McKell had supplanted as leader of the Labour Party in New South Wales).   17 Parl. Deb. (C. of A.), 1950, 206: 1415-20.

that 'no member of the House is allowed either to praise or to blame the representative of His Majesty the King', and charged him with disingenuousness, as he must be well aware that the Governor-General did not reply to statements made in parliament or enter into political controversies. Cameron's retort was to deny the patent fact that he had violated his own ruling, declaring that he had merely 'stated certain facts'.

Leaving aside such picturesque incidents, there remains the substantive question whether the appointment of an Australian, especially one with some political past, is likely to weaken the office of Governor or Governor-General. This problem has caused a certain amount of agitation in Canada, especially since the appointment of two successive Canadians to the post of Governor-General. Discussing the case of Mr Vincent Massey, one writer observed that the prestige of the head of state, in a democracy, depends either on popular election or on complete non-partisanship. The prestige of the Governor-General is important because he is the 'last line of defence' of the constitution, and any native Canadian with some history of political affiliation 'would be weakened in a constitutional crisis, however remote it may now appear'.[18] More recently, Professor Mallory has attacked the general assumption that the Governor-General not only is, but should be, a rubber stamp. The influence of constitutional monarchy may be only frail, but it is 'a necessary admixture of a non-party point of view at the summit . . . Cabinet government requires some meaningful role in the act of government by an impartial head of state who is to a degree independent of the administration of the day; otherwise the distinction between the confidential business of the Crown and the inner councils of the party in power is wholly lost'. He is particularly concerned at the view that cabinet office confers 'unlimited power on the government of the day—in particular, the right to appoint one's friends and remove the friends of one's political opponents from posts not protected by civil service tenure'.[19]

Professor Mallory's concern with political appointments to official positions may provide the clue to a species of concern almost unknown in Australia. Even in Canada, however, it could hardly be argued that the presence of a non-Canadian as Governor-General has been particularly efficacious in this direction. In this country, statutory control over public offices is fairly strict, and in

18 Thomas Franck, 'The Governor-General and the Head of State Functions', *Canadian Bar Review*, 1954, vol. 32, no. 31, p.1084.
19 J. R. Mallory, 'The Appointment of the Governor-General', *Canadian Journal of Economics and Political Science,* 1960, vol. 26, no. 1.

addition the influence of British convention has been strong. Such political appointments as have occurred have been commoner in the states than in the Commonwealth, and the Governors concerned have usually been Englishmen. If the question retains any life, it is now only in connection with the power to refuse a dissolution. There is some reason to think that the position of McKell in 1951 was rendered more delicate by the fact that he was a former Labour politician. Some Labour parliamentarians were apparently under the impression that McKell would resist the request for a double dissolution, especially as the Labour majority in the Senate believed it had circumvented the problem of 'failing to pass' the Bill over which a deadlock had taken place. It is doubtful whether any constitutional arrangement can serve as a complete antidote to the persistent forms of wishful thinking to which politicians and constitutional writers, in their various ways, are addicted.

Part IV

CABINET AND THE PARTY SYSTEM

9

THE POLITICAL FRAMEWORK

Parties and Governments

CABINET in Australia is best understood as the fulcrum of the party system. This applies equally in federal and in state government. In the states, where so much of the machinery of government consists of instrumentalities of economic intervention and regulation, cabinet is the focus of two distinct but related systems— on the one hand, the party system, and on the other, the politico-economic apparatus of economic intervention. Although the federal picture is more complicated, similar forces are at work. Each national party is a confederation of state political machines, and factions within cabinet and within the parliamentary party often correspond with greater or lesser exactitude to state groupings. Of the early federal cabinets it was said that 'to a very large extent the politics of the Commonwealth have been a mere projection upon a magnifying screen of the personal intrigues of New South Wales'.[1] Perhaps the most notable case was the conflict between the Scullin government and the supporters within the parliamentary party of the Premier of New South Wales, J. T. Lang. In composite non-Labour industries, inter-party conflicts regularly occur, as they did between the U.A.P. and the Country Party over tariff levels in the 1930s, or between the Liberals and the Country Party in 1950-1 over the revaluation of the currency. Such disputes readily acquire an interstate aspect, as in the argument over the fate of the Commonwealth Shipping Line in 1951-6, or in differences of opinion about the retention of uniform taxing powers by the Commonwealth. The interlocking of factional and interstate disputes is nowhere more clearly illustrated than by the repeated manoeuvres over the representation of various states in cabinet.

The relation between cabinet, and the party or parties which

[1] W. A. Holman, 'The Rise and Fall of the Federal Ministries', *Red Funnel,* 1 October 1905.

support it, is the resultant of attempts by a variety of interest groups to achieve their ends through the executive machinery. Interested pressures often crystallize around a particular set of policies or around the operations of a particular government agency. Tariff policy (and, more recently, import controls) are the unremitting concern of several of the most important pressure groups in Australia, whose interests may alternately conflict or overlap: the Associated Chambers of Manufactures, the Associated Chambers of Commerce, the organized farmers, and the trade unions in manufacturing industry. The arbitration system is a matter of constant concern to the Australian Workers' Union (A.W.U.), the largest and most bureaucratic of all the unions, whose size, ubiquity, and heterogeneity have enabled it to play a commanding role in Labour politics not unlike that of the great general unions in Britain. In the states, railway policy is perpetually affected by rural pressure, exercised through the Country Party, for differential freights and the operation of uneconomic lines, and by union pressure for improved wages and conditions. Not only the role but the very existence of the Country Party are due to the general acceptance of certain forms of government intervention, especially state fixation of wages, protective tariffs, and closer settlement, as the settled policy of the country in the two decades before World War I. Political commentators are often found refusing to classify the Country Party as a 'proper' party; it is called, with strongly pejorative undertones, a 'glorified pressure group', or the rural wing of the Liberal party. Australian politics is described as a 'two-and-a-half' party system—the Country Party forming the half. These views are, I believe, the product of an attitude related to that which treats cabinet government in Australia as an aberration from the British norm. In Britain, the function of the parties is, at least in theory, to lay down the broad framework of policy and to provide suitable machinery for recruiting members of the ministry. Once a ministry is formed, the functions of the party become subordinate, and the government is expected to behave with the 'prudence' which Burke regarded as the mark of statesmanship. In the Australian political system, the function of a party is rather to supply a convenient method by which the organs of government may be made to work in the interests of the 'syndicates' linked with the party. It is, then, the political and economic role of the state itself that is largely responsible for the character of the party system and for the relation between party and cabinet. If the Country Party differs, it is because its task is not complicated by the role of class antagonism which, in Australia as elsewhere, colours the relation between the parties of capital and labour, and also because, as a minority party, it is not concerned with the task of capturing a parliamentary majority. It has, therefore, fewer inhibitions about exploiting the situation to its logical extremity, and Country Party manoeuvres are often concerned less with policy questions than with access to certain portfolios (railways and agriculture in the states, the post office and the marketing portfolio in the Commonwealth) which offer important 'pork barrel' possibilities.

It may be pertinent to ask why, in view of all this, Australia should not have adopted a system of government closer to that of the United States, which sometimes appears expressly intended to facilitate the operations of pressure politics. If we leave aside the historical factors, it may be noted, firstly, that to some extent Australia does follow the American pattern, partly because the actions of the executive are circumscribed by judicial review, and partly because of the proliferation of rule-making bodies of a semi-judicial character. The crux of the difference lies in the enormous importance and general acceptance of what J. D. B. Miller calls 'ample government'—the central and inescapable necessity for large-scale government action to develop a large, remote, and difficult country. The American polity was designed in conformity with Madison's dictum that, since property is the chief source of contention among men, it should not be one of the concerns of government. Australian government was, from the beginning, actively concerned with economic matters. The United States constitution provides for weak government; the seven Australian constitutions for a strong executive. The point was explicitly recognized during the Federal Convention debates of the 1890s.

*

In the nineteenth century, the continuous jockeying for position between shifting coalitions of interest groups, especially where this was reinforced by struggles between conservative upper houses and more or less radical governments, led to a remarkable degree of instability. The absence of firm party differences encouraged emphasis on tenure of ministerial office as a means of manipulating the government machinery in the interests of the incumbent, or of the interest groups with which he was linked. It was a game, writes Harrison Moore, in which 'men exercise their natural combativeness and rivalry, and in which ministerial office is the trophy awarded to the victors, a trophy which they hold on condition of defending it against all challengers'. Instead of parties, there appears 'the habit whereby associations formed for some special purpose served as a point of union for general political action'. These conditions he concluded were 'not favourable to the smooth working of the Cabinet system'.[2] A gloomier view had been taken some years earlier by Jenks, who asserted that the three important conditions for the working of cabinet—personal cohesion among ministers, clear-cut party divisions, and accepted conventions—were absent. 'If the rather delicate traditions of Cabinet government break down, the system will degenerate more and more into a cynical struggle for office, in which, as the prizes are not very great, the competitors engaged will not necessarily be of a very high order of merit.'[3] The conditions for decline were already in evidence, because patronage had been severely limited through the setting up of independent controlling bodies like the Public Service Board. 'One very obvious result of the fact is that the party system is dying a natural death.'[4] It is generally assumed that this unstable situation began to change as the result of the emergence of the Labour Party in the 1890s, and the consequent coalescence of all other groups into a unified anti-Labour front. In fact, however, stable governments were already emerging in the 1880s, as the result of the growth of state intervention in connection with arbitration, protective tariffs, closer settlement, and the provision of public utilities required by the rapidly growing urban centres. Whatever the reason, there is no doubt that stable ministries became more and more the rule from the late years of the nineteenth century. Their lives were prolonged by successful exploitation of the economic agencies of the state to build a political machine whose reliable support could be counted on. (In addition, the use of electoral gerrymandering, which first became widespread at this time, was of some importance.) The Labour government in Queensland was able to remove yet another important source of instability by the abolition of the Legislative Council in 1922.

The change, however, has not meant the emergence of political bosses on the American model, with the possible exception of J. T. Lang in New South Wales. Bossism of this type depends on the existence of a large number of fragmented groups who are indebted to the boss for various favours. In Australia, interest groups are well organized, and it may be argued that the change as from the nineteenth to the twentieth centuries was to cement more or less stable alliances of the most important ones. From these has emerged the modern party system, which, so far from throwing up bosses, has been fertile in attempts to restrict the in-

2 In Atkinson (ed.), *Australia: Economic and Political Studies*, pp.98-100.
3 Jenks, *The Government of Victoria*, p.380.   4 Ibid., p.274.

dependence of government and to prevent it from making policy or exercising its administrative functions without reference to the party organization or to important interest groups influential in the party. Consequently, the allegation that governments are being dominated by 'outside interests' is one of the most frequent phenomena in Australian politics. A striking example of accusation and counter-accusation on this score occurred in Queensland in 1920. A Labour government led by E. G. Theodore had put through a number of measures which profoundly disquieted the business community, including the nationalization of the privately-owned tramways in Brisbane and an Act to abolish the upper house. It had also failed to appoint a new Governor.[5] The delegation that went to London, headed by Sir Robert Philp,[6] in addition to asking Lord Milner, the Colonial Secretary, to appoint a new Governor, also used its influence to prevent Theodore from getting a loan. The Brisbane *Courier* defended this action on the grounds that the government was setting up a dictatorship. Queensland was controlled by a 'junta' which had seized 'all the organs, instruments and functions of the State, except the judicature, and that is marked for an early capture'. Only a delegation of solid citizens could undo this situation by advising 'a cautious and waiting policy until Queensland comes under the administration of a Government which will restore responsible government'.[7]

Philp and his companions received a sympathetic hearing from the financial journals in London, which advised against a loan to Theodore until the government gave assurances against confiscation to investors. Theodore returned to Queensland in a towering rage, and declared on his return that the financial institutions in London had insisted on repeal of the offending legislation. Parliament was dissolved, and Theodore took the stump on the issue of 'self-determination' for Queensland. The capitalists, he thundered, were 'digging their claws into the industries and businesses of Queensland and gorging themselves on the life blood of the people'. It was the Nationalist Party, not Labour, that was ruled by outside interests. 'The Tories here talk of the junta of the Trades Hall. Why, we know nothing about outside influence or the power of a secret junta. We have to go to London to learn what that means.'[8]

5 See chapter 8.
6 Philp, a former Premier, had large interests in shipping, banking, insurance and merchandising.
7 *Brisbane Courier*, 15 March 1920. Quoted by E. M. Higgins, 'The Queensland Labor Governments 1915-1929', p.41.
8 Ibid., p.44.

The Stability of Governments
The instability of cabinets in the nineteenth century, superficially so striking, may easily be exaggerated. Contemporary observers were fond of likening the situation to that of France under the Third Republic. As in France, however, instability was apparent as well as real, as can be shown by an analysis of the differential tenure of office by ministers over a period.

Between 1856 and 1901, the actual number[9] of ministries in the various colonies was as follows:

New South Wales	29
Victoria	29
Queensland	21
South Australia	42
Tasmania	20

In New South Wales and Victoria, the average tenure of a government was 1.6 years; in Queensland, 2 years; in Tasmania, 2.2 years; and in South Australia, just over 1 year. Some periods were marked by an especially spectacular succession of short-lived governments. In South Australia, 1857 saw three separate ministries in office, one of which lasted eleven days, and another twenty-nine days. Another such year was 1868, when one of the three governments lasted only nineteen days, and yet another was 1899. In Victoria, 1875 saw three separate ministries (which occurred again in 1943). Although a number of very short incumbencies are on record, the all-time record-breaker occurred in New South Wales in 1921, with the 'Seven Hours Ministry' of Sir George Fuller.

South Australia is the most striking case, sometimes attributed to the great influence of Nonconformist religion. T. A. Coghlan wrote that 'it may be fairly proposed that Nonconformity and democracy are symptoms of a similar attitude of mind'. He continued:

There would be little exaggeration in saying that every member declared his own policy and every ministry called itself democratic. There was, in fact, a general agreement about most of the ordinary matters of government and administration. But while there was thus a consensus of opinion in favour of Liberal measures, each of the leading politicians had usually a special piece of legislation, as often as not belonging to the genus of

---

9 A few of these are, of course, separate 'ministries' only in a formal sense, owing their existence to reshuffles of the same government which, for constitutional reasons, required the swearing-in of a new Premier. The exclusion of these would not significantly alter the total picture.

fads, and for this he would endeavour to secure the attention of the public, and if successful, the attention of Parliament also. It generally happened that, the Opposition leader having defeated the Ministry, it might be on its principal member's pet fad, or Parliament having come to the conclusion that a change of Ministry should be tried, a new Ministry came in. This Ministry was allowed to govern in the ordinary way, passing the sort of measures which the general public approved of, until either its Premier, in his turn, chose to introduce his own legislative eccentricity without properly feeling his ground in the House or the country, or the country grew tired of the Ministry and its petty ways, and then another change was tried. This was group government, and every pettifogging politician had his chance of a little, if brief, authority.[10]

Another contemporary observer, William Pember Reeves, attributed the rapid succession of government not to Nonconformist opinions but to lack of personal scruple.

The almost French instability before 1891, the comparative fixity since, are worth a word here. Colonial ministries are often reconstructed for purely personal reasons. Such changes do not involve the coming in or going out of parties. Prime Ministers and their colleagues are seldom men of independent means. They usually have businesses which demand a share of their time, and every now and then some one has to leave office to attend to his private affairs. Again, ministerial life in the colonies is one of hard and harassing work. Ministers are not hedged about with any protective dignity. Many of them suffer in health, some of them break down, occasionally one dies in harness. Nearly all of them die poor. These things have a share in abridging the lives of cabinets. In the main, however, parliamentary parties prior to 1891 were always more or less fluid. There was little or no machine organization outside the Houses to compel discipline within. At public meetings candidates were pledged on certain prominent questions, and were usually accounted as owing allegiance to this or that leader. But the opportunities of disloyalty were innumerable, and full advantage was taken of them. Men would keep platform pledges to the letter and break them in spirit—could even, thanks to ignorance or apathy amongst their constituents, ignore them altogether. There was very little direct corruption; but unscrupulous men would support ministries for what grants they hoped to get for their districts. Men still more unscrupulous joined or deserted parties simply in the hope of office. There were members avowedly in-

10 *Labour and Industry in Australia,* vol. 4, p.1913.

dependent, who were occasionally the most honourable men in public life, but more often the reverse. On the whole, the experience of parliamentary parties without tight bonds and lasting lines of cleavage was depressing to most of those behind the scenes. It was emphatically a life in which it was wise to remember that your enemy might some day be your friend, while your friend would probably become your enemy.[11]

It is not surprising that under these circumstances there was a generally poor opinion of politicians and their works, reflected in the Press and in contemporary literature. As early as 1857 the Adelaide *Register* wrote:

> The grand struggle for office has now fairly set in. Representatives of the people are more or less engaged in a sublime scramble. Regardless of the decencies of political usage, careless of the ordinary courtesies of official intercourse, each is trying to elbow his neighbour in the great place-hunting mêlée. It is a spectacle worthy the contemplation of a free and enlightened community.[12]

Nevertheless, despite the superficially striking character of the figures, and the typically uncomplimentary view of politicians which was the result, it is possible to demonstrate that a stable core of politicians held office for long periods. The existence of this other side of the medal has also been demonstrated in France.[13]

In New South Wales, for example, politics between 1856 and 1891 were dominated by four men. Charles Cowper, the second Premier of New South Wales, held portfolios in six governments between 1856 and 1870. On each of these occasions he held the portfolio of Colonial Secretary, and on five of them was Premier in addition. His total incumbency of the portfolio of Colonial Secretary was seven years and two months. J. A. Martin was a minister in five governments between 1856 and 1872. On each occasion he was Attorney-General, and on three occasions Premier in addition. His total tenure as Attorney-General was five years and five months, and as Premier, three years and ten months. John Robertson was a member of ten governments between 1858 and 1886, and held office for twelve years in all. He was Premier

11 *State Experiments in Australia and New Zealand,* vol. 1, p.66.
12 Quoted by J. Blacket, *History of South Australia,* p.288.
13 J. G. Heinberg, 'The Personnel Structure of French Cabinets', *American Political Science Review,* 1939, vol. 33, no. 2; M. Dogan and P. Campbell, 'Le personnel ministeriel en France et en Grande-Bretagne', *Revue Francaise de Science Politique,* 1957, vol. 7, no. 3.

on five occasions, for a total period of three years and one month; Secretary for Lands on seven occasions, for a total of seven years and five months; and Colonial Secretary five times, for a total of four years and three months.

The outstanding position of Henry Parkes in New South Wales colonial politics is even more striking when statistically demonstrated. Between 1866 and 1891, he was five times Premier and once Colonial Secretary. His total tenure of office was sixteen years and three months, and his total period as Premier was thirteen years and nine months.

Although these four men stand out during the first period of responsible government in New South Wales, analysis also demonstrates the existence of a second tier of men whose tenure, in many cases of the same portfolio, was prolonged, and who, in consequence, exercised considerable influence in their day. Sir William Manning, for instance, was Attorney-General on five occasions between 1856 and 1870, for a total of three years and four months. Saul Samuel held office six times between 1859 and 1880, three times as Treasurer and three times as Postmaster-General.[14] His tenure of the latter portfolio totalled four years and two months, and of the former, two years and nine months. W. B. Dalley was Attorney-General on three occasions between 1875 and 1885, for a total period of five years and two months.

At a slightly later period where frequent changes of ministry were still the rule, we find once again that a small number of men held office for periods which marked them out from the ruck. G. R. Dibbs was in office for a total of six years and nine months in the years from 1883 to 1894. This included three years and one month as Premier, and three years as Treasurer (two months of which occurred while he was Premier). George Reid held office as Premier for a single period of just over five years between 1894 and 1899, and was Minister for Public Instruction in the Stuart ministry from 1883 to 1884, giving him a total tenure of office of slightly less than seven years over a lapse of sixteen years. W. J. Lyne held office in five governments between 1885 and 1901, for a total period of five and a half years. He was Minister for Public Works three times, with a tenure totalling three years and ten months.

An analysis of Victorian political history shows an even more striking concentration of office among a small number of men. The Victorian situation is all the more interesting because the turnover of ministries in the twentieth century has been almost as great as in

[14] In 1880 he was appointed Agent-General in London.

the nineteenth. From 1855 to 1901 there were twenty-nine governments; from 1902 to 1945, twenty-two. An analysis of the ninety years beginning with the Haines ministry, which took office in November 1855, to the resignation of the Dunstan ministry in October 1945, yields results as shown below.[15]

In the forty-five years from the inauguration of responsible government until federation, six men held office as Premier for total periods of more than three years. (Figures in parentheses denote the number of terms of office.)

TABLE 1

O'Shanassy	3 years	5 months	(3)
McCulloch	8 ,,	10 ,,	(4)
Berry	3 ,,	11 ,,	(3)
Service	3 ,,	5 ,,	(2)
Gillies	4 ,,	10 ,,	(1)
Turner	5 ,,	2 ,,	(2)

Between O'Shanassy's first term in 1857 and Turner's resignation to enter federal politics in 1901, there were altogether twenty-three ministries in office, but the six Premiers listed in Table 1 held office for a total of twenty-nine years seven months. Table 2 analyses the concentration of office between 1901 and 1945.

TABLE 2

Peacock	5 years	1 month	(3)
Bent	4 ,,	11 ,,	(1)
Lawson	6 ,,	2 ,,	(3)
Hogan	3 ,,	11 ,,	(2)
Dunstan	10 ,,	6 ,,	(2)

From Table 2 it can be seen that in the period 1901-45, when there were twenty-two ministries, five Premiers held office for a total of thirty years seven months. From the two tables it may be shown that during the whole period of ninety years, the Premiership was held for one-half of the time by only seven men, and for two-thirds of the time by eleven men.

A similar pattern may be shown to hold for the portfolio of Treasurer. From 1855 until federation, there were twenty Treasurers, of whom twelve held the portfolio for more than three years. The outstanding cases were as follows:

15 The material that follows is based on an unpublished study kindly given to me by Mr A. F. Davies.

TABLE 3

McCulloch	3 years	10 months	(3)
Verdon	5 „	10 „	(2)
Berry	5 „	2 „	(6)
Service	4 „	3 „	(3)
Gillies	4 „	9 „	(1)
Turner	5 „	5 „	(2)

From McCulloch's first term in 1863 until Turner's resignation in 1901, a period in which there were twenty ministries, six Treasurers held office for a total of twenty-nine years three months. In Table 4, a similar concentration is demonstrated for the period 1901-45.

TABLE 4

Peacock[16]	7 years	10 months	(5)
Bent	4 „	11 „	(1)
Watt	4 „	5 „	(3)
McPherson	7 „	2 „	(4)
Hogan	3 „	11 „	(2)
Dunstan	10 „	6 „	(2)

From Table 4, it may be seen that six Treasurers held office during 1901-45 for a total of thirty-eight years nine months, in a period when twenty-two ministries came and went. From the two tables taken together, it may be computed that, in the ninety years under review, the Treasurership was held for one-half of the time by only seven men, and for three-quarters of the time by twelve men. As all the Treasurers listed in Tables 3 and 4 were also Premiers, most of them for periods of more than three years, the concentration of power in the hands of a small core of individuals is even more marked. The extent of the concentration may also be shown by another method of analysis, set out in the following tables. Table 5 classifies the fifty-one ministries which were in office during 1855-1945 according to duration.

The most striking feature of this table is the demonstration that nine ministries were in office for almost one-half of the whole period. Table 6 shows how concentration of office in the hands of a small number of governments is accompanied by concentration of power in the hands of a small number of ministers.

16 Peacock had one term as Treasurer in the 1890s, which is included here for the sake of simplicity.

TABLE 5

Victorian Ministries, 1855-1945

Duration in years	No. of ministries in each class	Total years in office of each class	% of total period
Under 1	21	9	10
1-3	21	37.5	42
3-5	6	24	27
5 and over	3	19.5	21
	51	90	100

TABLE 6

Tenure of Office in Victorian Ministries, 1855-1945

No. of terms of office	No. of ministers in each category
1	134
2	69
3	40
4	26
5	10
6	3
7	3
8	1
13	1
	287

Forty-four of the 287 ministers in office during the period, i.e., about one-seventh, had more than three terms of office. One of the interesting consequences of the patterns already revealed is the occurrence of a cyclical process, occupying almost exactly one generation. At the beginning of each cycle, a large number of new men attains cabinet rank, and the number of new participants in cabinets diminishes steadily thereafter until the end of each thirty-year period. The remarkable regularity of the cycle is underlined by taking our analysis up to the assumption of office by the Bolte ministry in 1955.

TABLE 7

Participation in Victorian Ministries, 1855-1955

Decade	No. of ministers participating for first time	Progress totals
1855-1865	58	58
1865-1875	36	94
1875-1885	27	121
1885-1895	42	163
1895-1905	32	195
1905-1915	22	217
1915-1925	41	258
1925-1935	12	270
1935-1945	17	287
1945-1955	42	329

Table 7 shows a cycle in each of the periods starting with the years 1855, 1885, 1915, and 1945. The only imperfection of the cycle occurs during the decade 1935-45, and is readily accounted for. In 1943, a temporary breakdown of the alliance between the Dunstan (Country Party) government and the United Australia Party led to a Labour ministry taking office, which it retained for five days. Only one member of this government had previously held ministerial office. The others belong *effectively* to the period 1945-55, and if they are eliminated from the decade in question, the number of 'new entrants' falls to eleven.

*

As a postscript, some reference may be made to the unstable period of 'three elevens' in federal politics from 1901 to 1910. From federation until the defeat of the Fusion ministry in April 1910—a period of just over nine years—seven ministries were in office (three separate ones in the single year 1904), but a small number of men effectively held power. Alfred Deakin was Prime Minister for a total of four years and eleven months, and Attorney-General for two years and nine months. Sir George Turner, formerly Premier and Treasurer of Victoria, was Treasurer in every non-Labour administration until 1905—i.e., he held the portfolio for four years and two months in a period of four and a half years. Sir John Forrest and Sir William Lyne both held portfolios for more than seven years in all.

State Representation in Federal Cabinet

Not the least curious result of Australian federalism is the recurrent competition between various states for representation in federal cabinet. It was originally presumed by the authors of the Commonwealth Constitution that the Senate would act as a guardian of state interests. The Senate ceased to fulfil this role from an early date in its history, and cabinet became a more significant locus of state representation. The smaller states, especially Tasmania, have held from the beginning that this was a right and proper thing. In their case, party interests have sometimes been overshadowed by the fear that the policies of the Commonwealth would be dominated by the two large states of New South Wales and Victoria. When the first federal cabinet was constructed in the closing days of 1900, even before the first Commonwealth elections, the Press in Tasmania was quick to seize on the fact that the island state had been left 'out in the cold'. The excuse given by the Prime Minister, Barton, that a representative from Western Australia had priority, was condemned as a lame excuse, and one newspaper called on the voters of Tasmania to assert their claim to a representative in the ministry.[17]   In order to avoid antagonizing the Tasmanians, Barton included N. E. Lewis as an honorary minister, and when he resigned replaced him by P. O. Fysh.[18]

A few years later Tasmania again had a grievance when it had no representative in the Fusion ministry of 1909. 'No Tasmanian need apply', read the headline announcing the formation of the ministry. In 1920 a public meeting was actually held in Launceston to complain about the omission of any Tasmanian from the federal cabinet; the resolution was forwarded by the Premier with a note signifying his 'warmest support'.[19] On the other hand, when J. A. Lyons, formerly Labour Premier of Tasmania, was made Postmaster-General in the Scullin government, the Nationalist Premier of Tasmania moved in the House of Assembly that parliament should express its pleasure at the inclusion of a Tasmanian. In the debate on this motion, stress was laid on the fact that Lyons had a department, whereas Tasmanians were usually treated only to an honorary ministership or to the vice-presidency of the Executive Council. In 1941, the inclusion of a Tasmanian

17 Launceston *Examiner,* 31 December 1900, quoted by K. A. McKirdy, 'The Federalization of the Australian Cabinet 1909-1939', *Canadian Journal of Economics and Political Science,* 1957, vol. 23, no. 2.   McKirdy's article, which makes interesting comparisons between federal representation in the Australian and Canadian cabinets, provides some of the material for this chapter.   18 Both had been Premiers of Tasmania.
19 Letter to W. M. Hughes, *C.P.* 99, ser. 3 (C-A).

in the Curtin government was welcomed with the statement that 'he would be in a position to help assure recognition of Tasmania's claims for a fair share of Commonwealth expenditure'.[20]

Although Tasmania, with its special economic problems and its tradition of distinction from 'the mainland'[21] has been particularly notable for expressions of opinion on the matter of representation, other states outside New South Wales and Victoria have not been backward. An Adelaide newspaper noted with satisfaction in 1908 that there was a large number of South Australians in the Fisher government,[22] and when Hughes formed his first Labour ministry in 1915, a Liberal member of the South Australian parliament protested to the Premier about the 'injustice' done to South Australia by the absence of any representative in the new federal government.

In Queensland, the Press was also willing to disregard the fact that the Watson ministry of 1904 was a Labour administration in favour of the inclusion of two Queenslanders, who, it was believed, would be 'combative representatives' of their own state.[23] This satisfaction was all the more marked because Senator Drake, who had been a member of the first two federal ministries, had been a source of disappointment for all good Queenslanders despite the fact that his party was the one supported by the Press. A few years later, when L. E. Groom became a member of the Fusion ministry, it disapproved of him as being insufficiently disposed to defend Queensland's interests. His point of view was regarded as being 'too national'.[24]

On occasions, the federal government has gone out of its way to soothe the susceptibilities of the outlying states. In 1935, a special cabinet meeting was held in Perth shortly after the House of Commons had refused a petition from Western Australia for the right to secede from the Commonwealth. Similarly, a cabinet meeting was held in Tasmania early in 1939, during the parliamentary recess, as a special gesture to the Prime Minister, J. A. Lyons, who was spending his vacation at home.

[20] Launceston *Examiner,* 6 October 1941.
[21] Consciousness of 'the mainland' sometimes rises almost to the level of xenophobia. In 1954, the policy of the Commonwealth government was attacked during a state election as a 'mainland plot'.
[22] Adelaide *Advertiser,* 13 November 1908.
[23] *Brisbane Courier,* 27 April 1904.
[24] Ibid., 3 June 1909. Denham, a state minister, had written to Groom on a previous occasion when he became Minister for Home Affairs in the second Deakin government, that Queensland 'at last has a live representative in the Cabinet'. (Letter dated 10 July 1905; quoted in Lady Groom *et al., Nation Building in Australia,* p.41.)

The impact of federalism on the composition of Commonwealth cabinets can be seen in Tables 8 and 9.[25]

TABLE 8

Federal Ministers by States, 1901-51

State	Total	Liberal (etc.)	C.P.	Labour
N.S.W.	58	30	10	18
Vic.	50	29	6	15
Q'ld.	21	9	2	10
S.A.	20	8	2	10
W.A.	13	4	—	9
Tas.	13	5	—	8
	175	85	20	70

In Table 8, Labour men who later crossed the floor are shown under the heading 'Labour' if they held office in a Labour ministry before deserting their party. Eight such cases are included in the Labour total of seventy ministers, and similarly they do not appear under the heading 'Liberal'. In one case where a minister held office as a Country Party member, but later joined the United Australia Party, he is included in the Country Party total.

Table 9 demonstrates the discrepancies between the representation of each state in parliament,[26] and the number of portfolios which have gone to members from that state, in the fifty years under examination.

TABLE 9

Distribution by States of Ministers and Members of Parliament, 1901-51

State	% of seats in parliament	% of ministerial posts
N.S.W.	31	33
Vic.	24	29
Q'ld.	14	12
S.A.	11.5	11.5
W.A.	10	7
Tas.	9.5	7.5
	100	100

[25] McKirdy, op. cit., gives a table showing fluctuations in state representation in various ministries since federation.

[26] Allowance has been made in Table 9 for the increase in size of federal parliament in 1949 from 110 to 181 members (excluding the representatives

Certain points of interest emerge from these figures. There is a clear predominance of Victoria, especially in the Liberal Party. Victorians have held 34 per cent of portfolios allotted to Liberal ministers, as compared with 24 per cent of the seats in parliament and 29 per cent of portfolios in all governments. The smaller states have had grounds for their fear of under-representation (although this has varied as between the parties), but Western Australia and Tasmania have both had more than their proportionate share of portfolios in Labour ministries. In general, the representation of states in Labour ministries has been more even than in non-Labour ministries, and this may be attributed at least in part to the fact that Labour ministries are elected by ballot.[27]

The predominance of Victoria is one of the most interesting phenomena in Australian politics, which can be properly explored only in a full-dress study of the party system. Several observations may, however, appropriately be made here. The Liberal Party has always gained a higher proportion of Victorian seats than the national average, because of the relative weakness of Labour. The proportion of seats held by Labour members from Victoria has usually hovered around 21 per cent of Labour representation, as compared with a general figure of 24 per cent of parliamentary seats allotted to Victoria, and the former figure corresponds very closely to the state's share of portfolios in Labour governments. Labour's weakness in Victoria is largely the result of Liberal strength, which is partly due to a long tradition of readiness to use the state machinery for positive ends. On the other hand, the predominance of Victorian Liberals within the national party, and hence in cabinet, stems to some extent from the traditional role of Melbourne as a financial centre, to some extent from the united character of the Victorian Liberals as compared with the relatively fissiparous New South Wales Liberals, and to some extent from the influence of outstanding personalities like Deakin, Bruce, and Menzies.

It may be asked, finally, whether state representation in cabinet has achieved very much for the states concerned. In the case of Tasmania, there is reason to believe that the policy of the Menzies-

---

of the mainland territories). The only state affected significantly was Tasmania, whose proportionate representation declined slightly.

[27] The position of the smaller states is in contrast to the privileged role of the small maritime provinces of Canada, especially Prince Edward Island, which is regularly represented in the federal cabinet despite its minuscule representation in parliament. See R. M. Dawson, *The Government of Canada*, pp.232-3.

Fadden administration, which assumed office in 1949, was influenced in respect of decisions not to sell either the Commonwealth-owned airline, T.A.A., or the government-owned shipping line established by the preceding Labour administration. However, dissatisfaction has sometimes been expressed in the smaller states. In 1913 the Minister for Home Affairs, King O'Malley, was criticized for his failure to ensure that timber from his home state (Tasmania) was used in the manufacture of sleepers for the Trans-Australian railway. In 1922, a Hobart newspaper attacked a federal minister who hailed from Tasmania for being a 'big Australian' and not putting Tasmania first.[28]

It would be very difficult to discover to what extent conflict has taken place inside federal cabinets along state lines, but one or two pieces of evidence are available. In 1902, the former New South Wales Premier, Lyne, who was Minister for Home Affairs in the Barton ministry, complained to the Governor-General that 'the Victorian combination . . . disregard me and treat me with contempt'.[29] In more recent years, there has been evidence of New South Wales ministers, with the support of party members, forming something of a bloc over the election of a deputy premier and also over banking policy.[30]

The Demand for Elective Ministries

Dissatisfaction with the performance of colonial politicians found one of its expressions in the demand, put forward by some unorthodox radical parliamentarians and journalists, for the election of ministers by parliament in an effort to make them 'truly' responsible. An early exponent of the view that politicians were not to be trusted and that their responsibility to parliament should be rigorously safeguarded was the Victorian newspaper proprietor, David Syme.[31] In 1881, Syme published *Representative Government in England,* the burden of which was that the democratic principle of representative government, as stated for instance in Mill's famous essay, had been corrupted in Britain by the superimposition of responsible or cabinet government. Syme reiterated this point of view throughout his life and it was frequently expressed in the columns of his newspaper the *Age.* In an essay written shortly before his death, he described responsible government as 'a pernicious

---

28 Hobart *Mercury,* 21 November 1922.
29 Letter to Barton from Lord Hopetoun, 8 May 1902.
30 'Australian Political Chronicle', *Australian Journal of Politics and History,* 1957, vol. 2, no. 2.
31 Cf. J. D. B. Miller, 'David Syme and Elective Ministries', *Historical Studies,* 1953, vol. 6, no. 21.

method which is alien to a truly Parliamentary or representative system of government. Parliamentary Government is government by Parliament. Responsible government is government by party.' The poor standard of colonial administration was the result of party government, because the best qualified men were not appointed to portfolios. On the other hand, if ministers were individually elected by parliament, there might be some thought of their ability. It was this incapacity to manage affairs that had led to the tendency for decentralizing the administration of government to public corporations. Though parties will always exist, he concluded, 'we need not encourage party warfare by rewarding the successful party with office'.[32]

Syme's disgust with the kaleidoscopic reshuffles of colonial ministries was shared by politicians of various persuasions. The South Australian radical Cockburn advocated elective ministries in a speech in the House of Assembly in 1891, as a way of averting perpetual intrigues for office between the parties. He attacked the principle of collective responsibility as a cloak for the most sordid manoeuvres, and argued that election would increase the individual responsibility of each minister.[33] Other advocates of elective ministries included the Sydney *Bulletin,* and the Victorian politician W. A. Watt, who in a speech in the Victorian parliament in 1905 condemned the practice by which ministers, for reasons of party convenience, were compelled to vote for measures they opposed. Support for the elective principle was stimulated by developments in New Zealand, where a Bill to introduce election of the executive was actually brought before the House of Representatives. According to a contemporary observer, this move had been stimulated by the disinclination of ministries to resign except on a direct no-confidence motion, and their parallel readiness to sacrifice important principles in order to stay in office. 'As the ministry tends, therefore, to become a body which carries out the wishes of the whole House, and ceases to lead its own party the position would be simplified if the whole House elected the Executive for the fixed period.'[34]

The Labour Party showed some enthusiasm for elective ministries in its early years, and the platform of the New South Wales branch included a plank to this effect in 1897. Enthusiasm diminished as the party gained some experience of parliamentary life, and an attempt to include elective ministries in the federal platform was defeated at the Brisbane conference of 1908. This conference

32 Ambrose Pratt, *David Syme,* pp.304-12.　　33 Miller, op. cit.
34 H. de R. Walker, *Australasian Democracy,* pp.277-8.

also saw the adoption of election by caucus as the settled policy of the party.

In the early years of the Commonwealth parliament several motions were introduced supporting elective ministries. A motion by J. M. Fowler[35] in 1905 attacked collective responsibility, and criticized the transfer of parliament's authority to the cabinet. Fowler dwelt with favour on the example of Switzerland, where the divisive effects of party had been overcome. A motion in similar terms was moved by G. B. Edwards in 1910, and supported by Fowler. Edwards attacked cabinet as an 'engine of autocracy', and criticized the party system, which had 'nothing whatever to do with representative government'.[36] He drew heavily on Syme during the course of his speech.

The impact of the elective principle on Labour ministries is of course well known, and is discussed at length elsewhere. It remains to mention the extent to which the non-Labour parties have been influenced by moves towards election of ministers. In earlier years, election was occasionally used to resolve a deadlock. In 1894, for instance, the conservative Premier of Tasmania resigned, and advised the Governor to send for Fysh, leader of the largest group in parliament. Fysh declined the commission, and after protracted negotiations between the 'progressive' groups, a ballot was held in which Edward Braddon, who had recently returned from being Agent-General in London, was elected by a margin of one vote over his nearest rival, Andrew Inglis Clark. Some years later a similar situation arose in Queensland when the Premier, Denham, was about to leave for Britain and an Acting Premier had to be appointed. There was keen competition for this post and Denham resolved the problem by holding a secret ballot, with the Clerk of the Legislative Assembly acting as returning officer.

The Country Party has always been attracted by the elective principle, and its views were stated at length by a Country Party member of the federal parliament, P. G. Stewart, in 1925. Stewart, who had been a minister in the Bruce-Page government, made it clear that he was raising the matter because it was party policy. His speech recognized the existence of parties, but he believed that the party system could be circumvented. Ministers should be selected only because they were the ablest men, and parliament should control the executive. This would be done by reducing the

35 Fowler was a Labour M.P. with unorthodox views on a variety of matters. See *Parl. Deb.* (C. of A.), 1905, 25: 1105-19.
36 Ibid., 1910, 57: 3257-70. Edwards also favoured free trade and decimal coinage, on which he introduced several private motions.

powers of cabinet so that its functions were purely administrative, leaving parliament to deal with matters of policy through the extension of the committee system. Opposing the motion, the Attorney-General, Groom, pointed out that Stewart's proposal would simply encourage irresponsibility and infect the administration with party conflicts. In effect, parliament would express the popular will even less than it did under existing conditions.[37]

Stewart's motion represents the last serious parliamentary discussion of the question, and since then the Country Party has confined itself to electing its own ministers rather than to pressing for elected governments. The rules of the Country Party in Victoria, for example, provide for an exhaustive ballot along lines precisely similar to those observed in the Labour Party. In more recent years, the elective principle has had some success in the Liberal Party. In 1955, the Liberal and Country Party in the Victorian state parliament adopted a set of rules which included provision for election.[38] The rules provide that when the leader of the party has been commissioned to form a ministry, the party shall elect all members except two by secret exhaustive ballot. The party leader then appoints the two remaining members of the ministry and allots portfolios. The system extends to the filling of cabinet vacancies, which are dealt with alternately through election or through appointment by the Premier. The Victorian move appears to have been influenced by the results of a public opinion poll carried out in 1954, which showed that a large minority of non-Labour voters, as well as a majority of Labour voters, favoured the election of ministers by the parliamentary party.[39] Taking their cue from the Victorians, a special committee of the Federal Parliamentary Liberal Party recommended in 1956 that the question of electing all or part of the cabinet should be discussed and voted on by the parliamentary party. Since the report was made, however, no steps have been taken in this direction. More recently still, election was applied to the Country-Liberal composite government elected in Queensland in 1957, whose eleven members were chosen by exhaustive ballot among the parliamentary members of each party, acting separately.[40]

37 Ibid., 110: 864-71; 1598-1604.
38 G. Sawer, 'Political Review', *Australian Quarterly*, 1956, no. 1.
39 'Australian Public Opinion Polls', *Bulletin*, June 1954. In 1931, the All-for-Australia League, a professedly 'anti-party' organization which later merged into the United Australia Party, adopted a plank favouring elective ministries.
40 A. A. Morrison, 'Political Chronicle', *Australian Journal of Politics and History*, 1958, vol. 3, no. 2.

10

ALLIANCES AND COALITIONS

THE LABOUR PARTY, on its entry into politics in the 1890s, adopted a policy of 'support in return for concessions', which in the decade before World War I led to the formation of several alliances between Labour and radical groups on the non-Labour side. The most famous case was the agreement between Deakin and the Federal Parliamentary Labour Party, by which Labour supported Deakin in parliament in return for an agreed list of measures to be brought down by the government, notably those concerned with 'new protection' and industrial arbitration.[1] At a later date, similar arrangements were made between Labour and the Country Party in Victoria. A dissident group within the farmers' movement in Victoria, calling itself the Country Progressive Party, kept a Labour ministry in power in 1927 and 1928. Later, as a result of the union of the Country Progressive Party with the Victorian Country Party, the united body accepted the C.P.P.'s policy of not joining composite governments, unlike Country Parties in the federal sphere and in other states. Instead, it took office only as an all-Country administration with the support of one of the other parties in parliament. Between 1935 and 1942, a Country Party administration held power in Victoria, with Labour support, under the leadership of A. A. Dunstan, formerly leader of the C.P.P. Between 1950 and 1952, a Country Party government under J. G. B. McDonald again held office with Labour support. In both cases, support was ultimately withdrawn as a result of refusal by the Country Party to carry out sections of its agreement with Labour. From 1942 to 1943 Dunstan accepted the support of the United Australia Party, but after a crisis he was compelled to drop his opposition to composite governments and U.A.P. members were given portfolios in a new Dunstan ministry. In 1952, after the withdrawal of Labour support, the Liberal and Country Party (as it was now called) kept the McDonald ministry in office for several months, but without joining a composite government.

Labour has, in general, been opposed to coalition governments, as distinct from alliances of the kind just described. However,

[1] L. F. Crisp, *The Australian Federal Labor Party 1901-1951*, ch. 5.

Labour Parties in two states did participate in coalition governments during the decade before World War I. In 1905, the Butler (Liberal) government in South Australia was defeated at the polls. The largest party in the new parliament was Labour, which formed a coalition with a group of dissident Liberals led by Peake, who had split from the official Liberal Party because of its refusal to democratize the upper house by extending the franchise. Peake became Treasurer in a Labour ministry headed by Price, which remained in office for four years and carried out a mildly reformist programme. When Price died in 1909 and was replaced by Verran, the honeymoon ended because Peake refused to serve under another Labour leader. Labour, in its turn, refused to serve under Peake, who accordingly formed a minority cabinet and later a coalition with Butler. With the election of 1910, at which this government was defeated, the period of 'three elevens' came to an end in South Australia as it had recently done in the Commonwealth.

Another and more famous coalition took place in Queensland as the result of dissensions within the ruling Liberal Party in 1903. The Philp ministry resigned after an adverse vote in parliament, and negotiations took place between Labour and a small group of Liberal members led by Morgan, the Speaker. At first, the Labour Party offered to support a minority government under Morgan, but the latter seems to have insisted that Labour ministers be included in the cabinet in order to involve Labour directly in responsibility for the fate of the government. Two Labour men, Browne and Kidston, were included in the ministry. Kidston, who became Treasurer, had been one of the principal organizers of the downfall of the Philp ministry, one of whose members bitingly referred to him as an 'underground engineer'.[2] The parliamentary Labour Party was not entirely happy about the arrangement, and insisted that Browne and Kidston, who were leader and deputy leader of the party respectively, should give up their posts on assuming office. Airey became the new leader, and when Browne died in 1904 Airey, in his turn, became a minister.

When the government had been in office less than a year, further intrigues led to the defection of some of Morgan's Liberal supporters and the government was defeated by one vote on an amendment to the Address-in-Reply. Morgan was refused a dis-

[2] S. A. Rayner, 'The Evolution of the Queensland Labor Party to 1907' (unpublished M.A. thesis), p.205. Kidston had previously achieved some notoriety when, as Treasurer in the six-day Dawson ministry of 1899, he had uncovered and published details of some unsavoury transactions by the preceding Dickson ministry.

solution and resigned, but promptly resumed office when the Opposition leader, Rutledge, failed to form a government. A dissolution was then granted, and the Morgan government was victorious at the polls. During the election, the members of the two government parties stood separately and intra-coalition contests were avoided. By 1905, the Morgan government had passed all the reforms jointly desired by its supporters and by Labour, and friction on the Labour side became marked. A campaign began for more stress on socialism, headed by H. E. Boote, editor of the *Worker* newspaper, and Matthew Reid, then President of the Central Political Executive of the Labour Party. In 1905, the triennial Labor-in-Politics convention formulated a new objective for the party, aimed at 'securing the full results of their industry to the wealth producers by the collective ownership of the means of production, distribution and exchange'. Kidston did not take this implied rebuke quietly. Two months after the conference he issued a declaration signed by more than half of the members of the parliamentary party criticizing both the new objective adopted by the Labour convention and also its policy on the sale of Crown lands. The declaration pointed out the political difficulties that would confront Labour if it pursued these policies, referred to the refusal of the federal conference of the Labour Party to adopt an objective similar to the Queensland one, and concluded by warning that a 'ruinous division in the Party is inevitable'.[3] This document (known in Queensland political history as 'The Statement'), called for the holding of a new Labour convention on a 'wider' basis, a reference to the fact that the convention had included only eight parliamentarians out of thirty-eight delegates.

Although the statement was clearly distasteful to the Labour movement outside parliament, the situation remained quiet. Early in 1906, Morgan resigned, and a meeting of cabinet was called to appoint a new leader. Kidston himself proposed the Home Secretary, Denham, for the leadership, but cabinet did not accept this nomination, presumably because the coalition would have split if Denham had become Premier. Instead, Kidston was chosen, becoming now both Premier and Treasurer. Shortly afterwards, he again emphasized his opposition to the new Labour objective, and embarked on a series of actions designed to show that he would not tolerate interference from the party. He appointed five new members to the upper house, not one of whom was a Labour man. Despite efforts made by the Central Political Executive of the party and by the Australian Labor Federation, then the most important

3 Rayner, op. cit.

section of the Labour movement in Queensland, no reconciliation could be arranged. Denham made use of the situation to resign and rejoin the Opposition, but was unable to unseat the government. Early in 1907, Kidston challenged the Labour Party by declaring that although he was still a Labour man, he would only support those candidates for the forthcoming election who pledged their support for him. In March 1907, a Labour convention was held at Rockhampton. The leader of the parliamentary Labour Party, Kerr, moved that Labour support the government and avoid contests with the Liberal members of the coalition. However, the convention rejected this and resolved that all Labour candidates must pledge themselves to the new platform and refrain from making election compacts. Of the thirty-four Labour M.P.s only fourteen signed this pledge, the rest adhering to Kidston. These fourteen now sat on the cross benches in parliament, announcing their support for 'measures, not men'. In 1908, after the election which followed the constitutional crisis of 1907,[4] the Labour members opposed two railway measures introduced by the government. The Opposition, led by Philp, supported Kidston, and in November 1908 a coalition of the Kidstonites and Philpites was formed. Kidston was elected leader at a joint party meeting; Philp declined the party leadership and also refused to accept a portfolio. In 1909, a complete fusion of the two ministerial parties took place. This had apparently been suggested by Kidston when the coalition was formed, and a contemporary Press account praised Philp's 'public spirit' in standing down.[5] Kidston retained the Premiership until his retirement from politics in 1911, when he was succeeded by Denham.

Attempts to form a National Ministry, 1939-1941

The Labour Party's opposition to coalitions was emphasized during the political struggles in federal parliament in the period immediately before and immediately after the outbreak of war in 1939. Late in March 1939, the Prime Minister, J. A. Lyons, threw out some hints about the possibility of a 'national' government which would be necessary in view of the world situation. John Curtin, leader of the Labour Party, retorted that Lyons was only flying a kite to save his composite U.A.P.-Country Party government, in which dissension had been increasing for some time. Curtin declared:

4 See chapter 8.
5 Rockhampton *Morning Bulletin*, 18 October 1909; quoted by H. C. Perry, *Memoirs of Sir Robert Philp*, pp.271-2.

If there could be anything worse than a government consisting of two parties it would be a government consisting of three parties. Such a combination would not be a government, it would be a society of disputation and debate; decisions would never be reached; determinations could not be arrived at, let alone carried out. I say to Australia, quite seriously, that however good a government may be, it will be all the better if it is composed of men who subscribe to the one set of political principles, who are united in their outlook and upon the problems of the country, and who may as a team translate into reality ideas that they have as to the way in which the country should be administered. That government would be a government of leadership and action. And any government, even if it has the best policies, could do far better service to the nation if there were arrayed against it in Parliament an opposition courageous, intelligent and patriotic . . . all this talk about an all-party government . . . is designed merely to ensure the safety of the government against internal criticism, however necessary it may be in the interests of the nation that that criticism should be levelled.[6]

A national government was again suggested in May 1940, when the possibility was raised in parliament by a government backbencher. Both the Prime Minister, R. G. Menzies, and Curtin, as Leader of the Opposition, agreed that a national ministry would not necessarily promote national unity. During a debate on the motion, the suggestion was made for the first time that, as an alternative, an advisory war council including all parties should be set up. This was taken up at the federal conference of the A.L.P. in the following month, when a proposal for a national government was rejected in favour of a resolution calling for an advisory war council. The federal government refused to consider this suggestion; in the meantime, however, a change of heart had apparently taken place and in a letter to Curtin, Menzies offered him five or six portfolios in a national ministry. In addition, he offered to set up a Department of Labour with a Labour minister in charge, and to stand down himself if his presence constituted an obstacle to the formation of a national ministry.

The offer was rejected by the Labour caucus, but after the general election in September 1940, Menzies raised the matter once more. As a result of the election, the government had lost its majority and now depended on the vote of two independents. In October, Menzies conferred with the leaders of the two Labour

6 *Parl. Deb.* (C. of A.), 1939, 159: 14-15.

groups in federal parliament,[7] who agreed to refer the matter to their respective parties. The Labour caucus passed an evasive resolution, declaring Labour's determination to co-operate with all parties in prosecuting the war effectively. A further series of conferences between Menzies and the Labour Party leaders followed, but on 23 October the caucus finally rejected all these offers in favour of an advisory war council. The government accepted this view, and the council was actually set up five days later. Nevertheless, further hints about a national government continued to be thrown out until Labour finally assumed office in October 1941. At one stage, a group of Labour members headed by Dr Evatt was credited by the Press with wanting a national government, and there were even some references to the possibility of electing a Prime Minister from the floor of the house. In May 1941, Menzies appealed to the A.L.P. at a public meeting in Sydney, offering them half the portfolios in a national ministry. In August, when Menzies' leadership of his own party was in serious danger, he repeated this offer, with the addition of an undertaking to serve under Curtin if this was necessary. All these offers were refused by caucus, which was clearly influenced by the possibility that the government would fall and that a Labour ministry would take office on its own account.

The Advisory War Council, constituted under National Security Regulations on 28 October 1940, remained the nearest approach to a national ministry attained in Australia during the war. Its functions were to 'advise the Government with respect to such matters relating to the defence of the Commonwealth or the prosecution of the war as are referred to the Council by the Prime Minister and may consider and advise the Government with respect to such other matters so relating as it thinks fit'. The Council comprised eight members, four from the government parties and four from the Opposition.[8] All were under oath. According to Hasluck, the official war historian, the Council enabled 'a loose agreement [regarding] Executive action and legislative measures on questions vital to the prosecution of the war'.[9] Such an agreement was essen-

7 The A.L.P. and the A.L.P. (Non-Communist), comprising supporters of J. T. Lang, who had been responsible for the fall of the Scullin ministry in 1931.

8 The Labour members comprised three from the official A.L.P., chosen by ballot as usual, and J. A. Beasley, leader of the Non-Communist Labour group. When the Beasley group rejoined the official A.L.P. in March 1941, a ballot was taken for Beasley's place, which he lost to Dr H. V. Evatt. The A.L.P. then requested that the Council be increased to five members from each side of the house so that Beasley and Evatt could both be members, and the government agreed.

9 *The Government and the People 1939-41*, pp.272-3.

tial in the precarious parliamentary situation resulting from the 1940 election. It also had the important function of promoting co-operation in keeping industrial peace, which was constantly threatened by disputes whose origins lay in the depression years. This latter aspect ceased to be important when Labour became the government. Moreover, after the sweeping victory of the Curtin ministry in the 1943 elections, the parliamentary situation no longer mattered very greatly. As the war proceeded, the U.A.P. became increasingly restive about the value of the Council, and early in 1944, they decided to withdraw from participation, although this decision was defied by two of the U.A.P. representatives, Messrs Hughes and Spender.[10] In a situation where Labour was already becoming increasingly concerned with post-war policies, the U.A.P. had no wish to remain associated with a form of co-operation designed to meet an emergency which was now long past. The non-military aspects of the Council's discussions had been a source of difficulty from the beginning. In 1940, for instance, the Budget had been discussed by the Council and as a result traditional budget secrecy was greatly impaired. Important details of controversial provisions in the Budget were already appearing in the Press before the Budget speech had been made by the Treasurer.

[10] The move to withdraw from the Council was initiated by a 'cave' within the U.A.P. led by Menzies (referred to as the 'national service group' or the 'cavemen'). When Hughes and Spender refused to resign, they were expelled from the parliamentary U.A.P. The Country Party decided to retain its representation.

11

LABOUR IN OFFICE (1)

PERHAPS no aspect of Australian politics has attracted more attention than the long history of attempts by the Labour movement to control Labour governments, through the distinct but related forms of authority exercised by the parliamentary caucus, by the party machine outside parliament, and by the trade union movement. The methods of control which evolved between 1904 and 1916 were, in their turn, the outcome of the struggle inside the New South Wales Labour Party in the 1890s to establish 'solidarity', the principle that Labour members of parliament must be bound by the platform of the party outside parliament. At this stage, the struggle hinged on the introduction of a pledge by which Labour members bound themselves to support the party platform in parliament, and the problem of controlling a Labour administration would have appeared fanciful. Within ten years, however, the question had become real and pressing, and many of the participants in the early dispute were just as actively involved in its second phase.

Some sections of the party went so far as to deny the need for any leadership on the conventional pattern. In 1914, the Sydney *Worker* published an editorial declaring that the Labour Party was 'infinitely in advance of the days when the workers had to be "led". They have no use for leaders. In Conference assembled, they formulate their policies and decide their tactics.'[1] This passage gains a retrospective irony from the fact that the editor of the *Worker,* Hector Lamond, was one of the party members who seceded with W. M. Hughes at the time of the conscription crisis two years later. Nor was this the only case of historic irony. The three great advocates of solidarity in New South Wales in 1893-4 were W. A. Holman, G. S. Beeby and W. M. Hughes. In the space of twenty years, all three of these men found themselves at odds with the apparatus of solidarity which they helped to construct, but not before Holman and Hughes had exploited the apparatus to gain their own ends as political leaders. Shortly before, Ostrogorski had demonstrated how the exploitation of the 'caucus' in Britain had enabled the parliamentary leaders to tighten their grip

[1] Quoted, Evatt, *Australian Labor Leader,* p.340.

on the disciplined party whose discipline had originally been intended as a check on the parliamentary leadership.

More recently, an expert manipulator like J. T. Lang, after using the machine to give him almost absolute power in the New South Wales Labour movement, in the end was himself overthrown by it. At a time of unrest and unemployment, he was able to organize behind himself and the 'Lang Plan' all that solidarity which had been the pride of the Labour movement since the 1890s, and by a series of adroit manoeuvres to elevate himself to a position of power enjoyed by no other Labour leader before or since. Any opposition to him was ruthlessly destroyed. None the less, once the trade unions on whose unyielding support his power rested no longer found it expedient to support him, and set up their own 'Industrial Labour Party' in opposition, his grip soon slackened and he was rejected by the official party as it had rejected many of his antagonists of former years.

The legend of solidarity was built to a large extent on notions of class loyalty, closely linked with insistence on working-class origins and a trade union background as concrete evidence of class membership. In the earlier days of Labour governments, it was virtually impossible for a parliamentarian to be elected to cabinet without trade union backing. The fallacy of this situation was noted by one of Labour's early historians, Gordon Childe. He observed that in the New South Wales Labour government of 1910-16, the unions were amply represented.

> The Premier, McGowen, had been a boilermaker, yet in the 1913 gas strike he signed a proclamation appealing for scabs. Alf. Edden had worked in the coalmines, but he could not carry through the Bill the miners wanted for 8 hours from bank to bank. J. H. Cann had worked along the line o'lode at the Hill, Donald McDonald had shorn sheep, Fred Flowers, a painter, was a unionist of long standing . . . Thus unionism had no reason to complain that it was unrepresented in Cabinet.[2]

Childe goes on to lament, in a famous phrase, that from a band of inspired socialists the Labour Party had deteriorated into little more than a gang of office seekers. Although he has little trouble in demonstrating the intensity of the struggle for office, he provides little evidence for the existence of a socialist period in Labour history. In effect, his work suggests that the Labour movement, from the beginning, has been characterized by repeated cycles in which the existing leadership is overthrown by a trade union fac-

[2] V. G. Childe, *How Labour Governs*, pp.59-60.

tion, whose leaders achieve ministerial office through the use of the apparatus of solidarity. In turn, these leaders are then themselves overthrown by another faction or by a reshuffling of groups within the movement outside parliament. More recently, J. D. B. Miller asserts that

> the practices of the Labour Party . . . all tend towards a condition in which a Party clique can retain power within its hands . . . dictatorial authority in the Labour Party has always been exercised in the name of 'the Movement', and has fed upon a widespread suspicion within the rank and file of 'careerist politicians' and leaders who tried to exercise personal authority . . . one after the other, a series of Trade Union and Party cliques has at various stages of Australian political history used these arguments to destroy its rivals and in turn to be destroyed by them.[3]

The study of Australian political history has been dominated by analyses of these struggles, which, it can be argued, have made comparatively little impression on the actual conduct of governmental affairs. The use of a more or less Marxist scheme of analysis of political events leads to over-emphasis on conflicts and crises, whereas a study of the actual conduct of administration draws attention to the manner in which every cabinet, regardless of its party origin, mediates between the organs of government and the interests of various groups whose efforts are directed towards making government work for their benefit. It is possible that the early advent of Labour governments in Australia has left an ineffaceable impression of a militant working class whose unity and discipline enabled it to capture political power after only a short period. W. A. Holman, commenting on the impression made by the first federal Labour ministry under J. C. Watson, observed ironically that 'critics, confronted with the portent of a working-class cabinet, were unable to shake their imaginations free of the blood-curdling associations of the Committee of Public Safety, and looked forward with a groan, if not to bloodshed, at least to all-round confiscation and outrage'.[4] Echoes of this apprehension are plentiful in the literature of the period, where the Labour Party is personified as 'a blatant Hercules, low-browed, truculent, heavy-jawed, with an illimitable thirst and a lust for the property of others'.[5] Instead, Holman observes, 'the Labour Ministry, like all Ministries, generally followed established precedent. When as often happened,

[3] 'Party Discipline in Australia', *Political Science,* 1953, vol. 5, nos. 1-2.
[4] *Red Funnel,* 1 February 1906.
[5] John Dalley, *Only the Morning* (1930). For other examples see S. Encel, 'Political Novels in Australia', *Historical Studies,* 1956, no. 27.

they established precedents themselves, these were such that no subsequent occupant of their offices has since ever departed from.' Despite much surface froth, continuity of policy and administration on most major questions has been as characteristic of Australia as of all other countries with representative institutions.[6] Moreover, the 'catastrophic' theory of Labour politics is of little help in analysing the history of extremely long-lived Labour administrations whose leadership has rarely been in danger of defeat, even on comparatively minor questions of administration.

The Role of Caucus

Since Labour first assumed office, the allegation has been made that Labour ministries violate alike the principles of democratic individualism and of cabinet responsibility. Soon after the Watson government took office in April 1904, George Reid criticized the ministry because its policy was not its own but that of the Labour Party, a body outside parliament and not responsible to it. He remarked:

> Whilst pandemonium may rage in the caucus, whilst individual opinion may fearlessly and strongly exert itself . . . the moment a decision is reached, a change takes place. The voice which we hear in this Chamber is not the voice of the man who speaks . . . it represents the view, not of an individual conscience or an individual intellect, but of a collective conscience and a collective intellect.[7]

Labour members were not slow to retort with examples of influence on the policy of non-Labour ministries exercised by organizations of employers who were dictating the policy of the Deakin and Reid governments from outside parliament.

Some years later, Reid's accusation was repeated by a leading constitutional lawyer. During the parliamentary session, he wrote:

> The regular sittings of the caucus must . . . tend to supersede the deliberations of the Cabinet, to bring ministerial differences to the arbitrament of a party meeting, instead of to the Cabinet or the Premier; and to substitute for the collective responsibility of the Cabinet to Parliament the individual responsibility of Ministers to the caucus. The course of development might well be one in which the Cabinet was set aside in favour of direct government and administration by the caucus, acting, perhaps, through committees presided over by a Minister.[8]

6 This underlying continuity is examined further in later chapters.
7 Parl. Deb. (C. of A.), 1904, 19: 1354-5.
8 Harrison Moore, in Atkinson (ed.), Australia: Economic and Political Studies, p.117.

Harrison Moore's words were written shortly after the 1918 federal conference of the A.L.P., where a proposal had been put forward that in future Labour ministries each minister should be assisted in the administration of his department by a committee appointed by the parliamentary party. Both this motion and Moore's apprehensions about it display considerable detachment from the realities of government. Certainly, little has been heard of the suggestion since Labour ministries became a familiar feature of the Australian scene.[9] Such proposals can only be made in the belief that a Labour government is, or should be, an approximation to the dictatorship of the proletariat. W. K. Hancock, for example, argued that the theory of caucus control was a repudiation of the principle enunciated by Burke, in his address to the electors of Bristol, that a member of parliament is a representative and not a delegate. Labour's principles, he wrote, belong to 'an age in which there was no general agreement to maintain the existing social structure, but rather a determination on the part of an organized class to overthrow or modify that structure in its own interest (or, as it believed, in the common interest)'; under these circumstances, there was an insistence that 'the member of Parliament was a delegate or instrument of the will of the class that had chosen him'.

These principles, according to him, encourage the growth of heresy hunting and its exploitation as a stepping-stone to power. The logical end product of this will be Caesarism, of which J. T. Lang was a portent. The attempt at rigid control of the parliamentary leadership, he says, 'aggravates the very evil which it is designed to cure. Each individual revolt against the supremacy of the "party will" seems to prove the necessity for a more stringent control; but the tightening of control itself becomes a cause of new revolts.' Such a situation may be exploited by a man as adroit as Lang, whose 'consciousness of class was stronger than his sense of the State'. By making a pact with the party executive, Lang

won a power which no other Australian Premier has ever possessed. His own followers, his own ministers, became his slaves. Parliament became a machine for ratifying the decrees which Mr. Lang, after consultation with the Labor chieftains outside Parliament presented to it. Mr. Lang, bayed about by enemies on every hand, was nevertheless fashioning a dictatorship of the proletariat.[10]

9 The Savage (Labour) government in New Zealand made some experiments in this direction in 1935 and 1936.
10 'England and Australia', in W. K. Hancock, *Politics in Pitcairn,* pp.73-5.

Hancock concludes that Lang's dictatorship 'was something more than an accident of personal and temporary significance'; it was the natural outgrowth of an embryonic situation present almost from the inception of the Labour Party, and the forces making for its recurrence were permanent ones.

His words were written in 1934, at a period when dictatorship appeared to be growing as inevitably as democracy was waning, and there is more than a hint that Lang is in some way to be compared to Mussolini. This is both to exaggerate the significance of the Lang era and to obscure the extent to which machine politics has become established in other states of Australia in a less spectacular but perhaps even more effective fashion. Moreover, in two cases, those of Victoria and South Australia, the growth of the machine owes very little to Labour influence.

Not all observers outside the Labour movement have been as critical of caucus control. A. W. Jose, writing at almost the same time as Hancock, praised the caucus system, with its regular meetings and discussions of party policy, as a method of educating Labour politicians. Caucus, he wrote, was

> a studious and educative body, which met every week during sessions to consider coming legislation, directed certain members to study the problems involved and make an early report on them, and prides itself in knowing its opponents' arguments almost as well as its own . . . for a party which necessarily included men of little reading and almost as little political experience this system proved invaluable, and when its enemies jeered at it as a collection of 'professional politicians' it retorted with good humour that at any rate it practised its profession seriously.[11]

A Canadian observer suggests that the caucus system has produced far less change than was apprehended in its early years.

> It has merely changed some of the conventional rules of procedure without altering the basic nature of the Cabinet as the instrument of a single party, responsible for the Government of the country as long as it commands a majority in the legislature. Caucus may deliberate *in camera,* but what it decides upon must finally issue in measures for which the Cabinet is fully accountable before Parliament.[12]

Divergences in the views of outsiders are matched by considerable conflict of opinion among active Labour politicians, whose

11 *Australia—Human and Economic,* p.88.
12 Alexander Brady, *Democracy in the Dominions,* p.6.

outlook has been strongly influenced by their situation at the time. J. C. Watson, the first Labour Prime Minister of Australia, does not appear to have had much difficulty in his four months of office, although the Labour Party at the time was a heterogeneous body including socialists, single taxers, prohibitionists, and radical democrats. Holman ascribed Watson's success to 'a personal charm of manner which few had ever been able to resist'. It is nevertheless true that Watson had been opposed to the introduction of a pledge in New South Wales in the 1890s, and his subsequent career suggests that he was not as happy about the activities of caucus and the party machine as his lack of unfavourable comment might suggest. According to a contemporary historian, he complained privately a year or two after his term of office about the dominance of caucus, which made it difficult for him to have a free choice of colleagues and of business. At the 1908 federal conference, he opposed a resolution calling for the election of members of cabinet by caucus, and retired from the leadership of the parliamentary party before Labour assumed office in November 1908. Although this retirement was ostensibly for health reasons, the same source suggests that he was reluctant to take office again under the constraints imposed by caucus control.[13] In 1916, he was one of the Labour members who left the party with Hughes on the conscription issue.

Watson's successor, Andrew Fisher, is on record as not finding caucus supervision particularly irksome. Writing to the literary critic, A. G. Stephens, shortly after he had become Prime Minister, he wrote that caucus

> has never been a trouble to me. At present it is the finest battleground any political party could wish to have. We are pledged to each other to the same extent as we are pledged to our constituents. No organization has been successful which has not a guiding principle and a body to which it can appeal for a dicision [sic] on disputed points.[14]

It is doubtful whether Fisher was equally satisfied during his second term as Prime Minister, when he was forced by caucus pressure to bring down a Bill for the establishment of a Commonwealth Bank. He was also reported as complaining, after his resignation from the Prime Ministership in 1915, of harassment by caucus.

The two most successful Labour Prime Ministers, Curtin and

[13] H. G. Turner, *The First Decade of the Australian Commonwealth*, p.117. [14] Letter dated 20 November 1908 (ML).

Chifley, were complimentary to caucus in their public utterances. Both of them were able to get their way on all important matters, and it is likely that their published statements represent part of their technique for keeping on good terms with the parliamentary party. During the critical months of 1942-3, when Curtin made his successful endeavour to persuade the Labour movement to reverse its traditional policy on conscription for overseas service, he went out of his way to reject suggestions that there was hostility between himself and the party outside parliament. At the annual conference of the New South Wales branch of the A.L.P., he declared that 'no man has ever been pushed out if he had an idea to advance, and brought it before the party for an opinion and sought authority for it to be carried out'.[15] Two years later Chifley, then Acting Prime Minister, also stressed his good relationships with caucus and with the party outside parliament. During the debate on the Commonwealth Bank Bill, Opposition speakers continuously alleged that the government had introduced the Bill at the dictation of the A.L.P. federal conference.

> MR. FRANCIS: The trouble is that the Labor caucus has told the Government what to do.
>
> MR. CHIFLEY: I am proud to be the mouthpiece of the caucus of the Labor Government in this country. I have no objection to offer if my colleagues differ from me regarding some aspects of Government policy; we have a way of finally resolving our difficulties.[16]

In view of the factional struggles in which Chifley had already been involved, and of the even more violent ones that he was to endure shortly afterwards, we may suspect that this statement was at least as much intended to keep Labour M.P.s happy as it was an expression of Chifley's real opinions.

Early advocates of solidarity, like Holman and Hughes, came to condemn it when it resulted in their expulsion from the Labour movement. In 1909, Hughes wrote a famous defence of solidarity, 'The Labor Party and the Pledge', as one of the series of articles entitled 'The Case for Labor' which he was then contributing to the Sydney *Daily Telegraph*. The loyalty of Labour men to one another and to their principles was unfavourably contrasted with the double-dealing of the members of the Deakin-Cook or 'Fusion' ministry which had just taken office after overthrowing the Fisher government, where Hughes had been Attorney-General. In 1912, Hughes was successful in using the machinery of the federal conference to discipline the members of the New South Wales Labour

15 *S.M.H.*, 7 June 1943.   16 *Parl. Deb.* (C. of A.), 1945, 182: 2643.

government, including Holman, who opposed the submission of
a referendum to the electors asking for increased legislative powers
for the Commonwealth government. The conference forbade members of the party to oppose or to depart from its decisions. In
1916, this resolution proved to be a boomerang in the conscription
crisis, when both Hughes and Holman left the party. As Prime
Minister in a 'National' government, Hughes was untiring in his
attacks on the control of the Labour Party by extra-parliamentary
bodies. Speaking on a motion to extend the life of parliament,
which was opposed by Labour, Hughes attacked the 'junta' which
he declared, 'is behind honorable members opposite, which directs
every action of theirs, and without the approval of which they
cannot, and dare not, speak or move'. He also attacked the role
of the 'junta' in forbidding Labour members to accept his invitation to join the National ministry. Labour members, he declared,
could not accept his invitation to 'join hands' because they lived
in fear of the 'sword of excommunication' suspended over their
heads.[17]

Holman, after taking a leading part in the fight to introduce
the solidarity pledge in the 1890s, became a minister in the New
South Wales Labour government in 1910, and Premier in 1913.
Throughout his ministerial career until he left the party in 1916,
he had troubles with caucus and the state executive of the Political
Labor League (as it was then known).

In 1915 he was involved in a dispute with caucus over appointments to the Legislative Council. After he had made some appointments unpopular with the party, caucus carried a resolution in
Holman's absence, providing that no further appointments to the
Council should be made unless the names of the proposed appointees had been approved by caucus. The next day, Holman announced that he would ignore this decision. He said that caucus
was guilty of a 'confusion of the leading functions of legislation and
administration', and that 'no parliamentary government in the
world allows its parliamentary supporters to dictate administrative
acts'.[18] He announced, moreover, that so long as the resolution
stood he would make no further appointments to the Legislative
Council. To underline his defiance, he then promoted George
Black, who had been elected to cabinet with Holman's support
on the understanding that he would be only an honorary minister,
to the post of Minister for Public Health.[19]

Although Holman's attitude conformed to accepted British con-

17 Ibid., 1917, 81: 10569-75.   18 Harrison Moore, loc. cit.
19 Childe, op. cit., p.19.

vention, it was unlikely to commend itself to caucus, which is often concerned with details of administration rather than with legislation. Childe suggests that Holman's distinction between executive and legislative acts was not logical: 'A government is called upon to give an account in the House of its administration and therefore the Party must take responsibility for acts which they may have to defend in the Assembly.'[20] Holman's view was rejected at the 1916 state conference. Contemporaneously, the Ryan and Theodore governments in Queensland had adopted the practice of leaving the choice of Legislative Councillors to caucus and of submitting the names to the state executive of the party for endorsement, as in the case of Labour candidates for the Legislative Assembly.

In his reminiscences, Holman justifies his actions in terms of a great experiment in socialist planning that was frustrated solely by the unreasonable interference of conferences, executives, and trade unions. He described the state A.L.P. conference as the 'annual escape-pipe of the movement through which waste steam goes off'.[21] Holman's biographer, Dr Evatt, concludes that this theory will not bear analysis, and observes:

> During the period when the control of Labour's Party machine tightened, Holman raised little objection so long as he was the director of the machine. More and more he tended to regard his personal opinions on tactics (as well as on policy) as basic tenets of the whole of the Labour organization. If a contradiction arose, he concluded too easily that the organization was wrong.[22]

The ambiguity of the situation, in which opinions regarding party control over the ministry seemed to depend almost entirely on the success or failure of the people concerned in operating the system to their own advantage, is vividly illustrated in the autobiography of J. T. Lang, whose remarks show him well content with the system so long as it worked according to his directions. A story from Queensland underlines this basic ambiguity. At the Labour convention of 1922, a union delegate, Brice, attacked the Theodore government for its failure to intervene on behalf of the unions before the Queensland Arbitration Court, in a case where the court had reduced wages. The state president of the A.W.U., W. J. Riordan, defended the government as being only 'a reflex of the industrial movement'. As he could not pretend, however, that the industrial movement had supported the cut in wages, he

20 Ibid., p.20.   21 Evatt, op. cit., p.339.   22 Ibid., p.573.

added the disingenuous afterthought that 'no government could save the worker until he was in a position to save himself'. Brice retorted that this was no more than double-talk, and that if the government were only a 'reflex' of the unions it should have supported their case in court.[23]

The Influence of the Catholic Church

The role of Roman Catholics, especially those of Irish extraction, is one of the perennial themes of Australian Labour politics, and no attempt will be made to discuss it at any length in these pages. We shall be concerned only with attempts—or alleged attempts— by organized Catholic groups to influence the policy or administration of Labour governments. It will, however, be necessary to make some general remarks on the place of Catholics in the party before proceeding to an account of its actual manifestations.[24]

The minority position of the Catholic community, with its attendant discrimination against Catholics on religious, social and economic grounds, has resulted in the disproportionate attention paid by the organized Catholic laity to politics. Catholics are almost absent from the higher reaches of the business world, they are comparatively rare in the universities, they are under-represented in the higher (though not in the lower) strata of the public services, and they are disproportionately few in the professions. As in the United States, they are numerous in the police force, as well as the criminal classes. Perhaps by way of compensation, their political importance and their political solidarity have been out of all proportion to their numbers. The exact correlation between Catholic belief and Labour political affiliation has only become the subject of careful investigation by political scientists in the last few years, but it is generally agreed that about three-quarters of all Catholics consistently vote Labour. As Labour votes are generally in the vicinity of one-half of the total vote, it is probably a reasonable conclusion that about 40 per cent of Labour support comes from Catholics (who make up about 25 per cent of the entire community). When a minority becomes as large as this, it requires only a modicum of organization to become the dominant group.

Although the peculiar religious and social solidarity of the

[23] Higgins, 'The Queensland Labor Governments 1915-1929'.
[24] For more extended treatment of the question see James Murtagh, *Australia—the Catholic Chapter* (2nd ed., Sydney, 1959); Childe, op. cit.; Crisp, *The Parliamentary Government of the Commonwealth of Australia* and *The Australian Federal Labor Party 1901-1951*; T. C. Truman, *Catholic Action and Politics*.

Catholic community provide the basis for such organization, the problem is much more complicated than this, and within the community itself there have been sharp differences on the tactics, or indeed the advisability, of organizing Catholics specifically for political action. Nor should it be forgotten that a number of Labour ministers of the Crown have been Catholics without in any way conforming to a religious 'party line' in their political activities. It is possible to demonstrate that a very high proportion of Labour ministers have been Catholics, but in a number of cases this fact indicates no more than the denomination in which their parents were married. A striking illustration of the danger of facile correlation may be taken from the split which took place at the federal conference of the A.L.P. in Hobart in 1955. This represented a new high level in attempts to make political loyalty dependent on religion. As a result, seventeen delegates left the conference, of whom fifteen were Catholics; but of the nineteen who remained, eleven were also Catholics.[25]

It is also essential to distinguish various phases in the relations between the Catholic Church and the Labour movement. Until 1916, the leadership of the A.L.P. was largely Protestant, and politically active Catholics were concerned chiefly with lobbying in favour of the Church's major public objective—state support for the Catholic education system. With the support of the Archbishop of Melbourne, Dr Carr, a Catholic federation was formed in Victoria and New South Wales, which was active in pressing the Church's views, particularly on education, on Labour and non-Labour governments.[26] Before the 1913 election in New South Wales, the federation sent to all candidates a circular asking their views on matters such as bursaries and scholarships, free school materials, free medical inspection of all schoolchildren, and transport to school. The Labour Premier, Holman, issued a confidential letter to all Labour candidates, pointing out that the party conference had repeatedly forbidden the giving of pledges to other bodies, and that undertakings on these specific questions could not be given before they had been considered by the party as a whole. Holman's letter was attacked by the *Catholic Press* as a 'Machiavellian ukase' which was only one incident of a campaign 'that already has not been too clean'. Despite a vigorous campaign against Holman by Father M. J. O'Reilly, one of the leaders of the Catholic federation, he was returned with a comfortable majority,

25 One of the delegates to the conference kindly made this analysis.
26 Celia Hamilton, 'Catholic Interests and the Labor Party', *Historical Studies,* 1959, vol. 9, no. 33.

but the *Catholic Press* noted with satisfaction that nineteen
Catholics were now members of parliament as a result of the election.[27]

A watershed was the bitter struggle over conscription in 1916-
17, which cemented the already close relations between the Church
and the A.L.P. The leading figure in this struggle on the Catholic
side had been Archbishop Carr's successor, Dr Daniel Mannix,
who in 1913 had advocated a direct approach by Catholics to the
Labour Party. The ensuing period, which came to an end only in
1955, saw a steady increase in Catholic representation in Labour's
parliamentary caucuses, and more important for our purpose, in
the proportion of Catholics holding ministerial office. Since Labour
became the dominant party in Queensland in 1915, five of eight
Labour Premiers have been Catholics, and most of the ministers
in Labour governments have also belonged to the faith. Between
1941 and 1958, a period when Labour was continuously in office
in New South Wales, two of the three Premiers were Catholics, and
so were two-thirds of their colleagues in cabinet. In the federal
sphere, the proportion of Catholics and non-Catholics in the parliamentary party has been roughly equal over a period of fifty
years,[28] but the proportion of Catholics in the ministry changed
drastically as a result of the split in 1916. Among the seventy men
who had held office in Labour cabinets between 1904 and 1949,
forty were Protestants, twenty-seven Catholics, and three freethinkers. All but a handful of the Catholics belong to the period
1929-49. The long-term effects of the conscription schism can be
seen in the Scullin government of 1929-32. Out of the nineteen
ministers who held office in the three ministries which existed
during this period, twelve were Catholics, and in the third cabinet
to be formed, there were ten out of thirteen.

A new phase of the situation opened after World War II, with
the formation of the A.L.P. 'industrial groups' inside the trade
unions, whose avowed objective was to wrest control of the big
industrial unions which were dominated by officials belonging to
the Communist Party. From their early days, the groups were
closely linked with the Catholic Church, more particularly with
the Jesuits, and their activities came under great influence from
various Catholic lay organizations associated with the 'lay apos-
tolate'.[29] Their most consistent supporter in the church hierarchy

27 Ibid.; Evatt, op. cit., pp.331-2.
28 L. F. Crisp and S. P. Bennett, *A.L.P. Federal Personnel 1901-1954*.
29 Truman, op. cit.; D. W. Rawson, 'The A.L.P. Industrial Groups',
Australian Quarterly, 1954, no. 4.

appears to have been Archbishop Mannix, and the key figure among the laity was a Melbourne lawyer, Mr Bartholomew Santamaria, who was secretary of a group of organizations connected with the Catholic Action movement. Santamaria's activities were largely unknown to the general public until he was publicly denounced by Dr H. V. Evatt, then federal parliamentary leader of the A.L.P.; until then the ramifications of his influence had been known inside the Labour Party simply as 'the movement', a term which became nationally famous as a result of Dr Evatt's speech in October 1954. By this time, the industrial groups had succeeded in building up something of an *imperium in imperio,* and numerous allegations were being made of their influence on the election of cabinet ministers and on government policy. In 1952, it was subsequently alleged, a 'ticket' run by the 'groupers' had resulted in the election to the ministry of one of the most junior members of the Victorian parliamentary party, who subsequently became the sole survivor of the 'groupers' in parliament after the party had split and an election in 1955 brought about the defeat of the Cain Labour government.[30]

The life of the Cain government was punctuated by the rumblings of this intra-party conflict at cabinet level. In December 1953, the Minister for Lands, Mr R. W. Holt, walked out of a sitting of parliament after refusing to proceed with an amendment to the Land Settlement Bill. It later transpired that the minister had been waited upon by Mr Santamaria, in his capacity as secretary of the National Catholic Rural Movement. According to Mr Holt, Santamaria had requested him to amend the draft Bill so that Crown lands not required under it, or under the Soldier Settlement Act, could be made available to approved persons or organizations so that they could be brought into production. Such an amendment would have made it possible for migrants brought to Australia by the N.C.R.M. to be settled in groups. The amendment was introduced into the Legislative Council by the Minister for Labour, Mr A. M. Fraser, and was immediately attacked by the Opposition on the grounds that it would enable foreign or sectarian communities to be set up. The government was in a minority in the upper house, and depended on the vote of two independent members. Under pressure from these two, the amendment was modified, and Holt and several other ministers who had opposed the original amendment said they were now reconciled to the modified version. However, when Holt had moved the amendment in the Legislative Assembly, he made a sudden dramatic gesture, tore up his copy

---

30 An allegation made at the special party conference in March 1955.

of the amendment, exclaimed 'I cannot go on!' and left the chamber. After an initial refusal, cabinet finally accepted his resignation.[31]

The incident was recalled nearly a year later when Dr Evatt denounced Santamaria and his supporters, both in the party machine and in the state and federal parliamentary parties. The Victorian state executive of the A.L.P. was dominated at this time by adherents of the Santamaria faction, and one of the first steps in the battle following the speech was a declaration by the federal executive of the A.L.P., declaring the state executive to be 'bogus'. In the following March, a special state conference was called to elect a new executive. As the conference had been boycotted by the 'groupers', none of them was on the new executive. Seventeen Labour parliamentarians then refused to recognize the new executive, and the latter promptly suspended them from party membership. Four of these men were ministers, who refused to resign their portfolios. The Premier, Mr Cain, accordingly tendered his resignation to the Governor, and was immediately commissioned to form a new ministry, from which the dissidents were excluded. Three weeks later the new ministry was defeated in the Assembly when the dissident Labourites voted with the Opposition, and Cain was granted a dissolution. At the subsequent general election Labour was roundly defeated, and among the casualties were all the dissidents save one.

The Victorian case was the only one where a Labour government was directly precipitated from office by the action of the Democratic Labor Party (as it later came to be known), but both in New South Wales and in Queensland the existence of the 'movement' had its repercussions. In 1951, the McGirr ministry in New South Wales announced a scheme to grant a charter to a Catholic university. This proposal, which would have meant a radical departure from the traditional secularism of public education in Australia, aroused considerable public hostility, and opposition to the scheme from within the government was led by Mr Clive Evatt, then Chief Secretary.[32] Evatt alleged that the Catholic hierarchy was dictating to the government, and after public controversy had gone on for some time the scheme was dropped.[33] McGirr resigned shortly afterwards, to be replaced by J. J. Cahill.

The Queensland crisis of 1957 is discussed in chapter 13.

[31] *Age,* 14-15 December 1953.
[32] Younger brother of Dr H. V. Evatt.
[33] According to one account, the hierarchy became less enthusiastic about the scheme when its probable cost was investigated.

12

THE ELECTION OF LABOUR MINISTRIES

AN IMPORTANT COROLLARY of the relation between Labour governments and party organs is the practice of electing ministers by an exhaustive ballot of the parliamentary party. Originally, the New South Wales branch supported the radical-democratic demand for ministries elected by parliament, but by 1905 the party was moving towards election by Labour caucus. The idea was initiated by the West Australian branch, influenced by the history of the first Labour administration, under Daglish, which took office in that state in 1904. As a result of internal dissensions, Daglish demanded the resignation of his ministers, and then reconstructed the ministry with the omission of two former members. His action caused considerable criticism within the party, which was intensified in the following year when he resigned after an adverse vote in parliament. The government introduced a motion calling for the acquisition of the property of the Midland Railway Company, but when the House divided, a number of Labour men crossed the floor and voted with the Opposition. Accordingly, a motion was introduced at the 1905 federal conference of the A.L.P. in the name of the Goldfields Trades and Labour Council, to the effect that Labour ministries should in future be elected by caucus. The conference, however, would only agree to a resolution that the members of the ministry should be the subject of recommendation by caucus. The debate on the motion was long and controversial, and one of the principal opponents of the motion was Watson, lately Prime Minister. The suggestion that ministers be elected by caucus aroused concern in conservative quarters, and the Melbourne *Argus* uttered a warning that Labour caucus would become 'the Jacobin Club of Australian politics'.[1]

In 1908, the federal conference of the A.L.P. in Brisbane finally adopted the proposal that ministers be elected by caucus, again in the face of opposition by Watson and some other parliamentarians.

---

[1] 12 July 1905; quoted, D. E. McHenry, 'The Origins of Caucus Selection of Cabinet', *Historical Studies*, 1955, vol. 7, no. 25. A motion at the New South Wales state conference in 1906 was rejected because of opposition from parliamentary members.

The motion was acted upon very shortly afterwards when Andrew Fisher was commissioned to form the second federal Labour ministry. A meeting of the parliamentary party adopted a resolution that the remainder of the ministry be elected by ballot. In the debate, an amendment by Watson that voting be done openly was defeated; so was another motion that three portfolios should be reserved for members of the Senate. The Press was again generally hostile to the innovation, although the *Age,* which was still conducting a campaign for elective ministries, praised the move as a step towards its ultimate goal, and as 'a great improvement on the old system of secret selection'.[2] Another favourable comment came from the *West Australian* a few years later, surveying the results of the system in the selection of the Scaddan ministry in 1912. The newspaper concluded that 'the members chosen for executive office augur not altogether unsatisfactorily for an evenness of feeling and capacity for restraint characterizing the new Government . . . the country is likely to be satisfied. Possibly the best possible choice of those who could be eligible has been made'. The Leader of the Opposition in the Legislative Council, J. W. Kirwan, also said that the conduct of the election had almost converted him to the notion of ministers elected by the party in power, and added:

I think that the system of election is valuable inasmuch as it relieves the leader of embarrassment, and also I should imagine it prevents the jealousy that sometimes exists in parties where a particular individual may not be selected, and there is much subsequent irritation. Perhaps also that system which has been adopted with such eminently successful results in State and Commonwealth Parliaments may lead on to still further advancement towards possible elective Ministries.[3]

More typical, however, was the verdict of the Sydney *Daily Telegraph* after the election of the second Fisher ministry in 1910, when the Press was full of reports of 'tickets' and of canvassing for election. The *Telegraph* claimed that as a result of the elective principle, Labour had abandoned the principles of responsible government. 'The Ministry will be an automaton without political life or political responsibilities.'[4] Discontented voices were also heard within the Labour Party. George Black, who had been defeated in the ballot for the election of the McGowen ministry in New South Wales in 1910, wrote that

2 13 November 1908; quoted D. E. McHenry, loc. cit.
3 D. E. McHenry, 'Caucus over Cabinet', *University Studies in History and Economics,* September 1955.   4 28 April 1910.

such a method of selection was productive of destructive and disintegrating influences . . . out of a well of intrigue and barter arose a great deal of jealousy and much ill-feeling (for a time concealed), while some Ministers were burdened with preliminary obligations which they were obliged to honour when they would have preferred other courses.[5]

Black was even more scathing about the election of the Holman government in 1913. He recounts that one member 'strove to purchase a portfolio by buying drinks and dinners for members and by almost forcing loans on impecunious newcomers'. On the day of the ballot this individual checked his investments 'by scrutinizing the ballot papers of his debtors behind the roller maps in the Public Works Committee's room where the voting took place'. The system, Black declared, was rotten, because it 'relieves a Premier of all responsibility with regard to his colleagues and enables him, if so minded, secretly to select the sycophants and incapables best fitted to be his tools'.[6]

Black's words can easily be dismissed as the complaints of an unsuccessful candidate; it is probably not unfair to assume that, had he been elected in 1910, he would have regarded the system as wholly desirable. Nevertheless, he was not the only Labour man to raise his voice in criticism. Holman instances how J. R. Dacey, one of the ablest members of the New South Wales parliamentary party, had been defeated in the original ballot in 1910 because he had the misfortune to be an unattractive speaker, which caused him to be underestimated by the rank and file members of caucus.[7] Childe is caustic about the quality of the men selected, and after quoting a number of examples where faithful party hacks were elected time and again in preference to abler men, he observes: 'Such consistency in the choice of old favourites is sufficient commentary on the efficacy of this check in the hands of caucus.'[8] Black also gives the example of D. R. Hall, who resigned from federal parliament to enter New South Wales state politics because of repeated defeats in the balloting for office. 'He grew weary of being ignored in Federal politics for men of meaner calibre if of greater dimensions and yearned to re-enter the State sphere. He had been overlooked in the original Fisher Cabinet in favour of King O'Malley, and when E. L. Batchelor passed away, Hall was again disappointed.'[9]

There is reason to doubt whether election is 'democratic' in any

5 George Black, *A History of the N.S.W. Political Labor Party*, pt. 6, p.27.
6 Ibid., pt. 7, pp.20-4.   7 'My Political Life', *Bulletin*, 1934-5.
8 *How Labour Governs*, p.23.   9 Black, op. cit., pt. 6, p.30.

sense other than assuring a reasonably accurate representation of the balance of forces within (and sometimes outside) the parliamentary party. There is evidence that the jockeying for position which takes place during elections leads to considerable heartburning and mistrust. It is not feasible, as Disraeli said of the Conservative governments of the 1820s, 'to gratify so many ambitions, or to satisfy so many expectations. Every man had his double; the heels of every placeman were dogged by friendly rivals ready to trip them up.'[10] The formation of blocs during the voting is, of course, a commonplace. At the 1913 state conference in New South Wales, Black was involved in an argument with the leaders of the Australian Workers' Union, who had alleged that the ministry was flouting the will of the movement outside parliament. Black retorted that the A.W.U. was greatly concerned to oust members of the ministry by nominating its own candidates against them for endorsement in the impending election. The influence of the A.W.U. is strongest in Queensland, where it has been able to exercise considerable pressure on ballots for ministerial office, and no Labour government has long survived a conflict with it.

The election of federal ministries has traditionally exhibited not only the working of blocs but also the convention that each state should be represented in cabinet. As a result, the Prime Minister's position is weakened by thrusting upon him less able or congenial ministers than he would like to have, and he can only partly counterbalance this by allotting them minor portfolios and lowering their order of seniority. The phenomenon of blocs is closely connected with that of 'tickets'. Here, however, the Prime Minister may come into his own because his support for a candidate is extremely important, especially in cases where a ministry is re-elected following a parliamentary election. In 1941, for example, John Curtin was able to specify that he wanted a ministry with fourteen members from the House of Representatives and five from the Senate. He was, however, unable to have E. J. Ward excluded from the ministry; similarly, in 1943, A. A. Calwell was elected to the ministry against the known opposition of Curtin. In this case, Calwell beat R. T. Pollard, who had to wait until 1946 before he became a minister.

The chances of success of a ticket are considerably enhanced by the smallness of parliamentary numbers. Before 1949, when the size of federal parliament was enlarged, a ministry could constitute as much as one-third of the total membership of caucus. In such cases, the solidarity of the people on the ticket, or already

10 *Coningsby*, bk. 2, ch. 1.

in cabinet, can be decisive. As Mr Tadpole remarked to Mr Taper: 'Do you happen to know any gentleman of your acquaintance who refuses Secretaryships of State so easily that you can for an instant doubt of the present arrangement?'[11]

In 1912, the federal conference resolved that Labour ministries returned at a parliamentary election should in future always submit themselves to a new ballot. The process is popularly known as a 'spill'. Caucus is generally in favour of spills at every opportunity, because, as Crisp remarks, there is always 'a sporting chance of replacing one of the least popular Ministers in a new ballot'.[12] Spills may also take place as the result of a motion in caucus, and they have occurred on several important occasions in the federal sphere following changes in personnel which were not the result of an election. In 1915, when Andrew Fisher resigned the Prime Ministership to be High Commissioner in London, caucus decided that a spill should take place, and in the process two ministers were eliminated in the ballot for the new (Hughes) ministry. However, the rule is not invariable; for instance, following the death of Curtin in 1945 and the election of J. B. Chifley as Prime Minister, the single vacancy in cabinet was filled without a spill.

Spills (apart from those occurring after an election) have become rare in the state sphere, where Labour ministries are normally very long-lived and the weight of ministerial influence operates against the occurrence of a spill when a casual vacancy occurs. In the last thirty years, state ministries have grown in size steadily without any corresponding rise in the size of parliament, a fact which increases the value of cabinet solidarity.

The criticism that caucus election involves a modification of the position of the Prime Minister or Premier is, of course, beyond doubt. However, the heads of Labour ministries are almost invariably men of outstanding strength and capacity—qualities without which they could never attain the top of the greasy pole. Consequently, a Labour Prime Minister or Premier, although he may require considerable finesse to discipline dissentient colleagues, can usually find the resources to do so. Nevertheless, it is strictly true that no head of a Labour government can dismiss a member of his ministry. King O'Malley, a minister in the Fisher government, asserted that only caucus could dismiss a minister, because 'only that authority which elects possesses the power of withdrawal'.[13] It is of interest to observe that under the stress of wartime conditions, the federal caucus was prepared to accept the motion of

11 Ibid., bk. 2, ch. 6, p.100.
12 Crisp, *The Australian Federal Labor Party*, p.144.   13 Ibid., p.149.

J. H. Scullin, himself a former Prime Minister, that his successor, John Curtin, should be given power to dismiss a minister. Even in the heat of disputes with individual dissentients like Ward and Calwell, Curtin wisely refrained from making use of his authority.

There has been speculation regarding the effect of caucus election on the quality of Labour ministers. Conservative comment has usually been unfriendly, and a Labour sympathizer supports this with the cautious observation that caucus has been 'sober and not imaginative' in its selection.[14] The point is, in practice, somewhat academic, because the field from which a Prime Minister or Premier can select is very limited. In 1931, the Scullin ministry of thirteen was chosen from a total parliamentary party of fifty-six. In 1941, caucus was slightly smaller, and the number of ministers to be chosen had increased to nineteen. It is true that in future the selection of a federal ministry will not be equally hampered because of the considerable increase in the size of parliament in 1949, but the change would not be a dramatic one. Any hypothetical Labour government might expect to command between ninety and 100 parliamentary members, which leaves the proportions much as they were in 1910. In the states similar considerations apply *a fortiori*.

However, even if the point is largely academic, there are undoubtedly cases where the existence of tickets and of bloc voting has had the effect of keeping out men considerably more able than those included. The quality of speeches in parliament is not, of course, always a safe criterion, but if it is taken as having any reliability then there were several notable omissions from the Curtin and Chifley governments, and some of those included had played no very conspicuous part in parliamentary proceedings. In the states, it has seemed positively unwise for an aspirant to ministerial office to appear in *Hansard* except as a participant in a division.

14 Ibid.

13

STATE LABOUR GOVERNMENTS
SOME CASE HISTORIES

THE PROCESSES of interaction between Labour governments
and their supporting party organs emerge only sketchily from the
generalizations made in the preceding chapters. Substance may be
given them by looking in detail at some of the more notable cases
of struggle over policy or leadership. In this chapter, we shall be
concerned with incidents occurring in the three largest states, New
South Wales, Victoria, and Queensland, in each of which a remarkably consistent pattern has developed with the passage of
two generations.

New South Wales

Until 1941, Labour ministries were in a precarious position because of parliamentary weakness. Either their majority in the
lower house was tiny, or they were faced with a hostile majority
in the upper house. Every ministry had to engage in complicated
manoeuvres to obtain the support of powerful groups within the
party or the trade unions. Since 1941 Labour has held office un-
brokenly and, since 1950, has had a majority in the Legislative
Council. This has brought the consequence of increased efforts by
the trade unions and the party executive to bend the government
to their will. When Labour is apparently in a position to do all it
wishes, particular groups are liable to become disgruntled because
they are not being treated as well as they expect. Through this runs a
persistent feeling that the government should be directly responsive
to the wishes of the groups supporting it, that it should behave
as a reflex of the trade union movement. During the long and
chequered history of Labour governments in New South Wales
this attitude has been expressed with particular intensity and
frequency.

The first Labour Premier, J. S. T. McGowen, soon found himself in strife. In 1912, for instance, his government introduced a
Bill to grant land at Newcastle to the Broken Hill Pty. Co. for the
purpose of establishing steel works. This was in contradiction of
Labour's policy of establishing a state-owned iron and steel industry, and the Bill was introduced without caucus having been

consulted. McGowen had the further misfortune to be in office when dissensions arose over Labour's land policy. The Minister for Lands, N. A. Nielsen, favoured land nationalization and universal leasehold tenure. The opposition of members from rural constituencies led to a parliamentary crisis while McGowen was abroad in 1911. The situation was saved only by the skilful tactics of the Acting Premier, Holman, but it involved compromising with the dissident members of the party over the land question. Nielsen resigned and Labour back-tracked on its policy of leasehold tenure. Moreover, in 1913 the government used its influence to secure the re-endorsement of one of the dissident members, an action for which it was censured by the party conference.

McGowen also made himself unpopular over the question of appointments to the Legislative Council. Successive party conferences had decided that a Labour government should appoint sufficient members to the Council to create a Labour majority, and that each of the appointees should be required to sign a 'suicide pledge'. In 1912, the government appointed ten members, of whom only four had signed this pledge. One of them, moreover, was a known political opponent of Labour, and he and others were suspected of giving donations to party funds as a *quid pro quo*. McGowen was censured by the 1913 conference for this action, and also for his use of volunteers to operate the gas works in Sydney during a strike. In consequence, he resigned his leadership shortly before the elections which were due in 1913, and Holman was elected party leader and Premier.

The record of Holman's struggles with the party and the unions has been told in detail elsewhere.[1] Here, we shall be concerned only with those instances of particular significance for the operation of cabinet government.

Holman ran into trouble, like McGowen, over appointments to the upper house. In April 1914, the executive of the Political Labor League instructed the parliamentary party to abide by a decision of conference that the executive must be consulted before any appointments were made to the Legislative Council. Holman bitterly criticized this move and made a personal attack on R. D. Meagher, who was Speaker of the Legislative Assembly as well as being president of the P.L.L. executive. By 1915, tempers were so frayed that slanging matches took place on the floor of the house between Holman and Labour back-benchers. On one occasion

[1] Evatt, *Australian Labor Leader;* Childe, *How Labor Governs;* Holman, 'My Political Life', *Bulletin,* 1934-5. The succeeding paragraphs are based on these three sources.

Holman actually threatened to have a Labour M.P. expelled from the party. During one of the noisiest affrays, an Opposition member coolly asked Holman whether it would improve matters if Opposition members were to retire temporarily from the house.[2] The Labour conference of that year again introduced a censure motion on the government, reiterating all the complaints that had already been made against McGowen, with the addition of several other items of Labour policy that Holman had failed to carry out. By a series of manoeuvres Holman was able to gain a tactical victory at the conference, so that the censure motions were defeated. However, he was unable to prevent caucus from setting up a committee to examine all Bills before they were presented to parliament.

By the time of the 1916 conference, it was fairly clear that Holman could not stay much longer as Premier of a Labour government. The so-called 'industrial section' of the party, whose centre was the A.W.U., organized a campaign to capture the conference. A 'secret' committee of union representatives was set up at the Sydney Trades Hall, which organized a ticket for elections to the P.L.L. executive. According to Childe, Holman knew all about this committee and had suborned its secretary. He organized a rival ticket, but was defeated, and no politicians were elected to the executive, which was dominated for the next six years by the A.W.U. The conference actually passed a rule preventing active politicians from being members of the party executive. When it was clear that things were going against him, Holman offered to resign, but the conference disregarded this finesse and passed a censure motion on the government. Holman's next move was to call a caucus meeting, which agreed that the whole parliamentary party was affected by the censure vote, and a delegation led by John Storey was sent to the conference to explain that the ministry saw no choice but to resign. This would necessitate new elections by caucus.

The conference remained unimpressed, and Holman then carried out his threat to resign. His resignation, Childe observes, was handed 'not to the Governor, but to Caucus, and at the behest not of Parliament, but of an outside body'.[3] This 'interesting constitutional precedent' did not commend itself to the Governor, Sir Gerald Strickland, who in any case disapproved of Holman, and in a tart note he pointed out that the resignation was only constitutional if it was handed to the Governor. Caucus elected Storey as its new leader; but, unwilling to take Holman's place, he arranged

2 Evatt, op. cit., pp.380-2.   3 Childe, op. cit., p.40.

that the latter's resignation should not be handed to the Governor forthwith. He then returned to the conference, and explained that his position was impossible. A vote of censure affected the whole parliamentary party, and caucus could not properly accept the resignation of the government, especially as the latter had now promised to deal firmly with obstruction from the Legislative Council. A compromise resolution was worked out behind the scenes, a vote of confidence in Holman was carried by the conference, and he then gave his personal assurance that he would hold a referendum on the abolition of the Legislative Council. Shortly afterwards, the eruption of the conscription crisis enabled Holman to leave the Labour Party and to remain in office by arranging a coalition with the Opposition.

The A.W.U. was now in charge of the Labour machine in New South Wales, but its attempt to dominate the situation completely by securing a majority on the P.L.L. executive led to further strife at the conferences of 1919 and 1920. These were a triumph for the A.W.U., which was able to expel some of the leaders of the opposing faction, and when Storey became Premier early in 1920 the A.W.U. attempted to direct the government's affairs.[4] An article in the *Worker* indicated what its attitude would be. 'The Labor politician has loomed too large up to now. We leant heavily upon him and he was not strong enough to bear the burden. Then when he failed us, in our rage we struck out furiously, treating as a bad servant the man we had depraved by making him master.'[5] In fact, however, most of the prominent men on the executive were by this time themselves politicians. The daily Press commented that 'the hand in the machine glove is that of the A.W.U. Central Branch, or rather the hand of the small coterie of machine political officials who also control and direct the affairs of the A.W.U. Central Branch'.[6] As D. W. Rawson suggests, 'what was sought was not the domination of politicians by the executive but the domination of both executive and politicians by a particular group of men who included members of both'.[7]

The formation of the Storey ministry provoked a direct clash. There were no former ministers available for appointment, Labour having 'blown out its brains' in 1916, and competition for places was intense. The A.W.U. leadership, headed by John Bailey,

[4] It was alleged at the time that the real government of New South Wales was at 'MacDonell House' (the A.W.U. headquarters) or the 'Barley Mow' (a hotel where A.W.U. leaders regularly forgathered).

[5] *Australian Worker*, 9 September 1918; quoted by D. W. Rawson, 'The Organization of the Australian Labor Party 1916-41' (unpublished Ph.D. thesis), p.19. [6] *S.M.H.*, 9 January, 1920. [7] Rawson, op. cit., p.20.

president of the central branch of the A.W.U., made an attempt to unseat Storey before the ministry was sworn in. According to J. T. Lang, a group of parliamentarians met secretly under Bailey's leadership in Centennial Park on the day after the election, and drew up a 'ticket' on which J. J. McGirr was first and Bailey second. Storey, however, got wind of the meeting and sent W. J. McKell along to report. He then drew up a ticket of his own which was successful in the ballot.[8]

The ministry's troubles continued after Storey's death in 1921. He was succeeded by James Dooley, whose short term as Premier was marked by continuous strife with the party executive and the A.W.U. The A.W.U. pursued its feud with Dooley even after Labour had gone out of office in 1922, and attempted to have him deposed from the leadership of the parliamentary party by the state executive. Dooley's response was to attack his opponents publicly, describing them as a 'gang of uncouth crooks'.[9]

After the fall of the Dooley Government, controlling power in the Labour movement passed to J. T. Lang, who had been Treasurer in Dooley's administration. Lang was able to consolidate his control by channelling the payment of party funds through his hands, and by the time Labour returned to power in 1925 he was solidly entrenched both as leader of the parliamentary party and as boss of the party machine. He was supported by a group of left-wing unions which had gained control of the executive after the A.W.U. had been beaten at the 1923 conference. Lang's contact with the party and with the unions was chiefly through his Minister for Mines, A. C. Willis, who had been president of the Miners' Federation and a leader of the 'One Big Union' movement which had been defeated by the A.W.U. in a series of factional struggles between 1916 and 1920. Despite his grip on the party machine, Lang was faced with considerable opposition inside the parliamentary party, many of whose members owed allegiance to the A.W.U. In addition, there was resentment among the members from rural constituencies at what they regarded as Lang's excessive care for urban interests. About eighteen months after he had assumed office, Lang found himself confronted by a determined attempt to overthrow his leadership, now being widely attacked as the 'Lang dictatorship'. By this time he was at odds with most of his cabinet, Willis being his only supporter within the government. In October 1926, P. F. Loughlin, the leader of the 'rural' wing of the parliamentary party, and Deputy Premier, opposed Lang for the leadership when parliament reassembled

8 J. T. Lang, *I Remember,* p.167.   9 Rawson, op. cit., p.25.

after the winter recess. Loughlin was apparently instigated by the A.W.U. group on the party executive, which knew that the parliamentary party was divided almost equally between supporters and opponents of Lang. In order to strengthen his position, Lang appointed an independent M.L.C. to a position on the Metropolitan Meat Board, and then filled the casual vacancy so caused with one of his own supporters. He did this without informing caucus,[10] and the *Labor Daily,* which Lang controlled, justified this by asserting that caucus could not be trusted. 'Mr. Lang and the real workers' representatives do things and talk about them afterwards . . . the closeting of secrets in caucus is akin to trying to conserve water in a colander.'[11]

Loughlin's challenge to Lang resulted in a tie, so that Lang remained leader. In the following month, a special A.L.P. conference was called, at which a resolution was passed with only four dissenting voices, declaring the party's confidence in Lang, confirming his leadership, and authorizing him 'in the event of circumstances arising which in his opinion imperil [party] unity, to do all things and exercise such powers as he deems necessary in the interests of the movement'.[12] The conference also resolved that the parliamentary leader would in future be chosen not by caucus but by the annual party conference.[13] The high water mark of 'outside interference' in the affairs of Labour governments had apparently been reached.

Loughlin resigned from cabinet, and after an abortive attempt to organize a 'Country Labor Party' later went over to the non-Labour side. Two other country members, R. T. Gillies and V. W. Goodin, also voted against the government in divisions. The Opposition, taking advantage of this situation, introduced a motion of censure, but the three Labour rebels abstained on the division and the government remained in office.[14] To stabilize the situation, Lang signed a pact with Gillies and Goodin by which they remained in the party. The terms of this agreement were never disclosed, but they apparently involved an end to the Lang 'dictatorship', more regard for country interests, and the abandonment of the new rules (the so-called 'Red Rules') which were then being

10 *Parl. Deb.* (N.S.W.), 2nd ser., 1926, 108: 112.
11 21 August 1926; quoted, Rawson, op. cit., p.107.
12 *S.M.H.,* 13 November 1926.
13 The resolution was rescinded in 1939, at a 'unity' conference which deposed Lang from his position.
14 The Press had a field day; in the evening they were celebrating Lang's defeat, but by the following morning they had to cut short their jubilation. (*S.M.H.,* 23 and 24 November 1926.)

formulated to guide future party conferences. Caucus then met and unanimously elected Lang as its leader. He promised to seek an early dissolution, and in return for this no Deputy Premier was appointed, so that the occasion of a fresh split inside caucus should not arise. Parliament remained in session, and sixty Bills were pushed through.

Early in 1927, fresh trouble arose as a result of the introduction of the 'Red Rules'. They had already received this nickname because Lang's opponents declared that the rules would permit communists to join the Labour Party, from which they had been excluded some years before. When the proposed rules were finally published, the allegation was seen to be unfounded, but the name stuck because of its pejorative value. The approval of these rules was the main business before the Easter conference of the A.L.P. The executive, headed by W. H. Seale, was evenly divided between the A.W.U. faction and its opponents, but one member resigned and the A.W.U. was able to fill the vacancy, giving it a majority of one. The particular significance of the majority at this point was that the A.W.U. was hostile to the proposed new rules, because they would effectively prevent it from dominating conferences. As a tactical move, the A.W.U. majority on the executive now proposed to postpone the conference from Easter to June. Seale and his supporters then left the executive and carried on with arrangements for the conference at Easter. There were now, not for the last time, two Labour parties in New South Wales, one headed by the 'Seale Executive', the other by the 'Conroy-McGarry Executive'. The Easter conference took place under the presidency of Seale, and was attended by representatives from the bulk of the trade union movement, including all the important industrial unions. It reaffirmed Lang's leadership and instructed caucus not to interfere with it; adopted the 'Red Rules'; and expelled Gillies and Goodin from the party, a move which Lang did not favour because it was bound to provoke a parliamentary crisis and hence a dissolution.

While these storms were raging outside parliament, Lang was faced by continuous opposition within both caucus and cabinet. For the entire period under review he had ceased to call cabinet meetings and was assisted only by Willis, his two other usual supporters, J. M. Baddeley and W. J. McKell, being abroad. The Easter conference was attended by less than half of the members of the parliamentary party, and while it was proceeding cabinet met in Lang's absence and demanded that Willis resign. Having done so, it then went on to pledge its support for Lang. The conference riposted by giving Lang the power to reconstruct cabinet if he thought it necessary. Caucus replied by holding a meeting which reaffirmed the pact with Gillies and Goodin and voted for their readmission to the parliamentary party.

In the meantime, the federal conference of the A.L.P. decided to intervene. Meeting in January 1927, it decided that a 'unity' conference should be called in New South Wales and that in the meantime the 'Conroy-McGarry' executive was to be regarded as the only rightful executive of the party in New South Wales. The federal conference was under strong A.W.U. influence, which did not increase the willingness of Lang's followers to accept its decisions. In particular, they refused to accept the instruction that any decisions reached by the unity conference must be taken by a two-thirds majority. Faced with this resistance, the federal leadership gave in and agreed to simple majority voting. The federal leadership was concerned, in fact, less with the precise outcome of the conflict in New South Wales than with the necessity of presenting a united front at the next federal elections. As a result, the unity conference, held in July 1927, resulted in a complete victory for the Lang faction. Lang's over-riding authority was confirmed; the 'Red Rules' were adopted; the members of the 'Conroy-McGarry' executive were suspended from party membership for three years; and Lang's parliamentary opponents were wiped out in the pre-selection ballots which followed. (In the country, however, most of Lang's opponents retained their endorsement.) The A.W.U., in reply, disaffiliated from the party in 1928 and left Lang with a free hand during his second term of office from 1930 to 1932.

In the meantime, the crisis within parliament had reached the point where Lang decided to force a showdown. At the Easter conference in 1927, rumours were already circulating that caucus would expel Willis, and that the other ministers would request the Governor, Sir Dudley de Chair, not to dissolve parliament at Lang's request unless the whole ministry were consulted. It was officially denied from Government House, however, that some ministers had asked the Governor to dismiss Lang and Willis and to commission Dunn, the Minister for Agriculture, to form a government. Fears were expressed that Lang might forestall these moves by obtaining the Governor's agreement to a reconstruction of the ministry. In the event, Lang waited for more than a month after the Easter conference, and used the appointment of his private secretary to the new position of Director of Welfare, which was opposed by most of his cabinet, as a pretext. On 26 May he asked the Governor to convene a meeting of the entire Executive

Council, and executed the series of manoeuvres already described.[15] By resigning and reconstructing the ministry, Lang was able to get rid of his opponents within cabinet without precipitating a parliamentary crisis and bringing about a situation where a dissolution could have been granted to the Opposition.[16]

The story of Lang, one of the most paradoxical in all Australian political history, shows how the deep distrust of politicians held by the Labour movement as a whole, and the never-ending search for a way of ensuring that a Labour ministry remains nothing more than a reflex of the industrial movement, may lead to a situation where the head of a Labour government becomes an almost complete dictator. In his day, Lang was regarded as the great exception to the rule that politicians are untrustworthy. The solution to the perennial problem, therefore, was to give Lang plenary power over the other politicians. Curiously, it is people outside the Labour movement rather than inside it who have attacked Lang as a dictator. The journal of the A.W.U., the *Worker,* attacked him rather as a tool in the hands of militant union leaders, describing him ironically as 'the Sole Hope of Labour—half Saviour and half dictator'.[17] After the Easter conference of 1927, one of his supporters wrote a letter to the Press pointing out that so far from Lang being a dictator, he had himself been dictated to by 'the Upper House, the Nationalist party, the last conference, the present conference, the Parliamentary party, Goodin and Gillies, Willis and Voigt, Hugh D. McIntosh and Jock Garden . . . Lang wears a crown of thorns'.[18]

By 1930, Lang was so firmly entrenched that he could do practically what he liked. The opposition had been either thrown out of the party or had left it; his grip on the party machine seemed unbreakable; and he had achieved the reputation during his earlier ministry of being the champion of the poor. This was enhanced by his opposition to the plan to cut wages and prices, agreed to by the other Premiers in 1931 which, however, he ultimately signed. All important decisions in his second ministry appear to have been made either by him or by his immediate adjutants, especially by his private secretary, Harold McCauley. Light was thrown on this

15 See chapter 7.
16 The extraordinary intricacy and deviousness of Lang's intrigues cannot be conveyed in cold print. Dr Rawson has suggested to me that only in music could justice be done to them—perhaps in the form of a concerto for bassoon.
17 14 October 1926; quoted Rawson, op. cit., p.129.
18 *S.M.H.*, 22 April 1927. In his disingenuous autobiography, *I Remember,* Lang builds up the figure of an upright, radical working-class leader, obstructed by the scoundrels and the time-servers who surrounded him.

situation by the investigations of a Royal Commission into corruption in the Lang administration. One of the principal witnesses was the former Chief Secretary, Mark Gosling, who is on record as saying that the Lang ministry had 'one leader, who announced its policy. When he announces it, we follow, and as soon as he announces it, we know where we stand. We do not seek to know what he is going to do, and are prepared to surrender our judgment, if necessary, in advance.'[19]

Giving evidence before the Royal Commission, Gosling admitted that important decisions within his administrative competence had in actual fact been made by Lang and his immediate agents, in particular by McCauley and by some shady operators concerned with greyhound racing and the operation of 'fruit machines'. According to the Royal Commissioner's report, Gosling had stated that 'Cabinet had taken to itself the matter of the granting of permits for greyhound racing and that he had no responsibility beyond his collective responsibility as a member of the Cabinet'. The following extract from the evidence is revealing:

> Your view of the matter is that the granting of these licences was the responsibility of the whole Cabinet?—Yes.
> That is from start to finish?—Yes.
> You disclaim any individual responsibility for the administration of the Act?—I accept my share as one member of the Cabinet.
> You say that other members of the Cabinet had the same responsibility for what was done?—Yes.
> Do you say that with regard to every licence or permit issued there was a deliberation in Cabinet?—No.[20]

The Royal Commissioner's comment on these evasions was acid:

> It is apparent that the Minister's attitude was that the responsibility of administration which the Act laid upon him had been shifted from his shoulders and had been undertaken by Cabinet. He admits that matters went before Cabinet without any information being supplied, and without any inquiry as to the merits or demerits of any particular application, and he was unable to afford the Commission any light as to the basis on which applications were considered or granted by Cabinet.

The Commissioner went on to conclude that the real authority for the granting of dog-racing permits was a shady financier named Swindell, and that Swindell had been in close touch 'directly or

[19] Cited by J. A. McCallum, in W. G. K. Duncan (ed.), *Trends in Australian Politics*, p.164.
[20] Report of the Royal Commission on Greyhound Racing and Fruit Machines, 1932, p.20.

indirectly with some section of the Cabinet throughout'. It is not difficult to infer which section, or rather which member, of the cabinet was indicated by this statement. Commenting on another part of Gosling's evidence, the Commissioner observed: 'The contemporary minute appears to show that it was the Premier and Minister for Health who dealt with the applications and there is no evidence as to any other Minister having been present at a Cabinet meeting when a decision was arrived at.'[21]

The dismissal of Lang in 1932 was followed by a long struggle within the New South Wales Labour Party, which ended with the overthrow of Lang's power in the party in 1939. (There is a pretty irony in the fact that, shortly before his final defeat, Lang appealed to the federal executive of the Labour Party to intervene.) In 1941, a Labour government under W. J. McKell, who had been a minister under Lang, came into office. The great fights of the 1920s and 1930s were now largely over, and under the skilful leadership of McKell, the government became too firmly entrenched to be upset even by the subsequent violent conflicts in the Labour movement following the schism of 1954-5. Nevertheless, the history of Labour administration in New South Wales since 1941 is studded with attempts by various party organs and by the trade unions to direct government policy on certain specific questions. McKell's immediate successor, J. J. McGirr, ran into the difficulties already described in connection with the scheme for a Catholic university, and he was also in trouble when the party and the unions pressed him to abolish the Legislative Council—in which Labour now had a majority—in 1950-1. During McGirr's term as Premier, the ministry was repeatedly harassed by the supporters in caucus of Mr Clive Evatt, who held a succession of ministerial posts under McKell, McGirr, and their successor, J. J. Cahill. Evatt's ministerial career was punctuated by public disputes with other ministers over matters of both policy and administration, but as he had support in caucus there was little that any Premier could do to restrain him. In the 'spill' that followed McGirr's resignation in 1952, it was alleged that the official 'ticket' did not include him, and although he was elected to the ministry, his portfolio was changed and his seniority in the cabinet list was lowered.

McGirr, apparently becoming weary of his position, had himself promoted to the chairmanship of a public authority, the Maritime Services Board, and Cahill became Premier. The latter, having weathered the storm created by the emergence of the Democratic Labor Party in 1955-6, found himself in difficulties because of

21 Ibid., p.62.

demands that the government should more directly obey the wishes of the state executive. In February 1957, the executive asked for an assurance that all future legislation would be submitted to it for its approval. Cahill's comment on this proposal was: 'The views of little men do not worry me.'[22] Although he was later constrained to retract this statement, he did not give way on the principle that he would not agree to detailed scrutiny of the government's actions by the party executive. A few months later a further dispute arose over the decision by the government to build an opera house in Sydney. This proposal was opposed by a faction within caucus, but Mr Cahill stated publicly that he would not ask the state A.L.P. conference to act as arbiter in the matter. 'If the conference decides to oppose the building of the opera house', he observed, 'the Government will have to examine the decision carefully'; but, he added, 'I can't see that happening'.[23]

The longer a Labour ministry remains in office, the greater becomes its detachment from the trade union movement. An interesting comment on this is afforded by the changes in personnel of the New South Wales government since 1941. In the original ministry of fifteen members, five had at some stage been prominent union officials, and five others had some union background. Up to the end of 1958, an additional sixteen ministers had held office. Of these, only one had been a union official of any importance. Four were farmers, three were lawyers, one was a business man, one a schoolteacher.

Victoria

The history of Labour ministries in Victoria is less eventful, if only because Labour has held office in Victoria for a relatively short period since it entered politics. Labour governments have always been in a precarious situation, either because of the lack of a safe majority in the Legislative Assembly, or because of a hostile upper house. The first Labour ministry in Victoria to endure for any length of time was the Hogan government of 1927-8, which did not have a clear majority in the Assembly and held office only with the support of a dissident farmers' group, the Country Progressive Party, which had opposed participation by the Country Party in composite governments with the Nationalists. This first Hogan ministry ran into trouble with the unions not because it offended the ruling junta, but because of a split within the union movement itself. Hogan himself had been an organizer for the A.W.U., and was supported by it. In 1928, as a result of

[22] *S.M.H.*, 26 February 1957.   [23] Ibid., 9 May 1957.

deficits incurred by the state railway system, he attempted to introduce economies, and thus ran into trouble with the Victorian branch of the Australian Railways Union, which had only recently affiliated with the Labour Party and was antagonistic to the ruling junta in the state executive. The A.R.U. was supported in its attack on the government by the Melbourne Trades Hall Council, and although the ministry finally fell over an attempt to introduce electoral reform it had already been weakened by its dispute with the unions.

In 1929, the state conference of the A.L.P. resolved that in future the party leader was not to form a government without the consent of caucus. A further resolution was introduced, calculated to prevent Labour from taking office unless it had a clear majority, and although this resolution was defeated, murmurings continued within the party, especially when Hogan formed a second government in 1929 with the support of the Country Progressive Party. This support did not last, because in 1930 the C.P.P. amalgamated with the Country Party and left the Hogan ministry dependent on the support of three Independent members. By this time the effects of the depression were being acutely felt, and tension between the government and its trade union supporters grew rapidly. The Waterside Workers' Federation was at this time engaged in a bitter struggle with waterside employers, but the government refrained from any action in support of the union. For this it was censured by the Trades Hall Council. Late in 1930, a special party conference was called, which demanded that both state and federal governments should refrain from dismissing any government employees, and should not force them to work longer hours for reduced wages. It censured the state government for doing so little to relieve unemployment, and also attempted to instruct Victorian members of the federal parliament on their attitude to unemployment. As the conflict continued, an attempt to emulate New South Wales and exclude politicians from the state executive was made at the 1931 conference.

The breaking point came in Victoria, as elsewhere, over the attitude of the ministry to the Premiers' Plan of 1931. The party expressly instructed Labour members of parliament to vote against the plan. In spite of this, fourteen out of twenty-five Labour M.L.A.s voted with the Opposition in favour of it. Another special conference was called in July 1931, which passed a resolution instructing both federal and state members to vote against legislation which would reduce wages or pensions. Hogan ignored this thunder on his left and announced that he would go ahead with

the plan. He was strengthened by the inactivity of the state executive, whose members included a majority of parliamentarians. The
Trades Hall Council, in reprisal, set up a political apparatus of its
own, with the aim of defeating recalcitrant politicians in pre-selection ballots. A. A. Calwell, later a federal minister, who was at
that time state president of the party, retorted by accusing the
union leaders of 'Langism', and threatened them with expulsion
from the party.

The defeat of the Scullin ministry in the federal elections of
December 1931 led to a temporary healing of these differences,
and yet another special conference, held in January 1932, patched
up the quarrel between the unions and the party executive. It
resolved, however, that the Hogan ministry must renounce its
support for the Premiers' Plan, and in the elections to the executive
the unions hostile to the government gained a majority. In April,
the executive decided that the government must refrain from introducing the annual legislation which was required to keep the
Premiers' Plan in operation. The instruction was issued at a time
when Hogan was abroad, and Mr T. Tunnecliffe was Acting
Premier. When parliament met, Tunnecliffe was challenged by the
Opposition to state whether the government intended to renew the
legislation, and his reply that the time was not yet ripe for a statement on financial policy was denounced as an evasion. On 13
April the government was defeated on a motion of no confidence,
and parliament was dissolved.

During the election campaign, it was disclosed that Hogan had
cabled Tunnecliffe from England to the effect that the demands
of the A.L.P. executive revealed it to be the enemy of both state and
people. The cabled message insisted that the Acting Premier's policy
speech must stand by the Premiers' Plan. Tunnecliffe had ignored
this cablegram, which was not laid before cabinet, and in his policy
speech he declared the government's determination to protect wage
and salary earners against further attacks. Only higher government
salaries would be reduced by legislation, and others would be
referred to a classification board. Following this speech, two
ministers resigned from cabinet and attacked Tunnecliffe for breaking faith with the other governments who were parties to the Plan.
The accusation of 'Langism' was now levelled at the ministry. Two
more ministers announced that they opposed Tunnecliffe's policy,
but would remain in cabinet at Hogan's request to protect his
policy. Hogan himself was unopposed at the election, as the split
in his ministry occurred too late for his Labour endorsement to be
upset, and the two Opposition parties had carefully refrained from

putting up candidates against him. The election resulted in an absolute majority over all other parties for the United Australia Party, which had earlier been victorious in the federal elections. Three ministers in the Hogan government lost their seats. Hogan immediately sent his resignation by cable and by radio-telephone to the Lieutenant-Governor, Sir William Irvine, himself a former Premier of Victoria. One of Hogan's ministerial supporters, who had resigned after Tunnecliffe's policy speech, was included in the new composite ministry.

A by-product of the election was the expulsion of Hogan and his supporters from the Labour Party, and a curious attempt on his part to prove that the A.L.P. executive had acted illegally was invalidated by the High Court.[24] Hogan, who was a farmer, later became a minister in the Dunstan (Country Party) administration.

Following the defeat of the Hogan ministry, the state A.L.P. conference of 1933 again decided that Labour should not take office as a minority government. Instead, in 1935 Labour supported the Country Party administration under A. A. Dunstan. An agreement was reached with Dunstan by which he agreed to carry out certain legislative measures, especially for the relief of unemployment, which were desired by the Labour Party. In 1942, however, after growing friction, this support was withdrawn, but Dunstan was maintained in office by the support of the United Australia Party, led by T. T. Hollway. When this alliance in turn broke down, and the Dunstan government was defeated on a vote of confidence, the Labour leader, John Cain, was commissioned to form a government, as his party was the largest in the Assembly. The A.L.P. executive, ignoring the 1933 resolution, advised Cain to accept the commission. After only five days in office, the Cain ministry was defeated on the adjournment.

Cain's second ministry, which lasted from 1945 to 1947, was comparatively uneventful, but his third administration was broken up by the great schism in the A.L.P. in 1954. The dramatic incidents of this crisis have already been described in chapter 11.

Queensland

Since 1915, Labour has held power in Queensland with only two

---

[24] *Cameron* v. *Hogan* (1934), 51 C.L.R. 358. Hogan originally sued the A.L.P. executive in the Supreme Court of Victoria ([1934] V.L.R. 88), on the grounds that they had illegally withdrawn his endorsement, and by so doing had deprived him of the emoluments and entitlements of Leader of the Opposition, which he would otherwise have become. The Supreme Court awarded him one shilling damages, but the verdict was upset by the High Court on appeal. These two cases provide a rare example of the detailed political history of a period being recorded in court transcripts.

intervals, one in 1929-32 and one since 1957, but the government's relations with its extra-parliamentary supporters were by no means a prolonged honeymoon. For most of the time the ministry has been in absolute command of the situation, but violent disputes have occurred on several occasions, and on two occasions they culminated in the fall of the ministry.

Since World War I, the key to Queensland Labour politics has been the predominance of the Australian Workers' Union. A number of factors have combined to bring this about—the largely rural character of Queensland's economy; the heterogeneous and highly bureaucratic character of the union, in which rank-and-file control is almost impossible; and the relative weakness of the big industrial unions which play a much more important part in other states. During the period of the Kidston ministry (1906-11), however, the A.W.U. had not yet emerged as the leading force in the Labour movement in Queensland. That position was held by the Australian Labor Federation, established in 1889. The A.L.F., based on migratory pastoral workers, represented the zenith of attempts to achieve unity between the industrial and political wings of the Labour movement. It consisted equally of unionists and 'political' members. Its outlook and structure did not fit easily into an industrial community, nor into a situation where Labour had to exercise the responsibilities of office. The experiences of the Kidston ministry weakened it, and its back was finally broken by the failure of the Brisbane tramway strike in 1911.

Because of the miscellaneous character of the A.W.U., and also because of the enormous size and thinly spread population of Queensland, an unparalleled degree of centralization has developed. Labour conferences (known as the 'Labor-in-Politics Convention') are held not annually but triennially. Between conventions authority is delegated to the Queensland Central Executive of the party (universally referred to as the Q.C.E.). This is now an unwieldy body with more than sixty members, and the real work is done by an inner executive committee of seven members. The constitution of the Labour Party in Queensland provides that politicians must not form a majority on the Q.C.E., which normally meets every two months. The executive is usually dominated by an alliance between the A.W.U. and the parliamentary party. As long as relations between these two groups are harmonious, the position of a Labour government is almost impregnable. The two great crises in Queensland Labour history have been the result of disruption of this relationship.

An additional dimension of the situation which is peculiar to

Queensland is the absence of an upper house. After a long campaign, the Labour government which came to power in 1915, under T. J. Ryan, was successful in gaining a majority in the Legislative Council, which was an appointive one. Ryan's successor, E. G. Theodore, showed no eagerness to abolish the Council after Labour had succeeded in swamping it with its own nominees (using the fact that there was temporarily no Governor of Queensland, and that William Lennon, formerly a Labour minister, was Lieutenant-Governor). Theodore declared in 1920 that abolition of the Council would be the subject of a referendum, but soon afterwards the triennial Labour convention instructed the government to make abolition an issue at the next election. In October 1921, the parliamentary party decided that a measure to abolish the Council should immediately be introduced into parliament, and in 1922 the upper house disappeared from the scene. Since that time Labour governments in Queensland have been unique in that they have had no hostile upper house to contend with. In only one other case—New South Wales—has Labour succeeded in gaining a majority in the state upper house, and that did not occur until 1950. It is probable that the abolition of the Queensland Legislative Council was instrumental in strengthening the government *vis-à-vis* the Labour convention.[25]

Theodore became involved in a protracted struggle with the trade unions as a result of economic difficulties in Queensland in the early 1920s—difficulties accentuated, to some extent, by the failure of certain of the government enterprises set up under the Ryan administration. In 1922, the State Arbitration Court decided that the state basic wage should be reduced. The government applied to the Court for a reduction in the salaries of state employees, and also introduced legislation reducing government salaries not covered by awards of the Court. These measures were opposed in caucus, and only after Theodore had threatened to resign did caucus give way. The unions, as might have been expected, were hostile, and the Q.C.E. passed a resolution censuring the government. A special Labour convention was called in 1923 to discuss methods of controlling the policy of the government. At the convention a resolution was introduced, similar to the one passed a few years later in New South Wales, authorizing the Q.C.E. to lay down the correct interpretation of the party platform and to expel parliamentarians who opposed this. A proposal was also made that members of the Q.C.E. should be admitted to cabinet meetings as observers. Theodore and his ministers strongly

25 A. A. Morrison, 'The Abandonment of Bicameralism in Queensland'.

opposed both suggestions, and because of A.W.U. support for the government both motions were defeated. However, the convention resolved that the government should introduce a forty-four-hour working week as soon as possible. This move, like most of the other resistance to the government at the convention, was initiated by the Australian Railways Union, which was strongly left-wing and opposed to the A.W.U., whom it accused of 'poaching' railway workers to join its ranks. The A.R.U. had nursed a grievance against the government ever since a meat strike in Townsville in 1919, which Theodore had broken by importing 'scab' labour.

Theodore opposed the introduction of a forty-four-hour week, arguing that Queensland could not afford it. He pointed out that in carrying out party policy by establishing government enterprises, raising wages, encouraging preference for trade unionists, and attacking the big graziers, the Ryan-Theodore governments had incurred severe financial problems. For this the unions were largely to blame, because they had failed to co-operate in making the state enterprises work efficiently. Any attempts by the government to achieve economies in the working of public enterprises had been resisted by the unions, who were constantly demanding shorter hours and higher wages when this was not economically feasible. Theodore expressed the dilemma of many a Labour leader when he described himself as 'a Premier who wanted to keep railway rates low for farmers and carry out developmental works, who had control over only a very limited taxing field, and who had to deal with intransigent railway workers who did not care about the budget but wanted better conditions from the Government they had helped to put in'.[26]

The dispute over this question dragged on for several years. After his speech at the convention in 1923, Theodore was invited to the Trades Hall to explain his opposition to the forty-four-hour week. He argued that the state could not afford the cost; that the Arbitration Court, and not parliament, was the proper vehicle through which the shorter working week should be introduced; and that the unions could get what they wanted from the Court by more effective industrial action. The argument about the Arbitration Court was an equivocal one in view of the government's own application to the Court for a reduction in the salaries of state employees, and in order to justify his actions Theodore had to resort to other disingenuous arguments which he used to support the forty-four-hour week in principle and simultaneously to condemn it as impracticable. He asserted that the existence of the

[26] Higgins, 'The Queensland Labor Governments 1915-1929', p.70.

forty-four-hour week as a plank in Labour's platform did not bind the government to enact it. For this he was attacked by the Brisbane *Worker*. 'How can the whole movement strive to attain it while the Labour government resisted it or refused to enact it . . . if [the Labor Convention] instructed the movement as a whole, then quite obviously it instructed the government, which is a part of the whole, and no sophistry can obscure that fact.'[27]

In 1924, the militant unions were able to win over a majority of members of caucus. Before parliament convened in July 1924 an all-night session of caucus took place at which Theodore and his deputy, McCormack, threatened to resign after caucus insisted on the government introducing legislation to declare a forty-four-hour week and to restore cuts in salaries. Caucus accepted their resignations, and proceeded to elect Collins, spokesman for the industrial unions, as the new leader of the parliamentary party. However, before balloting for the other positions could proceed much further, Theodore and McCormack withdrew their resignations and undertook to introduce a Bill to establish a forty-four-hour week. Theodore also agreed to some of the salary demands, but rejected others.

After Theodore had admitted in parliament[28] that the government was threatened by dissensions among its own supporters, the Q.C.E. met to discuss the matter. The majority upheld the government. However, as union attacks continued, Theodore decided that the time had come for him to retire from state politics, and he obtained endorsement for the federal seat of Herbert in October 1924. In February 1925, at the beginning of the federal election campaign, he resigned to contest the seat. Although Herbert was normally a safe Labour seat, he was narrowly defeated, and it is suggested that his union opponents organized opposition to him during the election campaign.[29]

The government's troubles did not end with Theodore's departure. McCormack, who now became Premier, continued to have trouble with the railwaymen, who were locked out by the government in 1927. The great bitterness engendered by this action caused the A.R.U. to describe the McCormack ministry as the 'Scabinet', whose policy was 'scab or be sacked'. As a result of the

---

27 27 December 1923.
28 Quoted Higgins, op. cit., p.71.
29 Higgins, op. cit., p.76. In 1927, when Theodore stood for the New South Wales seat of Dalley, a mass meeting of building workers in Brisbane urged unionists in Dalley not to vote for him. Left-wing union hostility was also manifested in an article in the *Australian Seamen's Journal* in July 1924 which described him as 'King Theodore the First'.

defection of the industrial unions, the McCormack government was defeated at the elections in 1929. There is an historic irony in the fact that one of the leaders of the A.R.U. at this time was E. M. Hanlon, who as Premier in 1948 was the author of anti-strike legislation conferring unparalleled powers of coercion upon the government. Theodore may well have reflected that the whirligig of time brings its revenges.[30]

Labour was returned to power in Queensland in 1932 and enjoyed an unprecedented run until a further crisis developed in 1957, the occasion for which had an oddly familiar ring. The Q.C.E., whose president, R. J. Bukowski, was state secretary of the A.W.U., attacked the Gair ministry for its refusal to grant three weeks' annual leave to all workers in Queensland. This proposal had been a source of contention for some time, but it now flared up with particular violence because of the intrusion of another issue—i.e., the split in the Labour Party which had already taken place in Victoria and New South Wales, but so far had left Queensland unaffected.[31] In a New Year message, Gair declared that the government would not gamble with the security and welfare of Queensland wage earners by granting industrial benefits which the state's economy could not afford. Bukowski replied that the proposal had been fully discussed by the Labour convention, and that it was the duty of every Labour member to carry out the decisions of the convention. When invitations to two ministers to address the state conference of the A.W.U. were declined, Bukowski alleged that this was because of 'dictation' by the Premier. Only the Deputy Premier, J. E. Duggan, attended the A.W.U. conference, and attacked 'trouble-makers' within the A.L.P. A campaign began for the investigation of certain actions of the government, especially with regard to the liquor trade and to the use of the Premier's Fund, a sum of £12,000 which the Premier had discretion to use for party purposes. In February, a full meeting of the Q.C.E. adopted, by a large majority, a motion that all members of caucus should be reminded of the decisions of the Labour convention on three weeks' leave, of their obligation to obey the decisions of the convention, and of the power of the Q.C.E. to deal with them if they did not do so.

[30] Theodore retired from politics in 1932 and became an important figure in the mining world. He died in 1950.

[31] The A.W.U. had originally supported the A.L.P. industrial groups, until its leaders discovered that their own ascendency might be endangered by the growing power of the groups. The Premier, Mr V. C. Gair, and practically all the members of his cabinet, were Catholics and were accused of sympathizing with the Santamaria 'movement'.

When the letter conveying the resolution was received by the parliamentary party, Duggan moved that a conference should take place with the inner executive of the Q.C.E., but meanwhile fresh disputes broke out over two contentious measures introduced by the government. One of these was a Bill to control the distribution of motor spirit, which was the outcome of a long battle with the oil companies. The A.W.U. and other sections of the Labour movement, both inside and outside Queensland, had supported the Gair ministry in this struggle, but the Q.C.E. appears to have seized upon certain detailed provisions of the Bill as ammunition against the government. The other measure was an Act making a number of amendments to the University Act, including one setting up a board of appeals against academic appointments which was hotly opposed by the university staff association as a threat to university independence. A crowded public meeting was held to protest against the appeals scheme, and the students' union collected 30,000 signatures to a public petition for the withdrawal of the Act.[32]

On 31 March, Bukowski complained that the Q.C.E. had not been informed of the contents of these Bills, to which the Premier replied that no necessity existed for any such notification. A special meeting of the inner executive of the Q.C.E. decided that the contentious measures should be withdrawn, but cabinet decided to disregard this and voted that royal assent be recommended for them. After further comings and goings, a full meeting of the Q.C.E. on 18 April declared that Gair no longer had the confidence of the Labour movement and that he should come before a special meeting to show cause why he should not be expelled. Gair called a cabinet meeting, at which all members signed a declaration that cabinet had complete confidence in the Premier, that at no time had he done other than execute the decisions arrived at in cabinet, and that the cabinet regarded with the utmost gravity the attempt to impose on the Premier the responsibility for decisions for which cabinet as a whole was responsible. Nine out of ten ministers (the exception being Duggan) also signed a statement that they would regard any action against the Premier as action taken against each minister individually. After a long debate, caucus resolved by a narrow majority to pledge its support for the Premier who, it declared, had 'at all times scrupulously carried out the decisions of caucus'.[33]

[32] A. A. Morrison, 'Political Chronicle', *Australian Journal of Politics and History*, 1957, vol. 3, no. 1.
[33] Memories of Kidston's 'Statement' were revived by this episode.

The Premier came before a meeting of the Q.C.E. on the following day, and after a long debate the meeting decided by a narrow majority that he should be expelled from the Labour Party. He replied that he had no intention of resigning as Premier until defeated in parliament. He then called a meeting of his supporters, one of whose actions was to choose a new minister to replace Duggan, who had resigned from cabinet. This group called itself the Queensland Labor Party. The other Labour members of parliament then constituted themselves into a separate group with Duggan as leader. Parliament met on 11 June, and was dissolved after the government had been refused supply. The subsequent elections were won by the Country-Liberal alliance which had been in opposition since 1932. One of the first actions of the new government was to repeal the obnoxious provisions of the University Act.

14

FEDERAL LABOUR GOVERNMENTS

A FEDERAL Labour ministry's position differs greatly from that of a state government. Although it is in theory bound by similar sanctions, its freedom of action is in fact much greater, partly because national policies cannot be manipulated as directly as the affairs of state governments, and partly because not one but six distinct party organizations are involved, whose outlook and interests vary considerably. The necessity to achieve the highest common factor of agreement (which, in practice, may be no more than the lowest common denominator of disagreement), often prevents instructions issued by the federal party organs from being more than diffuse and general in tone. Remoteness also prevents close or continuous supervision by the federal party organs; the federal conference meets only biennially or triennially, and the federal executive only bi-annually. Moreover, the latter may act as a screen for the federal ministry rather than as a gadfly. Even its establishment was a slow and disputed process, being opposed for a number of years by parties in several states on the grounds of centralization and loss of state autonomy. Four Labour ministries had held office in the Commonwealth before the 1915 A.L.P. conference agreed to set up an executive, and even then its powers were strictly limited.

Nevertheless, the newly-established executive was very soon constrained to intervene in the government's affairs. The 1915 conference had recommended that a third attempt should be made to extend the powers of the Commonwealth by a constitutional referendum, following the failure of referenda in 1911 and 1913. Before the referendum could be held, the Prime Minister, W. M. Hughes, persuaded the state Premiers to agree to refer certain powers to the Commonwealth for the duration of the war and one year thereafter, and thus avoided the need for a referendum. When several state parliaments failed to pass the necessary legislation, Hughes was censured by the executive, but when he threatened to resign from the party unless the vote were reversed, the executive quickly backed down.[1]

[1] The problem of Commonwealth powers, whose extent was then uncertain, was solved by the broad interpretation of the defence power given by the High Court in the *Bread Case* of 1916.

The federal executive played only a small part in the conflict over economic policy in 1930-1, and again during World War II. In 1946, after some complaints within the party, the executive decided that ministers in the Chifley government should attend its meetings when matters within their jurisdiction were being discussed. The practical results of this decision, however, were small.[2]

An attempt to achieve more direct contact between the federal parliamentary party and the trade union movement was made in 1939, when the Federal Labor Advisory Committee was established, comprising two members from the federal executive of the A.L.P., two from the federal parliamentary party, and two from the Australian Council of Trade Unions. This committee exercised some influence until Labour took office in 1941, when it lapsed, and it was not revived until 1948. In that year the A.C.T.U. asked the federal A.L.P. conference to reactivate the F.L.A.C., and as a result two ministers were appointed to represent the federal parliamentary party. The committee met quarterly until it was disbanded in 1951.

With the passage of time, the position of a federal Labour ministry has come to bear some resemblance to that of a Labour government in Britain, especially inasmuch as the ministry becomes, for all practical purposes, the national executive of the party. The principle of 'solidarity' was evolved, in the first instance, to deal with a situation where individual Labour politicians had to be kept in line. It requires some effort of imagination to apply the principle to the affairs of state governments, but at least the rhetoric of solidarity can be employed without too much detachment from reality. A real flight of fancy, however, would be required to apply it to the formation of national policies, especially as the Labour Party is not, by its nature, suited to the task of formulating policies on a national scale.[3] Moreover, any Commonwealth Labour administration since 1942 has the strength derived from the financial pre-eminence of the Commonwealth over the states, whose situation as clients of the Commonwealth is, in the long run, more important than any pressure which can be exerted through the organs of the Labour movement.

[2] The Prime Minister, J. B. Chifley, made a point of always providing written answers to questions raised at executive meetings. See Crisp, *The Australian Federal Labor Party,* chs. 3, 10.
[3] The late Sir Frederic Eggleston, in a rather ambivalent chapter on the Labour Party, compared it to H. G. Wells' 'megatherium of Rampole Island, a prehistoric animal . . . with its grey matter distributed over its huge frame in small pockets . . . It has set the pace in Australian politics because of its rude strength . . . I do not believe that it is an adequate instrument for national policy.' (*Reflections of an Australian Liberal,* p.75.)

In the comparative absence of control by extra-parliamentary bodies, the role of the federal caucus becomes correspondingly more significant. Attempts to assert this role have been made at various times. Even so, caucus has not been eager to provoke a clash with the ministry, and the two most famous cases of disruption in 1916 and 1931 were brought about rather differently. In the former instance, the Prime Minister's own actions were the direct cause, and in the latter, a variety of additional factors were at work to produce disunity within caucus. Largely because of the heterogeneity of the parliamentary party, it is difficult for any one group to organize effective opposition to government policy or to force the government to carry out a policy on which it is reluctant to embark.

Even under the relatively secure Curtin and Chifley ministries, the interplay of state and federal politics within the Labour movement was the most important element of conflict. As early as 1908, the A.L.P. conference in Brisbane decided that Labour should seek an increase in the Commonwealth's constitutional powers. In 1911, a referendum to achieve this was defeated, and an important reason was the behaviour of the New South Wales Labour ministry. In 1910, Labour had come to power for the first time in the largest state, and the newly-fledged government was opposed to any action that might reduce its own importance.[4] When the referendum proposals were brought before the Commonwealth parliament by W. M. Hughes, Attorney-General in the Fisher government, his New South Wales opposite number, W. A. Holman, pointed out that they went beyond the 1908 resolutions, and to that extent his government could not support them. However, the New South Wales state conference instructed the government to support the referendum, and on the advice of his colleague, J. R. Dacey, Holman changed his tactics. During the referendum campaign, he carried out a series of ingenious manoeuvres which apparently convinced a large number of Labour voters in New South Wales that they could expect more from their state government than from the Commonwealth. Only two members of the New South Wales ministry campaigned actively in favour of the referendum, and G. S. Beeby, the Minister for Education, announced that he would vote against it. As a result of these diversionary tactics, a majority of electors in New South Wales voted against the referendum. The

---

[4] The New South Wales ministry regarded itself as having a more effective field of action than the federal government, and some of its members were disdainful of the personal calibre of federal ministers. One New South Wales minister referred slightingly to the 'Federal numb-skulls'. (Holman, 'My Political Life', *Bulletin*, 1934-5.)

federal government was incensed, and at the 1912 New South Wales state conference Hughes, who was a delegate, moved that only the federal conference had the right to interpret the federal platform of the party. The conference passed a resolution that failure to support a further referendum to be held in 1913 would be regarded as opposition to Labour policy, and members who behaved in this way would lose their parliamentary endorsements. In the event, when the referendum was held, Beeby resigned his parliamentary seat and left the Labour Party in order to oppose it. After the second referendum had been defeated, he stood again for the same seat as an independent candidate. The Holman ministry[5] gave him its secret support, which became public when they advised the electors to vote for Beeby in the second ballot. The state executive issued a counter-declaration instructing Labour voters not to support Beeby, but he was elected and the government was able to stay in power because of his vote.

A few years later, a similar interplay of state and federal politics played an important part in the struggle over conscription.[6]

In 1915, a body was formed to campaign for the adoption of compulsory service as the policy of the federal government. This association, the Universal Service League, was supported by a number of prominent politicians, including Holman and the former Labour Prime Minister, J. C. Watson. Conscription was also supported by some unions and by a number of Labour Party branches. The Prime Minister, Andrew Fisher, stated that he was 'irrevocably opposed' to conscription, and early in 1916 two important Labour organs announced their opposition. The Easter conference of the P.L.L. in New South Wales rejected it, as did an interstate trade union conference in Melbourne in the following month. The New South Wales Labour conference directed all affiliated unions and party branches to oppose Labour M.P.s who supported conscription, and gave the executive authority to refuse endorsement of conscriptionists.

These decisions affected both Holman and Hughes, now Prime Minister, who was a member for a New South Wales constituency. Holman argued before the New South Wales executive that they had no right to direct him in this matter because defence was a Commonwealth matter. In the meantime, Hughes had been con-

[5] Holman had become Premier in June 1913, after the resignation of McGowen.
[6] See the accounts given by L. C. Jauncey, *The Story of Conscription in Australia;* Scott, *Australia During the War;* Evatt, *Australian Labor Leader;* Childe, *How Labor Governs;* J. R. Robertson, 'The Scaddan Government and the Conscription Crisis 1911-1917' (unpublished M.A. thesis).

sulting party executives and trade union organs in various states, and, finally, on Holman's advice, decided to press for a referendum. Although he had been evasive at first on the question of conscription, his visit abroad in 1916 appears to have convinced him that Australia could only supply enough men for the Allied campaigns if voluntary enlistment gave way to conscription.[7] After deciding on the referendum, he spent several days trying to convince both cabinet and caucus that this action should be taken. Cabinet was almost equally divided on the matter, and as a result it was taken to caucus. Caucus having failed to decide, cabinet met again, and decided by a majority to recommend to caucus that a referendum on conscription be held. After a caucus meeting which lasted into the small hours, the terms of the referendum were endorsed by a small majority.

The difficulties confronting a federal Labour government, without any clear mandate from either the party or the electorate, were never more vividly apparent than in this case. It would have required a rare feat of perspicacity to recognize the true balance of opinion within the movement. Although caucus had barely given Hughes permission to conduct the referendum, the state party executives, except in Western Australia, condemned the decision. Simultaneously, the members of the state parliamentary parties supported Hughes, with the exception of Queensland where the Premier, T. J. Ryan, led the fight against conscription. When the decision to take the referendum was announced, Hughes was expelled from membership of the Labour Party by the New South Wales state executive. Hughes refused to accept this decision, especially as he remained a member of the federal parliamentary party, and the federal executive had made no direct move to censure Hughes. To complete the confusion, although the parliamentary party had agreed that the referendum be held, a majority of Labour members voted against the enabling Bill when it was brought before parliament. The legislation was enacted as a result of Opposition support.

Confusion also reigned inside cabinet. F. G. Tudor, Minister for Trade and Customs, resigned when the decision to hold the referendum was taken. The day before the vote was taken, three

---

[7] Scott, op. cit. There is some evidence that Hughes was also becoming concerned about Australia's security against Japanese imperialism, and his speeches on returning from Britain mingled references to the need for more troops with that for 'keeping Australia white'. In Adelaide he declared: 'We shall hoist the flag of White Australia to the highest minarets of our national civilization.' Cf. D. C. S. Sissons, 'Australian Attitudes to Japan and Defence, 1890-1923' (unpublished M.A. thesis, 1956).

other ministers resigned. Two of them, Senator Gardiner (Vice-President of the Executive Council) and W. G. Higgs (Treasurer) did so because of their refusal to sign an Executive Council minute dealing with voting at the referendum. Hughes had drawn up a regulation which provided that voters could be asked by the returning officer whether they had obeyed the order calling up single men for home defence. Answers which were 'unsatisfactory' could be noted by the returning officer for later action. The regulation was submitted to a meeting of the Executive Council in Melbourne with the usual quorum of three, two of whom were Gardiner and Higgs, who refused to confirm the regulation. Hughes then convened another Executive Council meeting in Sydney, where he was staying at the time, and the regulation was confirmed.

When parliament reassembled after the defeat of the referendum, caucus met and a motion of no confidence in Hughes was put to the meeting. The debate went on for a long time, and had to be adjourned for lunch. When the meeting resumed, Hughes 'made a statement after which he left the chair asking those who thought with him to follow him'.[8] He left the room followed by twenty-four other members; forty-three members of the parliamentary party remained in the room, including the ministers who had resigned. After the meeting, another two, Hugh Mahon and King O'Malley, also announced their resignation from cabinet. Caucus formally expelled Hughes and his supporters, and elected Tudor as the new leader of the parliamentary party, whose members now sat on the cross-benches.

These actions left Hughes and his supporters in an ambiguous position *vis-à-vis* the Labour Party. Confusion prevailed also in two states. In New South Wales, Holman had not been expelled from the party but had merely been refused endorsement at the next state election. When, however, he formed a coalition ministry with the Opposition, he and his supporters were expelled from caucus, a decision shortly afterwards ratified by the state executive. In Western Australia, on the other hand, the triennial state conference of the party in June 1916 had refused to commit itself for or against conscription. Tension grew within the parliamentary party, and the government fell in July because of the defection of several Labour members. Although the former Premier, Scaddan, and the majority of members of caucus campaigned in favour of conscription, no attempt was made to expel them from the party after the referendum had been defeated. When a special federal conference was called in December 1916 to make final decisions on all the

[8] Extract from federal caucus minutes, 14 November 1916.

matters in dispute, one of the delegates from Western Australia, Senator Lynch, was one of Hughes' supporters who had left the federal caucus with him. This conference tidied up all the loose ends left over, expelled all the conscriptionists, and made the rift in the party permanent. Hughes, in the meantime, handed in his resignation and was commissioned to form a new government, which found itself facing two opposition parties in parliament. In February 1917, after the final expulsion of Hughes and his supporters, a coalition ministry of Hughesites and Liberals was formed with Hughes as Prime Minister.

Labour did not return to power until 1929, and the Scullin government, which assumed office in that year, was in trouble almost from the day of its formation. Here, too, conflicts between state and federal governments helped to bring the crisis to a head, although they were only the most important ingredient in a situation with which no government could have dealt calmly. The world depression, a hostile majority in the Senate, and the known opposition of the Commonwealth Bank to the fiscal policies of the government, all contributed to the downfall which some observers predicted from an early stage in its history. Like its contemporary in Great Britain, the ministry was soon riddled with factions, each supporting a different approach to the problems of deflation and unemployment. For almost a year, factional strife was so intense that various sections of the party held their meetings in separate rooms and the noise of argument in the corridors of Parliament House was continual.[9] Scullin, moreover, increased factional bitterness by taking some decisions without consulting all members of cabinet. Although the chairman of the Commonwealth Bank Board, Sir Robert Gibson, was an active and vociferous opponent of the government's financial policy, he was reappointed by Scullin when his term expired in 1930. The appointment was made shortly before Scullin left Australia in August to attend the Imperial Conference in London, and the news was released only after he had sailed. Scullin had also arranged for a visit from Sir Otto Niemeyer, a director of the Bank of England, without informing all members of the cabinet or the parliamentary party.

Such actions were not all on one side. While Scullin and two other ministers were abroad, moves were made in caucus to force the Acting Prime Minister (J. E. Fenton) and the Acting Treasurer (J. A. Lyons) to agree to drastic financial measures against Scullin's wishes. On 4 November 1930, caucus passed a resolution moved by Frank Anstey, Minister for Health, calling for a twelve-

9 Warren Denning, *Caucus Crisis,* p.66.

months' moratorium on the repayment of Commonwealth bonds due to mature in the following month. Three days later, Lyons cabled to Scullin in London, describing these moves as repudiation. 'I notified the party I would not be prepared to carry out their decision, but would communicate with you and ask you if you approved their action to relieve me of my position in the Cabinet and appoint a successor.' Scullin replied supporting Lyons' attitude, and instructed him to proceed with his intention to recommend to the Loan Council the floating of a conversion loan. He also sent a message addressed to caucus as a whole, appealing to members to reconsider their views, which if put into effect would destroy the credit of Australia: 'It is a reversal of the party's declared policy to honor national obligations, and no self-respecting Government could agree to it.'[10] The Loan Council agreed to the floating of the loan, to support which Scullin sent a public message from London.

Although Scullin won this battle with caucus, the latter carried through another defiance a few weeks later when it successfully pressed cabinet to appoint two Labour men, H. V. Evatt and E. A. McTiernan, to be judges of the High Court, in spite of Scullin's cabled protests.[11]

The immediate cause of the fall of the ministry was the action of a group of New South Wales members, under instructions from J. T. Lang, who had been returned to power in New South Wales in 1930. Lang nursed considerable rancour against the federal government because of federal intervention in the New South Wales political struggles of 1926 and 1927. He was also personally hostile to E. G. Theodore, Treasurer in the Scullin ministry, who was now member for a New South Wales constituency and one of Lang's principal political opponents in that state. During the 1929 election campaign, Theodore had promised that a Labour government would settle the industrial trouble on the New South Wales coalfields, which had taken on great bitterness as a result of a shooting affray following the dispatch of police to the coalfields by the Nationalist state government under T. R. Bavin. When the Scullin ministry took office, the mining unions and the state executive of the A.L.P. demanded that the federal government take over the mines and disarm the police. Scullin rejected this proposal as un-

10 E. O. Shann and D. B. Copland (eds.), *The Crisis in Australian Finance,* pp.63-5.
11 Denning, op. cit. Evatt had been a member of the New South Wales Legislative Assembly since 1925; McTiernan was New South Wales Attorney-General in 1920-2 and 1925-7, and became member for the federal seat of Parkes in 1929.

constitutional, and was immediately attacked by the ruling faction in the New South Wales party, known at the time as the 'Inner Group'. An article in the *Labor Daily* hinted that the 'Inner Group' would destroy the Scullin government.[12]

In May 1930, a federal conference of the A.L.P. approved a scheme for the expansion of credit which had been devised by Theodore. A number of members of caucus were opposed to this scheme, which was pigeonholed when Theodore, as a result of allegations of corruption made against him in Queensland, resigned his portfolio.[13] At the beginning of 1931, Scullin invited Theodore to rejoin the cabinet, and the matter was put to the vote by caucus. Twenty-four members voted for his readmission, nineteen opposed it, and nine abstained. Lyons, Fenton, and Anstey, who had opposed Theodore's readmission to cabinet, then indicated that they would resign. A week later Lyons and Fenton did in fact resign and, with three other followers, crossed the floor and joined the Opposition. As a result, a 'spill' took place in which three members of the ministry lost their places. One of these, J. A. Beasley, was the leading supporter of Lang in the parliamentary party; Senator Daly had incurred Scullin's resentment because he was directly responsible for the appointment of Evatt and McTiernan to the High Court; and Anstey, a Victorian member, was hostile to Theodore and was the leader of a group of left-wing critics of the government's policy.

These changes in the ministry reflected deep divisions of opinion over the proper policy required to deal with the depression, divisions running right through the Labour movement. Although the 1930 conference had criticized Scullin's actions, it 'avoided taking a position on the specific situation which faced the Scullin government . . . having taken the position that its decisions were binding, the conference failed to make clear what its decisions were'.[14] Moreover, although the conference had supported the expansion of credit, the federal executive did not give the government a clear directive to proceed with this policy. As a result, Lang was able to appear as the leader of a left-wing policy and to gain the support of a large section of the movement that disapproved of his tactics

12 1 February 1930; quoted, Rawson, 'The Organization of the Australian Labor Party 1916-41'.
13 A Royal Commission found that corrupt practices had occurred in the acquisition and operation of smelters in the Mungana-Chillagoe district when Theodore was Premier of Queensland. The Nationalist Premier, A. E. Moore, hinted at court proceedings, but when Theodore resigned to contest any action the Queensland government evaded the issue.
14 Louise Overacker, *The Australian Party System*, p.154.

but felt that his views were right and those of the government wrong. In February 1931, Lang produced the so-called 'Lang Plan' at a Premiers' conference, calling for a policy of credit expansion. He opposed the measures put before the conference, including the reduction of wages, which were adopted as the 'Premiers' Plan' at a further conference in June, and produced his own scheme as an alternative. (It involved the repudiation of overseas debts, the lowering of interest rates, and the abandonment of the gold standard.) This scheme was supported by sections of the Labour movement in other states, but New South Wales was the only one which took the drastic step of instructing its federal members to support Lang's proposals. The A.L.P. in New South Wales thus reasserted the right it had claimed in 1928 to instruct federal members from its own state.

A by-election in East Sydney in March 1931 provided a convenient test of strength between Lang and the federal government. The New South Wales executive selected E. J. Ward as candidate for the constituency, decided that the main issue of the campaign should be the Lang Plan, and that only supporters of Lang would be allowed to speak in the campaign. The federal executive and federal parliamentary members refused to accept this decision, and federal ministers made election speeches in support of the policy of the Scullin government. One minister who represented a New South Wales electorate argued that if the decision of the New South Wales party were to become the rule, there would be nothing to prevent state executives elsewhere from imposing conditions on their federal members, so causing the disintegration of the Labour movement.[15]

Ward was elected, and delivered a maiden speech inviting members from other states to support him. He also hinted at a reconstruction of the ministry, possibly with Lang at its head. This open invitation to revolt followed the expulsion from the party by the New South Wales state executive of those New South Wales federal parliamentarians who supported Scullin rather than Lang. Several of these were associated with the A.W.U., which had disaffiliated from the party in New South Wales and was determined to destroy Lang's leadership. In reply, federal caucus voted not to admit Ward, and as a result six members, led by Beasley, rejected the Labour whip and formed their own group on the floor of the House of Representatives. A special federal conference was then held in Sydney, which retaliated against the New South Wales executive by expelling the entire state branch from the A.L.P. The conference

[15] P. J. Moloney, *Australian Worker*, 25 February 1931.

also set up a provisional executive for an 'official' New South Wales branch. The struggle between these two rival New South Wales Labour Parties went on until 1936.[16]

In June, the government introduced legislation to put the Premiers' Plan into effect. The Lang Labor group and ten other Labour members of the House of Representatives voted against it, but the measure was passed with the support of the Opposition. E. J. Holloway, who had been elected to the ministry as a result of the first 'spill', resigned his portfolio because of opposition to the legislation. A further 'spill' took place, which resulted among other things in the re-election of Senator Daly. The last six months of the government's life were relatively peaceful, until in November 1931 the Lang group demanded an inquiry into the activities of the 'federal' Labour Party in New South Wales, alleging that Theodore had used funds for the relief of the unemployed as a political weapon against supporters of Lang. The government refused, and was defeated on a motion by Beasley. Parliament was dissolved, and Labour was defeated in the election.

The occurrence of two re-elections of cabinet during the Scullin ministry's tenure of office provides a particularly interesting means of analysis of the forces at work inside a federal Labour government. When the ministry took office the federal parliamentary Labour Party had fifty-six members. Almost half of these—twenty-two—came from New South Wales. Victoria had fourteen; Queensland five; South Australia eight; Western Australia two; Tasmania four; and the Northern Territory one. In spite of this great preponderance of New South Wales members, the distribution of portfolios among the states went disproportionately against it. Four members came from New South Wales; five from Victoria; and one from each of the remaining states. This represented a victory for the Scullin-Theodore 'ticket', which was also an A.W.U. ticket. Only one supporter of Lang, J. A. Beasley, was elected to the cabinet. When the first 'spill' took place on 3 March 1931, five members, led by Lyons, had defected to the Opposition. This had the effect of strengthening the position of New South Wales. In the new ministry, New South Wales had five ministers, Victoria five, and Queensland, Western Australia and Tasmania had one each. South Australia was now without a representative because of the exclusion of Senator Daly. Although New South Wales representa-

16 The 'official' party was headed by two undying opponents of Lang, Theodore and Bailey, the A.W.U. leader, and was nicknamed by its antagonists the 'T-B' party.

tion had increased, the strength of the Lang faction was reduced by the exclusion of Beasley.

A second 'spill' took place on 26 June 1931, after the defection of the Beasley group. As a result of this ballot, New South Wales members secured six portfolios, Victoria four, and Queensland, South Australia and Western Australia gained one each. In this case, although the representation of New South Wales members had fallen by seven, the number of ministers from that state had actually increased. This increase reflected the growth of the influence of the A.W.U. In the first cabinet there were two members associated with the A.W.U. (Blakeley and Senator Barnes). In the second ministry there were four (Barnes, Blakeley, Dooley and McNeill). In the third there were five (Barnes, Blakeley, Cunningham, Dooley and McNeill). Both Barnes and Blakeley were federal presidents of the A.W.U., Blakeley from 1919 to 1922, Barnes from 1924 to 1938. Dooley was a former New South Wales state president. McNeill had a long career in the union in South Australia, and succeeded Barnes in the federal presidency. In addition, both Scullin and Theodore had been active in the A.W.U., and Scullin was the brother-in-law of McNeill. Finally, the Victorian (Hogan) government had the backing of the A.W.U. As on an earlier occasion, the test of strength between Lang on the one hand, and the Scullin ministry and the federal A.L.P. executive on the other, was to a large extent the projection of the conflict between Lang and the A.W.U. in New South Wales.

The predominance of Catholics in the Scullin ministry has already been referred to in an earlier chapter. It is ironic, however, that the leader of the Labour defectors who went over to the Opposition, J. A. Lyons, was a devoted Catholic. Scullin himself was a devout adherent of the Church.[17]

*

The episodes just described were of a character so complex and spectacular—Eggleston's megatherium rending itself to pieces— that they can easily distract attention from matters which, in the long term, may be more important. Of great interest, in particular,

[17] Scullin's direct influence on these reshuffles is illustrated by the case of John Curtin, member for Fremantle, who later became parliamentary leader and Prime Minister. On grounds of ability, the one portfolio assigned to a Western Australian member should have gone to Curtin. However, Curtin was an ex-Catholic who had become an active rationalist, he was a heavy drinker and he was unpopular with the A.W.U. Scullin was not only devout but puritanical, and there is reason to believe that he would not support Curtin for election to cabinet.

is the fate of attempts by caucus to influence the policies of successive governments. The methods adopted for this purpose underwent considerable evolution in the course of the early Labour administrations. For example, the principle was established from an early date that the acceptance of a commission to form a government should be approved by caucus. On 23 April 1904, J. C. Watson informed a special meeting of caucus that he expected to be sent for by the Governor-General, and the meeting agreed that he should accept a commission if it were offered. On the 12 November 1908, Andrew Fisher announced that the Governor-General had asked him to form an administration. (This meeting also saw the defeat of an attempt by Watson to give Fisher the right to select his own ministers.) In 1910, after receiving a commission from the Governor-General, Fisher asked for leave to report to caucus before accepting.

Another technique with which experiments were made was the appointment of committees of caucus to scrutinize proposed legislation. On the 21 July 1909, the executive of the parliamentary party recommended that committees be appointed to study the Bills introduced by the Deakin-Cook government. Four committees were appointed, each of them dealing with the affairs of two government departments. Two of the chairmen of these committees were former ministers who had been responsible for the administration of the departments their committee was charged with examining.

This procedure was continued after Labour assumed power in 1910, and during the early months of the government a considerable amount of time at caucus meetings was taken up with considering reports from the committees. However, their importance soon declined and in later years they reappeared only when Labour was in opposition. Instead, attempts were made to ensure that no contentious measure should be introduced by the government until caucus approval had been obtained. For example, on 17 November 1910, Hughes moved that

> when during a discussion of any measure not already decided by the party, strong objections are expressed in regard thereto, and the Whip has ascertained that a majority of available members of the Chamber in which the matter is being discussed so desire, then the Minister in charge shall postpone the consideration of the clause until a meeting of the party can be called to consider the case.

The motion was carried. In 1915, following a complaint from the executive of the parliamentary party that members were not regarding themselves as bound by party decisions, a resolution was carried to the effect that all government measures should be submitted to caucus before going to parliament. Shortly afterwards, an attempt to inquire directly into the affairs of a particular department, by a resolution that a special meeting of caucus be held to examine King O'Malley's administration of the Department of Home Affairs, was lost by only two votes.[18]

It is questionable whether these attempts had any significant effect on the conduct of government business except on one or two celebrated occasions. Apart from the conscription crisis, a famous example was when King O'Malley used the machinery of caucus to force the government to introduce a Bill setting up a central bank. The federal conference of the A.L.P. in 1908 had, at O'Malley's prompting, passed a resolution in favour of the setting up of a national banking system. When O'Malley was elected to cabinet in 1910, Fisher, who was not on good terms with him, gave him the portfolio of Home Affairs and took the Treasury himself. Although the scheme for a Commonwealth Bank had been included in the fighting platform for the 1910 federal election, neither Fisher nor Hughes, his Attorney-General, were in favour of the scheme, against which they had been advised by spokesmen of the private banks. When O'Malley drew attention to the government's failure to implement this policy, Fisher tried to silence him by threatening to have him dropped from the ministry. When this produced no effect, he endeavoured to exclude O'Malley from cabinet meetings by calling them without O'Malley being informed. This manoeuvre also was of little effect against the volatile and energetic O'Malley who determined to proceed by stealth and to build up his numbers in caucus. He organized support over a period, describing his supporters as the 'Torpedo Brigade', a nickname exploited by opponents who alleged that he was attempting to blow up the government. In October 1911, O'Malley introduced a motion into caucus that the government should be instructed to bring down a Bill setting up a Commonwealth Bank. The motion was carried, but Fisher succeeded in excluding O'Malley from any direct part in the measure by leaving the matter in the hands of Treasury officials. At no stage did he discuss the draft legislation with O'Malley, and the measure as introduced departed in some important features from the latter's scheme.[19]

At a somewhat later date, John Curtin found it necessary to resort to carefully-timed manoeuvres in order to persuade the party that it should change its attitude on conscription, formed under

18 The incidents described are taken from the minutes of caucus.
19 L. C. Jauncey, *Australia's Government Bank,* ch. 3.

such dramatic circumstances in 1916. In 1942 it was obvious that voluntary enlistment for overseas service would not provide sufficient numbers of men to carry on the war against Japan in the islands north of Australia. Curtin, who had been an active opponent of conscription in 1916, was acutely aware of the problem, and carried out a series of tactical moves which were calculated to prevent the issue from disrupting the party and the government as it had done nearly thirty years before. In 1942, a federal conference of the A.L.P. met in Melbourne. As Prime Minister, Curtin was invited to address the meeting, and without prior warning asked the conference, as a matter of urgency, to change Labour's policy on the use of conscripts outside Australian territory. The conference did not immediately decide the matter, but agreed that it should be referred to each state executive. There is every reason to suppose that Curtin had foreseen some such outcome, and that he had deliberately refrained from having a motion placed on the agenda so that no opposition to it could be organized before the conference met.[20] Within a day or two of the conference's decision, the A.L.P. executive in New South Wales announced that it supported Curtin's proposal, and soon afterwards three other states—South Australia, Western Australia, and Tasmania—followed suit. The Victorian and Queensland executives both rejected the scheme, but only by a small aggregate majority of their members.

As a result, Curtin was free to introduce the legislation, and in February 1943 the federal parliament passed an Act which provided that the conscript militia could serve anywhere in the South-West Pacific, which was carefully defined as an area south of the equator between the 110th and 159th meridians of longitude.

Although Curtin had outmanoeuvred his opponents in parliament and outside it, an attempt to censure him was made at the annual New South Wales Labour Party conference in June 1943, which was supported by some members of his ministry, including E. J. Ward. Curtin went to the conference, and with an outstanding display of oratory was successful in persuading it not to pass a motion of censure on his government.

A few years later, Ward was again the central figure in a controversy which provided another remarkable case study of the interplay of relationships between the various organs of the Labour movement. Following the conclusion of the Bretton Woods Agreement in 1944, providing for the establishment of an International Bank and an International Monetary Fund, Australia was required

20 Cf. Whitington, *The House will Divide*, ch. 13.

to ratify this agreement by the end of 1945 in order to enjoy the privileges of a foundation member of these two organizations.[21] However, there was considerable opposition within cabinet and within the Labour movement as a whole to the agreement, reflecting Labour's traditional distrust of 'international financiers'. The debates were, in fact, an echo of the struggle within the movement at the time of the Premiers' Plan. The federal government consequently moved slowly, and it was not until November 1946 that cabinet agreed to recommend to caucus that the agreement should be ratified. After two protracted cabinet meetings, a decision in favour of ratification was announced with the proviso that the government would review the question of continued membership of the fund and the bank when the outcome of discussions on the formation of an international trade organization was known. The decision of the cabinet was approved a week later by a meeting of the federal executive of the A.L.P. which was addressed by the Prime Minister, Mr Chifley. Voting was seven to five in favour, one of the dissentients being a federal minister, Mr A. A. Calwell.

Caucus met during the first week of December, but in the meantime Ward and Calwell had succeeded in rallying their followers against the government, and the meeting decided that the proposal should be submitted to a special federal conference of the A.L.P. Seven ministers were said to have voted against the decision of cabinet at the caucus meeting. This manoeuvre broke down when it appeared that sufficient support for the calling of a special conference was not forthcoming. The summoning of a conference required the approval of a majority of the six state branches of the party, and only three were prepared to support the proposal. The matter therefore returned to caucus, which finally came to a decision in March 1947. In the meantime, a short leaflet entitled 'The Case for Bretton Woods' had been circulated by Mr Dedman, Minister for Post-War Reconstruction, who was one of the principal supporters of ratification. In reply to this, Ward prepared a further leaflet entitled 'The Case Against the Ratification of the Bretton Woods Financial Agreement'. He also delivered a radio broadcast attacking the agreement, and challenged Dedman to a public debate on the subject—a challenge which was not taken up. Two days before the meeting of caucus, a further statement was circulated among members by Chifley, which gave a clear and simple explanation of what the agreement would mean to Australia.

[21] The date was later extended, so that the belatedness of ratification did not deprive Australia of these privileges.

In the event, caucus voted thirty-three to twenty-four in favour of ratification, having rejected two amendments designed to postpone a decision.[22]

The government immediately introduced a Bill into parliament to ratify the agreement, after arranging for Mr L. G. Melville, who had been Australia's principal delegate at the Bretton Woods conference, to address the Opposition parties in explanation of the agreement. (Melville had previously explained the agreement to cabinet while it was still trying to make up its mind.) The debate was very quiet; Chifley was the only member of the government to speak. J. T. Lang, who had been elected to parliament as an Independent member in 1946, provided the only lively note when he attacked the agreement as a betrayal of Australia, and said the government was handing over Australia to the control of 'an international financial cartel'. The Bill was carried with Opposition support. Ward abstained from voting.

[22] J. D. B. Miller, 'The Bretton Woods Controversy', *Australian Outlook*, 1947, vol. 1, no. 3.

15

LABOUR IN OFFICE (II)
AN ASSESSMENT

Democratic institutions awaken and foster a passion for equality which they can never entirely satisfy . . . [The people] is not very favourably inclined towards the superior classes of society, and it carefully excludes them from the exercise of authority. It does not entertain any dread of distinguished talents, but it is rarely captivated by them.—de Tocqueville

THE INCIDENTS recounted in the preceding chapters are testimony to the endemic conflict between the traditions of the Australian Labour movement and the conventions which the British example has led us to regard as the norms within which cabinet government operates. In particular, the principle of collective responsibility within cabinet is perpetually in danger of a clash with the theory of solidarity as expressed in the party pledge and in the powers given to, or claimed by, party and trade union organs. At the 1919 federal conference, *ministerial* solidarity was attacked by D. L. MacNamara, M.L.C., later federal secretary of the A.L.P., when he moved that a collegiate system of administration be introduced by which each minister would have as 'associates' a committee of five members of caucus.

It should mean more effective administration than what the people got at the present time. Ministers drawing high salaries had in a sense become a class apart, and they came to caucus in a solid body . . . and presented their proposals in such a way that it did not always make for the best in legislation, nor afterwards in administration.

Miller comments on this motion (which was defeated 17-11), that its gravamen was the inability of Labour members of parliament to influence administration in favour of their constituents. 'There was little complaint about Cabinet's legislative decisions; what the supporters of the motion objected to was the fact that Labor M.P.s were often unable to get what they wanted from the administrative departments, and that Labor ministers would not help them to do so.'[1] The reasons for this 'sundering' of ministers

[1] Miller, 'Party Discipline in Australia', *Political Science*, 1953, vol. 5, nos. 1-2.

from their parliamentary associates were stated long ago by Childe, in a famous passage:

> The Minister faced with the actual responsibilities of governing, administering the details of his department, surrounded by outwardly obsequious Civil servants, courted by men of wealth and influence, an honoured guest at public functions, riding in his own State motor car, is prone to undergo a mental transformation. He inevitably looks at administrative questions from a different angle to that in which they appear to the private member. The latter wants a lot of things—mostly apparently small and simple—done for himself, his constituents, his friends, or his union; the Minister seems to possess the power to grant most of such requests. But the Minister is painfully aware of the limitations placed upon his power by considerations of finance, by constitutional usage, by the traditional procedure of his department, and by the very multiplicity of conflicting claims upon his favour. He is more fully seized of the implications of each question than a private member can be. He must beware of creating precedents rashly, confidential information in his possession cannot be revealed, lest it should slip out if too many persons are privy to it. The members of the Cabinet become bound together by sharing such difficulties, by the mutual recognition of the more intimate and secret problems of Government and a common desire to maintain their positions in the House and the Party, and to ensure both their return by the country and their re-election by Caucus. For that reason they tend to preserve a solid front.[2]

In these circumstances, it is natural that the party should try to substitute for the collective responsibility of cabinet the individual responsibility of ministers to caucus and, beyond it, to the party and the unions; and equally natural that ministers, exposed to different influences, should resist such pressure. Applauding Holman's stand against instruction by caucus and the party executive, Harrison Moore wrote that 'specific instructions in particular matters are in substance a withdrawal of confidence'.[3] But this was written on the assumption that caucus should behave as a species of agent of the parliament on whose confidence, in the last resort, cabinet depends, and which cannot directly interfere with cabinet's administrative discretion except by a withdrawal of confidence. It is unlikely that without some radical change in Australian society this view will ever commend itself to a party which, *ex hypothesi* as it were, regards politicians as 'opportunists'. 'Once you allow the

[2] *How Labour Governs*, p.17.
[3] In Atkinson (ed.), *Australia; Economic and Political Studies*, p.118.

politician to boss the show, he will give away everything to save himself, because he believes himself indispensable to the show, and in fact ends by becoming the show himself, and making a holy show of the rest of us.'[4]

The results of this determination not to allow 'reasons of state' as interpreted by ministers to interfere with the realization of concrete political or economic objectives can be valuable and constructive, as in the case of O'Malley's campaign for a national bank, but in the majority of cases their effect is to interfere with the formulation and execution of policies which look beyond the immediate advantage of a particular interest group. Administration, de Tocqueville observed, calls for the exercise of qualities in which democratic government is deficient: 'A democracy is unable to regulate the details of an important undertaking, to persevere in a design, and to work out its execution in the presence of serious obstacles. It cannot combine its measures with secrecy, and it will not await their consequences with patience. These are qualities which more especially belong to an individual or to an aristocracy.'[5]

An important ingredient in this situation is the oft-quoted 'anti-intellectualism' which is in fact not exclusive to the Labour Party but may be explained, as Métin did at the beginning of the century, as a consequence of narrow concentration by interest groups on their own immediate objectives. It is irrelevant to argue, as many Labour sympathizers have done, that both the electoral appeal of the Labour movement and the position of a Labour government would be strengthened by developing the intellectual and educational side of party activities.[6] The failure of the A.L.P. and of the trade unions to enlist the services of intellectuals is not a matter of default, to be cured by demonstration or persuasion; its causes lie at the very roots of the Labour movement. As a result of this failure, party conferences tend to be less important as the venue for debates on policy than as battlefields where the membership of the next executive will be fought out. But, as this is the real object of the party conference, criticism on the other ground is hardly relevant. Confusion on this point readily extends to consideration of the proper relationship between the party conference and a Labour ministry. Writing of the 1929-31 crisis, Overacker criticizes the weakness and hesitancy of the federal bodies of the A.L.P.

[4] Matthew Reid, presidential address at the 1907 Labour convention in Queensland; quoted, Childe, op. cit., p.25.
[5] *Democracy in America* (World's Classics ed.), p.161.
[6] These arguments are well summed up by Crisp, *The Parliamentary Government of the Commonwealth of Australia,* pp.112-15.

In formulating federal policy the federal conference followed so hesitant and vacillating a course that its decisions were seldom clear-cut and were frequently open to varying interpretations . . . The adoption of a constructive, viable programme by the interstate conference of 1930 might have convinced Prime Minister Scullin that his government must either implement that policy or resign.[7]

This is to ask the party conference to carry out functions for which it was not intended. As Overacker herself observes elsewhere, party organs act as a brake rather than as a spur on the government,[8] or as Miller remarks, their interest is in administration rather than legislation. Party conferences realize their function above all when Labour is in power; when it is not, they fail to act as policy-forming bodies precisely because they are not designed for this purpose. (In Britain, by contrast, party conferences appear much more vital when Labour is in opposition; when it is in power, policy becomes the prerogative of the government and the National Executive Committee little more than an extension of the latter.)

An 'ideal' relationship between a Labour ministry and the Labour movement as a whole would presumably be one that combined the smooth functioning of cabinet with the execution of a programme of social improvement. In a number of actual cases such an 'ideal' may be said to have been realized—e.g., the Fisher Commonwealth ministry of 1910-13, the Ryan and Theodore governments in Queensland from 1915 to 1921, and the McKell government in New South Wales from 1941 to 1946. Although the Curtin and Chifley ministries from 1941 to 1949 were successful as governments, their course could by no stretch of imagination be described as smooth.

The question has become almost academic in the states, where Labour governments, with the exception of Victoria and South Australia, have been so long-lived that their members become little more than the public relations officers of government departments. In these instances, Miller's observation that 'no Labor leader can retain his position without the support of the trade union movement'[9] requires some modification, especially in the light of events since 1955. The split in the Labour movement which resulted in the emergence of the Democratic Labor Party suggests that conflicts of an ideological character *can* take place in the Labour Party, despite a good deal of evidence to the contrary, and that governments may be unseated in consequence.

7 *The Australian Party System*, p.153.   8 Ibid., p.110.
9 Miller, loc. cit.

The correct formula may be that Labour governments, in the states at least, now have little to fear from trade union hostility provided there is no major conflict between the industrial and political wings of the Labour movement outside parliament. This may not, however, be an 'ideal' relation inasmuch as it is due to the bureaucratization of Labour politics and the growth of an 'establishment' linking the government, the union leadership, and the administrative machine, in which Labour serves as the party of administration.

In the Commonwealth sphere, the situation is more complex, if only because Labour has held office for less than one-third of the period since federation. Possibly as a result, its activities when in office have had a strongly reformist character. It is significant that the Curtin and Chifley governments, whose activity was outstanding in Labour history, were carrying out policies most of which originated in the public service. The successful relationship between these cabinets and their official advisers introduced a new dimension into federal Labour politics, because it provided a substitute for the absence of broad policies emanating from the party. It was possible for a Labour ministry to exploit the resources of the public service to give legislative shape and content to reforms which had rarely gone beyond vague aspirations expressed at party conferences. Moreover, it gave the ministry a source of strength comparable to that which has long been available to a British cabinet, and the great ascendency of Curtin and Chifley as Prime Ministers can in no small measure be traced to this phenomenon. Such a prediction may be rash, but it is probable that the near-crisis over the Bretton Woods agreement was the dying flicker of an era now past. Any future federal Labour government will not only be able to assert its role in making policy, but will have the administrative resources to support its assertion.

16

THE EMERGENCE OF COMPOSITE
NON-LABOUR MINISTRIES

THE EVOLUTION of a system of checks and balances within
the Labour movement, designed to enforce the responsibility of
Labour ministries to the party and the trade unions, was closely
followed by the growth of a characteristic pattern on the non-
Labour side, whose effect has been to establish relations which are
similar in purpose though different in detail. Since the early 1920s,
almost every non-Labour government, state or Commonwealth,
has been a composite of the two parties of 'town and country capital', as Crisp describes them. These composite ministries operate
along lines which are no more to be interpreted by reference to
British criteria than are the workings of a Labour ministry. As with
Labour, they are calculated to enforce the responsibility of the
government parties to the interest groups that support them, to
check the operation of collective responsibility and to temper the
purely 'governmental' or 'administrative' outlook which any government, whatever its political colour, is bound to assume.

It has been widely supposed that this situation is the 'fault' of
the Country Party, which is vilified by spokesmen of Liberal[1]
and Labour Parties alike as the 'Old Man of the Sea' of Australian
politics. The Liberals have consistently attacked it for its refusal to
unite with them, and its history is studded with attempts to bring
about a merger, none of which has been complete or comprehensive in its outcome. (Even in South Australia, where a single
party, the Liberal-Country League, operates in state politics,
federal members may identify themselves with either party in the
Commonwealth parliament.) Such criticisms err, I believe, for
several reasons. They exaggerate the extent to which the Country
Party differs from the other parties in the Australian political
system, a point already discussed in the introductory chapter.
There is something of the famous 'mote-beam' mechanism at
work here: 'they' (the Country Party) are narrow, parochial, and

[1] When general references are made to the urban non-Labour Party, the
term 'Liberal' is used for the sake of simplicity. Specific references in time
use the name actually employed by the party at that time.

selfish, while 'we' (Labour or Liberal) are a 'national' party that recognizes its wider responsibilities to the community. The criticism also exaggerates the innovating influence of the C.P., which is held to be responsible for destroying the established principles of cabinet responsibility by insisting on the device of the 'composite' ministry—one where each party retains its separate identity, where ministers remain responsible to their own party, and where the Prime Minister's choice of his cabinet is restricted by the right of the Country Party to nominate an agreed number of ministers.

Against this, it may be argued that the peculiar role of the Country Party is no more than the apotheosis of tendencies which have been present in the Australian political system for a very long time. The 'French situation' that prevailed in all the colonies until the 1890s inevitably leads to cabinet-making along lines not greatly dissimilar to those that apply to composite ministries. 'Unnatural' coalitions, formed as a result of the entry of Labour into politics, were a feature of the period 1890-1910, and in some of them the equality of the leaders was deliberately emphasized, e.g., in the 'Griffilwraith'[2] combination in Queensland, the Reid-McLean coalition (1904-5) and the Deakin-Cook 'Fusion' (1909-10) in the Commonwealth sphere. In the Reid-McLean ministry, in particular, the two factions remained distinct and bargains were struck over policy. Another contemporary example, the Liberal-Labour coalition in Queensland headed first by Morgan and then by Kidston, was marked by the repeated assertion by the Labour Party of its separateness and its right to influence the actions of Labour members of the cabinet. That such coalitions encroached on the principle of cabinet responsibility was recognized by Reid himself, who wrote in his memoirs that they 'debase the political currency and prevent the proper working of the parliamentary machine'.[3]

The problems confronting organized farmers' groups on their entry into politics from 1914 onwards bore some affinity to those which had faced the Labour Party twenty-five years earlier. Like the early Labour Party, they were a minority group whose policy was 'support in return for concessions', and like Labour in the 1890s, they found it expedient to establish strict forms of control over their parliamentarians to prevent them from being seduced from their allegiance. The importance of these controls was even more apparent as it became evident that the role of the Country

2 Nickname given to the ministry headed first by Griffith (1890-3) and later by McIlwraith.   Griffith and McIlwraith had previously been opponents for many years.   3 *My Reminiscences*, p.232.

Party would regularly be that of junior partner in a non-Labour combination. The parliamentary party adopted practices much like the Labour caucus, including the election of ministers by exhaustive ballot and external solidarity after intensive debate. 'Within the parliamentary party', writes Overacker, 'there is a high degree of unity and solidarity . . . Dissenters are given an opportunity to talk themselves out, and leaders stress that "in unity there is strength".'[4]

The control exercised by the extra-parliamentary bodies is also close and explicit. The federal constitution of the party lays down that 'the Federal Council shall not form with any other political organization an alliance that does not preserve intact the identity of the party', and furthermore that 'acceptance of portfolios in any other than a purely Country Party government must be with the approval of a majority of members of the Federal Council'. Parallel provisions are to be found in the constitutions of the state Country Parties. In Victoria, no member can accept office in any but a purely Country Party government without the approval of two-thirds of the party's central council; ministers must contest elections as C.P. members and not as members of the government, and participation in a composite ministry may be ended by a majority of a joint conference of the central council and the parliamentary party. At caucus meetings, ministers are to regard themselves as party members and not as bound by cabinet decisions. They are also affected by the rule that on matters outside the party platform, M.P.s are to abide by decisions of caucus unless freed by a special resolution. The overriding authority of the party organization is cemented by a provision that M.P.s are not bound by a caucus decision if it conflicts with decisions of the party conference and the central council.

The Victorian provisions are of remarkable stringency, reflecting as they do the peculiarly intense struggle of the Victorian Country Party to retain a grip on the governmental machine. Not surprisingly, they also reflect a history of dissension within the party. During the currency of the composite Bruce-Page government in the Commonwealth, the Victorian central council of the C.P., emulating the Labour Party in New South Wales, tried to establish the rule that Victorian members of the C.P. in federal parliament were bound by the council's decisions. The federal members refused to obey this direction, and ran as 'Australian Country Party' candidates at the subsequent election. In 1940, a Victorian C.P. member, John McEwen, who had received a

4 *The Australian Party System*, p.232.

portfolio in a composite ministry, was accused by the central council of co-operating too closely with the United Australia Party, and was expelled from the C.P. He, in his turn, ran for the federal election of that year as a 'Liberal Country Party' candidate.

In other states, similar but less elaborate provisions exist. In Western Australia, as in South Australia, the Country Party, known as 'Country and Democratic League', operates as a separate entity in federal but not in state politics. A federal member must inform the party executive before accepting a portfolio, and the executive may, at its discretion, convene a joint conference with federal parliamentarians which can instruct a C.P. minister to resign from office.

That the Country Party, by skilful use of its bargaining position, has been able to gain a great deal for its supporters is undoubted. It is of some importance, however, to be precise about *what* it has gained. Country Party propagandists like to emphasize their party's success in influencing *policy*. One of the most prolific of all C.P. apologists has written that the Liberals have 'fallen into the error of supposing that the Country Party can be tempted to forsake their separate identity if they are offered portfolios, and asked to forget the all-important topic of policy'.[5] It is true that differences on policy have occurred, but the evidence suggests that what the Country Party really cares about is access to certain key portfolios, i.e., about administration rather than policy. In 1910, the president of the Farmers' and Settlers' Association of New South Wales attacked the administration of the Wade (Liberal) government and declared that 'until that administration has been improved, the F.S.A. will refuse to be a single joint in the Liberal tail'.[6] In his memoirs, J. T. Lang attacks the C.P. for frustrating much-needed projects to relieve traffic congestion in Sydney by insisting that priority be given to country works. Premier Bavin, he observes, made his greatest mistake in forming a composite ministry: 'The Country Party merely moved in and took control of the Nationalist party. It has virtually been in control ever since . . . The tail has wagged the dog so long now that it can't even raise a bark of protest.'[7]

The most interesting attack on the Country Party comes from the late Sir Frederic Eggleston, who was a minister in a composite

5 U. R. Ellis, 'History of the Country Party', *New South Wales Countryman,* April 1949.
6 Ibid., April 1948. The account of C.P. policy given by J. P. Abbott, M.H.R., in A. C. Garnett, *Freedom and Planning in Australia,* is little more than a catalogue of administrative steps to increase the returns to primary producers.   7 *I Remember,* pp.363-5.

government in Victoria for close on three years. In a chapter entitled 'The Cost of the Country Party', he reviews the damaging effects of preferential administration in the immediate interests of the farmers on various important aspects of Australian development. Composite ministries, he asserts, have frustrated 'the role which the best Liberal influences have played in Australian politics, that of sound policy in administration and financial measures and of a scientific approach to and control of State undertakings'.[8] Moreover, he writes, the presence of Country Party ministers is a positive liability to the Liberals in the discharge of cabinet business: 'The parliamentary and administrative capacity of the Liberal members is, as a rule, considerably greater than that of Country members, and they are called upon to do a very large proportion of the work of the Cabinets.'[9] Hostility between Liberal and Country supporters of a composite ministry becomes particularly evident at the approach of a general election. In both parties there are groups who oppose the granting of electoral immunity to sitting members of the other party, which is one of the regular occasions for bargaining when a composite ministry is formed. In 1953, for instance, the Country Party indicated that it would nominate candidates for three federal seats held by Liberal members, and in reply a move was made in the Liberal Party to nominate a candidate against McEwen, Country Party minister for Commerce and Agriculture. The latter uttered a warning that 'all sorts of serious possibilities' might follow if he were opposed, and declared his astonishment that a candidate from 'the other party' might stand against him.[10]

Relations within composite governments are often little better than the 'snarling unanimity' which was said to characterize an early ministry in Queensland.[11] Liberal apologists are wont to blame this on the influence of the extra-parliamentary organs of the Country Party. Yet there is evidence that the Liberals are no less susceptible than the other parties to 'outside influence', and that their supporting party organs are also prone to regard responsibility to one's supporters outside parliament as more important than cabinet responsibility. At the same time, the Liberals are normally at pains to stress the independence of the parliamentary party and the government from control by party organs. A few

8 *Reflections of an Australian Liberal*, p.138. This complaint is an echo of the earlier attack made in *State Socialism in Victoria*, where Eggleston describes the impossibility of efficient administration of government undertakings whose rates are constantly manipulated in the farmers' interests.
9 Ibid., p.137.   10 *S.M.H.*, 18 November 1953.
11 A contemporary reference to the Herbert ministry, 1859-66.

COMPOSITE NON-LABOUR MINISTRIES 201

years ago, a flutter was caused when the Prime Minister, R. G. Menzies, conferred with the federal executive of the Liberal Party in the cabinet room at Parliament House, Canberra. Some members of the parliamentary party expressed alarm at this action as a 'dangerous precedent'.[12] Forty years earlier, in launching the National Federation, W. M. Hughes had included 'responsible government' as one of the planks of the new Nationalist Party's platform—an implied thrust at the Labour pledge he had helped to establish. Yet the new organization was itself an admission that from now on the structure of the main non-Labour party would embody principles similar to those at work in the Labour movement. Until this time, Liberal leaders had espoused the accepted British theory that party leadership resided in parliament, and the party organization in the country did not exist to exercise any direct influence on the government, whose members were individually and collectively responsible to parliament. The formation of the National Federation was a tacit departure from this principle. In practice, the party machine conducted its affairs not in public, as had originally been intended, but became a 'background organization' whose influence on the government could only be inferred, especially from outbursts during times of crisis.[13] The central body had particular strength because of its tight control of party funds and the absence of active party branches and affiliated bodies which, in both the Country and Labour Parties, act as a check upon a monopoly of authority by the party executive. The constitution adopted by the Victorian branch of the United Australia Party in 1932 included a pledge, and gave sweeping powers to the central executive, whose exercise led to repeated conflicts in later years.

The strength of trade union influence in the Labour Party derives partly from the importance of union contributions to party funds —a situation not confined to Australia. In the Liberal Party, the control of finance by a special committee has given this group a controlling influence both on party affairs and on the activities of Liberal or composite governments. Such finance committees became characteristic of the Liberal Party after the Labour victories of 1910 in the Commonwealth and in New South Wales. During their history they have had various names—the Constitutional Union, the National Union, the Consultative Council (especially in New South Wales, where Holman was instrumental in estab-

---

[12] *S.M.H.*, 26 February 1957.
[13] Cf. Crisp, *The Parliamentary Government of the Commonwealth of Australia*, pp.131-7.

lishing it in 1919), and most recently, the Institute of Public Affairs. Eggleston denies that the policy of the Liberal Party is dictated by the 'background organization'. He adds, witheringly, that 'the personnel of this background organization know so little about politics that they could not effectively interfere. They have no ideas, and no guts'.[14] There is no reason to doubt the sincerity of Eggleston's remarks, but it should be recalled that his career in active politics was only of short duration, and his own direct experience of 'dictation' when holding ministerial office derived from the Country Party. The case histories of non-Labour governments which follow suggest that successful or attempted dictation from outside has emanated equally from the extra-parliamentary organs of the Country Party, the finance committees of the Liberal Party, and individual interest groups.

14 Eggleston, op. cit., p.136.

17

COMPOSITE MINISTRIES IN THE STATES

THE EMERGENCE of the Country Party in the states soon led to political changes and the appearance of the composite ministry as the standard form of non-Labour administration. In Tasmania, where a Nationalist government under W. H. Lee had been in office since 1916, Lee was deposed in 1922 as the result of pressure from the recently formed Country Party, which had gained an accession of strength through the adherence of some breakaway Nationalist members. The Country Party was successful in insisting that J. B. Hayes, another Nationalist minister, should become Premier, and Lee was relegated to the portfolio of Treasurer.

In Western Australia, the Country Party entered politics in 1914, when eight Country members were returned to the Legislative Assembly. The party had adopted a strict rule against participation in any coalition government, but in 1916 a Country member accepted the Treasury portfolio. After a series of negotiations in 1919, the party changed its policy on coalitions, and three members entered a composite government with the Nationalist Party under Mitchell. However, the ministry was troubled by continuous friction between the two parties, especially when, as the result of an election in 1921, the Country Party gained more seats in parliament than the Nationalists. Despite this, the Country Party still had only three portfolios, and after disputes between the party executive and the parliamentary party, fifteen Country members withdrew from the official party. Labour was returned to office in 1924, and the Country members split into one group allied to the Nationalists, which was the 'official' party; the other group, insisting on the independence of Country members, called itself the 'united' Country Party. In later years the distinction between the two groups disappeared and non-Labour governments in Western Australia have ceased to be 'composite' in the original sense, although the Country Party organization outside parliament, known as the Country and Democratic League, retains its separate identity.

In Queensland, the Country Party first entered politics as a group of five Country members inside the Queensland Liberal Party in 1915. In 1916, this became a separate party both inside and outside parliament, but in 1924 it fused with the Nationalists to form the Country and Progressive Nationalist Party. The leader of this group was the former Country Party leader, A. E. Moore, who became Premier after the election of 1929. In 1936, four years after the defeat of the Moore government, the Country Party again constituted itself as a separate organization, and has remained so ever since, becoming the larger of the two non-Labour parties. In 1957, the Country and Liberal Parties fought the election jointly but separately, and it was the leader of the Country Party, G. F. R. Nicklin, who became Premier in the composite government. When the ministry was formed, the Country Party elected its members by exhaustive ballot in the customary fashion, but, unusually, the Liberals followed suit.

The role of the Country Party has been most significant in New South Wales and Victoria, where the basic conflict of interests between the Country and Liberal parties led to stresses within successive state governments. The Country Party first became important in New South Wales politics in 1921. At that time the Dooley Labour administration was in office, with two Opposition parties, Nationalists and Progressives, the latter being an amalgam of Country Party members and dissidents from other parties formed in 1919. The Labour government had a majority of only one and depended on an Independent, Daniel Levy, who had accepted the Speakership. Towards the end of 1921, Levy was persuaded by the Nationalists to resign as Speaker. A Labour member had to be appointed to fill the vacancy, the government was deprived of its majority, and as a result was defeated on a motion of censure. Sir George Fuller, the Nationalist leader, then negotiated with the Progressive Party for a coalition ministry. The Progressives refused to participate, proposing instead that a purely Nationalist administration should take office which the Progressives would support if no legislation were introduced which was unpalatable to them. When the matter was referred to the Progressive caucus, it was found that seven out of the thirteen members favoured joining a coalition, and as a result, the question was referred to the central council of the Progressive Party. The council split evenly and the chairman used his casting vote against a coalition, which was supported mainly by members from urban constituencies.[1]

Negotiations with Fuller continued, and an agreement was finally reached by which four Progressives were to be included in the ministry, the separate identities of the parties outside Parlia-

[1] Ulrich Ellis, *The Country Party*, p.70.

ment were to be maintained, and a joint party executive was to be set up with equal representation. Almost as soon as the coalition ministry had been sworn in, however, it foundered on the unexpected opposition of Bagnall, the Nationalist Whip. When the ministry met parliament he declared that he could not reconcile himself 'to the men who were the chief assassins of the last Nationalist Government being placed in the high and honourable positions of Ministers of State jointly with the leading members of the Nationalist Party'.[2] To break the deadlock, Levy then allowed his name to be put forward for the Speakership, and the new government was defeated on a motion of no confidence. Fuller requested a dissolution, was refused, and resigned from office, which he had held for just seven hours. The Dooley government resumed the Treasury benches and carried on until parliament was dissolved early in 1922.

The seven members of the Progressive Party who had opposed the coalition, all of them representing rural constituencies, became known as the 'true blues'. One of them, D. H. Drummond, who later held office in two composite ministries, attacked the proposal for a coalition as 'a cunning climax to the long continued Nationalist efforts to smash the Progressives, thoroughly discredit the Federal Country Party and give a strong setback to the New States Movement'.[3] Dissension within the Progressive Party continued, and in January 1922, the central council resolved that it would not enter any coalition with the Nationalists, that it would support a Nationalist government provided its policy was in accord with the platform of the Progressive Party, and also resolved that the party should contest no more metropolitan electorates. This decision was not to the liking of several Progressive members of parliament, and when Fuller formed his second government in April 1922, three of them joined it under a coalition agreement similar to that which had been repudiated by the 'true blues' a few months earlier. Within a few months all three of these had joined the Nationalist Party. A change in the attitude of the Progressives occurred in the following year, after the formation of the first federal composite government headed by S. M. Bruce. The party changed its constitution to provide for the possibility of entering into a composite government, but to make the *volte-face* less abrupt, the resolution stated elliptically that the party could 'enter into any arrangements which might be deemed necessary by other

[2] *Parl. Deb.* (N.S.W.) 2nd ser., 1921, 85: 301. This was a reference to the hostility of the Progressives towards Holman, the previous Nationalist Premier.   [3] *Land,* 17 December 1921; quoted Ellis, loc. cit.

political parties having similar aims or interests'.[4] In the meantime its position in parliament remained awkward, and J. T. Lang, then leader of the Opposition, exploited the situation by repeatedly bringing forward censure motions on the government for acts which had not endeared it to the Progressives. The same game had been played by the Labour Party in the Commonwealth parliament, but Lang actually succeeded in getting the Progressives to vote for two censure motions.

After the fall of Lang in 1927, the Nationalist leader, T. R. Bavin, approached E. A. Buttenshaw, leader of the Country Party (the name had been adopted in 1925), and offered him two portfolios in a composite ministry. The central council of the Country Party advised the parliamentary members to enter a 'composite government on liberal lines, the party to maintain its separate identity'.[5] Fortified by this support, Buttenshaw held out for five portfolios, and a bargain was finally struck by which four went to the Country Party as against ten to the Nationalists, with Buttenshaw as Deputy Premier. The four portfolios were those of Works and Railways, Local Government, Education, and Agriculture, all of special interest to the Country Party, which was anxious that the government should spend more money on these matters in rural areas.

In 1932, after Lang had been dismissed from office by the Governor, Sir Philip Game, the latter commissioned B. S. B. Stevens, leader of the United Australia Party, to form a government, and granted him a dissolution. The caretaker administration comprised six U.A.P. and four Country Party ministers. The election resulted in an increase of Country Party representation from twelve to twenty-five members, and as a result a ministry was formed with nine U.A.P. and five Country Party ministers. M. F. Bruxner, leader of the Country Party, became Deputy Premier, with the portfolio of Transport and Local Government. The other portfolios held by the Country Party were those of Lands, Education, Agriculture, and Mines and Forests. Despite reshuffles during the course of the Stevens administration, the Country Party retained Transport, Education, and Agriculture. It was a period of acute depression both in city and country areas, and the Country Party had successfully manoeuvred to obtain portfolios, such as those of Transport, which were concerned with public works expenditure. Bruxner, as Minister for Transport, had considerable success in arranging public works projects in country areas. In addition, the Country Party Minister for Edu-

4 Ellis, op. cit., p.74.   5 Ibid., p.104.

cation, Drummond, was able to resume the policy of expenditure on education in the country which he had inaugurated during the Bavin government, and in particular was responsible for the establishment of the New England University College at Armidale, in the rich north-western area of the state which was the centre of the New State movement with which Drummond had been associated for many years.

Throughout the Stevens ministry, there was friction between the U.A.P. and the Country Party, aggravated by the economic situation and by the resentment among U.A.P. members representing urban constituencies who were resentful at heavy expenditure in rural areas. Sections of the metropolitan press echoed this resentment, complaining that the parliamentary U.A.P. was moribund and that Stevens was aloof towards the rank and file of the party. The All-for-Australia League's support for the election of ministers was recalled, and there was talk of the annual re-election of the leader of the government. Discontent crystallized around the figure of E. S. Spooner, who became Minister for Public Works in 1935 when the ministry was reconstructed after an election. Spooner also became Assistant Treasurer (the Treasury portfolio being held by Stevens) and in this dual capacity he was regularly at loggerheads with his Country Party colleagues. By 1938, relations had become so strained that Stevens relieved Spooner of his post as Assistant Treasurer and transferred the Treasury portfolio to A. Mair, a U.A.P. member from a country constituency. The Stevens government was also becoming affected by the political crisis in the federal sphere, where a composite U.A.P.-C.P. government under J. A. Lyons had begun to disintegrate in the latter half of 1938. The end of the Lyons ministry following Lyons' death in March 1939, and the hostility shown towards the U.A.P. by Page, Country Party leader in the federal parliament, produced their effects in New South Wales State politics. In July 1939, Spooner resigned from the ministry, and attacked the financial policies pursued by Stevens, accusing him of being a prisoner of the Country Party. The Country Party, he alleged, were no less socialistic than Labour when it suited them, and Bruxner, as Minister for Transport, was ruthlessly carrying on the Lang policy of placing all metropolitan passenger transport under a government monopoly. The functions of local government were being encroached upon by the Country Party's policy of establishing state-owned abattoirs, and the proper role of private enterprise was threatened by the government's extension of state control over electricity supply. During the Budget debate in August,

Spooner moved a motion of censure on Stevens' financial policy and proposed that a new policy should be adopted for the current financial year. In reply, Stevens made a bitter attack on Spooner, accusing him of personal ambitions, and declared that he had raised no objections to the government's financial policy when he had been a member of cabinet. He defended the role of Bruxner as Deputy Premier.

When the vote was taken, several government supporters were absent from Sydney, and with the support of ten members of the U.A.P., the Labour Opposition, and an Independent member, the motion was carried by forty-three votes to forty-one. Stevens promptly resigned, advising the Governor to send for Mair, who formed another composite government in which Stevens did not participate.

Victoria

Antagonism between country and urban members of the non-Labour parties in Victoria has been an endemic feature of Victorian state politics since the early years of the century. For a long time this antagonism was fed by the existence of a gerrymandered electorate which gave a country vote considerably more value than a city vote. Between 1913 and 1952 governments came and went regularly over the question of electoral reform, with the Country Party for many years succeeding in playing both ends against the middle. In 1913, before the Country Party had entered state politics, a split occurred in the government party when the Premier, W. A. Watt, introduced a Bill providing for the redistribution of seats. The Labour Opposition joined with country members of the Liberal Party to defeat the Bill, and Watt resigned. After he had been refused a dissolution, Labour took office in a minority government under G. A. Elmslie. When the Elmslie ministry had been in office for thirteen days, the anti-Labour groups patched up their conflict and the government was defeated on a motion of no confidence. Watt then resumed office, after Elmslie in his turn had been refused a dissolution.

After the emergence of the Country Party, such events became a commonplace. Within the Victorian Farmers' Union, which appeared on the scene in 1917, there were two factions—the majority, including a large number of parliamentarians, favouring co-operation with the Nationalist Party and participation in composite ministries, while the minority, led by A. A. Dunstan, favoured a more flexible policy of support in return for concessions and were willing to ally themselves with Labour for this purpose.

Dunstan had won his seat from Labour, and as leader of a group composed chiefly of small wheat and dairy farmers, was in favour of the policy of 'agrarian socialism' which did not appeal to the larger landholders who for some time formed the majority of the Country Party.

In 1922 the Lawson (Nationalist) ministry, lacking a majority in the Legislative Assembly, invited two members of the Farmers' Union to join a coalition. Neither side was satisfied with this arrangement and when, in 1924, a redistribution Bill was introduced, the Farmers' Union voted with Labour to defeat it. At the election that followed, Labour gained seven seats to become the largest party. A Nationalist ministry was formed by Peacock, but after less than three months in office it was defeated on a motion of no confidence by the combined votes of Labour and the Country Party (as it had now become). Peacock resigned and the Labour leader, G. M. Prendergast, formed a ministry supported by the Country Party. Within four months, the Nationalists and the C.P. had compounded their differences, and Prendergast was defeated on his Budget. In the composite ministry which then took office, John Allan, the C.P. leader, who had been a minister in the Lawson government, was Premier, and three other portfolios also went to the C.P.

The history of the Allan government was marked by friction over various matters, especially railway policy. The farmers were pressing the government to introduce differential freight charges in their favour on the state railways, at a time when the railways were in financial difficulties. In 1926, the Nationalist Minister for Railways, F. W. Eggleston, resigned his portfolio, which was then taken over by Allan himself. In the following year, three Nationalist members broke away to form the Victorian Liberal Party, and a breakaway Country group was formed under Dunstan, calling itself the Country Progressive Party. After the state elections had been held in 1927, these two groups, with seven members between them, held the balance in the Legislative Assembly. The new Labour leader, E. J. Hogan, who was himself a farmer, moved a vote of no confidence, which was supported by the two splinter groups. On the defeat of the government, Hogan formed a Labour administration which survived for sixteen months, promising to satisfy the demands both of the Liberals (who wanted electoral reform) and the Country Progressives, who wanted more government aid for small farmers. The ministry had no chance of achieving its objectives, as it had only six members in the Legislative Council, where the Liberals and Country Progressives were unrepresented. The immediate cause of its defeat was the rejection of an electoral reform Bill by the upper house.

A new twist to the situation came in 1935. In 1932, a composite U.A.P.-C.P. government had been formed under Sir Stanley Argyle. Allan was Deputy Premier and Dunstan was Minister for Lands, the Country Progressives having reunited with the Country Party in 1930. In 1933, on Allan's resignation, Dunstan became leader of the C.P. Before the 1935 election, it was agreed that the two government parties should support a joint ministerial policy, leaving Dunstan free to express the special objectives of his own party. As a result of the election, the Country Party won three seats from the U.A.P. and was consequently in a position to drive a harder bargain. Argyle offered Dunstan the post of Deputy Premier, which he accepted, but only a few days later the central council of the Country Party directed Country Party ministers to withdraw from the government. As soon as parliament assembled, Dunstan moved a vote of no confidence, which was carried with Labour support, and after some hesitation Argyle decided to resign. During the debate on the motion, Labour disclaimed any intention of forming an alliance with the Country Party, but finally agreed to support Dunstan in return for certain concessions. So was ushered in the unprecedented situation whereby a purely Country Party administration held office as the result of an alliance with one of the other parties in parliament. Its formation represented a triumph for the policy which Dunstan had espoused consistently ever since he entered politics, and to which he had finally succeeded in converting the majority of the Country Party. His tenure of office broke all records, as he remained Premier for an unbroken period from 1935 to 1942, and after a very brief intermission, again from 1942 to 1945.

The attitude of the A.L.P. in this transaction remains obscure. Had they refused to support Dunstan, the outcome could only have been another composite ministry, and presumably it was felt that Dunstan was the lesser evil. Whether he was or not can only be a matter of opinion, but there is little doubt that Labour's gain from the alliance was very meagre. Although it was apparent after only a short time that the C.P. could not be expected to introduce electoral reform, and that the parsimonious financial policy of the Dunstan government was doing little to promote economic recovery, the A.L.P. continued to support Dunstan for seven years. Victoria had, at the outbreak of war in 1939, the lowest rate of taxation in Australia, and the lowest expenditure on social services,[6] at a time when the U.A.P.-C.P. government of Stevens in New South Wales had gone to considerable lengths to 'prime the pump'. It is not surprising that Eggleston attacks the A.L.P. for its 'irresponsibility' in supporting Dunstan, and accuses it of nourishing 'hereditary feuds' against the Liberals.

By 1940, relations between Labour and the Country Party were becoming greatly strained, and the former's restiveness increased after Labour governments had come to power both in New South Wales and the Commonwealth in 1941. The Country Party began to look for new allies, especially after the emergence of T. T. Hollway as leader of the U.A.P. Dunstan's ascendency had increased the hostility of the U.A.P. towards the Country Party but Hollway, after becoming parliamentary leader of the U.A.P., advocated a more flexible policy with the ultimate object of achieving electoral reform. In 1942, when Labour finally withdrew its support for Dunstan, the U.A.P. agreed to keep Dunstan in office. However, the inevitable conflict over electoral reform, which had also been the immediate cause for Labour's withdrawal of support from Dunstan, soon broke out between the Country Party and the U.A.P. In September 1943, the Labour leader, John Cain, introduced a motion of no confidence. The U.A.P. thereupon decided to enter into negotiations for the formation of a composite ministry, but without result. The motion of no confidence, with some amendments, was put to the vote and the U.A.P. voted with Labour in support of it. Dunstan resigned, and the Governor commissioned Cain, whose party was the largest in parliament, to form a ministry. After only five days in office, the Country Party and a majority of U.A.P. members combined to defeat the Cain ministry on the adjournment. Dunstan was now forced to accept a composite ministry, with Hollway as Deputy Premier.[7]

After the end of the war in 1945, Macfarlan, the Attorney-General, resigned from the ministry and became leader of a group of dissident Liberal members who opposed the continuance of the composite ministry. Macfarlan was outspoken in his attacks on 'outside interests' who, by pressing the Liberals to remain in the ministry, were preventing the realization of any electoral reforms. During the supply debate in September 1945, Labour moved a

[6] Cf. H. P. Brown, 'Federal-State Financial Relations', in Sawer (ed.), *Federalism, An Australian Jubilee Study:* and a letter from a former Commissioner of Taxation, Mr L. S. Jackson, *S.M.H.,* 29 June 1959.
[7] *Age,* 31 August-18 September 1943.

series of hostile amendments, which were supported by the Macfarlan group. The government was twice defeated when the house divided, and after unsuccessfully attempting to reconstruct the ministry Dunstan handed his resignation to the Governor. After Cain had reported his failure to gain majority support in the Legislative Assembly, Hollway was summoned and failed, in his turn, to find a majority. The Governor then commissioned Macfarlan to form a caretaker government, which was granted a dissolution after it had obtained supply with the support of the Labour Party.[8]

The imbalance in Victorian politics remained. In 1947, an election resulted in the formation of a composite government under Hollway, followed by a series of attempts to resolve the instability of the political situation through a merger between the Liberals and the Country Party. In 1948, some Country Party M.P.s joined the Liberal Party, which thereupon changed its name to Liberal and Country Party (L.C.P.), but the majority of Country Party members refused to join the merger, which was also opposed by the central council. The L.C.P. remained anxious to secure an electoral redistribution, and the Country Party remained determined as ever to obstruct any redistribution which would inevitably reduce its importance and probably deprive it of its key position. After the election of 1950, the two parties failed to agree on a new composite administration, and as a result the Country Party, now led by J. G. B. McDonald, again allied itself with Labour to form an all-Country administration. This time, the Labour Party entered the alliance on condition that the government should introduce certain specific measures, including the establishment of a Greater Melbourne Council and a redistribution of electoral boundaries. In June 1952, the government finally refused to implement these two undertakings, and Labour withdrew its support. The L.C.P. agreed to support the McDonald government, but in the meantime a leadership crisis occurred which involved the deposition of Hollway and his replacement as L.C.P. leader by L. G. Norman. Hollway now insisted that he would support only a government pledged to introduce a redistribution based on federal electoral boundaries. (This redistribution, popularly called the 'two for one' scheme, involved the division of each federal electorate into two state electorates; as there were thirty-three federal electorates in Victoria, the size of the Legislative Assembly would become sixty-six, an increase of one.) He gathered round him a group of followers who styled themselves the

8 Ibid., 28 September-3 October 1945.

Electoral Reform League, and in September 1952 the group voted in support of Labour on a division in which the government was defeated. The A.L.P. and the Electoral Reform League then signed an agreement by which the A.L.P. undertook to support a government under Hollway pledged to bring in electoral reform. A month later, the Labour leader in the upper house introduced a resolution refusing supply to the McDonald ministry. With the support of two members of the Hollway group, this resolution was passed and a parliamentary deadlock ensued. The government had already obtained supply in the Assembly, and McDonald accordingly asked for a dissolution. The Governor summoned all the party leaders in turn. Norman, leader of the L.C.P., emphasized that he would continue to support the McDonald ministry. Hollway undertook to form a government which would obtain supply and pass an Act providing for a redistribution of seats on the 'two for one' basis. Cain stated that Labour support would be given only to a ministry headed by Hollway, to which Labour would grant supply on condition that it introduced an electoral reform Bill. The Governor finally decided to commission Hollway to form a ministry, but after less than three days in office the Government was defeated on a motion of no confidence and was refused a dissolution.[9] The Governor then recalled McDonald, commissioned him to form a government, and granted him a dissolution which resulted in the return of the Labour Party.

This series of events had some picturesque sidelights. During the early stages of the crisis, allegations were made that a group of city businessmen had approached Liberal members of parliament in an attempt to bribe them to vote against the McDonald ministry. These allegations were investigated by a Royal Commission, which held only one meeting and then adjourned indefinitely, on the grounds that the matter was beyond its jurisdiction because a libel action had been brought in a court of law. After his unsuccessful attempts to form a ministry, Hollway made attacks on 'outside interests' which had put pressure on members of the L.C.P. to prevent them from supporting him and thereby giving him a majority in the Assembly. The election campaign was marked by a remarkable degree of vituperation between the official L.C.P. and the followers of Hollway. Hollway himself left his electorate of Ballarat to oppose the L.C.P. leader, Norman, in the metropolitan electorate of Glen Iris, and won a resounding victory.

After the election, the Cain government brought down a Bill

9 Ibid., 23-31 October 1952.

for redistributing the electorates on the 'two for one' principle. The measure passed the Legislative Council because of the support of two members of the Hollway group (which later formed itself, perhaps with some consciousness of past history, into the Victorian Liberal Party). The 1955 election, which was the first to be fought on the new electoral boundaries, resulted in an absolute majority for the L.C.P. for the first time since 1932, and a reduction in Country Party representation. It appeared that Victoria, like the other states, had entered a period of stable governments.

18

FEDERAL NON-LABOUR GOVERNMENTS

WITH FEW EXCEPTIONS, conservative governments in the Commonwealth sphere have been coalitions or composite ministries, their careers marked by internal dissensions which have, on several important occasions, culminated in their downfall. Until 1909 there were, in Deakin's phrase, 'three elevens' in the field and governmental stability depended on alliances like those between Deakin and the Labour Party, or coalitions like the Reid-McLean ministry, where the Free Trade Party led by Reid combined with some of Deakin's more conservative followers. The 'Fusion' ministry of 1909-10 was little more than a nervous alliance between groups whose views conflicted on several questions of major policy. Deakin himself observed wryly that behind him sat all his political opponents since federation, and some members of the conservative faction, who distrusted Deakin's radicalism, preferred to sit on the cross-benches. A contemporary writer observed that although the fusion was officially described as 'Liberal', it was really a conservative party, 'led by men who are the bitterest enemies of Mr. Deakin and his party'.[1]

The formation of the Fusion ministry was attacked with great bitterness and vehemence in parliament, especially by Deakin's former colleague Sir William Lyne, who made Deakin's life embarrassing by interjecting 'Judas' whenever Deakin entered the chamber. In a speech garnished with details of discussions inside cabinet, Lyne accused Sir John Forrest, one of the leading conservative members of the ministry, of being the 'baneful influence', which had impelled Deakin to enter the Fusion.[2] He gave circumstantial stories about intrigues conducted by Forrest at various periods, accusing him of being responsible for the resignation of C. C. Kingston in 1903 and of trying to induce followers of Deakin to preserve the Reid-McLean government. Labour members were equally caustic in their criticism, all the more since the formation of the Fusion had led to the fall of the Fisher ministry which had previously been kept in office by Deakin's support. F. G. Tudor deplored the fact that the intrigues of Deakin and Cook had de-

---

[1] Quoted by Crisp, *The Parliamentary Government of the Commonwealth*, p.124. [2] *Parl. Deb.* (C. of A.), 1909, 50: 1010-32.

stroyed the 'sincerity' which had distinguished Australian politics. 'The terms of the coalition are that the Cookites approve Mr. Deakin's policy, and that Mr. Deakin makes no attempt to carry it out; but, of course, the real purpose of the coalition is to get into office.'[3] One of Deakin's followers who refused to support the Fusion, G. H. Wise, alleged that Deakin had originally said he would not accept the leadership of a non-Labour coalition. According to this account, Reid had then proposed Cook as leader, but the latter, realizing that the Liberals would not join a coalition unless Deakin were its leader, had proposed the latter. In all this, Deakin had been made the puppet of men like Forrest whose sole anxiety was to gain office.[4]

A brief interlude of tranquillity followed in 1913, when Cook was Prime Minister of a Liberal government following Deakin's departure from politics, but a fresh series of convulsions occurred after the split in the Labour Party in 1916. After Hughes had left the party, he at first formed a government consisting only of former Labour men, but his minority position in the House of Representatives was too precarious to last. In the meantime, negotiations had been going on for the formation of a new party which would bring together Hughes and the Liberals. The National Federation, as the new party was known, was launched at a meeting in the Melbourne Town Hall to which admission was by invitation only; the names of those invited were selected from lists drawn up by Hughes and his principal collaborators, one of whom was J. C. Watson, first Labour Prime Minister of the Commonwealth. Another was Peter Airey, who had been parliamentary leader of the Labour Party in Queensland and a minister in the Kidston government. On 17 February 1917, Hughes resigned and requested a new commission from the Governor-General, which was immediately issued. He then formed his third government, which included six Liberals and five ex-Labour men.

After the federal election of May 1917, resulting in the return of the Nationalist ministry, and a second referendum on conscription, the rumblings of discontent made themselves heard. The conservative members of the government, led by Sir William Irvine and W. A. Watt, were opposed to Hughes' policy of not introducing conscription unless it were accepted at a referendum. A group of Western Australian members, led by Sir John Forrest, were discontented with Hughes, and Forrest himself aspired to become Prime Minister. In the early days of 1917, he told the Press that at a cabinet meeting he had refused 'to place himself unre-

3 Ibid., 1909, 49: 1172-3.   4 Ibid., 1909, 49: 1174.

servedly in Mr. Hughes' hands'.[5] Despite these dissensions, a party meeting lasting five hours passed by sixty-three votes to two a resolution expressing its confidence in Hughes, and declaring that 'in the best interests of country and Empire, Mr. Hughes should retain the leadership of the party'.[6]

Dissension was not stilled and a New South Wales member, W. H. Kelly, who had been a minister in the Cook government and was a supporter of Irvine, put forward a proposal that a Nationalist government be formed under a stop-gap leader, for which post he nominated G. H. Wise. At an adjourned meeting of the party, moves to replace Hughes continued, and a motion was introduced urging that the government should resign and that Austin Chapman (who had been a minister in several governments from 1903 to 1908) should be asked to form a ministry. An amendment to leave the matter in the hands of the government, which was in effect a negative of the motion, was then moved and carried with only seven dissentients. Strengthened by this support, Hughes waited on the Governor-General, and tendered his resignation. The Governor-General, Sir Ronald Munro-Ferguson, asked him to continue as Prime Minister pending the issue of a new commission; Hughes gave no advice as to a possible successor. Munro-Ferguson then interviewed a large number of party leaders, the last one being Forrest, who was closeted with His Excellency for two hours, during which he pressed his own claim to become Prime Minister. According to Munro-Ferguson's own account, Forrest treated the Nationalist Party's vote of confidence in Hughes (for which he had also voted) 'as "une politesse", having no practical significance. He denounced the Prime Minister's autocratic ways, frequently reiterated the phrase aut Caesar aut nihil, his want of method in the conduct of affairs, and asserted that all real business was hung up in favour of limelight exhibitions on the platform.'[7] Munro-Ferguson apparently toyed with the idea of commissioning Forrest, but was assured emphatically by Cook and Watt that there was no chance of Forrest obtaining sufficient support. In the evening of the same day, he accordingly sent for Hughes and commissioned him to form a new government.

This manoeuvre, whose outcome Hughes must have guessed in advance, enabled him to fulfil his election pledge not to carry on without a vote of confidence from the electors, while simultaneously retaining his Prime Ministership. Justifying his actions in parliament, he declared that he had fulfilled his pledge, stressed

5 Scott, *Australia During the War*, pp.431-2.
6 Ibid., p.432. 7 Ibid., p.434.

that the Governor-General had 'exhausted every effort to obtain information as to the state of the House', and had then come back to Hughes and asked him to accept the commission. Tudor, the Labour leader, moved a vote of no confidence in Hughes for the handling of the affair, which was defeated by forty-three votes to nineteen. Hughes now proceeded to remove the embarrassment of Forrest's presence in the ministry by the unprecedented expedient of putting his name forward for a peerage. Forrest retired from the ministry so that he could take his seat in the House of Lords, but died at sea before he reached England. He was replaced by W. A. Watt, and in addition Hughes appointed four assistant ministers on whose support he could rely.

Hughes was now firmly in the saddle, but he continued to suffer from the heterogeneity of his cabinet and his party, while his dictatorial mode of behaviour intensified the antagonisms that already existed towards him. His autocratic habits were particularly evident in his handling of the Commonwealth Shipping Line which he had been responsible for establishing in 1916, and the wheat pool which he had organized during the war for the bulk shipment of wheat to Britain. The members of his cabinet were suspicious of him and his trips abroad were the subject of particular concern. When he left to attend the Imperial War Conference in London in April 1918, Cook, who was Minister for the Navy, accompanied him—according to one account—so that he could watch Hughes on behalf of the cabinet.[8] When, not long afterwards, he went abroad to attend the Versailles Peace Conference, there was suspicion among ministers that he intended to make some shipping deals without informing cabinet. Hughes, aware of the disquiet among his ministers, left Sydney by train ostensibly to embark in Melbourne for his voyage to London. However, he alighted from the train *en route* to Melbourne, doubled back to Sydney and embarked on the *Niagara*, travelling to London by way of the Pacific. The reason for this stratagem became apparent when it transpired that Sir Denison Miller, Governor of the Commonwealth Bank, was also a passenger on the *Niagara*. The acting Prime Minister, Watt, suspecting that Hughes was up to something, then cabled him requesting that no financial commitments should be made without the approval of the Treasury. Hughes gave a non-committal reply, and while he was abroad did in fact sell some of the Commonwealth ships without consulting the ministry. Watt was then authorized by a meeting of cabinet to inform Hughes that they did not approve of his taking this action without consultation.[9]

8 Crisp, op. cit., p.198.   9 *Parl. Deb.* (C. of A.), 1920, 94: 5801-2.

The antagonism between Hughes and Watt, which dated back to the early years of the war, flared up in a celebrated incident when Watt, who had been sent abroad to conduct negotiations with the British government, resigned from cabinet while still in London, after the disclosure that Hughes had cabled directly to the British government without informing Watt or instructing him to modify his stand in the negotiations. Hughes took the precaution of giving his own version of the incident at great length in parliament while Watt was still abroad, and by the time Watt returned to defend his action the impression was fairly general that he had behaved like a prima donna and deserved little sympathy.[10] Watt, for his part, delivered a bitter attack on Hughes when he returned to Australia, accusing him of conducting business behind his back and of giving an *ex parte* account of their correspondence. He explained that he had already had some discussion with the British Ministry of Munitions concerning the Australian share in the sale of the wartime wool clip, but in the meantime Hughes had sent further cables directly to the British government

> as if I were not in London . . . I was nonplussed when I heard from the press that the Prime Minister had been developing problems so intimately connected with my mission without my knowledge . . . never for a moment did I imagine that he would communicate those proposals direct to the British Government, and ignore the presence in London of the man who had been sent there to deal with them.[11]

He was critical of Hughes for comparing the position with the protest which he had sent to Hughes in the preceding year about the sale of ships. He also denied Hughes' allegation that the Press had been informed about his resignation before the news was cabled to Hughes. This, he alleged, was a manoeuvre on Hughes' part to make his conduct appear reprehensible.

Hughes did not take these remarks quietly, and in his turn attacked Watt for high-handedness and for his insistence on being given plenary authority. 'He insisted upon greater authority than it is possible, under representative government, to give a Minister who represents his Government abroad.'[12] With conscious virtue, he described himself as Watt's 'protector' in cabinet, where the latter's highhandedness had given rise to frequent trouble. The Country Party leader, W. J. McWilliams, called for a plague on

[10] *Age*, 21 October 1920, remarked that the clash between Hughes and Watt would have come sooner or later, mission or no mission.
[11] *Parl. Deb.* (C. of A.), 1920, 94: 5793.   [12] Ibid., 1920, 94: 5810.

both their houses. Hughes was to blame for sending a cable to the United Kingdom which had wrecked Watt's mission, when it should have been sent to Watt himself with a request that he pass it on to the Colonial Secretary. Watt was to blame for reacting so sharply, instead of simply informing Hughes that the cable had made his position impossible. He also regretted that cabinet business of this sort should have been brought before parliament and not simply submitted to a party meeting.[13]

As the life of the Hughes government wore on, pressures mounted on it from various directions. With the end of the war, Hughes' policies evoked discontent among a number of powerful groups that supported the Nationalist Party. His difficulties were typical of the dilemma of a conservative Prime Minister who depends on the support of a heterogeneous collection of interests. The high tariff of 1921 alienated pastoral and commercial interests; the manufacturers, who supported the tariff, were suspicious about Hughes' attitude to industrial arbitration; the shipping interests opposed his policy of a government shipping line; and conservative groups in general opposed his attempt to extend Commonwealth powers by a referendum in 1919. When Cook resigned in 1921 to become High Commissioner in London, the National Union was able to force Hughes to replace him with S. M. Bruce, a comparative newcomer to politics, who belonged to a prominent commercial family in Melbourne.[14] In 1922, with the approach of a general election, a group broke away from the National Union to form the Liberal Union, which its supporters hoped would be strong enough to replace the Hughes government by an alliance with the Country Party. Although this scheme misfired, pressure from the National Union seems to have been instrumental in Hughes' resignation early in 1923.[15]

The immediate cause of Hughes' downfall was the refusal of the Country Party, which had entered federal politics in 1919, to support any government of which he was the leader. Country Party members were particularly hostile to Hughes for his management of the wheat pool and for regulations fixing the price of meat which he had issued in 1918.

During the Budget debate in 1920, a Victorian Country Party member, W. C. Hill, quoted lengthy extracts from the minutes of the Wheat Board, of which he and Hughes were both members, to show that Hughes was committing Australia to lose money on

13 Ibid., 1920, 94: 5814.
14 B. D. Graham, 'Finance Committees in Non-Labor Politics 1910-30'. *Australian Journal of Politics and History,* 1960, vol. 6, no. 1.   15 Ibid.

the sale of wheat to Great Britain.[16] It was inevitable that Hughes should resist the demands of the farmers for the sale of wheat at higher prices, as this would infallibly have caused the domestic price of bread and flour to rise. Hill's attack on Hughes was symptomatic of the whole period, which was also marked by attempts on the part of the Labour Party to manoeuvre the Country Party into supporting motions of censure and no confidence in the government. Adroit parliamentary tactics were successful in averting this embarrassing possibility.

The years 1921 and 1922 saw Hughes making repeated efforts to meet the Country Party half way. His first step, in 1921, was to offer to take the Country Party into coalition. The offer was rejected, and a motion introduced in the Country Party caucus that the party should join the coalition if it were given a majority of portfolios, as well as the Prime Ministership, was defeated. The federal election of 1922 brought about a crisis. The Nationalists gained twenty-nine seats in the House of Representatives, and in addition had the support of three independents. Although they still had an absolute majority in the Senate, the vote meant that the Country Party now held the balance of power in the lower house. Labour won nine seats at the election, raising its numbers to twenty-nine and the Country Party increased its representation to fourteen. A meeting of the parliamentary Country Party issued a statement declaring that the results of the election were a 'distinct vote of censure by the people upon the present administration',[17] and it was plain that the Country Party felt itself in a position to drive a hard bargain. Hughes' first reaction to the election results was a policy of masterly inactivity. He refrained from calling cabinet for a whole month after the elections, but finally had to do so because five of his ministers had been defeated at the polls and would automatically lose their portfolios after the lapse of three months following the dissolution of parliament. The defeated ministers having returned their commissions, an approach was made by the Nationalists to the Country Party, which appointed its leader, Dr Earle Page (who had replaced McWilliams in 1921), its deputy leader, Gibson, and the party Whip, Stewart, as its negotiators. They were instructed that the party would insist on preserving its separate identity and that Hughes' retirement was an absolute precondition for any coalition. They offered four alternatives: a Nationalist ministry led by someone other than

16 *Parl. Deb.* (C. of A.), 1920, 92: 2241-7.
17 Ellis, 'History of the Country Party', the *New South Wales Countryman*, March 1948.

Hughes, which the Country Party would agree to support; a composite ministry, in which both parties retained their separate identities, to be led by a member of the Country Party; a composite ministry led by a Nationalist, with the Country Party having seven portfolios; or, finally, a coalition of 'equals' on the pattern of the Reid-McLean government.[18] The Country Party managers were also instructed that detailed agreement about portfolios should not be a condition of negotiations, and that agreement on a composite government or on an alliance depended upon a satisfactory programme of government policy.

In reply, the Nationalists tried to insist that the demand for the retirement of Hughes be dropped as a condition for a Nationalist-Country Party combination. Page's response to this was a public statement that Hughes must go, followed by a resolution of the Country Party caucus that it would not support any ministry in which Hughes was a member.[19] Hughes himself had already refused to resign in order to make way for another Nationalist who would lead an all-Nationalist ministry acceptable to the Country Party. He offered, however, to support a Country Party ministry led by Page. The latter had, in the meantime, been in close touch with Bruce, Treasurer in the Hughes government, with whom he had conversations at the home of J. G. Latham, a Victorian Nationalist member who later became Attorney-General in the Bruce government.[20] On 2 February 1923, after receiving a visit from his old associate Senator Pearce, Hughes advised the Governor-General to send for Bruce.[21] The latter was summoned, asked for time to ascertain whether he could form a ministry, and after consulting Page advised that he could do so. Hughes' resignation was accepted on 9 February.

The Bruce-Page Ministry

There is some discrepancy in accounts of the balance of forces within the Bruce-Page government, as it became generally known. The Press reported an agreement that cabinet, which comprised eleven members, would act only on policy decisions which were approved by more than six members of cabinet. This reported 'six to five' agreement appears to have misled some writers into the belief that five of the portfolios in the cabinet were held by

---

18 A. N. Smith, *Thirty Years*, p.247.   19 Ibid., p.248.

20 Latham had been elected in 1922 with the support of the Liberal Union.

21 Pearce came to see Hughes at his country home at Sassafras, in the Dandenong Ranges outside Melbourne, and apparently informed him of the National Union's decision to support Bruce for the Prime Ministership; cf. Smith, loc. cit.

the Country Party.[22]   In fact, that party held four: Treasurer, Postmaster-General, Minister of Works and Railways, Vice-President of the Executive Council, and one senator became an honorary minister. Contemporary newspaper reports provide the only evidence for the 'six to five' agreement. A procedure was, however, adopted to ensure agreement on policy. In effect, this was to be that all major questions would be presented to cabinet only after they had been discussed between Bruce and Page.[23] Ellis's account asserts that 'equal power in the Cabinet was conceded' to the Country Party.[24]

The Bruce-Page administration was, indeed, notable for the influence of the Country Party. The government was responsible for reorganizing the postal administration, with an extension of rural services and a reduction of country telephone charges. A board was established to direct the activities of the Commonwealth Bank, with heavy representation from primary producers. The first marketing boards for controlling the export of primary products were set up, under the control of the producers themselves. The wartime wheat and wool pools were wound up. A scheme for stabilizing prices in the butter industry, worked out by the dairy farmers, was adopted by the government. A primary producers' representative was appointed to the Tariff Board, set up by the Hughes government in 1921. A scheme of grants-in-aid for the construction of roads in rural areas was introduced. The holders of leases of Crown Land were relieved of the necessity to pay land tax. A rural credits department of the Commonwealth Bank was established. Country Party influence was also evident in some major policy acts of the Bruce government such as the attempt, in 1926, to give the Commonwealth increased powers by a constitutional referendum. The financial policy of the government was largely determined by Page as Treasurer. Nevertheless, it is fallacious to assume, as many contemporary political observers did, that the policy of the government was entirely dominated by the Country Party. Bruce was a strong Prime Minister and not a man to accept dictation easily. Moreover, although the Country Party had come into existence partly as a response to the

22 The Australian volume of the *Cambridge History of the British Empire* reports both the agreement and the allocation of portfolios, p.607, as do Overacker, *The Australian Party System,* p.230, and Crisp, op. cit., p.198. The allocation of portfolios is correctly stated by Ellis, loc. cit., and Sawer, *Australian Federal Politics and Law 1901-1929,* p.227.

23 The evidence for this is a letter written by Bruce to Page (with some characteristic spelling mistakes!) which is in the possession of Mr Ulrich Ellis.   24 Ellis, loc. cit.

acceptance of high tariffs as the settled national policy, it was obliged to acquiesce in a very marked increase in tariff protection during the 1920s, an increase so marked that the government found it necessary to appoint a committee of investigation to decide whether tariff levels were not too high. Other accusations of 'outside influence' on the government were plentiful during the campaign preceding the 1926 referendum. Sections of both the Labour movement and the Nationalist Party were opposed to the referendum, on the grounds that it was in fact a plot to gain advantages for particular interests. An editorial in the *Worker* alleged that Mr Bruce was not the author of the referendum proposals, which had been devised by a more ingenious intelligence. He was, the editorial continued, 'acting at the instigation of the Inner Council of the Capitalist class—of those rich men who meet in Melbourne in conspiratorial secrecy, and issue commands which Bruce and his colleagues dare not disobey'.[25] The amendment of the constitution was simply a device to consolidate the class ascendency of this group (obviously the National Union). The editorial chose to ignore the fact that a leading member of the 'capitalist class', Sir Arthur Robinson,[26] was one of the principal opponents of the referendum. Bruce, nettled by talk of this kind and also by allegations that he was acting as the puppet of the Labour movement, which by some species of superior cunning had persuaded the government to introduce these obnoxious proposals, described attacks on him as 'panic talk' and declared forcibly: 'No individual or body controls my Government and there is no one I cannot say, "go to hell!" to.'[27]

Accusations of pressure from the National Union were current also in connection with the Crimes Act of 1926. In the previous year, an attempt by the government to deport the leaders of the Seamen's Union, Walsh and Johnson, had been invalidated by a High Court judgment which bore on certain aspects of the exercise of the executive power.[28] At the general election in 1925, the dangers of 'Bolshevism' had figured prominently in the Nationalist campaign, a leading part in which was played by the president of the National Union, Sir William McBeath.[29] Early in 1926, when

[25] 25 August 1926; quoted in D. Carboch and A. Wildavsky, *Studies in Australian Politics*, pp.95-6.
[26] Sir Arthur Robinson, a lawyer and company director, had been a minister in several Victorian governments and was a spokesman for the Associated Chambers of Manufactures.
[27] Quoted in the *Australian Worker*, 25 August 1926; cf. *Argus*, 21 August 1926.
[28] *Ex parte Walsh and Johnson, in re Yates* (1925), 37 C.L.R. 36.
[29] Sir William McBeath, K.B.E., was a leading merchant in Melbourne

the Crimes Bill had been presented to the first sitting of the new parliament, he cut short a holiday voyage to press for the inclusion of certain provisions in the legislation. Bruce refused to let McBeath have an advance copy of the Bill, and even after the latter had managed to obtain one he found Bruce deaf to his suggestions. After a long interview Bruce was overheard to exclaim, 'I am committed to the party and the country', to which McBeath replied: 'Very well. You know what that attitude means.'[30] The Act was passed in its original form despite this hint, and although Press rumours of a cloak-and-dagger conspiracy to oust the government continued for some time, Bruce remained comfortably in office for a further three and a half years.

The spectacle of the first composite ministry in Australian political history was the subject of acrimony from political groups on all sides. In a parliamentary debate shortly after the installation of the government, Labour members accused the Country Party leaders of being 'hungry for office'. They had sought power, according to the Labour leader in the Senate, Albert Gardiner, 'with the activity and spirit of a fox terrier after a rabbit'. Page, he said, was flouting all the conventions of cabinet government by saying in a speech at Grafton that if the Country Party did not secure its objectives 'they would be able to pull out just like an army corps, with their lines of communication and all their forces intact'. Gardiner went on to ask how Page could, with a clear conscience, make such a speech

> after the Cabinet had been formed and its members had sat around the Cabinet table? He preferred to pose before the electors as a narrow party man rather than as a Minister who had taken the oath to administer the laws and who, by virtue of his acceptance of office, accepted the policy of the Prime Minister under whom he served.

The formation of the government was 'the most discreditable piece of bargaining, intriguing and huckstering for office that has ever disgraced' any government anywhere.

Gardiner made play with Page's professional role as a surgeon. He had, Gardiner declared, 'cut the guts out of the Nationalist party' and added: 'It does look as if an anaesthetic had been administered to the Nationalist party, rendering them unfit for fur-

---

who had served in various public capacities. He was chairman of the Victorian State Savings Bank Commissioners, a delegate to the League of Nations Assembly, 1924, and chairman of the Royal Commission on Navy and Defence Administration, 1917-18.
[30] Graham, loc. cit.

ther service as His Majesty's Government, though possibly useful as attendants on the Sultan of Turkey.'[31]

In the House of Representatives, Blakeley remarked that Hughes had been 'taken to the bathroom, where his political throat had been cut'.[32] Anstey recalled a speech made by Bruce only a few months earlier pledging his loyalty to Hughes, and asserting that if Hughes were put out he would go out with him. He recalled that in this speech Bruce had named Hughes as the only man whom he regarded as capable of governing Australia, apart from W. A. Watt. He had also attacked the Country Party, referring to Page as the leader of a party of men of paralysed intelligence. The mental paralysis of the government had now been confirmed by the absence of any policy in the Governor-General's speech. A South Australian member described the composite ministry as a 'morganatic marriage', and Scullin, later Prime Minister, likened Bruce and Page to Siamese twins. He recalled the allegation by Page that Nationalist policy under Hughes was socialism disguised by a fig-leaf, although at the same time he had called for continuation of the wheat pool. 'The fig-leaf Socialists,' Scullin said, 'have now combined with the Wheat Pool Socialists, and they are one in opposition to Socialism.' The Labour member for Melbourne, Dr Maloney, recalled that a leading member of the Nationalist Party, Sir Granville Ryrie, had called Page a 'blob' in an election speech, and produced a cartoon from a Melbourne newspaper showing Bruce in the character of Svengali with Page as Trilby. The picture, he said, should be reversed.[33]

It was not only the Labour Party which disapproved of this apparently unnatural union. Stresses soon developed within the government parties themselves, and the history of the ministry was marked by a series of resignations over various matters of policy and administration. In 1925 P. G. Stewart, the leading figure in the Country Party in Victoria, resigned from the ministry after an election pact had been announced by which sitting members of either party would not be opposed by members of the other party. Stewart refused to accept this pact and resigned. (In the following year, he left the Country Party and formed a breakaway group, the Country Progressive Party, whose state wing was led by A. A. Dunstan.) Stewart was a member for a wheat-growing electorate, and retained considerable support among the wheat farmers, who were particularly antagonistic to the high tariff policies supported alike by the Nationalists and the Labour Party.

31 *Parl. Deb.* (C. of A.), 1923, 102: 47-63.
32 Ibid., 1923, 102: 18-19.   33 Ibid., 1923, 102: 72-109.

In a speech on the Budget in 1927, he launched a bitter attack on Page, whom he accused of 'stabbing him in the back' in his own constituency. He also accused other Country Party ministers of 'ratting' on their own principles by accepting a high tariff, and by dropping their demands for the establishment of new states (which Page had once declared to be the most important issue in Australian politics). In 1921, he recalled, present Country Party ministers had attacked the Nationalists as profiteers and spendthrifts, and the most outspoken of all had been Page, who had described the Nationalists as 'looters and burglars'. It was now the Country Party which deserved these unflattering epithets. It had made a 'base political surrender' to the Nationalists; it had become a 'kept party'; it was a 'spurious' party that had betrayed its own supporters, the primary producers. He recalled the circumstances under which he had joined the Bruce-Page government.

> I was in the Ministry as the result of appeals by ... the Treasurer. I agreed to a certain party arrangement for the sake of the party, but I was never in favour of it. Before I joined the Ministry I was candid enough to go to the Prime Minister and to tell him that I was accepting the portfolio only in ... the interests of the party ... when the day came that I could be loyal to it no longer I would hand in my resignation.[34]

Stewart's attack on the Budget was joined by several other Nationalist members and by Stewart's supporters from the Victorian wheat electorates. A slashing criticism of Page was delivered by H. S. Gullett, a Victorian Nationalist member, who reminded his audience that Page, before becoming a minister, had made sweeping attacks on governmental extravagance. Nevertheless, he had turned out to be even more extravagant and to pay for this extravagance he was increasing the burdens of those least able to bear them by increasing indirect taxation in proportion to direct taxation. Three-quarters of the government's revenue was now being raised by indirect taxes, 'a policy that is inimical to the majority of the Australian people and the interests of our nation, and particularly to the primary producers whom he represents in this House'. He went on:

> I say, frankly, to the Treasurer, that if he cannot devise a better financial policy for this country, the sooner he gets out of the job the better ... I make that statement as a Nationalist member sitting behind the Treasurer, whom I do not recognize as my leader, but merely as the leader of the Country Party.

34 Ibid., 1927, 116: 1496-8.

I have made it clear that I am opposed to the Treasurer's policy, root and branch. I regard him as the most tragic Treasurer that Australia has ever known.

Gullett's speech reflected the recurrent ambiguity in the relations between the two non-Labour parties, especially as he declared that he 'repudiated' Page as his leader, but retained 'a deep personal respect for him'.[35]

The fall of the Bruce-Page ministry came about in 1929, when, to the dissident Country Party and Nationalist members who already formed a harassing force on the government's flank, there was added a small group led by Hughes who were opposed to the government's policy of reconstructing the industrial arbitration system so that federal authority over industrial disputes would be reduced. Hughes was thus able to turn the wheel full circle and expel from power the party which had been responsible for his downfall almost seven years earlier. As a result of the refusal of the Speaker, Sir Littleton Groom, to exercise his vote in favour of the government, the ministry was defeated by a single vote in committee and parliament was dissolved. During the debate on the Maritime Industries Bill, which was to put into effect the government's policy on arbitration, many past misdeeds of the ministry were disinterred. Particular interest attaches to the speech made by W. M. Marks, member for the New South Wales seat of Wentworth, who had been Parliamentary Under-Secretary for Foreign Affairs under Hughes in 1922. Marks, who had business connections with the entertainment industry, attacked the government both on its arbitration policy and on its proposed increase in amusement tax. He condemned Bruce for making policy decisions without consulting the party, and criticized Bruce's statement that, although the Bill was not part of the Nationalist Party's platform, some latitude must be allowed to the leader of the nation. Though Marks conceded that this was so, he added: 'When he [the Prime Minister] brings down major matters to this House his party should be consulted.'[36] Although the increase in amusement tax was part of the Budget, on which cabinet did not normally consult the party, the tax proposal was exceptional because a Royal Commission had only recently reported on the motion picture industry and had not advocated any increase in amusement tax.

The Lyons Governments

The resulting election campaign led to the return of the Scullin

35 Ibid., 1927, 116: 1491-5.   36 Ibid., 1929, 121: 860-3.

Labour government. Bruce himself was defeated, and did not figure in the negotiations which took place in 1931 for the formation of a new composite ministry in the event of an election victory. The political situation in that year was particularly confused, fissures having appeared both in the Labour and Nationalist Parties. The Nationalist Party in New South Wales had been overshadowed by the 'All for Australia League', formed largely as a reaction to the policies of the Lang government. In 1931 the United Australia Party emerged out of this welter and J. A. Lyons, who had been Tasmanian Labour Premier and later Postmaster-General in the Scullin government, became federal parliamentary leader in place of J. G. Latham, Attorney-General in the Bruce-Page government and Leader of the Opposition following Bruce's election defeat. The choice of Lyons was evidently, as in the case of Bruce, the result of pressure from the National Union. Eggleston was clearly referring to this when he wrote:

> On one occasion the leaders of the background organization told the head of a party facing an election, who was supposed to have no popular appeal, that unless he handed over the leadership to someone else, the funds would not be forthcoming. I do not know whether the story is true or not, but the person selected by the organization actually did lead, rather to the misfortune of Australia.[37]

By the latter half of 1931, the defeat of the Scullin government seemed a foregone conclusion, and the U.A.P. and the Country Party began to concert plans for a united election policy. A 'unity' conference was held at the end of October, which adopted a joint programme including an agreed policy on tariffs, the establishment of new states, and the elimination of overlapping functions between Commonwealth and state governments. By far the most important question at issue between the two parties was the tariff. To combat unemployment, the Scullin government had imposed unprecedentedly high tariffs on an enormous range of imported goods, and had thereby incurred the great hostility of the farming community. However, the U.A.P. was supported by manufacturing interests who were concerned to maintain high tariffs. The

[37] *Reflections of an Australian Liberal*, pp.135-6. In a series of articles in the *Sun-Herald*, Sydney, in 1959, the former Clerk of the House of Representatives, Mr F. C. Green, makes similar statements about the manner in which Lyons became leader of the U.A.P. It has been suggested to me privately that some leading members of the Associated Chambers of Manufactures in Melbourne had become friendly with Lyons in 1930, and that his decision to leave the Labour Party was the result of an offer to make him leader of a new non-Labour Party.

compromise reached at the unity conference was that the Scullin tariff should be revised on 'scientific' lines, that only 'efficient' local industry be encouraged, and that a series of reciprocal trade treaties be negotiated. A joint advisory council was formed early in December to supervise the election campaign.

After the unity conference, misgivings were expressed by manufacturers' organizations about the effects of this agreement. Lyons then hedged the joint policy by emphasizing that the U.A.P. was not a low tariff party. In his policy speech at the Sydney Town Hall in December, he reminded his listeners that the U.A.P. was the heir of the Liberal party, which had been responsible for Australia's adoption of protection, and recalled that the U.A.P. had not objected to the Scullin government's emergency tariff proposals. He promised that the very high tariffs imposed by the Scullin ministry would be submitted to the Tariff Board for review, and that there would be no arbitrary ministerial decisions on tariff questions. Simultaneously, Page was proposing that immediate reductions should be made and that all tariffs must be ratified by parliament. He described the Scullin tariff as a 'Frankenstein monster'.[38]

On 15 December, four days before the election, Lyons made a speech at a dinner given to him by the Associated Chambers of Manufactures. He refuted Scullin's allegation that he intended to let the existing tariff schedules lapse, repeating that they would not be altered simply by ministerial action. All tariff charges would first be referred to the Tariff Board and would have to be ratified by parliament. The Country Party promptly described this speech as a 'stab in the back'.

The election resulted in a landslide victory for the U.A.P., but although Lyons was now in a position to negotiate from strength, he continued to state his hope that the Country Party would join forces with him. Page, accompanied by T. W. Paterson, deputy leader of the party, conferred with Lyons and Latham, and a joint statement was issued on 31 December. Page had insisted that the portfolio of Trade and Customs be given to a Country Party minister; Lyons, not surprisingly, had refused. He also refused a Country Party proposal that tariff revision should be conducted with the 1928 tariff schedules as a basis instead of those inherited from Scullin. After the breakdown of these negotiations, Page hinted darkly that the government might not long be in office, and blamed the Associated Chambers of Manufactures and

38 Ellis, 'History of the Country Party', the *New South Wales Countryman,* January 1949.

the Melbourne *Herald* for declaring the Country Party 'black'.[39] (The mention of the *Herald* was a reference to the fact that its editor, Sir Keith Murdoch, was generally believed to be a prime mover in the installation of Lyons at the head of the U.A.P.)

When parliament assembled, the Country Party immediately launched its promised attacks on the tariff policy of the government. In October 1932, Lyons tried to relieve the situation by offering to take the Country Party into a composite ministry. He wrote to Page, offering him three portfolios, on condition that the Country Party ministers should be selected by Lyons, that the government's policy would continue to be as laid down during the election campaign, that the parties should have joint meetings on major policy questions, and that the Country Party should approve the policy of the government on the Ottawa Agreement. In reply to the Country Party's offer to negotiate, Lyons replied in a manner which made it clear that this was a 'package' offer. Page then replied, in a letter refusing to accept Lyons' demand that he should have the right to select Country Party ministers.

> If this Party is to retain its separate existence, selection must be made after consultation with the Leader of the Country Party . . . the Country Party is prepared to co-operate in the business of government subject to definite and clear understandings about policy and satisfactory safeguards for its continued existence.[40]

Lyons' reply was that he was not prepared to give a guarantee against any future merger of the parties.

It was observed at the time that this entire exchange was carried out by letter, although the offices of Lyons and Page in Parliament House were only a few yards apart, and that while it was going on Bruce, in a speech to the visiting English Test cricket team, had advocated the settling of arguments by face-to-face discussion.

Lyons returned to the question of a merger in June 1934, when a federal election was approaching, stressing that 'the only permanent and satisfactory solution is a complete union of the two parties'. Page refused to consider the suggestion, and in the end an electoral pact was concluded with only one definite agreement on policy—the setting up of an Australian Agricultural Council and a more active policy of rural development. The election campaign resulted in the loss of nine seats by the non-Labour parties. The

[39] *Australian National Review,* January 1932; cf. *S.M.H.,* 1 January 1932.
[40] Ellis, 'History of the Country Party', the *Countryman* (New South Wales), June 1949.

U.A.P. was reduced to thirty-two members in the House of Representatives; the Country Party, after losing one seat, had fifteen members. A composite ministry was now unavoidable, and a long series of negotiations began. Lyons wired to Page asking the Country Party to take an 'active share of responsibility for stable government'. He offered Page three posts, including one of assistant minister. When this was refused, Lyons made what he described as a 'final offer', comprising three posts in cabinet, one of which was now to be the vice-presidency of the Executive Council. The Country Party was to nominate its own ministers subject to veto by the Prime Minister. Portfolios would be allotted by the latter, who would also determine the order of precedence of ministers. He also offered the Country Party the post of Speaker, or failing that of Chairman of Committees, and gave some vague assurances about tariff policies. Page continued to insist on more definite assurances about tariffs, demanded that representation in cabinet should be proportional to strength in the House of Representatives, and that the Country Party leader should be Deputy Prime Minister. At the beginning of November, 'final finality' was reached when Lyons acceded to all the Country Party's demands. Page became Minister for Commerce and Deputy Prime Minister. The Country Party also received the portfolio of Interior (which included Works), and two other Country Party members were made assistant ministers. Lyons tried to insist that, despite Page's position as Deputy Prime Minister, he should not be Acting Prime Minister during Lyons' absence from Australia, but he was forced to concede even this point.[41]

The history of the second and third Lyons ministries was marked by growing tension. In 1935 Hughes, who was then Minister for Health, published a book in which he opposed the imposition of sanctions against Italy. As the government had just introduced a Bill to impose sanctions in conformity with a decision of the League of Nations, Lyons demanded Hughes' resignation.[42] In 1937, Sir Henry Gullett, Minister for Trade and Customs, resigned as a result of disagreement with the government's trade policy, and as a back-bencher also became a critic of defence policy. By 1938, the ministry had drifted into a state of chronic crisis. A rift

41 Ibid., July 1949.
42 The book, *Australia and War Today,* was published on 30 October; the Bill was given its first reading on 31 October. On 6 November, Lyons wrote to Hughes requesting his resignation, and quoted Hughes' criticism of sanctions as 'an empty gesture'. However, the disagreement did not last long, and Hughes returned to office at the end of February 1936. (*Parl. Deb.* [C. of A.], 147: 1306-7.)

appeared over the question of the policy of national insurance, which Lyons had announced in his policy speech at the 1937 elections. A Bill was introduced into parliament early in 1938, but while it was still being debated Lyons began to have doubts about proceeding with it.[43] He asked the Postmaster-General, Senator A. J. McLachlan, who was leader of the government in the Senate, to withdraw the Bill. The Treasurer, R. G. Casey, who had charge of the Bill in the House of Representatives, threatened to resign if it was withdrawn and Lyons then backed down. (Although the Act was finally passed, it was never proclaimed.) According to McLachlan's own account, he told Lyons that in the event of the withdrawal of the Bill, several ministers would have to consider their position as members of the government, and personally he would not continue under such circumstances. McLachlan's suspicions had now been aroused that he was being edged out of cabinet by his opponents, and his suspicions were apparently confirmed when, in October, a Labour member, George Lawson, gave notice of a question concerning the letting of contracts by the Post Office to a company of which McLachlan was chairman. He found that the matter had been discussed by cabinet in his absence, and 'obtained information that the real reason [for the question] was to remove from Cabinet one who it was felt would never yield on the question of national insurance'.[44] (Apart from McLachlan, the leading supporters of the national insurance scheme in cabinet were two Victorian ministers, Casey and R. G. Menzies, the Attorney-General.) McLachlan asserts that his opponents knew him well enough to be sure he would resign 'as a matter of honour' without even asking for an inquiry into the allegation, and that Lawson's question had been a put-up job. He wrote a letter of resignation to Lyons which he then read in the Senate, stressing that he must protect his honour and the honour of the government.[45] Opposition members taunted the government with its own disintegration, pointing out that eight former ministers were now back-benchers. The government was being run by the Country Party, and Page was the 'real element of disintegration'.[46]

[43] This, it has been suggested, was due to pressure from private insurance interests.
[44] A. J. McLachlan, *An F.A.Q. Australian*, p.258.
[45] Ibid. Insult was added to injury when Casey, who had remained in cabinet despite the *volte-face* on national insurance, was made a Privy Councillor and McLachlan was not. McLachlan's correspondence with Lyons on the matter is given, ibid., pp.259-62.
[46] Cf. Paul Hasluck, *The Government and the People 1939-41*, p.111.

Lyons, whose greatest attribute as a politician was his benevolent public personality, was faced with a situation quite beyond his capacity to control. Moreover, he appears to have been terrified at the prospect of war, and his health was failing. As a result, he had come more and more to depend on his older colleagues such as Page, with whom he had become personally intimate. One of the younger members of his cabinet then took the remarkable step of attacking his leadership from outside. R. G. Menzies, who had become Attorney-General in 1934, was strongly opposed to the Country Party and made no secret of his low opinion of the ability of Country Party ministers. In October, he delivered a speech at a luncheon in Sydney in which he discussed Australia's need for 'inspiring leadership'. Australians, he said, could no longer

> remain smug and self-satisfied with democratic platitudes . . . democracies could not maintain their place in the world unless they were provided with leadership as inspiring as that of the dictator countries. The first lesson for the governments of Australia is that in these times of emergency we must not hesitate to take the people fully into our confidence, and give them leadership along well-defined lines.[47]

The general belief that this speech was aimed at Lyons and Page was reinforced when the ministry was reshuffled only a few days later, and at the same time a 'policy committee' was formed which was widely described in the press and in parliament as an 'inner Cabinet'. Both Menzies and Casey were members of this committee, and the latter was promoted from eighth on the cabinet seniority list to fifth position.

It has never been quite clear what kind of support Menzies commanded at this stage and, in particular, whether the National Union of the U.A.P. in Victoria, which had helped to promote Lyons as Prime Minister in 1931-2, was behind him in his criticism of the leaders of the government.[48] One school of thought is that the same group of party notables (including the editor of the Melbourne *Herald*, Sir Keith Murdoch) who had helped to bring about the formation of the U.A.P. in 1931 with Lyons at its head had now lost confidence in him and were preparing to have him replaced by Menzies. On the other hand, says another school, the *Herald* continued to support Lyons during this period, and support for him was also expressed by the secretary of the National Union, Mr Willis, and by the chairman of the Consultative Council of the

---

47 *S.M.H.*, 25 October 1938.
48 Green, loc. cit.; *Nation*, 30 January and 13 February 1960.

U.A.P. in New South Wales, Mr Telford Simpson, a leading Sydney solicitor. However, the existence of a group of business-men in Melbourne who were interested in Menzies' becoming Prime Minister was admitted before a Royal Commission in 1941 by Mr Staniforth Ricketson, a leading stockbroker.[49]

The reconstruction of the ministry aroused further taunts from the Opposition, and Curtin made a sharp attack on the government when its new membership was announced. 'It is now almost certain', he said on a motion of no confidence,

> that the Prime Minister is about to engage once again in that most popular pastime of his, the game of political musical chairs. The right honourable gentleman proposes to set the Government revolving around the chairs in the Cabinet room, and we shall discover that one, two, or three newcomers will occupy chairs to the exclusion of one, two or three of their present occupants. This will be given to the country as evidence of a reconstruction of the Ministry. The Prime Minister has made very many reconstructions of the Ministry. As a matter of fact I should say that, sitting behind him today, the number of his ex-Ministers almost totals the number of his present Ministers . . . I regard it as a rather despicable piece of political manoeuvre that, whenever the Government discovers that its hold on the country is weakening, two or three of its junior ministers are selected as scapegoats . . . the Ministers who are to be sacrificed have not been responsible for the national leadership which we have been told on the authority of the Attorney-General himself has not been satisfactory because the results do not attest to satisfactory leadership . . . These changes are to be made merely to placate certain powerful inter-ests which stand behind this Government. Apparently to satisfy these interests the Prime Minister and the Minister for Com-merce, who are the leaders of the parties which formed this Government, are once again, metaphorically speaking, to throw some Christians to the lions. The Prime Minister's tenure of office seems to demand that more or less annually he must sacrifice some of those who serve in his Ministry. One can regularly see in what is known as the ex-Ministers' alley justi-fication for that statement. There will be new recruits in the ex-Ministers' alley next week.[50]

One of the by-products of the promotion of Casey was that T. W. White, Minister for Trade and Customs, had his precedence lowered. He apparently knew nothing of this until the new mini-stry was being sworn in at Government House, and interrupted the ceremony when he discovered that Casey had been placed ahead

49 Crisp, op. cit., pp.132-6.   50 *Parl. Deb.* (C. of A.), 1938, 157: 1093-4.

of him. He promptly wrote a letter of resignation to Lyons, which he read in parliament on the same day. His letter read, in part, as follows:

> My dear Prime Minister,
> I was surprised to read in the press this morning in an 'official announcement' attributed to you that, inter alia, 'it was proposed that a senior Cabinet group should deal with major matters of national significance and Government policy. The remainder of the Cabinet would be divided into two sub-committees to be presided over by one of the three senior Cabinet Ministers'. The names of the Prime Minister, the Minister for Commerce, the Attorney-General, the Minister for External Affairs, the Treasurer, and the Minister for Civil Aviation, defence and other works, were mentioned as comprising the Cabinet group.
> I had intended to question the wisdom of such action in putting government policy into the hands of a coterie as being a departure from the best democratic principles, and did suggest, after you had mentioned that I was to be a member of such a Cabinet group, that if expedition in attention to Cabinet matters was the objective, it could be attained by more ordered discussion.[51]

Although White was apparently taking his stand on a matter of principle, the very next paragraph suggested a rather more elementary reason for his resignation, because he went on to recount how Lyons had called for him immediately after the cabinet meeting and informed him that, owing to a mistake, he had been wrongly told that he would be a member of the policy committee. An angry clash with Lyons followed. The Prime Minister denied that the policy committee would be a 'coterie', adding: 'Only this morning in Cabinet in your presence I made it clear that while for reasons of promptness and time-saving, matters of policy would in the first instance be thrashed out by the committee the results of their deliberations would in all cases be brought to Cabinet.' He went on:

> It is interesting to note that your resignation was not tendered while you were (as was tentatively decided this morning) a member of the policy committee, but was tendered only when you discovered that there was to be a change and that the Minister for Defence was to take your place . . . I should add that your attitude comes as no surprise after the discreditable manner in which only yesterday you indicated your annoyance at the Treasurer being placed above you in the order of precedence in the Cabinet.[52]

51 Ibid., 1938, 157: 1324.
52 Ibid., 1938, 157: 1325. Casey and Menzies were apparently responsible

The formation of the inner cabinet aroused widespread comment both in parliament and in the press. The Labour Party exploited the general confusion with repeated questions about the real significance of the innovation. Lyons, for his part, denied repeatedly that there was an 'inner group', a term which had acquired significance at the time of Lang's domination of the New South Wales Labour Party in the early 1930s. In reply to one series of questions, Lyons reiterated that the seven senior ministers merely constituted a policy committee.

No powers whatever are given to members of the committee that are not given to every other member of the Cabinet. Their duties are to investigate policy questions and to make recommendations to the Cabinet, members of which, as a whole, take official responsibility for all matters dealt with by the Cabinet and dealt with by the policy committee.

He added that the only 'inner group' that he knew of was the one associated with the Labour Party.[53]

The change did not improve relations within the ministry, and the press continued to be full of reports of dissensions. It was widely reported that cabinet meetings were being thrown into turmoil because Menzies took every opportunity to score off the Country Party. In the following March, Menzies resigned from cabinet and from the deputy leadership of the U.A.P., giving as his reason the final abandonment of the national insurance scheme by the government. In a public statement, he declared that for several months he had been at variance with the majority of cabinet, but 'on each occasion I refrained from resigning, feeling that at a time like this a common front should be observed. The decision of the Cabinet regarding national insurance is the last but weighty straw.' He declared that he must honour his commitments to his electors.[54]

A few weeks later Lyons died after a sudden illness, and a period of confusion followed. Although Menzies had the backing of a large group in the U.A.P., the Country Party was extremely hostile to him and other sections of the U.A.P. were not prepared to support him. Before Lyons' death, there had been rumours that he proposed to retire from the Prime Ministership, but at all events he had not indicated any preference for a successor. At the time, S. M. Bruce was passing through Australia on a mission to the

---

for the reversal of Lyons' original decision not to include the Minister for Defence in the policy committee; cf. Hasluck, op. cit., p.107.
53 Ibid., 1938, 157: 1332-3. 54 *S.M.H.*, 15 March 1939.

United States, and a move was made to bring him back into federal politics with the object of becoming Prime Minister. The prime mover in this was Sir Earle Page, who had been sworn in as Prime Minister in the absence of any clearly defined successor to Lyons as leader of the U.A.P. It had been generally agreed that Page would only act as a 'caretaker' Prime Minister until the U.A.P. could elect a new leader to replace Lyons. The move to re-call Bruce was supported by Casey, who announced his belief that Bruce was 'the only individual under whom the united and full effort of Australia can be achieved'.[55] Page cabled to Bruce, offering to resign his seat in the latter's favour. Bruce declined, but said he would re-enter politics provided he was not connected with any party. If he became Prime Minister, he wanted the right to call meetings of all his parliamentary supporters at any time (which had not been the case in the Bruce-Page govern-ment), and to bring anyone he wished into the government irre-spective of party or even of membership of parliament. As this was a demand for plenary powers such as no Prime Minister had ever possessed, Page readily assumed that it would be unpalatable to the public, and his public utterances interpreted it as a request for the formation of a 'national' government.[56] Page's object, which was to prevent Menzies from becoming Prime Minister, was indicated when he announced in parliament on 20 April that he had returned his commission to the Governor-General and had advised him to send for Menzies. (Menzies had been elected leader of the U.A.P. at a meeting in Sydney two days earlier.) His speech indicated that he could not possibly co-operate with Menzies in a composite government.

In an unprecedented personal attack, he declared that the new leadership of the U.A.P. had resulted in a 'change in the relation-ship of the two parties composing the Government. The general basis for the successful functioning of a composite government must be the fullest mutual confidence and loyalty between parties composing it.' The threat of war meant that not only was this confidence essential, but that the leader of the government must inspire co-operation from the community. He must possess 'cour-age, loyalty and judgment'. He went on to recount three instances in Menzies' past career which showed that he possessed none of these three qualities. His courage was in doubt because of his failure to enlist in the A.I.F. during World War I; his judgment was in doubt because of his resignation over the issue of national insurance at a time when war was threatening; and his loyalty

[55] Ibid., 17 April 1939.   [56] Hasluck, op. cit., 112-13.

was in doubt because of his public attack on Lyons at a time when he was a member of the cabinet. It was because of his inability to have any confidence in Menzies that he had invited Bruce to return and become leader of a national government, offering to vacate his seat in order to make this possible.[57]

There was little debate on this remarkable speech. Curtin, leader of the Opposition, said that personal antagonisms had been one of the most important factors in making orderly government in Australia almost impossible during the past two years. If Menzies had been as candid as Page in replying to him, he would have shown how unfit was the leader of the Country Party for his position. If neither party had confidence in the other, good government was impossible.

The Menzies Government, 1939-1941

The first Menzies ministry contained no members of the Country Party. Inside the Country Party itself Page's leadership suffered as a result of his public outburst, and four Country Party members absented themselves from party meetings in protest. Upon the outbreak of war, Menzies entered into negotiations for the formation of a composite ministry. These broke down over the old question of the right of the Country Party to select its own ministers. Page stood down as leader of the party, and A. G. Cameron, a South Australian member, was elected in his place. The four dissidents then rejoined the party caucus.

The ministry was reconstructed early in 1940. Casey was appointed first Australian Minister to the United States, and another minister resigned over an incident involving a racehorse. The by-election to fill Casey's seat in parliament resulted in a victory for Labour, and Menzies sought Country Party support. In March, he wrote to Cameron offering him five posts in cabinet. Cameron was to be deputy leader of the government, two ministers were to have portfolios and the other two would be without portfolio. He agreed to 'consult' Cameron on the appointment of Country Party ministers.[58]

One item of this agreement concerned the dispute which had arisen between the U.A.P. and the Country Party over the government's scheme to encourage the manufacture of motor cars in Australia. In December 1939, the government had introduced the Motor Vehicle Engine Bounty Bill, laying down conditions under which bounties would be paid for car engines manufactured in

[57] *Parl. Deb.* (C. of A.), 1939, 159: 14-18.
[58] Hasluck, op. cit., p.206, gives the text of Menzies' letter.

Australia. The Bill was passed as a result of Labour support, the Country Party voting against it. In the meantime, J. N. Lawson, Minister for Trade and Customs, had negotiated an agreement with a leading industrialist, W. J. Smith, head of Australian Consolidated Industries Ltd. Shortly afterwards, Smith gave Lawson the lease of a racehorse which he owned. The incident received publicity in the press, and as a result Lawson resigned from the ministry.[59] Cameron, who was still in opposition at that stage, demanded a Royal Commission into the relations between A.C.I. and the government. When the composite ministry was formed, agreement was reached that the ratification of arrangements between A.C.I. and the government should be on a free vote.[60] In May, Menzies introduced the Motor Vehicles Agreement Bill to ratify the agreement by which A.C.I. became sole producer of motor vehicles in Australia. He announced that members of the government parties would be permitted to vote according to their opinions. Although no Country Party minister spoke in opposition to the Bill, it was attacked by several Country Party members, and in the divisions Country Party ministers and members alike went into the 'No' lobby. Only one Country Party member voted in favour.[61]

As a result of the elections of September 1940, the ministry found itself with a reduced majority. After the election of a Speaker, it depended on the votes of two Independent members. A dispute arose in the Country Party over the election of a leader. In November, caucus met and John McEwen, now a minister in the composite government, was nominated. The nomination of Page followed, with Cameron's name only in third place. Cameron left the meeting in a huff, and though he was persuaded to return and preside, he refused to accept nomination for the leadership or even to vote. The result was a deadlock, and to resolve it A. W. Fadden, also a minister and one of the members who had refused the whip in 1939 after Page's attack on Menzies, was elected deputy leader and asked to act as leader in the absence of a final decision. Cameron then resigned from the leadership of the Country Party and from the government. In a letter of resignation, he wrote that intrigue within the party had

---

59 The 'case of the rented racehorse' provided an opportunity for further allegations about the influence of big business. Menzies described Lawson's action as a 'foolish blunder'.

60 In his letter to Cameron, Menzies stated he was willing 'to depart from the usual Cabinet practice and agree that on this matter Cabinet ministers shall be free to vote as individuals'.

61 *Parl. Deb.* (C. of A.), 162 *passim*.

reached its zenith in ruptures of the seal of Cabinet secrecy which must ultimately make any minister's position inside either a party or a Cabinet untenable. No party can function if its internal state is a stew of simmering discontent, spiced by insatiable personal ambitions and incurable animosities. No leader can lead successfully if he must devote most of his time to outwitting rivals or to be outbidding them for support, or to be watching every football lest he stumble on a mantrap or a mine.[62]

From the back benches he became a relentless critic of wartime administration.[63]

By August 1941, public and party discontent with the state of war administration had reached a point where a revolt against Menzies' leadership within his own party came to a head. A protracted cabinet meeting in Melbourne ended with the withdrawal of the Country Party ministers. At this truncated meeting, Menzies announced his intention to resign. Several ministers, led by E. J. Harrison, expressed their support, but the majority refrained from supporting him. Although the question did not go to a vote, it was clear that the Prime Minister had lost the confidence of his own party. A joint meeting of the government parties was then held, at which Menzies announced his resignation and refused to accept nomination for re-election as leader of the joint government parties. Fadden was then elected unopposed, and after Menzies had handed his resignation to the Governor-General, was commissioned to form a ministry.[64] Menzies had already been attacked in public by several back-benchers of the government parties, who had hinted that they would vote against the government in the House of Representatives if Menzies did not resign the leadership. In a public statement on his resignation, he said that many of his colleagues 'feel that I am unpopular with large sections of the press and the people, that this unpopularity handicaps the effectiveness of the Government . . . and that there are divisions of opinion in the Government parties themselves which would not, or might not, exist under another leader'.[65]

A variety of groups were blamed for the intrigues preceding Menzies' resignation. The Victorian Independent, A. W. Coles, who had joined the parliamentary U.A.P. in June 1941, now resigned and stated publicly that he had witnessed a 'lynching' which was 'something so unclean I will never excise it from my

---

62 Hasluck, op. cit., p.206.
63 Cameron's criticisms were so sweeping that he was described as a locomotive with a full head of steam but no rails to run on; his retort was that some others had a fine set of rails and no steam.
64 Hasluck, op. cit., pp.501-5.   65 S.M.H., 29 August 1941.

memory'.[66] The president of the Country Party in Queensland declared that the intrigue against Menzies had been promoted by a
group of U.A.P. and Country Party members from Queensland,
calling themselves the Queensland National Organization, during
Menzies' absence abroad early in 1941.[67] Various members of
the U.A.P. who had not been appointed to the cabinet were blamed
for engineering the downfall of Menzies in revenge for their exclusion from the ministry. Another account emphasized the hostility of Sydney business interests to Menzies.[68]

Hasluck, whose account is sympathetic to Menzies, remarks
that the incident 'throws a curious light on the conventions of party
government in Australia'. Instead of ministers resigning because
of a loss of confidence in the Prime Minister, they had allied themselves with dissident elements in the party to force his resignation.
The 'traditional expectation' would have been that a party meeting
should have declared its lack of confidence in the leader; instead,
he had been forced to resign after a series of personal campaigns.[69]

The Menzies-Fadden Government

In 1949, the wheel came full circle when Menzies was returned
as Prime Minister of a composite government with a sweeping
majority in the enlarged parliament. In this ministry his dominance
was undoubted from the first and the role of the Country Party was
reduced to that of a very junior partner. In the original ministry
of nineteen, the Country Party held five portfolios—those of the
Treasury, Commerce and Agriculture, Health, Postmaster-General, and Repatriation. The number of ministerial posts was
raised to twenty-two in 1956. After the Commerce and Agriculture portfolio was split in 1956 into the portfolios of Trade and
Primary Industry, McEwen, who had been Minister for Commerce
and Agriculture, took the portfolio of Trade, which had become
one of the most important preoccupations of the government. A
Liberal, W. McMahon, became Minister for Primary Industry, but
following the general elections of 1958 the portfolio reverted to
the Country Party under C. F. Adermann. A. W. (later Sir
Arthur) Fadden, held the Treasury portfolio continuously from
1949 until he retired from politics in 1958, and Sir Earle Page
held the portfolio of Health continuously from 1949 to 1956.

Although conflicts over policy and administration continued,
the life of the Menzies-Fadden administration was halcyon by

66 Ibid., 30 August 1941.   67 Ibid.
68 Sydney *Daily Telegraph*, 24 November 1941. The *S.M.H.* was consistently hostile to Menzies during the war.
69 Hasluck, op. cit., p.502.

comparison with its predecessors. Strife was reported over a number of important questions, but it never took the form of violent outbursts as in past years—a reflection, perhaps, of general prosperity and an accompanying apathy towards politics. Where divisions were evident, they did not always follow party lines, although in 1950 suggestions that the Australian pound might be revalued to parity with sterling produced reports that Sir Arthur Fadden had declared this would be done 'only over his dead body'. Country Party ministers, especially the Treasurer, were reported to be hostile to reorganization of the Commonwealth Bank, first announced in 1957 after repeated lobbying by the private banks. In the outcome, the legislation was passed, but it provided for a Development Bank with extensive powers to provide rural credits. This was palatable to the Country Party, but it produced resistance among Liberal back-benchers.[70]

The increase in parliamentary numbers after the 1949 election was responsible for the entry into parliament of a number of younger Liberal members whose parliamentary activities were marked by criticism of the government for failing to adhere with sufficient enthusiasm to 'Liberal principles'. These men, sometimes described as the 'Young Guard', were reportedly resentful at the influence of the Country Party and the limitation of opportunities caused by its presumptive right to a certain number of portfolios.[71] At any rate, the passage of time brought several of these younger men into the ministry, whose enlargement in 1956 also increased the opportunities of promotion.

[70] 'Political Chronicle', *Australian Journal of Politics and History*, 1958, vol. 3, no. 2.
[71] Henry Mayer, 'Liberal-Country Party Rivalry', *Voice*, December 1955.

Part V

PERSONNEL AND PROCEDURE

19

THE COMPOSITION OF CABINET

The Calibre of Ministers

AUSTRALIANS have a notoriously poor opinion of the capacity, political morality, and attainments of their politicians. Cabinet ministers are as susceptible as other members of parliament to this low valuation, which is to be found among a wide variety of political and social groups. This might be expected in a political system where faithful adherence to party interests is, in practice, the overriding political virtue. George Higinbotham, in a farewell speech to his constituents in 1876, declared that factional struggles made the electors care little or nothing about the quality of their government.

> I protest to you, gentlemen, that if you sent out the bellman into the streets, and let him select fifty men from whom to choose by ballot nine Ministers of the Crown, I believe that nine Ministers would be elected who would be quite as well deserving of the confidence of the people of this country as any of those Ministers who have been competing for power for years past.[1]

An Australian journalist, satirically praising politics as the one 'mirth-provoking attribute' in a dull society, suggested that it was essential to be a man of promise rather than of achievements. 'It is not necessary to do great things, but to act as if you could do them, or wished to do them, or would be certain of doing them if you got the chance.' With a modicum of good luck, he concluded, and some good management, 'almost any one can rise to Ministerial rank in Australia, or for that matter obtain . . . the Premiership'.[2]

A more recent critic condemns the 'clique of professional politicians' whose interest is to favour safe, mediocre men rather than able administrators. 'A party which, by the admission of its leader, was full of mediocrity, collectively turned up its nose and looked

---

[1] Morris, *Memoir of George Higinbotham*, p.198.
[2] Alfred Buchanan, *The Real Australia*, pp.79-80, 90.

the other way' when faced with the possibility of recruiting able ministers. Only six men on either side of parliament, he concluded, were 'really worth a place in the team'.[3]

A criticism often made by those people whose interests are not mainly political is the absence of high standards to which aspiring ministers are required to conform. In these cases, there is usually a direct or implicit comparison with the level of education and attainments of ministers in Britain (although one may recall W. Somerset Maugham's remark that the cabinet ministers he had met were persons of very ordinary character). The essayist Francis Adams once wrote a sketch of a typical political career:

> A butcher in a little Queensland seaport carries through his claims, after a struggle as severe as it was protracted, to the lion's share of the richest gold-mine in the world—enters, an untried man, into a powerful ministry—shows himself the worthy antagonist of the strongest politician in Australia—expels the politician from the leadership of the party which he had created —grasps the Treasury and administers it admirably, and is only hurled from an office by an unscrupulous Coalition (and all this done in the most characteristically simple Australian temper and style).[4]

In this, as in other writings, Adams oscillated between dislike of the crudity of Australian politicians and admiration for the opportunities that colonial society held for the man of energy and determination. A more recent critic is untroubled by ambivalence on this score:

> A butcher or a clerk who has done nothing more noteworthy than carve meat or add figures for a decade suddenly becomes active in local politics. He gets the local political 'selection', and another decade may find him a cabinet minister. Push and talk did the trick. Every one of his constituents realize it, and comment on the fact. A tram-guard may become a National Park trustee, a giggling bush doctor may be placed in complete charge of the finances of the nation. A few years ago a museum of scientific specialists found themselves under the jurisdiction of an ex-coalminer. Don't get me wrong here. Coalminers are pleasant folk, and as people I prefer them to the shareholders. But if a man has been a coalminer until he is thirty it seems insane to make him a minister of the Crown.[5]

[3] Warwick Fairfax, *et al., Men, Parties and Politics,* p.12.
[4] *The Australians,* pp.59-60. The protagonist of this little tale was W. Pattison, Secretary for Mines in the McIlwraith ministry of 1888, and Treasurer in the Morehead ministry, 1888-90.
[5] A. J. Marshall, *Australia Limited.* Marshall, a leading zoologist, wrote

It is easy to misconceive the nature of these complaints. For a start, they are directed at least as much against the 'uncouthness' and obvious lack of culture of a large proportion of ministers as against their lack of ability, which is not necessarily correlated with surface polish. For another thing, the critics sometimes appear unaware that they are actually complaining not about Australian politics, but against certain universal characteristics of democracy, especially its alleged failure to provide inspiring political leadership. The only effective answer to such an attitude is the famous remark attributed to Sir Winston Churchill: 'Democracy is the worst form of government, except for all the others.'

On the other hand, there are certain inherent obstacles to the recruitment of an able team of ministers in an Australian ministry. One of these is the narrow field of choice imposed by the small size of parliament. The British cabinet system is very much a product of the enormous size of the House of Commons. If we exclude junior ministers, any British government needs to select only one-tenth of the parliamentary party in the Commons to fill all ministerial posts—and this with no mention of the House of Lords. No government in Australia, whether federal or state, is in a position even remotely comparable. State governments, in addition, have functions which are closer to the responsibilities of a British county council or county borough than of a sovereign state, and they are never likely to attract a large number of individuals of outstanding calibre. As a result, state ministries have a large 'tail' of comparative nonentities, although in most cases the Premier stands head and shoulders above his colleagues. The federal government is in somewhat better case since the Commonwealth parliament was increased in size in 1949, but even so the selection of a ministry absorbs about one-fifth of the total parliamentary party.

A Sociological Analysis of Ministers

Whatever the subjective evaluations that can be made of the ability and character of cabinet ministers compared with their counterparts in other countries, the existence of objective differences in terms of social origin, career, professional and educational background, etc., can readily be demonstrated from the evidence now available.[6]

Wherever such studies have been made, it appears that by far the greatest number of men holding ministerial office have been re-

his provocative little book as part of a wartime series entitled 'Think—or be Damned'. His 'giggling bush doctor' is Sir Earle Page.
[6] For a fuller account see S. Encel, 'The Political Elite in Australia', *Political Studies*, 1961, vol. 9, no. 1.

cruited from the upper-middle classes, are university graduates, and practised one of the liberal professions, particularly law and journalism, before entering politics. The series of studies published by the Hoover Institute, for example, shows this to be true of Britain, France, and the United States. In Britain, aristocratic descent is also important, and the main difference between the parties lies in the relative absence of this element on the Labour side, coupled with a greater stress on the professions.[7] A recent study of the sixty-one members of the four Labour cabinets between 1924 and 1951 shows that thirty-one were drawn from the professions, with academics and lawyers the most prominent. Twenty-two had attended preparatory and public schools, and eighteen had been to either Oxford or Cambridge.[8]

A similar bias is to be found in the United States, where 'regardless of democratic institutions and values, political decision-makers will tend to be chosen from among those ranking high in America's system of social stratification'.[9] According to this analysis, United States senators and political officials are drawn predominantly from professional and business circles, and their general level of education and attainment is well above the average for the community as a whole.

The picture in Australia differs from this in several ways. To begin with, the occupational background of cabinet ministers is more representative of the population as a whole. Of the 176 ministers who held federal portfolios between 1901 and 1951, the largest single number were lawyers (thirty-seven in all); but these were closely followed by manual workers (thirty-five), farmers and graziers (thirty-six), and business managers or proprietors (twenty-eight). Lest it be thought that federal ministers differ significantly from state ministers, the following figures may be of interest. They relate to ninety-one out of the 138 ministers who held office in both state *and* federal governments from 1945 to 1958. Out of this total number, the largest group were farmers or graziers (twenty-two), followed by lawyers (seventeen), business managers or proprietors (sixteen), and manual workers (thirteen). This occupational distribution, moreover, is very similar to that found among members of parliament as a whole, unlike the situation in both Britain and the United States, where the studies

[7] W. L. Guttsman, 'The Changing Social Structure of the British Political Elite', *British Journal of Sociology,* 1951, vol. 2, no. 2.
[8] Bonnor, 'The Four Labor Cabinets', *Sociological Review,* 1958, vol. 6, no. 1.
[9] D. R. Matthews, *The Social Background of Political Decision-Makers,* p.23.

already quoted find that the liberal professions are represented more strongly among ministers than among members of the legislature. The only exception is the legal profession, which is practically a passport to cabinet office, especially in the Labour Party, where there are fewer lawyers.

A second difference relates to educational standard. Unlike the other countries mentioned, only a minority of the men already described were university graduates. Out of the 176 federal ministers from 1901 to 1951, fifty-four had some form of tertiary education; in the 1945-58 group, thirty-eight out of the ninety-one had tertiary qualifications.

Thirdly, there is a great difference to be found between the parties—much greater than in Britain, for example, or even in France. Taking the 1901-51 group, we find that thirty-four out of the thirty-five manual workers were Labour men, but only six out of the thirty-seven lawyers were Labour, and only seven out of the thirty-six rural proprietors. In the 1945-58 group, where the numbers of Labour and non-Labour ministers were almost equal, seven of the twenty-two rural proprietors were Labour men, as against twelve of the thirteen manual workers. The discrepancy in educational levels was also great. In the 1901-51 group, only nine of the fifty-four possessing tertiary qualifications were Labour; in the other group, the proportions were eleven out of thirty-eight.

Social differences between members of opposing parties are hardly to be wondered at, but Australia is perhaps distinctive in the acuteness of these differences and in the fact that the disparity between ministers of different parties is almost as great as that between the various parliamentary groups, taken as a whole.[10] One of the sharpest of all contrasts is to be found in religion. In the 1901-51 group of federal ministers, seventy were Labour and 106 non-Labour. (The 'Labour' group includes those who defected from the party *after* holding office in a Labour administration, and they do not appear in the 'non-Labour' group; however, men who entered parliament as Labour members and first held ministerial office under a non-Labour government are classed as non-Labour.) Of the Labour men, forty were Protestants, twenty-seven Catholics, and three were freethinkers. The situation among the non-Labour ministers is complicated by defections from the Labour side. Altogether, thirty-one Labour men crossed the floor in 1916 and 1931, of whom thirteen were ministers. Five of these thirty-one

[10] The greater homogeneity of ministers as compared with M.P.s in Britain is shown by J. F. S. Ross, *Parliamentary Representation* (2nd ed., London, 1948), pp.52-7.

defectors were Catholics, including three who had been ministers. As five non-Labour ministers were also Catholics, the outcome is that ten men who at any time held office on the non-Labour side were Catholics. Five of these were former Labour men, three of whom held office in Labour governments. The most prominent was J. A. Lyons, who holds the distinction of being the only Catholic to become leader of a non-Labour Commonwealth government. (His widow, Dame Enid Lyons, who was for a short time a minister in a subsequent non-Labour government, is included in the above statistics.)

In the 1945-58 group, seventeen of the forty-four Labour men were Catholics, twenty-five were Protestants, one was a freethinker, and one a Jew. However, as this study was based on a postal survey, it is important to check the non-respondents, and it is curious that out of the thirty Labour ministers who failed to reply, at least twenty were Catholics. Among the forty-seven non-Labour ministers, only one was a Catholic.

Two oddities may be noted in conclusion. Medical men have been reasonably prominent among ministers. Since 1920, nine doctors and one dentist have held cabinet office, mostly as Minister for Health. Women, on the other hand, have hardly figured, despite the fact that universal suffrage has existed throughout the twentieth century. Only two women ministers are on record—Dame Annie Florence Cardell-Oliver in Western Australia (1947-53), and Dame Enid Lyons in the Commonwealth (1949-51).

The Prime Ministership

The difficulties confronting an Australian Prime Minister were made apparent in Part IV. How have the personal characteristics of the men who filled the office helped or hampered them in their task?

It may be observed, for a start, that the party system effectively eliminates uncertainty as to the choice of the leader of a new government. The Governor-General has no such problems as may sometimes perplex a British monarch or the president of a republic with a parliamentary executive. Only the first Governor-General, Lord Hopetoun, was faced with a real exercise of discretion, and his famous 'blunder' may serve as a cautionary tale for all his successors. Acting on apparently unimpeachable premises, he invited Sir William Lyne, as Premier of New South Wales, the senior colony, to form the first federal ministry. (As no federal election had yet been held, there was no parliamentary party to consult.) Lyne, who had taken no part in the campaign for federation, was regarded with hostility by most of the leaders of the federal movement, especially in New South Wales and Victoria, and after strenuous efforts on his part to win their support, and equally strenuous efforts on their part to prevent him from forming a ministry, he reported his failure to Lord Hopetoun. The latter, by now fully aware of the hornets' nest he had brought about his ears, then called on Barton, the leading figure in the federal movement in New South Wales, to form a government, which he did largely under the guidance of Alfred Deakin of Victoria. Deakin, whose manoeuvres had been mainly responsible for Lyne's failure, received the sobriquet of 'Alfred the king-maker'.[11]

Since then, no Governor-General has been faced with similar difficulties in divining who is the acceptable leader of the majority party. The choice of party leaders takes place with such ceremony and with so much public advertisement that no special exercise of political acumen is necessary. When a quandary does occasionally arise, the Governor-General's path is rapidly smoothed. In 1941, after Menzies had been deposed as Prime Minister and the Fadden ministry had soon afterwards been defeated on its Budget, Fadden advised the Governor-General, Lord Gowrie, to send for Curtin, the Labour leader. In 1945, when Curtin died in office, a commission was issued to the Deputy Prime Minister, F. M. Forde, but it was generally understood that he was a stop-gap until the Labour caucus met to elect a new leader. When it chose J. B. Chifley, the Treasurer, Forde returned his commission and the Duke of Gloucester sent for Chifley.

The 1945 incident presented less uncertainty as it followed not long after the death of J. A. Lyons in 1939. Lyons' sudden death occurred at a time when the deputy leadership of the U.A.P. was vacant owing to Menzies' resignation a few weeks earlier. The Deputy Prime Minister was Sir Earle Page, whose party was the smaller of the two partners in the composite ministry. A speech by Page shortly afterward relates how a constitutional precedent was made.

> His Excellency the Governor-General spoke to me in the afternoon and asked whether it would be possible for him to get advice from Mr. Lyons regarding the nomination of his successor. His Excellency had a discussion with two of the doctors attending Mr. Lyons and they informed him that such a direc-

---

11 The full story is told by J. A. La Nauze in *The Hopetoun Blunder*, where all the documentary evidence is presented. Lyne's own record of events only reached the archives in 1945, after the retirement of his former private secretary.

tion from the patient was impossible. Consequently, when the right honorable gentleman died, no advice had been tendered to the Governor-General by the only person constitutionally competent to give it.

The position then was that the United Australia party, which was in partnership with the Country party in the government of the country, and which being the larger party, had always provided the leader of the Government, was temporarily without a deputy leader; therefore, no officer of that party could rightly be said to be in the direct line of succession. In those circumstances, and without any advice from me, the Governor-General decided to commission me to form a government to carry on the affairs of this country. As honorable members will agree, it was obvious to all at that time that at any moment Australia might find itself at war, and that it was imperative there should be a government fully clothed with all powers—not merely an interim government carrying on temporarily pending the choice of a new leader—but one with complete and absolute power to deal with any situation that might arise. The Governor-General issued his commission to me without any qualification whatever. I discussed the position with him and with my colleagues in the Government, pointing out that for twelve years I had co-operated with members of the United Australia party or of the Nationalist party in the government of this country, and stating that, in my opinion, a composite government was likely to be permanently successful only if led by the leader of the numerically stronger party, who should deal with the general problems of government as a whole. Although I had been given an unqualified commission my wish was that the *status quo ante* should be re-established at the earliest possible moment. I told my colleagues, without any pressure at all, and without the signature of any document—the existence of which I absolutely deny, because no such document was ever drawn or signed—that when the United Australia party elected its leader I would tender my resignation to the Governor-General and give him whatever advice he sought. That is the position I am still in. As I have said, as soon as the right honorable member for Kooyong (Mr. Menzies) was elected, I indicated my readiness to take immediate action.[12]

If we exclude the two 'caretaker' Prime Ministers, Page and Forde, there have been fourteen incumbents since federation. They are a heterogeneous collection, viewed from any direction. In terms of previous occupation, five were lawyers (Barton, Deakin, Reid,

12 *Parl. Deb.* (C. of A.), 159: 15. The reference to a 'document' is a comment on Press reports that a written agreement on this procedure had been prepared. Despite Page's denial that advice had been sought, I have been informed that the Chief Justice, Sir John Latham, was consulted.

Hughes, Menzies); three had been trade union officials (Hughes, Scullin, Curtin); two, coalminers (Fisher, Cook); two, skilled workmen (Watson, Chifley); one, a journalist (Curtin); one, a schoolteacher (Lyons); one, an accountant (Fadden); one, a merchant (Bruce). As speakers, they ranged all the way from Deakin, from whom 'words flowed in a silver stream . . . audiences felt that they were being honored above their deserts'.[13] Deakin, like Disraeli, also had the capacity of giving life to the most technical discussion. In 1902, he kept the House of Representatives in a state of rapt attention for more than three hours while, as Attorney-General, he expounded the intricacies of the Judiciary Bill. He was cheered from both sides of the House when he finished.[14] At the other extreme were Cook, the most taciturn of politicians, who came to life only in opposition, and Chifley, another 'strong man' who preferred the detailed work of administration to speech-making. Among eloquent Prime Ministers, there have been as many styles as there were men. Barton's speeches were 'inlaid thought on thought, word upon word, qualifying phrase on qualifying phrase'.[15] Hughes was a master of invective. Curtin had a gift for the withering *mot,* but he was also fond of literary allusions and rotund periods in his public speeches. Reid was a crowd-pleaser, who shone when dealing with interjectors, but like Lord Hartington, who yawned during his own maiden speech, found long addresses tedious. On one occasion, Deakin arranged that complete silence should be observed on the Opposition benches while Reid, as Prime Minister, was opening a debate. Reid became bored and sat down prematurely.

The ability of a Prime Minister to dominate his cabinet depends, in the long run, on the political situation, but within this given framework qualities of personality can be decisive. The instability of the Lyons government was the product of the weak, though amiable, character of its leader and not only of the political tensions of the 1930s. Scullin, a gentle, devout, and austere character, was not well suited to cope with the enormous problems of the depression. Hughes, on the other hand, survived as Prime Minister for more than seven years during a period of almost continuous upheaval. Writing about Winston Churchill, he has unwittingly left an unmistakable likeness of himself: 'It is usually quite impossible to shift him by argument. He is so fertile of expedient and so mercurial that one can never corner him. He is here, he is there,

---

13 Buchanan, op. cit., p.259.
14 Walter Murdoch, *Alfred Deakin—A Sketch,* p.218.
15 Buchanan, op. cit., p.256.

he is gone, and again he is where he was before.'[16] Hughes' strength as a Prime Minister lay in the fact that, in addition to his considerable intellect, he possessed a mental agility and a political flair unrivalled among his contemporaries. His fellow-ministers were quite unable to keep up with his energy and unpredictability. A hostile back-bencher attacked them for this failure.

> It was almost certain that his egotism, his autocratic disposition, and his craze for notoriety would plunge them into adventures which might seriously compromise them all. The cable messages, now imploring, now threatening, now demanding information, which followed Mr. Hughes on his course round the world, have cost the country a pretty tidy sum, though the gentleman responsible for them no doubt regards them merely as tributes to his greatness.[17]

Among non-Labour Prime Ministers, Bruce and Menzies have been the only ones to enjoy periods of complete personal ascendency. Bruce's education[18] and social position, according to one critic, 'combined to give him a confidence which confounded his maturer critics, and an agility which carried him safely over many dangerous situations'.[19] Eggleston, though unable to discern any qualities of statesmanship in Bruce, admits that he was 'unquestioned leader of his party and disciplined recalcitrant members without suffering in his own prestige, a thing rarely found possible in Australia'.[20] Menzies, on the other hand, did not achieve the remarkable dominance which characterized his second term as Prime Minister until he had re-established the leadership so humiliatingly terminated in 1941. A biting criticism published during the 1943 election campaign compared him to Hamlet.

> Mr. Menzies is acutely conscious of his central position and convinced he deserves it . . . However, as the play runs its appointed course, the other characters, being immensely impressed by Hamlet at the start, take him less and less seriously. They grow increasingly doubtful that he will ever do anything but talk, and they can seldom understand what he is talking about.[21]

[16] W. M. Hughes, *The Splendid Adventure*, p.138.
[17] J. M. Fowler, *Statesman or Mountebank: An Australian Study*, p.20. A few years earlier, a panegyric inspired by Lord Northcliffe had celebrated Hughes as a 'Nelson of politics'. (Douglas Sladen, *From Boundary Rider to Prime Minister*, p.4.) Earlier still, Melbourne *Punch* had called him 'the Mirabeau of the proletariat' (23 June 1904).
[18] Bruce, a Cambridge graduate, is the only Prime Minister to have been educated at an English university. [19] Denning, *Caucus Crisis*, p.42.
[20] *Reflections of an Australian Liberal*, p.12.
[21] Fairfax, *et. al., Men, Parties and Politics*, p.67.

Many other critics at the same period dwelt on Menzies' inability to condescend gracefully to colleagues of lesser intellect, with the result that he lectured his ministers like a schoolmaster; on his perpetual tendency to regard forensic brilliance as a substitute for genuine policy, and to postpone decisions on awkward problems in the hope that they would solve themselves. Menzies' history exemplifies the defects of a brilliant legal career as a preparation for politics, which have been described by a life-long legal and political opponent, Dr H. V. Evatt. Writing of C. G. Wade, who became Premier of New South Wales in 1907 after making his name as a Crown prosecutor, Evatt observes that 'the path from the Bar to the legislature is seldom an easy one'. Wade had 'a safe seat handed to him, accompanied by many trimmings including the adulation of a great metropolitan newspaper', and became a minister 'with a speed that was almost indecent'.[22] The Premiership, for him, did not represent the end of a long struggle to reach the top of the greasy pole, and his appreciation of the political responsibilities of the office was consequently defective. It may be the lack of humanity often attributed to successful barristers that accounts for the nickname of 'Ming the Merciless' which became attached to Menzies during his first term as Prime Minister.[23]

The personalities of Labour Prime Ministers run a wide gamut from the fireworks of Hughes to the stodginess of Andrew Fisher, who was described by a parliamentary correspondent as 'painfully inefficient in the public expression of his own thoughts and even in repeating official expositions of Bills of which he had nominal charge'.[24] Holman damned him with faint praise by describing his virtues as 'simplicity, frugality, rugged candor and a single-minded devotion to righteous causes'.[25] Fisher belonged to a period when Labour pronouncements viewed leadership as an evil that was not even necessary. The neutral colouring of men like Fisher and Watson, or McGowen in New South Wales, was largely the outcome of this strong prejudice. Until the emergence of Curtin and Chifley, there had been no successful combination of strong leadership and assured party loyalty. Both men found themselves in a situation that favoured the exercise of initiative by the Prime Minister, but their personal methods were immensely different. Curtin played the role of a prima donna, who, when irritated, would assume 'the acid and icy tones of a headmaster addressing

---

[22] *Australian Labor Leader,* pp.246-7.
[23] The name derives from a somewhat repulsive tyrant depicted in a syndicated American comic strip.
[24] L. V. Biggs, in *Forum,* 12 March 1924.
[25] *Bulletin,* 27 March 1935.

an unruly sixth form'.[26] On more than one occasion he was known to threaten resignation, and in one climactic episode he did in fact deliver his resignation to the cabinet. The crisis was smoothed out at a hurried meeting of caucus which declared its complete confidence in the Prime Minister. Curtin was an aloof, isolated personality, troubled by intense doubts about his course of action on many critical occasions, and he lacked the sense of humour that most successful politicians either possess or cultivate. It is probably fair to say that without the continuous and loyal support of his much calmer lieutenant, Chifley, he would have given way earlier under the great strain that finally killed him. Chifley lacked any of Curtin's 'inspirational' qualities, but made up for them by great administrative competence, and by his ability to evoke great personal affection and confidence. Although some of his critics have regarded him as better suited to the role of lieutenant than of captain, he undoubtedly dominated his cabinet.

Chifley's success as an administrator underlines one of the weaknesses of a Prime Minister's position, especially as compared with that of a British Prime Minister. The fact that the latter is also First Lord of the Treasury is, as Jennings remarks, not entirely an accident of history.[27] The unity of administrative direction which it symbolizes is marked, for instance, by the rule (formally established by Treasury minute in 1920) that the Prime Minister's consent is required for the appointment of the four principal officials of every department of state, and it was taken further when this side of Treasury activities was, in 1956, placed under the control of one of the joint permanent secretaries of the Treasury.[28]

An Australian Prime Minister is in a different position. His influence over appointments is restricted by laws designed to minimize political intervention in the control of the public service, which is vested in a statutory body, the Public Service Board. Only the heads of departments are appointed directly by the Governor-General-in-Council—i.e., by cabinet, which also exercises some influence over the appointment of diplomatic representatives. The members of the Public Service Board are appointed by the Prime Minister, who is responsible for their work in parliament, but not in any other important sense. Moreover, the division between control of establishments and control of finance prevents any centralization of authority such as is possible in Britain. One way in which a Prime Minister can strengthen his control is by

---

[26] Fairfax, op. cit., p.78. [27] *Cabinet Government,* p.132.
[28] D. N. Chester, 'The Treasury—1956', *Public Administration* (London), 1957, vol. 35, no. 1.

taking the portfolio of Treasurer, but this involves him in detailed administrative duties which most Prime Ministers prefer to avoid. In only one case has the combination been tried successfully—by J. B. Chifley from 1945 to 1949, although J. A. Lyons also acted as his own Treasurer from 1932 to 1935. Chifley's case, although a special one, does suggest that the growth of the Commonwealth administrative machine since 1939 gives the Prime Minister a source of strength which has previously been lacking from the office.

It should be recalled that Chifley was Treasurer for about four years under Curtin. In this time he had acquired a remarkable grasp of administrative detail and had surrounded himself with a group of trusted advisers, who would no longer have had direct access to him had he relinquished the Treasury on becoming Prime Minister. It is possible, moreover, that he sensed the political advantages of being his own Treasurer. There are few sanctions that a Labour Prime Minister can apply against recalcitrant colleagues in the ministry or in caucus, and Treasury control is one of them, especially as the policy-making role of the Treasury had grown so notably compared with the period before 1939.[29] Chifley continued to develop the resources of the Treasury, and when he left office he bequeathed an instrument to his successors of great importance both politically and administratively. Nevertheless, there are grounds for believing that Chifley's tenure of the two offices had some disadvantageous consequences. In administration, it sometimes led him to take the 'Treasury view' too wholeheartedly, when a Prime Minister should perhaps have been concerned to temper it. As a political leader, he may also have been influenced too heavily by the Treasury view. In 1949, the Liberal Party outbid Labour during the election campaign by promising to abolish petrol rationing and to increase child endowment payments. Chifley's resistance to these proposals may have been justifiable from the viewpoint of a Treasurer, but it may equally have been fatal from the viewpoint of a Prime Minister facing an election.

The Position of the State Premier

A state Premier is, in the nature of things, in a simpler position than a Commonwealth Prime Minister. Even in the nineteenth century, when factional shifts occurred continuously, individual figures like Parkes could command personal loyalties that were

---

[29] The financial predominance of the Commonwealth also meant that a federal Labour government was in a far stronger position *vis-a-vis* Labour Parties in the states, especially if Labour were in office, than ever before.

more important than any policy. With the 1890s came the emergence of figures like Reid in New South Wales, Kingston in South Australia, and Forrest in Western Australia, whose terms of office were long and continuous. These men were as unlike as can be imagined. Reid was well known for his indolence, especially as he often appeared to be dozing on the front bench. His laziness was sometimes attributed to his great girth, which he regularly exploited as a source of humour in his speeches. On one occasion, when a stout member of the Opposition side complained that the House was too thinly attended for proper debate, Reid drawled in reply: 'It will never be a thin House while the honourable member and I sit in it.'[30] One of Reid's successors, McGowen, was also stout and indolent. He was reputed only to notice the passage of time because he lay on the office sofa with his coat off in summer, and in the winter with his coat on.

At the other extreme was Kingston, a man of passionate temper and extravagant behaviour, who was personally responsible for much advanced social legislation that brought him into violent conflict with the conservative upper house and particularly with its President, Sir Richard Baker. After an exchange of pleasantries in which Kingston had described Baker as 'false, treacherous, mendacious and untrustworthy', he sent Baker a letter challenging him to a duel outside the latter's office, and enclosed a pistol and cartridges. Baker accepted the challenge, but took care to inform the police, who arrived at the appointed hour and arrested Kingston, who had come suitably armed. He was charged with 'unlawfully, wickedly, wilfully and maliciously' attempting to provoke a duel, and bound over to keep the peace.[31]

In the present century, the central problem of state government has been that of obtaining funds for public works, and as a result most Premiers also take the Treasury portfolio. This, coupled with the long life of most state governments, has had a considerable effect on the position of the Premier and also on the qualities required for a successful incumbent. Picturesque, erratic or indolent individuals like Reid, Kingston, Parkes and other nineteenth century 'giants' are at a discount. A twentieth-century Premier must, above all, be a man with a capacity for hard work and detailed administration, as well as a shrewd political manager. For two generations, the bulk of state government has comprised the operation of large public utilities and of various agencies of economic and social regulation. The most important function of a state

30 A. B. Piddington, *Worshipful Masters*, p.57.
31 Cf. Coghlan, *Labor and Industry in Australia*, vol. 4, ch. 12.

ministry is to provide the budgetary framework for these 'semi-government' bodies, and in this the Premier is the key figure, even if he does not actually hold the Treasury portfolio.

The most important element in this situation is the financial predominance of the Commonwealth government, especially since the establishment of the Australian Loan Council in 1925 as a federal-state consultative body to deal with the flotation of loans and the management of the National Debt. (The powers of this body were entrenched by an agreement that was written into the Commonwealth constitution by an amendment approved in 1928.) The Commonwealth Treasurer of the period, Dr Earle Page, described this body magniloquently as a 'Cabinet of governments'. The establishment of the Loan Council gave a new significance to the meetings of the Premiers' conference, which had met more or less regularly since the 1880s.[32] This body has been the venue of various attempts to secure interstate co-operation on matters such as the reference of constitutional powers to the Commonwealth, the unification of railway gauges, uniform laws on a variety of topics, education and health. Until the Loan Council was set up, the Commonwealth Prime Minister attended the Premiers' conference by invitation. Since then, Loan Council meetings have become part of the normal proceedings of the Premiers' conference, which is held annually in Canberra. With the introduction of uniform income tax levied by the Commonwealth in 1942, the most important items of business at the conference have become the regular wrangle over tax reimbursements and the Loan Council meeting. For a few years after 1945, the meetings of the National Works Council were also a feature of the conference. This body was set up by the Chifley government as an instrument for planning a steady level of public works expenditure in order to buttress the policy of full employment contained in a White Paper published shortly after the end of the European war. However, its importance in a period of steadily rising public expenditure and labour shortages soon withered, and instead of becoming an administrative counterpart of the Loan Council, it disappeared as a separate body.

In all this, the crucial role is the Premier's, and as the financial dependence of the states on the Commonwealth has become more marked, so has the Premier's overriding authority increased within his own bailiwick. In the last twenty years, it has become increasingly common for major statements of government policy to be made by the Premier, even when they are clearly within the prov-

[32] A. J. A. Gardner, in Spann (ed.), *Public Administration in Australia.*

ince of a particular departmental minister. In earlier days, it was not unknown for ministers and even for departmental heads to announce policy decisions independently of the rest of the ministry. The strength of the Premier's position is enhanced by the generally long-lived character of state governments and the accompanying tendency of Premiers to remain in office for periods running into double figures. This strength makes it possible for a well-established Premier to resist pressures from within his own party (or parties) and to cope successfully with situations that would have led to his downfall not so many years ago. The late Sir Albert Dunstan, though leader of a minority government, ruled Victoria for ten years with an interruption of only five days. Sir Thomas Playford became Premier of South Australia in 1938 and was still in office in 1960. In 1946 he was easily able to subdue a rebellion inside his own party against the scheme to bring the electricity generating industry in South Australia under public ownership. The careers of Dunstan and Playford are paralleled by those of Cosgrove in Tasmania, Forgan Smith in Queensland, Collier in Western Australia, Stevens and Cahill in New South Wales. The qualities exhibited by these men show a remarkable degree of homogeneity, and they differ sharply from Commonwealth Prime Ministers both in their similarity to one another and in the nature of their abilities.

Ministerial Responsibility

'For all that passes in Cabinet', said Lord Salisbury in 1878, 'each member of it who does not resign is absolutely and irretrievably responsible'. In consequence, writes Jennings, 'a minister who is not prepared to defend a Cabinet decision must, therefore, resign'. The principle of collective responsibility means, moreover, that a minister 'must vote with the Government, speak in defence of it if the Prime Minister insists, and that he cannot afterwards reject criticism . . . on the ground that he did not agree with the decision'.[33] As Lord Melbourne told his cabinet on a famous occasion, he did not care whether the price of flour was to go up or down, so long as all ministers told the same story.

Nothing, perhaps, illustrates more clearly the differences between cabinet government in Australia and cabinet government in Britain than the frequency with which the convention that the first loyalty of a minister is to his colleagues has been overriden, both in state and federal politics. The case histories related in Part IV of this book suggest that, in Australia, the basic convention

[33] *Cabinet Government,* pp.257-8.

is not collective responsibility within cabinet, but the individual responsibility of each minister to his party. In times of stress, this may go even further and involve loyalty first and foremost not to the party as a whole, but to a particular section of the party or the extra-parliamentary organization.

Jennings[34] formulates a number of rules that emerge from the practice of British cabinets since the Reform Act of 1832. If a minister does not resign, he is 'responsible'. Secondly, collective responsibility can operate so long as there is agreement on fundamentals, but compromise on incidentals is essential to avoid frequent splits that would weaken the institution of cabinet government. For this reason, he regards the well-known 'agreement to differ' on tariff policy within the MacDonald 'National' ministry in 1932 as out of keeping with the general practice. Thirdly, individual ministers are expected not merely to refrain from opposing a cabinet decision, but to support it publicly. Fourthly, public controversies between ministers, or criticisms of one minister's administration by another, are breaches of collective responsibility.

Finally, Jennings makes three points regarding the action of the Prime Minister, or any other minister, in committing the whole government on his own responsibility. A minister should not express personal opinions on future policy without consultation; a minister should not announce a new policy without previous cabinet consent, but if he does, cabinet must either support him or request his resignation; and the Prime Minister is usually in a position to pledge the support of his colleagues, otherwise he must resign.

These conventions are but facets of the one central principle of cabinet solidarity, and it is this principle that repeatedly comes under attack during disputes over policy and administration in Australia. In Britain, a cabinet *contretemps* may involve the violation of one, or perhaps two, of these rules, but it can also take place without any such violation. In Australia, not only is it unlikely that the latter will occur, but in the cases already described it has been usual for practically all the rules to be broken simultaneously. During the struggle within the New South Wales Labour Party in 1926-7, public disagreements were common; decisions were taken by the Premier and his one cabinet supporter, Willis, without cabinet meetings being held; votes of no confidence in the Premier were moved and supported in caucus by members of the government. But not a single minister resigned until Loughlin, the Deputy Premier, had been defeated in a ballot for the leadership of the government. In 1951, opposition to the policy of the McGirr

34 Ibid., pp.260-9.

government in New South Wales to establish a Catholic university was led by a minister, C. R. Evatt, who did not resign despite his disagreement with government policy and his participation in public controversy over the scheme.

Two Labour governments in Victoria fell from office as the result of crises where similar disregard of the rules was exhibited. In 1932, public dispute between the members of the Hogan government over the implementation of the Premiers' Plan went on during the election campaign. When the Premier instructed his deputy, Tunnecliffe, that his policy speech must stand by the Premiers' Plan, the latter did not resign in order to attack the government's policy, but delivered a policy speech in defiance of Hogan's instructions. Although two ministers then resigned, two others remained in cabinet while expressing their public disagreement with Tunnecliffe, and the Premier himself did not resign. In 1955, on the other hand, following the split in the Labour movement outside parliament, four ministers refused to recognize the authority of the new state executive of the A.L.P., but did not resign, and refused to do so when the Premier requested their resignations following their suspension from the party.

Federal Labour governments have been troubled by similar difficulties. Scullin, like Hogan, left a dissident party behind when he went abroad in 1930. During his absence, ministers who were dissatisfied with the government's financial policies supported motions in caucus aimed against those policies, and shortly afterwards, two appointments were made to the High Court against Scullin's express wishes. The life of the Curtin government was punctuated by a series of remarkable infractions of collective responsibility, involving all of Jennings' rules at one time or another. Thus, after the success of Curtin in 1942 in persuading the A.L.P. to change its traditional policy on conscription, a censure motion against him was publicly supported at the New South Wales Labour conference in 1943 by one of his ministers, E. J. Ward. During the struggle over the ratification of the Bretton Woods agreement in 1946, Ward was again the leading figure, but he was supported by other ministers, who opposed in caucus the decision in favour of ratification made by cabinet. Ward's most important supporter, A. A. Calwell, also a minister, voted against approval of the government's decision by the A.L.P. Federal Executive, of which he was a member.

On the non-Labour side, we have already seen how the rules of the Country Party are fundamentally in conflict with the principles of cabinet responsibility. In the composite ministries that are the normal form of non-Labour governments, the 'agreement to differ' is virtually institutionalized. Jennings is probably right in arguing that such an 'agreement' makes cabinet government almost unworkable, but this would only be the case if it were taken literally. The willingness of the Country Party to compromise its long-term views, such as resistance to high tariffs, in return for access to certain key portfolios, makes it possible for the appearance of cabinet solidarity to be maintained fairly convincingly. Nevertheless, the second and third of Jennings' rules are regularly violated even when no crisis is in train. For instance, it is not unknown for divergent statements of policy to be made by the party leaders in a composite ministry during election campaigns, when separate policy speeches are regularly made by the leaders of the Liberal and Country Parties.

The tension between Liberals and Country Party in Victoria led to repeated disputes over electoral reform in which the solidarity of the ministry was broken. In 1924, the Nationalist government led by Lawson, which included two members of the Victorian Farmers' Union, approved a Bill to redistribute the electorates, but the two V.F.U. ministers did not immediately resign, although their party was opposed to redistribution. They did resign when the Bill was presented to parliament, when they crossed the floor with the rest of their party and helped to defeat the government. The history of the Hollway composite ministry (1947-50) was marked by public disputes and tension over Hollway's scheme for electoral reform, but the ministry remained in existence until the general election of 1950, when the C.P. took office with Labour support.

Federal non-Labour governments have exhibited similar phenomena. The formation of the Hughes Nationalist government in 1917 led to incidents such as the public announcement by Sir John Forrest of his disagreement with Hughes. The resignation of W. A. Watt in 1920, during his mission to London, was accompanied by parliamentary discussion of the differences between Watt and Hughes, garnished with quotations from ministerial correspondence. Fifteen years later Hughes, now a minister in the second Lyons government, publicly attacked the defence policy of the ministry in a book, and it was only after the resulting embarrassment had been fully exploited by the Opposition that Lyons asked for his resignation. In 1938, R. G. Menzies made a speech which was undoubtedly an attack on Lyons, but there is no indication that his resignation was asked for, and he did not in fact resign until five months later.

During Menzies' own Prime Ministership some little time later, there was an outstanding case of an agreement to differ in connection with the Motor Vehicles Agreement Bill of 1940. In this instance, a composite ministry was formed on the understanding that a free vote would be allowed, and when the Bill came to the floor of the House of Representatives the Country Party ministers went into the 'No' lobby.

One of the outstanding features of the operation of collective responsibility is the strength it lends to the position of the Prime Minister, who can on occasion take a major policy decision without consulting his colleagues—or at any rate, not more than one or two of them—in advance. This is a point that Australians seem reluctant to concede, perhaps because it is this, more than any aspect of the cabinet system, that cuts across the accepted norm of responsibility to the party and arouses suspicions about 'leadership' which are never far from the surface in a country so self-consciously democratic. The hostility aroused by Hughes with regard to the Commonwealth shipping line and other wartime policies has already been described, and we may at this point briefly consider the most celebrated recent case, that of Chifley and bank nationalization. The decision of the Labour government in 1947 to nationalize the private banking system was widely interpreted as a personal and 'hasty' decision by Chifley himself, which was sprung on an unsuspecting and reluctant party. Sir Frederic Eggleston's observation was typical: 'Mr. Chifley at once [after a hostile judgment by the High Court] decided to nationalize the whole of the Australian banks. This decision was taken without even the formality of a Cabinet meeting.'[35] A similar line was taken by the Press and by Labour's political opponents at the time, and Labour sympathizers have always been somewhat embarrassed by this 'accusation'. Their embarrassment about the affair is, of course, also based on the obvious fact that Chifley's action was an error of judgment in dealing with the situation caused by the Court's decision, and a political error whose long-term consequences for the Labour Party were unfortunate. Nevertheless, the abiding interest of the matter appears to reside in the controversial question whether Chifley made the decision on his own, or whether it was a cabinet decision. Evidence has been adduced on both sides. The possibility of nationalization had been discussed by cabinet in

35 Eggleston, op. cit., p.84. Eggleston may have been misled by erroneous Press reports. Chifley's announcement was made after a cabinet meeting had endorsed his views. For a full account, see L. F. Crisp's biography, *J. B. Chifley* (Melbourne, 1961).

1945 at the time of the Banking Act, and a cabinet meeting *was* held immediately after the High Court's decision in the *State Banking Case*. As against this, it is argued that Chifley was an inveterate—nay, a 'fanatical' believer in nationalization, which he had urged in his minority report as a member of the Royal Commission on Banking and Monetary Systems before the war. Also, he had apparently noted the reference to nationalization made by Dixon J. (later Chief Justice) as an *obiter dictum* in the course of his separate judgment.

It is possible to maintain that much of this argument is beside the point. We must distinguish two levels. If the accepted norm is to be that any major policy decision requires previous ratification by the party, then it may plausibly be held that Chifley acted 'precipitately' and without a 'mandate'. At the same time, nothing is gained by refusing to recognize that the operation of cabinet government concentrates power in the hands of the Prime Minister, whose discretion as to its use is governed largely by his estimate of whether he can carry his ministry and his party with him. Chifley's estimate of this was certainly accurate, and his action is all the less remarkable in that it was a possible outcome of Labour policy, and not a reversal or a major deviation. It cannot, for instance, be compared with the problems faced by Curtin a few years earlier over conscription. At all events, Chifley's dominance of his cabinet and party was unaffected by the bank nationalization episode, as evidenced by his decision to devalue the pound in 1949. The possibility of a British devaluation had been discussed by cabinet in consultation with its economic advisers, and Chifley was given discretion to follow suit provided that Britain did not devalue excessively. As a result, when Sir Stafford Cripps announced the devaluation of sterling, Australia followed suit almost immediately. As no meeting of federal cabinet had been held in the interim, the announcement was treated by the Press and the Opposition as yet another snap political decision by the Prime Minister.

One other facet of ministerial responsibility concerns the assumption of responsibility by the ministry as a whole for the actions of an individual minister. Although Jennings suggests that here, too, certain rules may be extracted from actual practice, a recent study has shown that the outcome of cases where the actions of an individual minister are in dispute is governed by no other principle than what happens to be politically expedient at the time.[36] It is

36 S. E. Finer, 'The Individual Responsibility of Ministers', *Public Administration* (London), 1956, vol. 34, no. 4.

not strictly true, in the light of the cases analysed by Professor Finer, that 'the Government does not accept responsibility for an error of judgment or bad administration by one of its members'.[37] In some instances it may find it politically necessary to do so, the history of defence policy in Britain and Australia alike being a good example.

Another one of Jennings' observations is not borne out by Australian experience. He writes that cabinet 'must leave to each minister a substantial discretion as to what matters he will bring before it. If he makes a mistake, then he must accept the personal responsibility. On the other hand, a minister cannot hide behind the error of a subordinate'.[38] Some recent contraventions of this rule may be quoted. In 1948, it was discovered that a temporary member of the staff of the Commonwealth Department of Territories, J. S. Garden, had been involved in a series of shady transactions over timber leases in New Guinea. Garden was an old political associate of the Minister for Territories, E. J. Ward. An investigation by a Royal Commission took place, the report of which exonerated Ward from any knowledge or complicity in Garden's dealings, but suggested that he had been 'ill-advised' to allow Garden the latitude he had enjoyed. Under British conditions, there is virtually no doubt that a similar series of incidents would have spelt *finis* to the career of the minister concerned, but this did not happen in Ward's case. Even if the Prime Minister, Mr Chifley, had wished Ward to resign, this would have required action by caucus.

On another occasion, the Minister for External Affairs, R. G. Casey, found himself embarrassed by newspaper reports concerning Australian policy in the Far East, and proceeded to pin the blame on subordinates by an outburst regarding a 'nest of traitors' in his department. In 1955, the Minister for the Interior, W. S. Kent Hughes, was attacked for a muddle in the building of houses in Canberra, for whose administration he was responsible. In reply, the minister blamed faulty co-ordination between the Departments of Interior and Works (for which he was also responsible). In conformity with the common practice, the Prime Minister, who was reported to be 'horrified' at the muddle, did not ask for Kent Hughes' resignation, but excluded him from his next ministry after the subsequent general election.

On the basis of these and similar incidents, it may be concluded that the Australian convention is for the acceptance of responsibility both by cabinet and party for the actions of an individual

37 Jennings, op. cit., p.463.   38 Ibid.

minister. Only where the 'error' becomes the subject of an adverse decision by a Royal Commission or a court of law, or leads to actual strife within the party, will this protection be withdrawn.

Honorary and Assistant Ministers

No distinction between 'cabinet' and 'ministry' existed in Australia until 1956, when it was introduced by the Menzies government. For a long time, however, distinctions in status have been recognized by designating certain ministers as 'honorary', 'assistant', or 'without portfolio'. These designations are, in most cases, literally untrue. Honorary ministers are paid, ministers without portfolio usually have portfolios, assistant ministers are often in sole charge of departments. This semantic oddity is the result, not merely of colonial perversity, but of political and constitutional exigencies. The term 'assistant minister' will here be used generically, as of the three it is closest to the truth.

The expressions 'honorary' and 'without portfolio' are older than 'assistant' minister, and were at one time accurate descriptions. In the nineteenth century, several Premiers of Tasmania held office without salary. In that case as in others, a contributory reason was the general provision that ministers, on being appointed, must stand for re-election to parliament. A minister who assumed an honorary office, like that of Premier, not listed in the schedule to the constitution as an office of profit under the Crown, could evade the necessity for re-election. More important was the fact that governments could increase their number, for political or administrative reasons, without an amendment to the schedule. These ministers, being 'honorary' or 'without portfolio', were then actually paid by deductions from the salaries of ministers with 'constitutional' portfolios.

Constitutionally speaking, an honorary minister was enabled to exercise executive office by being sworn in as a member of the Executive Council. A letter from the Commonwealth Solicitor-General, Robert Garran, illustrates both the subterfuge and the manner in which it was legally cloaked. Garran wrote:

> An Assistant Minister is a member of the Federal Executive Council, and as such may countersign Executive Minutes and all other documents for signature by the Governor-General. And he may, of course, perform all administrative acts and decisions which are not by statute required to be done by a Minister of State. An Assistant Minister is not one of the King's Ministers of State for the Commonwealth within the meaning of Section 64 of the Constitution. Consequently he is not a 'Minister' within

the meaning of Section 17(h) of the Acts Interpretation Act of 1901 or within the meaning of any provision in the Commonwealth Statutes in which the word 'Minister' is governed by that definition.[39]

The financial subterfuge appears in a further letter from the then Prime Minister, S. M. Bruce, written to the Premier of South Australia in response to an enquiry about conditions of appointment of honorary ministers. Bruce stated that:

Honorary Ministers do not draw any emolument under the Ministers of State Act, but an amount is paid to them—varying with the circumstances of each particular case—out of the salaries paid to Ministers with portfolio. This latter amount is represented by a lump sum specially provided by the Act, and which is allocated in accordance with the wishes of each Administration.[40]

The device of appointing a minister without a seat in cabinet was no novelty. In 1861, the Cowper ministry in New South Wales created a ministerial portfolio of Postmaster-General (which until then had been non-political) and appointed a parliamentarian to this office. He was sworn in as an Executive Councillor, but without a seat in cabinet.[41] One or two similar appointments were made between 1861 and 1878, variously referred to as 'a member of the Government without a seat in Cabinet', or 'without a seat in the Executive Council'. In most cases the portfolio in question was that of Attorney-General; thus, in 1870, Cowper appointed Sir William Manning as Attorney-General without a seat in cabinet. The last case was that of W. J. Foster, Attorney-General in the Farnell ministry of 1877-8, who was originally appointed without a seat in the Executive Council but became a member of it during his tenure of office.

State governments have been able to overcome the difficulty, mentioned by Garran, regarding the Acts Interpretation Act. The difficulties raised by the Commonwealth Constitution, which makes it virtually impossible to introduce posts corresponding to those of junior ministers in Britain,[42] are accentuated by the intractable problem of amendment. The amendment of state constitutions is a

[39] Letter to Atlee Hunt, Secretary of the Department of External Affairs, 23 September 1914. *C.P.* 103, ser. 4 (C-A).
[40] 30 August 1924, *C.P.* 103, ser. 11 (C-A).
[41] According to Parkes, Cowper did this as an inducement to Parkes to join him. When the latter refused, the portfolio was given to another member. (Parkes, *Fifty Years in the Making of Australian History*, pp.154-5.)
[42] See chapter 3.

relatively simple matter, and in at least two cases state parliaments have provided that ministers without portfolio can act for other ministers. The New South Wales Constitution Act, as amended in 1902, provided that the holder of any office of profit which is created as an office of the executive government was not disqualified from membership of the Legislative Assembly, thus avoiding the restrictive effect of the second schedule to the constitution. Similarly, Section 36 authorized the Governor to transfer functions from one Executive Councillor to another. These provisions became necessary because of an amendment passed at the same time requiring all ministers to be members of the Executive Council. In the Wade ministry (1907-10) two ministers without portfolio were members of the Executive Council.[43]

In South Australia, the Administration of Acts Act, 1910, gave the Governor power to commit the administration of any statute to a minister other than the one provided in the Act in question. Similarly, any offices which were by statute attached to a particular portfolio, could be transferred to another minister. This legislation reinforced the statutory provision made in 1908 for one honorary minister.[44] Another state which has introduced constitutional provisions regarding honorary ministers is Victoria. A constitutional amendment in 1944 provided that allowances should be paid to not more than three honorary ministers, and in 1947 it was further provided that one of these should be secretary to cabinet, with a specified allowance. In 1950 the Ministers of the Crown and Parliamentary Salaries Act reduced the number of non-salaried ministers to two. In Tasmania, where the salaries of all ministers have long been fixed by statute, differential salaries are provided for the Premier, for ministers, and for honorary ministers, each of whom has a portfolio.

No other states have constitutional provisions regarding honorary ministers, although all states have used them. The nomenclature used in each case seems to be a matter of personal taste. The McLarty ministry in Western Australia (1947-53) originally had two honorary ministers, both of whom were given portfolios, but were not paid. During the life of the government, salaries were

---

[43] Reality became confused with protocol, however, in 1910. An honorary minister, acting as Minister for Agriculture, made the mistake of signing a notice in the *Gazette* as if he officially held the portfolio. (*Parl. Deb.* [N.S.W.], 2nd ser., 1910, 39: 409.)

[44] Repealed in 1921. The provision that another minister may act for the minister mentioned in a statute does not, of course, apply only to honorary ministers. Victoria was the first colony to legislate for this purpose. (Acts Interpretation Act, 1890, sec. 6.)

granted to them and the prefix 'honorary' was dropped. In New South Wales, the title is varied from time to time; the most popular one is 'minister without portfolio', but some governments have preferred the other terms, and there have been cases of ministries including both an 'assistant' minister and an 'honorary' minister.[45]

It will be seen that the status, functions, and salary provisions for these posts are as confusing as the names attached to them. One may now legitimately ask whether there are any differences at all between assistant ministers and others. The letters already quoted have some bearing on the question of their duties. Bruce stated that they were appointed 'primarily for the purpose of assisting Ministers in carrying out the work of the Public Departments'. Garran said that an assistant minister 'may countersign Executive Minutes and all other documents for signature by the Governor-General. And he may, of course, perform all administrative acts and decisions which are not by statute required to be done by a Minister of State'. A British writer, explaining the puzzling phenomenon to his readers, observed that 'a colonial friend' had told him that

> distances are great in Australia, and very frequently a Minister, say of Lands or of Mines, has to travel far for inspection or other purposes, and may thus be absent for a time from Parliament. Consequently it is advisable to have an extra Minister or two to take his place in Parliament for the time being to answer questions relating to his Department.[46]

More recently, a former federal minister has related how he was originally appointed honorary minister in the Bruce government to deputize for the Attorney-General, who was abroad. Later, he became 'a sort of offsider to the Prime Minister, taking the work of any Minister who was ill or absent'.[47] Labour governments have found a special use for honorary ministers as representatives of the government in the upper house of parliament, especially in Western Australia. The most curious reason of all for appointing an honorary minister arose in 1910, when the ballot for ministers in the second Fisher government (Commonwealth) produced a tie for tenth place. The ministry was thereupon enlarged to eleven.

Whatever their title, assistant ministers always sit in cabinet and take a full part in cabinet discussions. As most of them also hold portfolios, it is apparent that the differences between a minister

---

[45] e.g. the Fuller and Lang governments (1922-7) and the Stevens government (1932-9).
[46] W. F. Trotter, *The Government of Greater Britain,* p.95.
[47] McLachlan, *An F.A.Q. Australian,* p.130.

without prefix and an assistant minister are less important than the similarities. The differences are that an assistant minister is paid less,[48] and that his name appears at the very end of the list of ministers in order of seniority. Far from an assistant minister being what his name suggests, he is frequently appointed to look after one of the responsibilities of a more senior minister who has been saddled with more than one task. For example, R. G. Casey was appointed Assistant Commonwealth Treasurer in 1934, but he was in effect Treasurer for the ensuing year while the portfolio was nominally held by the Prime Minister, J. A. Lyons.[49] Assistant ministers in the Commonwealth have also been made politically responsible for the activities of independent statutory bodies. In a recent case, the Curtin government gave some of its members, in addition to their own portfolios, the task of assisting certain other ministers. This was in 1942—i.e., at the height of the war against Japan. The same government took the practice further by appointing certain members of parliament to assist ministers without altering their parliamentary status.[50]

A few declarations of principle on the subject have been made in federal parliament. In the debate on the Ministers of State Bill, 1941, the then Prime Minister, R. G. Menzies, expressed himself as opposed to the continuance of the post of assistant minister. In his speech on the second reading, he remarked that

> the system of having assistant ministers is not altogether satisfactory. I have felt myself since I became Prime Minister, and I am quite sure some of my predecessors have felt the same, that it is desirable that every person who sits in Cabinet should do so as a Minister of State with a specific responsibility for some department of State and with specific accountability to Parliament for the way in which he administers that department. Consequently, it seems to me to be desirable to dispense with the post of Assistant Minister, and to take steps to see that each man who is in fact a Minister shall be a Minister of State with responsibilities for a department of State.[51]

Menzies returned to the topic in the debate on the Ministers of State Bill, 1946.

> MR. MENZIES: . . . I always had great difficulty in understanding that an assistant Minister who was paid a certain sum of money out of the Cabinet fund —

[48] The difference in salary is usually of the order of £300-£400.
[49] In 1935, he was officially given the portfolio and the Ministers of State Act was amended accordingly.
[50] *Parl. Deb.* (C. of A.), 171: 1455.   [51] Ibid., 167: 323.

MR. CHIFLEY: The same as honorary Ministers are in the States.

MR. MENZIES: Quite so. I had great difficulty in understanding that an assistant Minister was not, in fact, holding an office of profit under the Crown. For many years, the practice continued, the view being that assistant Ministers were remunerated, not by the Crown for services rendered to the Crown, but by Ministers of State for services rendered to Ministers of State. That put the assistant Ministers in a very queer and anomalous position.

In the same debate, Chifley, then Prime Minister, defended the institution, whose object was

to enable Ministers with full Cabinet rank to be relieved in cases of sickness or when they can be spared to take a holiday and, generally, to relieve them of some of the heavy burden of work which falls upon their shoulders . . . the practice of appointing Ministers without portfolio is adopted by the State Governments and the Government has merely carried into the Commonwealth sphere a practice originally inaugurated by the States. As to the legal and constitutional position I concede that the Constitution may not have contemplated the appointment of assistant Ministers. The exigencies of the present day, however, are such as to justify their appointment.[52]

One curious aspect is that assistant ministers have always, apart from the one or two instances mentioned above, ranked as full members of cabinet. In 1917, a former honorary minister deplored the practice. Ministers, he declared,

meet in Cabinet not to consider the general policies that are best in the country's interest, but to solve some tangles concerning individual members of the Government in connection with the administration of their Departments. It is then devil take the hindmost, and the man with the loudest voice has his grievance first heard. The Cabinet . . . is not what it ought to be . . . a thinking machine for the consideration of the country's destinies.[53]

The remedy, according to Kelly, was to delegate the routine duties of administration to under-secretaries who would not be members

[52] Ibid., 189: 1146-9. In 1958, Menzies again referred to the dubious constitutional position, arguing that a salaried assistant minister would hold an unauthorized office of profit under the Crown. (Ibid., 7 Eliz. II, H. of R., 18: 434.)

[53] W. H. Kelly, M.H.R. for Wentworth; ibid., 83: 2796. Kelly had been a member of the Cook ministry, 1913-14.

of cabinet. There is evidence that Kelly's description of cabinet meetings has remained an accurate one, and in the circumstances the work of an assistant minister would be positively handicapped by absence from cabinet. But the more important reason may lie in the weakness of collective responsibility. Difficult as this is to enforce at any time, the introduction of a hierarchical principle by placing some ministers 'below the line' could be simply asking for trouble. As most Australian ministries are small, the problem of unwieldiness has not been important. It is only since the size of federal cabinet rose to nineteen in 1941 that this consideration became significant, and even there the hierarchical principle did not become established until 1956.

Parliamentary Under-Secretaries

Until the Menzies government was, in 1956, split into ministers of cabinet rank and ministers not in cabinet, the post of assistant minister was the closest Australian equivalent to the British practice of appointing ministers 'below the line'. There is, however, no analogue at all to the thirty or so junior ministers to be found in any British government. In the states, ministries are too small to necessitate such posts, and parliaments too small as a source of recruits. Successive Commonwealth governments have tinkered with the possibility, but the constitutional difficulties are severe, and where appointments have been made the duties have approximated those of a parliamentary private secretary in the House of Commons rather than a parliamentary under-secretary. The first example was the appointment of W. M. Marks as parliamentary under-secretary for External Affairs in 1921.[54] At this time W. M. Hughes, as Prime Minister, was responsible for External Affairs. The portfolio then included the external territories of New Guinea, New Britain, etc., some of which were new accessions as a result of the war. What Marks' precise duties were is not clear but he regularly answered questions in parliament about the territories.

The next appointment was made by the Lyons government in 1934. In November, the Governor-General's speech promised that the unemployment problem would be the special concern of the Minister for Commerce. In the event, the government appointed F. H. Stewart, M.H.R. for Parramatta, who had been Minister for Commerce in the first Lyons ministry, 1932-4, as parliamentary under-secretary for employment. Stewart was to work with a special

[54] The appointment was announced on 21 December 1921, as part of a reconstruction of the ministry, and came to an end with Hughes' resignation in February 1923.

sub-committee of cabinet on the unemployment problem. The appointment was severely criticized by the Opposition, which harassed Lyons with questions about Stewart's functions, about his lack of an office, about the government's breach of faith in not appointing a full minister to take charge of unemployment, and so forth. There was particular emphasis on the fact that Stewart did not answer questions on the employment problem in the House of Representatives. The Speaker was himself at a loss on this matter, as Section 92 of the Standing Orders refers only to Ministers of State and other members who have charge of any business on the notice paper. His conclusion was that the Prime Minister could authorize the minister in charge of the department concerned (i.e., Commerce) to deal with these matters. It was alleged by the Opposition, among other things, that Stewart's inferior status was the result of a deal with the Country Party, which had not been represented in the first Lyons government. The leader of the Country Party, Dr Earle Page, had been given the Commerce portfolio in the second Lyons ministry.

The anomalous character of Stewart's position was underlined when the Prime Minister stated, in response to a question, that Stewart attended meetings of cabinet at which unemployment was discussed. Finally, after prolonged Opposition pressure, Lyons agreed that Stewart should be given the right to answer questions in parliament as Marks had done.[55] The experiment was discontinued when Stewart resigned in February 1936, but was revived two years later when the Lyons government appointed two parliamentary secretaries, one for Defence and one for the Treasury. Once again, they were not to answer questions in the house or to reply personally to letters; their function was to 'co-operate with ministers in administrative work'.[56] The appointments lapsed after the death of Lyons in 1939 and the reconstitution of the ministry, although one of the two, G. A. Street, became Minister for the Army in the first Menzies government in 1939.

The abandonment of this experiment was referred to with regret in a debate in 1941. The Labour M.H.R. for Bourke, Mr Maurice Blackburn, deplored the fact that the experiment had not been repeated. He supported the appointment of under-secretaries because they would be 'buffers between Ministers and members of Parliament. One source of trouble to all Ministers is the manner in which they are bombarded by letters by honorable members who have not approached the department concerned, or are dissatisfied with a departmental decision.' The Prime Minister, Menzies,

---

[55] *Parl. Deb.* (C. of A.), 145: 650-741 *passim*.   [56] Ibid., 157: 6-7.

pointed out that if the under-secretaries were to be paid the constitution would first have to be amended. Blackburn's retort was that the payment of assistant ministers was not a violation of the constitution, and he saw no reason why parliamentary under-secretaries should not be paid out of the cabinet fund in the same way as assistant ministers.[57]

Perhaps the main reason why any interest should be taken in the question of parliamentary under-secretaries arises from the comic opera episodes in federal parliament in 1952. Shortly after the Menzies-Fadden administration took office in 1949, it appointed four parliamentary under-secretaries. The Nicholas committee on parliamentary salaries suggested that the duties of these men were 'necessarily more arduous and more constant than those of private members and their expenses are higher'. Recognizing the constitutional difficulty, the committee cautiously recommended that subject to the proper interpretation of the constitution, under-secretaries be paid an additional salary of £500.[58] A few months after the publication of the committee's report the status of the under-secretaries blew up in the government's face.

After having provided accommodation for the under-secretaries in Parliament House (where all ministers' offices are located), the Speaker, A. G. Cameron, a stormy petrel of long standing, decided to withdraw his recognition and instructed the officers of parliament to remove the names of the under-secretaries from the doors of their rooms. The Opposition, delighting in this opportunity to irritate the government, proceeded to draw the Speaker out on his reasons for this action. Cameron stated that, in his view,

> the officers concerned are not officers of this Parliament; they are officers of the Crown. For that reason I have refused to recognize them in this House. I went so far, and I think that I was in error in doing so, as to provide certain accommodation for them in this building. As the House knows, I am a small farmer and not a lawyer, but I think that I can read English.[59]

He went on to rule that ministers could not delegate their authority and that a member who accepted the position of under-secretary had rendered himself liable to disqualification because he held an office of profit under the Crown. In support of his views, Cameron cited British practice, in particular the report of a committee of the House of Commons in 1941, which had argued that

[57] Ibid., 167: 379.
[58] Report on Salaries and Allowances of Members of the National Parliament, 1952, p.19.   [59] Parl. Deb. (C. of A.), 217: 717.

the real test was not whether a member had received money for performing certain duties, but whether he held an office. At this stage the government decided to intervene, and the Acting Prime Minister, Sir Arthur Fadden, made a prepared statement. The appointments, he said, had been made

> informally, in an announcement by the Prime Minister. The object of the appointments was to provide assistance for certain Ministers. The Parliamentary Under-Secretaries have made enquiries, conducted correspondence, and occasionally received deputations on behalf of ministers. There has, however, been no delegation of the authority of a Minister to do any executive act which a Minister is, by law, required to perform.

He pointed out that parliamentary under-secretaries were not paid salary but only travelling allowances, and cited the legal opinion given by the Attorney-General, who had stated that under-secretaries did not, in law, hold an 'office', and certainly not an office of profit.[60]

The Leader of the Opposition, Dr Evatt, declared himself dissatisfied with the statement, and asked Sir Arthur Fadden to table opinions given by previous Solicitors-General on this question.[61] The government did not respond to the request, but a few months later the Prime Minister made a lengthy statement on the subject which traversed the ground once more. In the course of his remarks, Menzies foreshadowed the possibility of assistance being given to ministers by parliamentary under-secretaries in the House. It would be useful, he said, if an under-secretary

> could, during the committee stages of a Bill, sit at the table and relieve his Minister in the discussion of clauses and amendments as they arise. We would therefore think it an extremely useful thing if the Standing Orders permitted a Parliamentary Under-Secretary to sit at the table and to relieve his Minister from time to time in the committee stages of Bills . . . I shall take a suitable opportunity of inviting the Standing Orders Committee to consider this problem and to make a recommendation to the House about it.[62]

In spite of this last statement, the government took no further action in the matter, and although the posts of parliamentary under-secretary remained during its lifetime, their significance remained minimal and there was no instance of one of the incumbents being promoted to ministerial rank.

[60] Ibid., 217: 818-19.
[61] Ibid., 217: 819.   Sir Robert Garran's views were cited above.
[62] Ibid., 218: 618-21.   The statement carefully dodges the constitutional problem, on which Menzies' views have already been quoted.

20

SOME PROBLEMS OF OPERATION

Ministers as Administrators

T H E R E I S general agreement that cabinet ministers in Australia take a great deal of direct interest in the details of administration. As a consequence, departmental work may suffer from lack of delegation, and in addition ministers become identified in the public eye not only with policy but with responsibility for individual acts of administration. On occasion, ministers may exploit this fact to earn approbation (as in 1942, when a minister in the Curtin government was accused of being a 'cheer chaser'); more often, however, they incur odium. A Premier of Victoria, Graham Berry, was attacked for his administration of land policy, and a bad season was popularly blamed on the 'Berry blight'. In 1935, the Minister for the Interior in the Lyons government, T. W. Paterson, was personally identified with attempts to prevent a certain Mrs Freer from entering Australia, and in consequence a well-known agricultural pest known as 'Paterson's curse' was nicknamed the 'Mrs. Freer weed'.[1] R. G. Menzies, during his first term as Prime Minister, received the sobriquet of 'Pig-iron Bob' on account of his attitude towards the export of this material to Japan. In 1948 and 1949 the Minister for Immigration, A. A. Calwell, received considerable adverse publicity because of his emphasis on the rigorous administration of the 'White Australia' policy, which led to the deportation from Australia of Asian nationals who had married Australian citizens.

Perhaps the outstanding case of unjustified odium incurred for acts of administration was that of J. J. Dedman, Minister for War Organization of Industry in the Curtin government. Dedman's department, as the one chiefly concerned with restrictions on civilian consumption, launched a number of schemes to rationalize the production of various consumer goods in order to conserve scarce materials. This led to a number of lurid stories in the press, of which the most famous was the allegation that the minister had 'killed Santa Claus' by prohibiting the manufacture of pink icing for cakes. The personal abuse heaped on Dedman overlooked the

1 Paterson's Curse (*Echium plantagineum*) is a large herb with purple flowers, common in southern parts of Australia.

fact that this and other schemes of rationalization had been devised by trade associations in the industries concerned and had
merely been gazetted by the Department of War Organization of
Industry.

Another consequence is that ministers are reluctant to take decisions, and have a tendency to send far too many matters of a
routine character to be dealt with by cabinet. As a result, cabinets,
especially in the Commonwealth, frequently resort to the appointment of *ad hoc* sub-committees to deal with matters which could be
competently disposed of by a single minister. Federal cabinet is
said to be particularly prone to this tendency; for instance, Budget
discussions sometimes go on for a long time and, in conformity
with Parkinson's famous law, spend far too much time on matters
of comparatively trivial detail. Similarly, needless pains are sometimes taken over details of international agreements whose outlines have already been approved.

Lack of delegation has been adversely commented upon on
various occasions. The Royal Commission on Postal Services
(1910) criticized attempts by the Postmaster-General to interfere
with the day-to-day administration of the department.

> There have been nine Postmasters-General since the inaugura-
> tion of the Commonwealth, and the evidence discloses that
> most of the Ministerial heads endeavoured to effect signal alter-
> ations of policy. Ministers are apparently anxious to signalize
> their occupancy of office by some new and distinct act of
> administration; but due regard does not appear to have been
> paid to the effect of such actions . . . there also seems to have
> been a strong inclination on the part of Postmasters-General to
> give too much consideration to, and interfere with, details, in-
> stead of confining themselves to the broader principles of ad-
> ministration.[2]

In 1916 a Royal Commission on the public service in Victoria
made similar criticisms. Its report pointed out that too much work
was placed on cabinet because of statutory provisions requiring the
most trivial matters of administration to have the assent of the
Governor-in-Council. Thus, cabinet had had to approve the
granting of overtime for a workman employed by the Public
Works Department, the retirement of a cook in a government
insane asylum, and permission for a bailiff employed by the Lands
Department to act as a poundkeeper. Lack of delegation extended
from ministers to the permanent heads of departments, some of
whom attempted to deal with every important question entering

2 *Report of the Royal Commission on Postal Services,* 1910, p.15.

their department. This was accompanied by lack of co-ordination both between ministers and between departments, and the Commission ironically suggested that some departments should place over their entrances the notice 'no connection with the shop next door'.[3] In 1927, another Royal Commissioner made similar criticisms.

> When I observe the trivial matters which are placed before Ministers for their approval, I feel sorry for them. I am sure that Ministers would appreciate being relieved of such minor matters of routine, but because whatever they do is likely to be criticized, and because no doubt there is always something of a feeling of 'here today and gone tomorrow' about their office, it is difficult to institute reform.[4]

Sometimes, however, this direct concern with administration has been regarded as a virtue rather than a vice. A former Attorney-General of New South Wales asserted that ministers in Australia were legitimately exercising their discretion on administrative questions because of the absence of routine. 'There are few official traditions handed down from one permanent secretary to another; there are seldom precedents in any matters; whatever is done must be done on the direct responsibility of the Minister.'[5] Another observer defends a strong attitude towards officials by ministers on the ground that the mediocrity of most Australian ministers gives public servants an exaggerated view of their own importance.

> The standard of ability displayed by the average member of parliament who reaches office is not very high. Thus the door is left wide open for the application of the bureaucratic 'departmental view', and 'government by public service' accordingly tends to become an established organization.[6]

A similar view to Denning's has been stated most forcibly by J. T. Lang, who gives an account of how the under-secretary of the New South Wales Treasury tried to pressure him, when he first became Treasurer, into signing important papers without reading them, as his predecessors in the office had done. 'The oldest trick in the Public Service is to buffalo a new minister with the "file treatment" . . . too often the bureaucrats win the "battle of the files". They bluff their ministers into submission. Then they destroy the government but manage to survive themselves.'[7]

[3] Report of the Royal Commission on the Public Service of Victoria, 1916.
[4] Report of the Royal Commission on the Victorian Public Service, 1927.
[5] B. R. Wise, The Commonwealth of Australia, p.232.
[6] Denning, Caucus Crisis, p.70.   [7] I Remember, pp.173-7.

A striking case study of the important relationships which occur in the administrative process is to be found in the events connected with the approval of tenders for constructing extensions to the General Post Office in Sydney in 1939.[8] Two departments, the Post Office and the Department of Works, were concerned. The Director-General of Posts and Telegraphs, Sir Harry Brown, agreed to the acceptance of the second lowest tender, because it provided that the building be faced with terra-cotta tiles, rather than the lowest tender, which provided for a sandstone facing. The Minister for Works, H. V. C. Thorby (Country Party), who had been a builder in private life, disagreed, and recommended the acceptance of the lowest tender. This view was accepted by the Postmaster-General, A. G. Cameron, on grounds of economy in expenditure. A copy of the correspondence was sent to Sir Harry Brown, who instructed his assistant to communicate with Canberra (the headquarters of the Post Office being in Melbourne) requesting that the matter remain in abeyance until Brown had spoken to the Postmaster-General. As it happened, there was now a new Postmaster-General, E. J. Harrison, as the Lyons ministry had in the meantime been replaced by the first Menzies government. Harrison agreed that a terra-cotta facing should be used, and asked Brown to draft a letter to the new Minister for Works, Senator Foll. The latter, however, saw no reason to vary the decision of his predecessor. When a copy of Foll's letter to Harrison reached Brown, he said to his political superior: 'But, Mr. Harrison, he cannot do that in the face of the recommendation of these men who are paid to advise Ministers, these experts of the Department.'[9] Harrison now drafted a further letter to Foll in which he emphasized his strong preference for terra-cotta, and Foll then wrote to the Director of Works in Sydney, instructing him to accept the appropriate tender.

Thorby, hearing of these events, moved the adjournment of the House of Representatives to discuss the matter. In emphatic terms, he explained that he was personally in favour of the sandstone facing, and declared: 'I defy the Commonwealth architects, or any others, to justify a terra-cotta faced building.'[10] Harrison, in reply, defended his action in taking the advice of his departmental officers: 'When all is said and done they are the experts and the Minister is only a layman.'[11] Cameron took up this gage, and retorted that Harrison's remarks suggested that

[8] *Report of the Royal Commission on Additions to the Sydney G.P.O.*, 1939.   [9] Transcript of Evidence, p.544.
[10] *Parl. Deb.* (C. of A.), 158: 670.   [11] Ibid., 158: 676.

anyone would think that we have arrived at a stage when it is an offence on the part of a Minister of State to have an opinion, or a policy, of his own . . . [it appears that] the honourable gentleman has no opinion whatsoever excepting that which is placed before him by the head of his department . . . if we are to accept the position that Ministers of the Crown are running this country, and not the heads of departments, then the method should be that a Minister of State hears the reasons advanced by the heads of his department for and against any particular proposals and arrives at his own decision . . . it appears as though the Minister for Works was at fault in daring to disagree with the recommendation of the head of his department.[12]

By this time, animosity between the U.A.P. and the Country Party had become explicit. U.A.P. members alleged that Harrison, who had been Assistant Minister for Works in the Lyons government, had not been consulted about the contract. Mr Lane, M.H.R. for Barton, accused Cameron and Thorby, as 'cobbers' in the Country Party, of ignoring Harrison. 'A strong-minded agriculturist walked into the office of the Assistant Minister and, in his usual dictatorial manner, said to him, "We two Ministers have decided this." ' He concluded pointedly: 'A departmental officer is an advantage to some Ministers.'[13]

The responsibility of ministers for administration is affected by the absence of a well-defined echelon of senior officials such as the administrative class of the British civil service, whose role in advising on policy is explicitly recognized. Criticisms have often been made of the poverty of staffing of government departments in Australia at the policy-making level. Eggleston wrote that

the lower ranks are over-staffed and the thinking staff starved. The prejudice against the 'tall poppies' prevents enterprising and capable men from joining the service, and results in scanty staffs in the highly paid sections. The few officers there are, are immersed in routine, and have no leisure to think out policy.[14]

Nor are ministers able to seek assistance to any large extent from their private secretaries. Whereas any British minister has a principal private secretary whose rank in the civil service is that of under-secretary, and a staff of subordinates, Australian ministers

---

[12] Ibid., 158: 679.
[13] Ibid., 158: 686-7.   The Royal Commissioner (Mr Justice Maxwell) refuted suggestions that Sir Harry Brown's behaviour had been 'officious', and observed that 'the extent to which a departmental head will seek to influence a ministerial decision depends not only upon the circumstances of the case, but on the particular departmental head'. (*Report of the Royal Commission on Additions to the Sydney G.P.O., 1939.*)
[14] *State Socialism in Victoria*, p.299.

normally have only one private secretary, who may be a junior officer of the minister's department, or else a political friend whom he brings with him when he takes office.[15]

The Payment of Ministers

The constitutional position regarding the payment of cabinet ministers in Australia follows the tradition established by the Act of Settlement. All holders of offices of profit under the Crown are debarred from membership of parliament, except the officers of parliament and those listed in a schedule which in the states is appended to the Constitution Act, and in the Commonwealth is contained in successive Ministers of State Acts. The various Constitution Acts all provide for an appropriation to pay ministerial salaries until parliament otherwise provides. The first constitution to come into operation in Australia, that of the colony of Victoria in 1855, provided £14,000 for this purpose. In this, as in all succeeding cases, no statutory rule was laid down as to the distribution of the amount, and it is still the general custom to appropriate the 'Cabinet Fund' in a lump sum. Changes in the amount, to provide for additional portfolios or for rises in ministerial salaries, are usually made by amending the constitution of the state in question, or, as in the Commonwealth, by amending the Ministers of State Act. There have only been one or two instances where the amount paid to a particular minister was provided by statute. In 1883, the Victorian Officials in Parliament Act provided for the appointment of a Minister of Defence to be paid £1,500. In Queensland, an Act of similar title in 1885 provided a special allowance of £750 for the Vice-President of the Executive Council. In Queensland this office, which is always held by the Premier, provides the statutory basis for the salary differential between that functionary and his fellow ministers.

The level of ministerial salaries prevailing, at least in the larger colonies, at the end of the nineteenth century is illustrated by the salary arrangements of the Gillies-Deakin ministry in Victoria in 1886. In this, the Chief Secretary (i.e., the Premier) and the Treasurer each received £2,000; the Attorney-General, £1,600; the Minister of Defence, £1,500; and the other six ministers, £1,400 apiece. The equivalence in salary between Premier and Treasurer is unusual, being the result in this case of the two-headed character of the ministry.[16]

15 In 1953, three-quarters of ministerial private secretaries in the Commonwealth were junior officers of the minister's department, and only a small proportion had been in the job for any length of time.
16 Jenks, *The Government of Victoria*, pp.277-8.

On the establishment of the Commonwealth, salaries at about this level were adopted as the norm. Section 66 of the Commonwealth Constitution appropriates the sum of £12,000 for the payment of seven 'Ministers of State'. Out of this the Prime Minister received £2,100, and the other ministers £1,650 each. Funds had also to be found to pay £750 to the Vice-President of the Executive Council, who was the eighth member of the cabinet, as well as the whips. This was provided by deducting an amount from each of the Ministers of State. That this contribution continued to be normal was indicated in a debate in federal parliament in 1935. During a discussion on the status of assistant ministers, the Minister for Trade and Customs, T. W. White, stated that 'Assistant Ministers in the present Cabinet are paid the difference between the Parliamentary salary and their present salary by the full portfolioed ministers'. He added that the exact amount deducted in this way had never been disclosed since federation. The assistant minister in question was the Assistant Treasurer, R. G. Casey, who had been promoted to the position of Treasurer, which necessitated an amendment of the Ministers of State Act. The Prime Minister, J. A. Lyons, pointed out that Casey could now be paid on the same basis as other ministers, who up till then had contributed towards his salary.[17]

An official comparison of salary provisions in the states is to be found in the *Commonwealth Year Book* for 1920.

N.S.W. Premier: ministerial salary + £500
     Attorney-General: £1,520
     6 other ministers: £1,370
     Solicitor-General: £1,000
     Vice-President of the Executive Council: £800

Vic.   £8,400 for 8 ministers

Q'ld   8 ministers, paid £1,000 each; one designated by the Governor to receive an additional £300

S.A.   6 ministers, paid £5,000 in all. One minister to be 'honorary' (a provision later abolished)

W.A.   6 'principal officers of State', paid a total of £6,200

Tas.   Ministers paid £700 in addition to their allowance as M.P.s, except for the Premier, in whose case the amount was £900

17 *Parl. Deb.* (C. of A.), 147: 351-9. Details of ministerial salaries are also given in *Parl. Deb.* (C. of A.), 1917, 83: 2793-4; 1938, 158: 1676-7; 1952, 216: 210-17. Exact figures for the early cabinets were kindly supplied by Mr J. H. Starling, former Secretary of the Prime Minister's Department.

Ministerial salaries remained at much the same level until the depression of the 1930s, when there were widespread cuts in salaries and wages throughout the community. These cuts were gradually eliminated by 1939, but ministers received increases only through general rises in parliamentary salaries. The only important exception to this rule was the provision made by federal parliament in 1938 for a special allowance of £1,500 for the Prime Minister.[18]

A new era opened in 1952 with the publication of the report of a special committee of inquiry appointed by the Commonwealth government. Previously, there had been criticism of the secrecy attached to ministerial salaries. In the Senate debate on the Ministers of State Act of 1935, Senator Duncan-Hughes said he could see no reason why ministerial salaries should not be published. 'Secrecy in such matters', he added, 'gives rise to curiosity and causes unnecessary, and sometimes adverse, comment.' He was supported by Senator Hardy who compared the situation unfavourably with that in Canada, where ministers were both better paid and where their salaries were published.[19] Criticism was renewed three years later when the Act was again amended. W. V. McCall, a government back-bencher in the House of Representatives, made an unfavourable comparison with the British Ministers of the Crown Act, passed in the previous year, where ministerial salaries were listed.

In 1951, following pressure for a general increase in parliamentary salaries, the Menzies government appointed a committee headed by a member of the New South Wales Supreme Court bench, Mr Justice H. S. Nicholas, to make a complete review of the matter. Mr Justice Nicholas was a distinguished constitutional lawyer who had been counsel to the Royal Commission on the Constitution in 1927-9, and the report of his committee is a model of analysis. It makes the simple point that while a politician's salary should not be excessively attractive, it should not be so small as to act as a deterrent to entering politics; conversely, it should be large enough not to involve him in financial embarrassment. The report is the first official document ever published in Australia to contain a rational discussion of the various financial commitments to which ministers and members of parliament are liable. It criticized the numerous wrong-headed letters about ex-

---

[18] Act no. 2, 1938. The Ministers of State Act, 1946, increased federal ministers' salaries and raised that of the Prime Minister to £3,400, exclusive of the special £1,500 allowance. The states also increased ministers' salaries shortly after the war.　　　[19] *Parl. Deb.* (C. of A.), 147: 396.

cessive salaries for politicians that had been received from members of the public during the inquiry. 'We have borne in mind' says the report, 'the danger of encouraging the so-called professional politician . . . the danger exists but in our opinion its magnitude has been exaggerated.'[20]

The report demonstrated how the salaries of senior government officials had risen steadily since 1901 so that in every case except that of the Prime Minister, a minister received less than the permanent head of his department, whereas in 1901 ministers had received from two to three times as much. It also made certain general comments about the hierarchy within cabinet, which represent the first official recognition of a situation that has grown up steadily in Australia, as in other countries. The committee recommended that the Treasurer should be paid more than the other ministers; that the Deputy Prime Minister, not being the Treasurer, should be paid a special allowance of £300; and that out of the other ministers approximately six should be classified as 'senior ministers'. It also recommended a considerable increase in the Prime Minister's differential, by which he would receive, in addition to his parliamentary salary, an amount of £4,000 plus an entertainment allowance of £3,500.

The example set by this committee was soon followed in other cases. In Victoria, a committee headed by a former member of the Nicholas Committee, Sir Frank Richardson, produced a similar report in 1954, and subsequent reports were produced for Tasmania in 1955 and for New South Wales in 1956. All three of these accepted the principle of a high differential for the Premier; Victoria and New South Wales accepted the recommendation that the Deputy Premier be paid a special allowance, which had not been adopted by the Commonwealth government. The New South Wales report, made by Mr E. S. Wolfenden, also recommended that the differential possessed by the Attorney-General should be discontinued—a practice already adopted elsewhere.[21]

The practice of having ministerial salaries fixed by an independent committee now seems to have taken firm root in Australia, although the convention of appropriating the amounts in a lump sum and not including separate statements in the Budget has

20 *Report on Salaries and Allowances of Members of the National Parliament*, 1952, p.13.
21 The Wolfenden report (not to be confused with a contemporary English document) gives a table of parliamentary and ministerial salaries current in 1956. Commenting on the disparity between ministerial and official salaries, it suggests that a minister's remuneration 'should at least approximate that of the Under-Secretary of the Department'.

remained. That this may still lead to acrimony was well illustrated in 1956, when the reconstruction of the Menzies ministry necessitated a further amendment to the Ministers of State Act. In the previous year, a committee of inquiry headed by the ubiquitous Sir Frank Richardson had recommended increases in parliamentary salaries without, however, suggesting any changes in the additional amounts paid to ministers. The debate was conducted with notable lack of finesse by the Treasurer, Sir Arthur Fadden, who tried to rush the Bill through and provoked a minor revolt among government back-benchers. The number of senior ministers had been increased through the division of the government into ministers of cabinet rank and other ministers, but as only a lump sum was appropriated, suggestions were heard that unjustified increases in ministerial salaries were being made, out of keeping with the Nicholas and Richardson reports. The Treasurer was able to soothe these fears by pointing out that the Nicholas report had emphasized the Prime Minister's right to fix the number of senior ministers at his discretion, which had been exercised in this case.[22]

Secrecy

In view of all that has been said, it is hardly surprising that secrecy of cabinet proceedings is frequently breached in Australia, although the situation is not as extreme as in the United States. Formal safeguards, such as the Executive Councillor's oath, are much the same as in Britain, but, as Jennings observes, the only effective sanction is practice.[23] In Australia this sanction frequently operates to encourage disclosure rather than to preserve secrecy.

When cabinet solidarity is genuine and the conventions of collective responsibility are respected, secrecy will be much easier to enforce. Neither of these conditions is secure in Australia, where the disclosure of cabinet information has not infrequently been used as a political weapon. Another possible reason for the lack of secrecy arises from the large volume of routine administrative business transacted by cabinet. Harrison Moore observed many years ago that 'the secrecy of Cabinet proceedings is guarded well enough in matters of the first importance, but . . . the number of departmental matters dealt with in Cabinet is very large, and this has probably been responsible for recent practice whereby frequently a *communiqué* is made to the Press'.[24] In the states,

22 *Parl. Deb.* (C. of A.), 4 Eliz. II, H. of R. 1: 39-90.
23 *Cabinet Government,* p.248.
24 In Atkinson (ed.), *Australia: Economic and Political Studies.* Moore's article was originally written in 1914.

neither matters of policy nor of administration have ever been concealed for long. Perhaps more interesting is the extent to which important policy matters of national policy have been disclosed by members of the federal cabinet.

The relationship between cabinet and the Press is also of importance. In Australia, as elsewhere, the Press regards it as its duty to disclose whatever it can discover. The principle enunciated by Delane, editor of *The Times*, London, that 'the first duty of the press is to obtain the earliest and most correct intelligence of the events of the time, and instantly, by disclosing them, to make them the common property of the nation' finds general observance.[25] However, few Australian journalists would share Delane's reticence with regard to confidential documents. When a minister offered to supply him with secret information in return for the political support of *The Times* Delane is said to have remarked: 'I don't much care to have confidential papers sent to me at any time. The possession of them prevents my using the information which from one source or another is sure to reach me without any such condition of reserve.' The absence of an Official Secrets Act in Australia, at least in peacetime, removes any legal obstacle to the recurrent practice by which confidential documents have been quoted in the Press. Thus, in 1917, the daily papers in Sydney quoted freely from a secret memorandum on conscription prepared by W. A. Holman.[26] In the following year, the contents of the first report of the New South Wales Royal Commission on the Public Service were disclosed in the Press before the document was presented to parliament.[27] Again, in 1929, the Sydney *Sun* published extracts from a confidential memorandum prepared by the Commonwealth Attorney-General, J. G. Latham, on industrial policy.

In the latter case, a fencing match took place in the House of Representatives, Opposition speakers attempting to trap the government into admitting that such a memorandum existed, ministers doing their best to avoid the admission. Finally, the Prime Minister, S. M. Bruce, admitted its existence but accused the Press of misquoting.

The document from which the newspaper paragraph purported to quote, but which it did not quote accurately, conveying quite

25 Quoted by Wickham Steed, *The Press* (Penguin Special ed.), p.76.
26 Cf. Evatt, *Australian Labor Leader*, pp.450-1; Lang, *I Remember*, p.95-100.
27 I am indebted to Dr V. A. Subramaniam for drawing my attention to this incident, where a threat of action for contempt of parliament was made.

an erroneous impression as to its contents, was circulated by the Attorney-General, and sent not only to me, but to every other member of the Cabinet, and was marked as a Cabinet document. No one outside Cabinet except an officer could have any knowledge of its contents, unless the document was stolen, or its contents had been improperly disclosed in dereliction of duty by some public officer.

It was lamentable, he declared, that the Press should behave like this, for 'government would be rendered impossible in any country if the members of the Cabinet could not circulate among themselves documents freely expressing their opinions on important matters of public interest'.[28]

Bruce's view was challenged by an Opposition member, Anstey, who argued that the important question was whether the theft had led to the disclosure of information which should be made known in the public interest. 'If it is true that a Cabinet document was stolen, the thief has rendered good public service by enabling the wisdom of the Attorney-General to be broadcast to a listening and gaping world.'[29]

On several occasions, ministers or ex-ministers have quoted the actions of other governments as a weapon of debate. In 1909, Sir William Lyne, in his celebrated diatribe against the Fusion ministry, gave a circumstantial account of intrigues conducted by Sir John Forrest in a number of governments, and accused him of being personally responsible for the resignation of C. C. Kingston over the Arbitration Bill of 1903.[30] During the debate W. H. Kelly, M.H.R. for Wentworth, pointed out that the private ministerial conversations which Lyne had disclosed were subject to cabinet secrecy, and could not be answered by other ministers lest they be themselves forsworn. In another case, W. Angwin, a member of the Scaddan government in Western Australia, quoted a minute written by the former Colonial Secretary. This document, he claimed, showed that the previous (Wilson) government had intended to flood the state with cheap labour.[31]

In 1916, the Leader of the federal Opposition, F. G. Tudor, gave a circumstantial account of a meeting of the Executive Council in Melbourne where he and another minister, W. G. Higgs, had refused to approve a regulation under the War Precautions Act which would have affected the conduct of the impending refer-

[28] *Parl. Deb.* (C. of A.), 121: 19.   [29] Ibid., 121: 61.
[30] Ibid., 49: 1010-32. It may be recalled that Kingston had caused an uproar by disclosing details of the Bill to a correspondent of the *Age*.
[31] *Parl. Deb.* (W.A.), 1915, 51: 847-8.

endum on conscription. Sir William Irvine, rising to a point of order, declared:

> The Honourable Member can, of course, read any regulation that was passed, and received the assent of the Governor-General-in-Council; but the honourable member stated that this regulation had been turned down at some meeting of the Executive Council. If that is true, it is a revelation of facts, which ministers present at the council are bound by their oath of office not to reveal, and to which this House should not for one moment listen.[32]

The Speaker refused to make a ruling on Irvine's point, declaring that 'if honourable members who were members of Cabinet desire to make statements as to what takes place in Cabinet I cannot rule their remarks out of order'. When the Prime Minister, Hughes, commented that in his opinion the reference to Executive Council proceedings should not have been permitted, the Speaker instructed him to withdraw his remark as a reflection on the Chair, stating that 'if I did anything wrong in allowing the honourable member for Yarra[33] to make those references, the obvious duty of the Prime Minister was to prevent my error'.[34] Later in the debate, Higgs defended the disclosure. 'I do not', he said,

> support the proposition that the members of a Cabinet should follow the example of thieves when they keep that honour which is said to distinguish them. We were loyal to the Prime Minister until the Prime Minister was disloyal to us . . . Does not the honourable member for Flinders consider that ministers have some responsibility to the Parliament of the Commonwealth? Does he suggest that ministers, because they have an oath of secrecy, are bound to smother up every act of every colleague? I take it that each minister is the judge as to what he should disclose, and must take the responsibility for his actions.[35]

In 1942, the Minister for Labour and National Service, E. J. Ward, referred to a cabinet submission by his predecessor in the portfolio (H. E. Holt) regarding the employment of women in wartime. Before he could proceed with his expressed intention of quoting the submission, Holt interjected, asking the Speaker whether Ward was in order 'in divulging publicly in the House the contents of an official document presented to a Cabinet, the members of which are sworn to secrecy? I submit that the Minister is violating the oath of secrecy by proxy, as it were, in divulging

---

32 *Parl. Deb.* (C. of A.), 80: 9246.   33 F. G. Tudor.
34 *Parl. Deb.* (C. of A.), 80: 9277.   35 Ibid., 80: 9280.

the contents of such a document.' The Speaker's reply was that 'any confidential document submitted to Cabinet, as this one apparently was, must, in the public interest, remain entirely confidential. The document itself must not be quoted, nor its contents be referred to.'[36]

This ruling was challenged by a Labour member, Frank Brennan, former Attorney-General in the Scullin government, who reminded the House that when confidential communications between Scullin and members of his cabinet were disclosed in parliament no one had challenged the propriety of the discussion. He added: 'There is no precedent for a declaration from the Chair that a minister may not say in this Chamber that some previous minister made a submission in certain terms to a Cabinet. With great respect, sir, I submit that it is not a part of your function to censure honourable members as to the propriety of how they acquire information.' He pointed out that there was no standing order forbidding a minister to state in the house what a previous minister had submitted to cabinet. 'It does not come within the province of the Chair to pass judgment upon the matter. It is entirely for the minister himself, knowing the history of the document which he proposes to quote, to decide whether or not he should divulge its contents.'[37]

The Speaker (Mr W. M. Nairn) refused to accept this argument, and ruled that the minister was debarred from making the document public, and also from revealing its contents. About eight years later, when a similar incident occurred, the Leader of the Opposition (Mr Chifley) asked the Prime Minister (Mr Menzies) for a ruling on this point. In 1950, the Minister for the Army, Mr Francis, quoted from a cabinet minute to prove his allegation that the policy of the preceding Chifley government had been to favour the release of Japanese war criminals. Chifley asked the Prime Minister 'whether he approves of a minister using secret and confidential documents, or documents which purported to be so, in debates in the House?'[38] In a statement prepared in reply to this question, the Prime Minister said:

I have no doubt that it is a sound general principle that submissions made to Cabinet by individual ministers are confidential to that Cabinet, as are Cabinet communications between ministers . . . It is quite clear to me that the Minister . . . was drawn into reading the precise terms of a ministerial recommendation made to Cabinet because of the controversial course the debate had taken . . . I want to reaffirm my belief as leader of

36 Ibid., 171: 1440.   37 Ibid., 171: 1441.   38 Ibid., 206: 933.

the government that it would be a sound practice that no reference should be made to Cabinet files except for the purpose of (a) discovering what operative decisions have actually been made; and (b) ascertaining the contents of communications in fact made between the government and outside persons or authorities.[39]

In one or two cases, internecine conflicts between members of the same government have been aired in parliament, to the accompaniment of quotations from cabinet documents designed to prove the truth of statements on either side. In the exchange between Hughes and Watt in 1920, Hughes made a statement justifying his decision to table correspondence between Watt and himself. The correspondence had been edited by Hughes with the concurrence of the Leader of the Opposition (Tudor) and the leader of the Country Party (McWilliams), so that the two latter might agree that Watt's position would not be misrepresented through publication. Glossing his action, Hughes stated that it was 'without precedent for a government to table the secret correspondence that has passed between its various members',[40] but that the circumstances of the case were equally unprecedented. A minister who had been sent to represent Australia in financial discussions with the British government, and to represent Australia also at several international conferences, had resigned precipitately, leaving his country without any representation. Moreover, Watt himself had asked that the correspondence be published.[41]

In the same year a Country Party member, W. C. Hill, attacked Hughes for his handling of the wheat pool, administered by the Wheat Board of which Hughes was chairman and Hill a member. After the debate had been adjourned, Hughes quoted from the minutes of the Board in a Press statement replying to his Country Party critics. On the resumption of the debate, Hill followed suit with lengthy extracts from the Board's minutes. When Cook, Minister for the Navy, queried the propriety of quoting the minutes of a public body, Hill retorted: 'I presume that what the Prime Minister can read I can read.' Cook admitted the point, with the rider that Hughes and Hill had been equally unwise in their actions.[42]

---

[39] Ibid., 206: 1145-6.   [40] Ibid., 92: 2521.

[41] This did not prevent Watt from complaining later that he *had* been misrepresented.

[42] In 1948, the Deputy Leader of the Opposition, A. W. Fadden, quoted a statement made to the British cabinet by Chifley, the Prime Minister, and one made to the Executive of the Council for Scientific and Industrial Research by its responsible minister, Dedman. He acknowledged that these were 'confidential'. *Parl. Deb.* (C. of A.), 198: 1038.

Some years later, confidential cables between Scullin, then in London, and his cabinet colleagues in Australia were disclosed in the Press during 1931. Tension inside the Scullin government was such that there is little doubt that the information was divulged to the Press by dissident members of the Labour caucus in an attempt to influence Scullin's policy.[43] On this occasion, although the statements made in the Press were quoted in parliament, no challenge was made on the grounds of secrecy. Incidents of this kind have continued to occur when dissensions arise inside cabinet over matters of policy. During the life of the Curtin government, disclosures appeared periodically in the Press regarding new economic controls to be imposed by the government for wartime purposes. The chief target of these disclosures was the Minister for War Organization of Industry, Mr Dedman, whose department was responsible for most of the controls directly affecting civilian consumption. There is reason to believe that advance information on these matters was 'leaked' to the Press by other members of the ministry who were anxious to embarrass Dedman.[44] In 1952, a dispute within cabinet over the disposal of the government-owned airline, T.A.A., was publicized in the Melbourne *Herald,* which revealed that cabinet opinion was evenly divided on the question. The public reaction to this disclosure had considerable effect in inducing the government not to wind up T.A.A. The Prime Minister, Menzies, was reportedly incensed by this episode, and having failed to discover the identity of the minister responsible for the 'leak', instructed all members of cabinet to have no conversations with journalists except in the presence of their private secretaries or another minister.[45] In 1956, the Minister for External Affairs, Mr Casey, was accused of deliberately making disclosures to the Press concerning Australian policy towards the dispute over the nationalization of the Suez Canal by the Egyptian government. Shortly before a meeting of cabinet, the Melbourne *Herald* published a statement that Casey would make 'an impassioned plea' to cabinet not to support the use of force in the dispute.[46] Allegations were made that this statement was a manoeuvre to make it clear to other countries that the Commonwealth government was not unanimous in its support for the

---

[43] Cf. Denning, op. cit., p.66.
[44] The unpopularity of Dedman with the Press (whose hostility was influenced by its principal advertisers, the large retail stores) was matched by the relative popularity of J. A. Beasley, Minister for Supply, whose department had frequent clashes with W.O.I. on matters of economic policy.
[45] This instruction proved enforceable for only forty-eight hours.
[46] 11 September 1956.

British stand on the matter, which the Prime Minister was then publicly espousing in London.[47]

The most recent case of disclosure involved yet a different twist to the situation. In this case, the Prime Minister quoted confidential documents on defence policy in parliament in order to rebut allegations made in public by a former member of the Military Board. Following criticism of the excessive cost of construction of an ammunition filling factory at St Mary's, near Sydney, the former Master-General of the Ordnance, Major-General Legge, wrote a letter to the Melbourne *Age* accusing the government of disregarding the advice of the chiefs of the armed services. There had, he alleged, been 'gross and inexcusable waste of public money at St Mary's, not, as the Prime Minister seems to imply, on the advice of the Chiefs of Staff, but in fact contrary to the recommendations made'.[48] Two days later Major-General Legge repeated the allegations in a public statement accusing the government of ignoring the advice not only of the Chiefs of Staff, but also of a whole galaxy of advisory committees on defence. These allegations were followed by a series of articles in the *Sydney Morning Herald* which subjected the government's defence policy to a blistering criticism. As a result, the Prime Minister, Mr Menzies, attacked the *Sydney Morning Herald* for accusing him of 'evasiveness and prevarication' in his statements on defence, and then quoted a series of documents to prove that the government had in fact acted on the advice of the Chiefs of Staff. These documents included a letter from the Chairman of the Chiefs of Staff Committee, Vice-Admiral Sir Roy Dowling, a copy of a brief signed by Major-General Edgar on behalf of the Chief of the General Staff, and a further brief for the Minister of Defence Production signed by Major-General Legge. Justifying his action, the Prime Minister argued that this was a special case.

> Documents passing between the government and its Defence advisers are confidential. Any belief that they are liable to disclosure would gravely, and perhaps fatally, impair the mutual confidence and utter frankness which is of the essence of defence communications . . . The Chiefs of Staff, through their Chairman, have, to prevent a grave public misconception, felt it necessary to make a partial waiver of the rule . . . I hope there will be no further occasion for a departure from the general rule of non-disclosure of defence documents.[49]

47 Adelaide *News,* 12 September 1956.   48 23 September 1957.
49 *Parl. Deb.* (C. of A.), 1957, 6 Eliz. II, H. of R. 16: 1354-8. Opposition members accused Menzies of putting pressure on the Chiefs of Staff to agree to the disclosure.

If any conclusions are to be drawn from this selection of cases, it is that cabinet secrecy, like other conventions of cabinet government, will almost invariably yield to considerations of political advantage.

The Problem of Outside Interests

One of the less fortunate consequences of the Australian attitude to government is the prevalence of easy-going standards regarding the possibility of conflict between a minister's official position and his private interests. Moreover, the use of a ministerial position to advance the material interest of its incumbent, although officially frowned upon, is only on occasion subject to effective sanctions. Jennings observes that ministers must not only be honest and incorruptible, but should also appear to be so.[50] The history of British politics is marked by a succession of rulings on this point made by various Prime Ministers since Palmerston, whereas Australian politics is marked rather by repeated evasions of the problem.

On several occasions, the private legal practice of a minister has come into conflict with his official position. In 1893, the Attorney-General (Edmund Barton) and the Minister for Justice (R. E. O'Connor) in the Dibbs ministry in New South Wales were involved in a law-suit between a firm of contractors and the New South Wales Railways Commissioners. Before the case came to court, Barton ruled that the Railways Department was not under the shield of the Crown. The effect of this was that the Attorney-General was entitled to appear against the Railways Commissioners in a court of law. According to one hostile critic, Barton's announcement was clearly made in order to permit the heads of the Crown Law department—himself and O'Connor—'to earn large fees by appearing for the great railway contractors . . . Barton's audacious and abusive quibbling in defence did not better the position, nor did his *ad misericordiam* statement that an adverse vote would cover him, an honourable man, with infamy and dishonour'.[51] (The vote was on a motion of censure launched by the opposition.) During the debate, Joseph Cook, then a member of the Labour Party, said that Barton's plea 'sounded like an appeal from Dr. Jekyll for mercy to Mr. Hyde'.[52] The censure motion was carried, but the Premier, Sir George Dibbs, evaded resigning by an unconstitutional manoeuvre which

50 *Cabinet Government*, pp.96-102.
51 Black, *A History of the N.S.W. Political Labor Party*, pt. 3, p.9.
52 Ibid.

enabled him to prorogue parliament on the day after the vote was taken.

In 1905, a case arose regarding the Attorney-General of the Commonwealth. Cook, now Deputy Leader of the Opposition in the House of Representatives, pointed out that the government of South Australia had retained Isaac Isaacs (Attorney-General in the Deakin ministry) and Josiah Symon (Attorney-General in the previous Reid ministry) in connection with possible litigation over the use of the waters of the river Murray. Cook asserted that 'the Attorney-General of the Commonwealth ought not to be in a position in which his functions as the representative of the Commonwealth Government may conflict with obligations which he has undertaken to a State Government'.[53] During the debate, reference was made to the actions of George Reid, who was accused of accepting a brief from a shipowner against the Newcastle Marine Board when he was Premier of New South Wales. Another speaker recalled that Sir Henry Parkes had laid down that a law officer of the Crown should not take part in any proceedings in which the Crown might be involved.

Isaacs, defending his position, was supported by most of the lawyers in the Chamber. He pointed out that he could not afford to give up all his practice, of which he had relinquished a great deal, to attend to his parliamentary duties. Comparisons with Great Britain, which had been freely made during the debate, were irrelevant because of the large salary paid to the Attorney-General to enable him to relinquish private practice. The Commonwealth was unlikely to be involved in this case, but if it were he would certainly withdraw, nor would he give advice which reflected on the position of the Commonwealth.

Much of the 1905 debate revolved around the exact significance to be attached to a 'retainer', and the point arose again in 1913, when the Opposition criticized Irvine, Attorney-General in the Cook ministry, for accepting a retainer from the Marconi Company, which was then litigating with the Commonwealth concerning patent rights. The Opposition claimed that Irvine should not keep his retainer, and that he was acting in a manner 'detrimental to the best interests of the Commonwealth'. A number of references were made to contemporary events in Britain (including another case involving the Marconi Company) and several speakers suggested that the rule recently laid down by Asquith should be adopted in Australia. One speaker reminded the house that Mr Agar Wynne, Postmaster-General, had resigned his directorship

53 *Parl. Deb.* (C. of A.), 26: 1329.

of a private bank on becoming a minister, and that in an earlier instance, George Higinbotham had given up his private practice when he became Attorney-General of Victoria.[54]

Australian governments have, on the whole, evaded suggestions that rulings should be laid down regarding the holding of directorships by ministers, although the links between governments and large private firms have occasionally reached almost scandalous proportions. In the 1880s, successive governments of Queensland were so closely linked with the Queensland National Bank, the principal financial institution of the colony, that Opposition critics described the ministry as merely a branch of the bank. In the Morehead ministry (1888-90) the Premier was himself a director; the Treasurer, Sir Thomas McIlwraith, was a former director and one of the largest shareholders; A. H. Palmer, President of the Legislative Council and a former Premier, was also a director. McIlwraith's successor as Treasurer, Pattison, was the largest shareholder in the bank, and in addition was chairman of the Mount Morgan Mining Company, one of the largest industrial concerns linked with the bank. When McIlwraith resigned after a series of intrigues in which he was displaced by Pattison, he condemned the influence of 'Mount Morganism' on the government. Corrupt practices were freely alleged, and the Brisbane Press attacked 'the Mount Morgan speculators who controlled the private fortunes of the leading members of the dominant party'.[55] A later Premier, T. J. Byrnes, launched a prosecution against three former directors of the Queensland National Bank, including Morehead. Fortunately for the defendants, Byrnes died suddenly. His successor, Dickson, did not press the case, and the defendants were acquitted.

It may have been some memory of this affair, as well as a desire to emphasize the determination of his government not to be involved in scandals like those in which members of the preceding Gair ministry were involved, that led G. F. R. Nicklin, on becoming Premier of Queensland in 1957, to instruct all ministers to surrender their directorships.[56]

The problem of directorships assumes particular significance because of the large volume of public works carried out under contract, and the fact that ministers are frequently concerned with

54 Ibid., 70: 944-1001.
55 *Brisbane Courier*, 3 May 1890, quoted S. A. Rayner, 'The Evolution of the Queensland Labor Party to 1907'.
56 In 1956, for instance, the Minister for Lands, T. A. Foley, was found guilty of corrupt practices by a Royal Commission, and resigned his portfolio (but not his seat).

the details of such contracts. In 1904, the Minister for Water Supply in Victoria, George Swinburne, was attacked in the Victorian parliament because he was a director of a large engineering firm which occasionally tendered for government works contracts.[57] The most notable case was that of Senator A. J. McLachlan, Postmaster-General in the Lyons government, who resigned after a series of criticisms on this point. In 1936, Maurice Blackburn, a member of the Labour Opposition, asked Lyons in the House of Representatives whether any ministers were company directors. Lyons replied that 'no reason can be seen why information of this personal character should be supplied to the honourable member'.[58] Blackburn's question had been prompted by two articles in the *Bulletin* drawing attention to the fact that McLachlan was a director of several important companies, including one which was the largest manufacturer of concrete pipes in Australia, and consequently had considerable business with the Post Office. The question, he said, was not personal. 'The people of this country have a vital interest in knowing what are the business interests of members of the Cabinet. We live in an age in which government and business are closely associated.'[59]

Two years later, the matter flared up once more under circumstances which, according to McLachlan, were deliberately provoked to embarrass him. Notice of a question was given by a Labour member about the letting of tenders to the Hume Pipe Company Ltd., of which McLachlan was chairman. McLachlan writes that he had 'taken the precaution before being sworn in of asking whether my position as chairman of directors of the Hume Pipe Company would in any way conflict with my duties as Postmaster-General'.[60] McLachlan's behaviour in parliament does not suggest that he was as innocent of the implications of the matter as his account suggests. Both Lyons and McLachlan had emphasized the fact that the position of chairman of directors of a public company did not mean an intimate knowledge of all the company's activities, and McLachlan himself argued that, as Postmaster-General, he could not be expected to know the name of every company with whom his department had contracts. Curtin, leader of the Opposition, expressed his astonishment at these statements. It was extraordinary, he remarked, that the chairman of a company should be no more than a 'guinea pig' and take so

57 E. H. Sugden and F. W. Eggleston, *George Swinburne*, pp.163-4.
58 *Parl Deb*. (C. of A.), 151: 637.   59 Ibid., 151: 1021-2.
60 An *F.A.Q. Australian*, p.255. In the light of subsequent events, McLachlan accepted assurances on this point rather too lightheartedly.

little part in determining its policy. He reminded the house that the company had been supplying the Post Office for a number of years, and that government contracts had been specifically mentioned at its last annual meeting.

I cannot understand a Minister being ignorant of important contracts involving substantial expenditure . . . the Postmaster-General knew he was Postmaster-General, and he also knew that he was chairman of directors of the Hume Pipe Company Ltd. It would be extraordinary to me if, in that capacity, he did not know that the Hume Pipe Company Ltd. was tendering for government contracts.[61]

Lyons was finally pushed into making a statement of principle on the matter in reply to Curtin's critical remarks on the adjournment. He said:

It does not seem to me to be practicable or desirable to lay down a general rule that no Cabinet Minister shall be a director of any company. It would be plainly anomalous if one Minister could retain the whole of the proprietorship of some business or enterprise, while another minister was debarred from being one of several directors conducting an exactly similar business or enterprise . . . If a contract which the Government makes with such a company is one which results from the exercise of individual judgment or selection, as in the case of the supply of goods of some special kind, it seems clear that a directorship of the company concerned would be inconsistent with the discharge of ministerial duty. But some arrangements which are technically contracts are made on a non-selective or non-discriminating basis . . . if there is the slightest element of judgment or choice involved in the placing of government business, no minister should be a director of a company which is the recipient of that business.[62]

Perhaps the most spectacular case of all is one to which publicity has been given very recently. From 1955 onwards, there was frequent public comment on the fact that the Minister for Transport in the Bolte ministry in Victoria, Sir Arthur Warner, was also a leading industrialist with extensive interests in the manufacture of electrical equipment. It was pointed out that the Railways Department, of which he was ministerial head, was supplied with electrical gear by this particular group of companies, Electronic Industries Ltd. Publicity became more intense when it was also revealed that automatic soft-drink machines manufactured by a

61 *Parl. Deb.* (C. of A.), 157: 1313-14.
62 Ibid., 157: 1373-4.

subsidiary firm were being installed on Victorian railway stations, and that ordinary water fountains were being removed from the same stations. Despite considerable public agitation, neither Sir Arthur Warner nor the Premier felt moved to make any public rejoinder. A contemporary account remarked that 'Warner himself scarcely deigns to enter into a discussion on the matter, while Premier Bolte, who used to depend very much on Warner as the grey eminence in Cabinet, simply reiterates his confidence about the integrity of all members of his Cabinet'. The same account stresses that the real significance of the case lies not in the individual instance but in the precedent which it represents.

> The real criticism . . . is the dangerous precedent that his dual role is setting for later politicians whose personal standards might be less securely above temptation. To some observers, the provincial character of the Cabinet he is sitting in, so far from being a justification for waiving the rules expected elsewhere, is the strongest reason for insisting on them, for it is an unhappy fact that the tendency for corruption is greater in Australian State parliaments than in the national assembly at Canberra.[63]

Finally, there is the curious instance of the large gift presented to W. M. Hughes in 1921 for his services to Australia during World War I. In 1921, a Labour member, Frank Brennan, moved the adjournment of the House of Representatives to discuss the acceptance by Hughes, then Prime Minister, of a gift of £25,000 from 'admirers in Australia and London', which had been presented at a public meeting in Sydney a few months earlier. The names of the people who had been on the platform at the meeting, observed Brennan, suggested that they 'may safely and not unjustly be presumed to have had something more than an academic interest in legislation passed through this House publicly, as well as in certain secret regulations passed from time to time by this government'.[64] The acceptance of gifts, he argued, was an infringement of the constitution, and he also recalled that in 1881 Henry Parkes had written to a testimonial committee refusing a gift of money before he made a trip to England. 'It is clearly my duty', Parkes had written, 'as far as lies in my power, to preserve my public position from personal entanglements which at the present or some future time might be made the ground of reproach or suspicion.'

Hughes disposed of this motion without much ceremony, re-

63 *Nation*, 22 November 1958.
64 *Parl. Deb*. (C. of A.), 95: 7698-710.

minding his hearers that in spite of Parkes' letter, he had in the
event accepted the money.

Corruption

The problem of 'outside interests' owes some of its significance to
the fact that many active politicians have, under Australian conditions, little source of income other than their parliamentary
salaries. Only a minority are able to continue earning substantially,
while occupying ministerial office, from such sources as directors'
fees, legal partnerships, landed property, and authors' royalties,
which are more important in countries where the greatest number
of politicians are drawn from the professional or business classes.
For a Labour man, moreover, a political career is liable to become
his only profession, and there is evidence that Labour men can be
tempted successfully by monetary offers. W. J. McKell, on becoming Premier of New South Wales in 1941, appealed to his ministers not to be tempted by offers of money in addition to their
ministerial salaries. 'I ask you to do nothing that would undermine
and destroy the confidence of the public or besmirch the reputation of my government. Your salaries are sufficient for your requirements.'[65]

A bibliography of the inquiries held by Royal Commissions,
select committees, and courts of law into alleged cases of corruption would fill several pages, and it may be assumed that not
every case which had occurred has been the subject of inquiry.
The attention paid to detailed matters of administration by ministers under Australian conditions infallibly provides opportunities
for them to succumb to corrupt offers in connection with such
matters as the disposal of Crown lands, the issue of licences, or
the sale of government assets. All the states and the Commonwealth can display a record in such matters, but it is not the intention of this comparatively short note to make a survey. It will
be sufficient to note briefly some of the more outstanding cases,
especially where Premiers have been personally involved. In
1881, for instance, E. A. Baker, Minister for Mines in the Parkes
government, was found guilty of corruption by a Royal Commission inquiring into the disposal of mining leases. Another member of parliament was also implicated. The minister was expelled
from parliament by a vote of the Legislative Assembly, and the
member was censured. Sir John Robertson, a former Premier and
at this time Vice-President of the Executive Council, resigned
office because of his connections with the member who had been

[65] *Daily Telegraph*, 28 October 1941.

censured. (He later rejoined the government as Minister for Lands.)

Another celebrated New South Wales case in which the disposal of Crown land was concerned took place in 1905, when a Royal Commission investigated the activities of the Minister for Lands, W. P. Crick, in connection with charges of extortion. He was placed on trial, together with another member of parliament, but two successive juries were unable to agree, and no conviction was recorded. Crick resigned his post and his seat, and was struck off the roll of solicitors by the New South Wales Supreme Court.[66] Some years later, the Premier of New South Wales, W. A. Holman, was mentioned in a Royal Commission of inquiry into a contract for the sale of wheat granted to a certain Georgeson in 1919. Despite a Press campaign of insinuations, the Royal Commissioner found no evidence that Holman had in any way been responsible for maladministration or corruption alleged in connection with the contract. However, Holman, like many other Premiers, seems to have neglected to supervise his colleagues with sufficient care, and his position was weakened by persistent allegations about his close connections with a well-known financier, H. D. McIntosh, whose name figured in several other inquiries at this time.[67]

The most famous case of all was that of J. T. Lang, who was clearly regarded by a Royal Commission in 1932 as the moving force behind a series of corrupt practices in the issue of licences for greyhound racing while he was Premier of New South Wales from 1930 to 1932. The same Royal Commission also dealt with the use of 'fruit machines' to raise money for public hospitals, a scheme which was illegal in its intention and corrupt in its administration. The Royal Commissioner commented sharply:

> It appears that a feeling is gaining ground that governments are not bound to observe strictly the terms of the laws which they administer. Mr. Gosling, when asked whence a certain power was derived, said that the Cabinet 'arrogated it to itself.' . . . In the case of mechanical coursing the Act gave authority to race on licensed grounds. Instead of licensing grounds the Minister issued permits to conduct racing. There was no authority vested in the Minister to do this, but nevertheless it became the practice.[68]

[66] The rather lurid details of this episode are recounted in Cyril Pearl, *Wild Men of Sydney* (1958); see also Evatt, op. cit., ch. 25.

[67] Evatt, op. cit., chs. 54-5.

[68] Report of the Royal Commission on Greyhound Racing and Fruit Machines, *P.P.* (N.S.W.), 1932, p.3.

Dealing with the operation of fruit machines, the Royal Commission report declared:

> It was distinctly improper that ministerial sanction should have been given to such a scheme as was evolved. It meant, in effect, that the hand of the police was to be stayed, that there were to be no prosecutions in certain cases, that immunity was not to be granted to all hotel-keepers who installed fruit machines, but only to such of them as used the machines belonging to the syndicate.[69]

Lang's autobiography contains some characteristically evasive comment on the Royal Commission report. He was not, according to his account, interested in the people who obtained the licences. 'That was a matter for the Chief Secretary.' As the Chief Secretary, Gosling, was by his own admission a person who acted only on the instructions of the Premier, one may be forgiven for regarding this remark as disingenuous. Lang concludes: 'Nothing was proved. No action was taken.'[70]

A Premier of Victoria also came to grief through dealing in land. In 1909, a Royal Commission inquired into the acquisition of certain estates by Sir Thomas Bent, Premier from 1904 to 1909. The accusations made against Bent in the course of this inquiry were so serious that they put an effective end to his political career. A case of a Premier who got into trouble over the disposal of mining leases was that of E. G. Theodore, although in this instance the accusations were made some years after the events were alleged to have taken place. In 1930, when Theodore was federal Treasurer, a Royal Commission of inquiry found that he had a case to answer concerning the operation of the Mungana-Chillagoe mines in northern Queensland. The Queensland government declared its intention to prosecute, and Theodore resigned his portfolio to contest the case. In 1931, a jury absolved him on all counts.

Tasmania has also been the scene of several notable accusations against ministers. In 1928, A. G. Ogilvie, who had completed a term as Attorney-General and became Premier in 1934, appeared before a Royal Commission in connection with his administration of the Public Trust Office. Twenty years later, another Premier, J. A. Cosgrove, resigned his portfolio to appear before a court on charges of corruption. The court's verdict was favourable to him, and he was promptly re-elected to the Premiership by Labour caucus. Ten years later, however, the Treasurer, Dr R. J. Turnbull,

69 Ibid., p.74.   70 *I Remember*, pp.358-9.

although acquitted on a charge of extortion in connection with the issue of a lottery licence, was instructed to resign and was expelled from the Labour Party.[71]

The general picture suggests that charges of corruption against ministers in Australia, so long as they are not conclusively proved, do not constitute a fatal threat to the political career of an individual. Ministers are not regarded in the same light as Caesar's wife; not only suspicion, but conclusive proof of guilt, is necessary before corruption becomes a ground for removal. In this sphere, as in others, it is the attitude of the party towards the individual which determines the result.

[71] He was reinstated as Treasurer, but his resignation was demanded after a clash with the parliamentary party.

21

THE ADMINISTRATIVE STRUCTURE
IN THE STATES

Ministerial Portfolios

CONSTITUTIONAL PROVISION was originally made in the colonies for 'officials liable to retire on political grounds', who were exempt from disqualification for parliamentary membership normally applying to holders of an office of profit under the Crown.[1] Each Constitution Act includes a schedule of such positions, of which there were initially five—Colonial (or Chief) Secretary; Attorney-General; Treasurer; Commissioner (or Secretary) of Crown Lands and Survey; Commissioner (or Secretary) of Public Works. Although the term 'Minister' has become general in the present century, some portfolios retain their archaic titles.[2] In New South Wales, the Treasury portfolio still resides in the 'Colonial Treasurer', and a few ministers in several states are officially described by the title 'Secretary'. In Queensland, the latter term applied to most portfolios until 1957, when 'Minister' was adopted generally.

Governmental responsibilities expanded rapidly at the end of the nineteenth century, and the number of portfolios grew, although some functions were surrendered to the Commonwealth at federation. In 1919, the states had the following portfolios in common:[3]

Premier (linked with Chief Secretary in Q'ld, S.A., and Tas.)
Chief Secretary (Home Secretary in Q'ld)
Treasurer
Attorney-General (linked with Justice in N.S.W.)

[1] Cf. Davies, *Australian Democracy*, pp.109-20; Spann (ed.), *Public Administration in Australia*, ch. 3; Department of Political Science, University of Melbourne, *The Government of Victoria;* S. R. Davis (ed.), *The Government of the Australian States.*
[2] In the states, it appears to be etiquette to refer to a 'Minister of the Crown', although not every state has established this as the formal constitutional usage. In the Commonwealth, both etiquette and constitutional prescription have been set from the beginning by the use of the term 'Minister of State' in the Constitution Act.
[3] *Commonwealth Year Book,* 1919, no. 12, p.924.

Lands (in S.A., Crown Lands and Immigration)
Public Works
Mines
Education (called Public Instruction in N.S.W., Vic., and Q'ld)
Agriculture (except Tas.)
Railways (except N.S.W. and Tas.)
Labour (Labour and Industry in N.S.W.; Industry in S.A.;
  Industries in W.A.; absent in Q'ld and Tas.)

Public Health portfolios existed only in New South Wales and Victoria, and Water Supply only in Victoria and Western Australia. Victoria also had a portfolio of Forests; New South Wales of Local Government; and South Australia of Marine.

The states vary considerably in their grouping of portfolios, and also in the order of seniority in cabinet. Seniority, or precedence, is officially determined by the order in which ministers are presented to the Governor for swearing-in, and is the prerogative of the Premier or Prime Minister. It is influenced by the party standing of the individual minister, by the importance of his portfolio, and (in the Labour Party) by his order of election in the caucus ballot. The variations between the states are illustrated by the following table,[4] which shows the situation at the end of 1958.

New South Wales (16 ministers; 25 departments and sub-departments)

Premier, (Colonial) Treasurer
Deputy Premier, Minister for Education
Attorney-General, Justice
Colonial Secretary, Immigration, Co-operative Societies
Health
Child Welfare, Social Welfare
Local Government, Highways
Transport
Housing
Public Works (Secretary)
Conservation
Lands (Secretary)
Agriculture, Food Production
Labour and Industry
Mines
Minister without portfolio

4 Ibid., 1959; and cf. Davies, op. cit., pp.118-19.

Victoria (14 ministers; 19 departments and sub-departments)

Premier, Treasurer, Conservation
Chief Secretary, Attorney-General
Transport
Agriculture
Public Works (Commissioner)
Health
Water Supply, Mines
Education
Housing, Immigration
Crown Lands and Survey (Commissioner), Soldier Settlement
Labour and Industry, Electrical Undertakings
Local Government
Forests, State Development
Minister without portfolio

Queensland (11 ministers; 18 departments and sub-departments)

Premier, Chief Secretary
Labour and Industry
Education
Justice
Treasurer, Housing
Development, Mines and Main Roads
Public Lands and Irrigation
Health and Home Affairs
Agriculture and Stock
Public Works and Local Government
Transport

South Australia (8 ministers; 14 departments and sub-departments)

Premier, Treasurer, Immigration
Chief Secretary, Health, Marine
Attorney-General, Industry and Employment
Lands, Repatriation, Irrigation
Works, Marine
Agriculture, Forests
Education
Local Government, Roads, Railways

Western Australia (10 ministers; 20 departments and sub-departments)

Premier, Treasurer, Child Welfare
Deputy Premier, Works and Water Supplies
Transport, Housing, Forests
Railways, the North-West, Supply and Shipping
Health, Justice
Education and Labour
Lands, Agriculture and Fisheries
Native Welfare and Police
Mines, Chief Secretary
Industrial Development, Local Government and Town Planning

Tasmania (8 ministers; 13 departments and sub-departments)

Premier, Attorney-General
Deputy Premier, Agriculture
Chief Secretary
Treasurer
Lands and Works
Education
Housing
Forests

Note. The Tasmanian cabinet usually has had nine members in recent years, but in this case no separate Attorney-General had been appointed following the resignation of the previous incumbent.

The position of Premier evolved only slowly during the last quarter of the nineteenth century. The Constitution Acts as originally passed gave precedence to the Chief (or Colonial) Secretary, who was customarily head of the government in the early years. In New South Wales he was frequently referred to as the 'Prime Minister', but the appellation was no more than honorific. The separate office of Premier began to assume its own importance when the head of the government ceased to be Chief Secretary as a matter of course. The first Premier of Victoria to use the title in this way was G. B. Kerferd in 1874, who was Attorney-General in his own ministry. A Premier's office was first established as a separate unit in Victoria in 1883, followed by Tasmania in the same year, and New South Wales in 1886. The latter was the first state to give separate statutory recognition to the office, which was included in the schedule to the Constitution Act in 1920. In other cases, the designation of a separate payment for the Premier has established the separateness of the office and its precedence over the others. In Queensland and Tasmania, on the other hand, the traditional link with the office of Chief Secretary is preserved by the existence of a department of 'Premier and Chief Secretary'.

Towards the end of the century, the link between the premiership and the treasurership emerged. Premier Berry of Victoria was the first man to set this fashion in 1875, and it soon became common in all the colonies. In the twentieth century there have been only occasional exceptions to the rule that the Premier is also Treasurer, especially in Tasmania, where six out of fourteen premiers from 1901 to 1958 had held other offices.

The convention that the Premier is always a member of the lower house of parliament was set very early. The only colony where there were notable departures from the rule was Tasmania, where ten premiers between 1856 and 1887 sat in the upper house, but since then there have been no further cases. Two instances occurred during the twentieth century, both of short duration. B. R. Wise, who was government leader in the upper house in New South Wales, was Acting-Premier of the state for a few months in 1904. In Western Australia, H. Colebatch, M.L.C., became Premier for one month during a political interregnum in 1919.

New South Wales and Queensland formally appoint one member of the ministry as Vice-President of the Executive Council. The Martin ministry in New South Wales (1866-8) was the first government to take this step; in Queensland, the position was established by statute in 1874. The New South Wales practice has usually been to confer the title on the government leader in the Legislative Council, who is frequently Attorney-General; in Queensland, it is almost invariably held by the Premier. The Wade ministry in New South Wales (1907-10) made the post a salaried one, and in 1932 it was included in the schedule to the Constitution Act. A contemporary observer wrote that:

> An increase was needed of Ministers who would do their work and who would not leave everything—decisions, details, and administration—to their under-secretaries and to the heads of departments. The Vice-President of the Executive Council is very hard worked while Parliament is sitting, and bills are pouring in on him . . . he is entitled therefore to payment by the State, and should not be dependent on the charity or kindliness of his colleagues.[5]

5 Black, *A History of the N.S.W. Political Labor Party,* pt. 5, p.45.

Victoria, although it has not adopted the name, achieves a similar effect by appointing an 'unofficial' government leader in the upper house, who has, since 1940, received an allowance in addition to his ministerial salary.

The position of Attorney-General exhibits some curious features. This minister is normally one of the senior members of cabinet, as well as being principal law officer of the Crown, and head of a department responsible for the judiciary and other legal functions of the state. In the beginning, the inclusion of the Attorney-General in cabinet followed the precedent of the Executive Council under gubernatorial rule. Its main justification is that Australian parliaments (and governments), especially in the states, contain few trained legal men, which is a particular handicap in view of the problems that arise from written constitutions subject to judicial review.[6] Some lawyers have deplored the situation, on the grounds that the Attorney-General's office 'has a political rather than a professional character. It has, in fact, been held by people who were not members of the legal profession at all.'[7] Various expedients have been employed to overcome the dearth of lawyers. In Western Australia, a constitutional amendment passed in 1899 provides that the Attorney-General must be a lawyer. In the absence of a lawyer, a Minister for Justice is appointed to administer the Crown Law Department, whose head effectively becomes the principal law officer of the government. In New South Wales the Attorney-General is forbidden to delegate his functions (which prevents them from being exercised by a non-lawyer). In 1908, a Royal Commission in Tasmania inquired into the possibility of making the office of Attorney-General permanent and non-political.

The post of Solicitor-General has also had a curious history, in parallel with that of the Attorney-General. Before responsible government, colonial governors had both an Attorney-General and a Solicitor-General on the British pattern; the former was a member of the Executive Council, but not the latter. In New South Wales, the ministerial post of Solicitor-General was abolished in 1872, and replaced by the portfolio of Minister for Justice.[8] The permanent head of the Attorney-General's de-

---

6 A former state minister described in an interview how the Attorney-General used to sit on the right of the Premier at cabinet meetings to prevent him from making unconstitutional or illegal suggestions. In the short-lived Watson government, 1904, the Attorney-General was H. B. Higgins, a member of the radical wing of the Liberal Party.   [*Studies*, p.97.

7 Harrison Moore, in Atkinson (ed.), *Australia: Economic and Political*

8 Henry Parkes, who was responsible for this, criticized slavish adherence to the British practice of having two law officers of ministerial rank.

partment was invested with the title of Solicitor-General. The two portfolios are linked to a single department called Attorney-General and Justice, which in recent years has been headed by a single minister bearing both titles.

In Victoria, the posts of Solicitor-General and Minister for Justice were filled only intermittently in the nineteenth century, and rarely both in the same ministry.[9] The Solicitor-General, like the Attorney-General, was empowered by the Acts Interpretation Act to perform the duties of a law officer of the Crown. In 1952, after long disuse, the post became a permanent one in the Law department.

A number of other portfolios have had a transitory existence as the result of special circumstances, the most idiosyncratic being that of Minister for Motherhood in the New South Wales Labour government of 1920-2.[10] A case where the title of the position remains long after its practical importance has vanished is that of President of the Board of Land and Works, a distinction borne by the Victorian Minister for Lands. In 1857 the Haines ministry placed the portfolios of Lands and Works 'in commission', and set up a Board of five, the President and Vice-President being members of cabinet. The subsequent Nicholson ministry restored the two separate portfolios, and in 1860 the Lands Act reconstituted the Board with the Minister for Lands as President. The Governor-in-Council is empowered to appoint other ministers as Vice-Presidents, of whom there are currently three, one always being the Minister for Public Works.[11]

The Character of State Administration

Administrative activity in the states is dominated by a network of public utility corporations and statutory boards which account not only for the bulk of employment and expenditure, but also for the most important fields of legislative activity and political interest. State executive functions may be classified as follows:[12]

[9] In the Munro ministry, 1890-2, Deakin was Solicitor-General, and the portfolio of Justice was held separately.

[10] According to J. T. Lang, his function was the distribution of layettes. (*I Remember,* p.172.) The portfolio was actually created to administer a scheme of child endowment.

[11] The Board also has official members. Its statutory functions are to approve works contracts and sales of Crown land. See Jenks, *The Government of Victoria,* pp.285-6; *Report of the Royal Commission on the Civil Service of Victoria,* 1859, Appendix.

[12] Department of Political Science, University of Melbourne, *The Government of Victoria.*

1. Legal, protective, and registry services
2. Regulation of primary production
3.   „   „ industry and commerce
4.   „   „ labour
5.   „   „ standards
6.   „   „ professional and occupational standards
7. Conservation and development
8. Social welfare
9. Education and recreation
10. Public health
11. Industrial health

The most important single heading is 'conservation and development', under which, for reasons apparent to anyone acquainted with Australian political history, appear most of the public utilities just mentioned, operating in the fields of electricity supply, railway transport, gas supply, savings banks, roads, housing, water supply and drainage, port control, grain elevators, urban transport, food supply and storage, loans for land settlement, soil conservation, and forestry. Apart from railways, which came under public control at an early stage, most of these enterprises were established in the present century, and it is their existence which has given state government its characteristic flavour. Water supply came under public control under the inspiration of Victoria, where the State Rivers and Water Supply Commission was set up in 1905, closely followed by most other states (except Tasmania, where a state-wide commission was set up only in 1958). Urban transport became a state responsibility during and after World War I, taken over in most cases from municipal control. Electricity generation was taken over by the states after World War II, except for Victoria, where the State Electricity Commission dates from 1919, and Tasmania, where the Hydro-Electric Commission was set up in 1930. All the states entered the field of public housing in a big way after World War II under an agreement with the Commonwealth, although small beginnings had been made earlier.

Davies has analysed the results of this situation as it affects the structure of state politics. It means, for one thing, that most important state legislation originates with the big public authorities, and that the permanent officials who run them are in a better position to make policy decisions than the minister who is theoretically responsible. Ministers, he remarks, 'though often made to feel personally very concerned with a particular corporation's success or lack of it, are normally in an extremely weak position to formulate, let alone enforce, useful modifications of policy'.[13] The comparative absence of important issues in state politics leads to a general preoccupation with administration, and in this officials will inevitably play a central role. Indeed, it might be contended with some plausibility that, apart from a few outstanding figures, state politicians have been of less consequence than the administrators and engineers who built up the great public enterprises. Perhaps the archetypal figure among these was Sir John Monash, Commander-in-Chief of the Australian Imperial Forces during World War I, who became first chairman of the State Electricity Commission of Victoria, and was said to deal with recalcitrant cabinets in the manner of Napoleon with the Directory.

Despite variations between the states, the universal tendency is for each state administrative system to become a collection of satrapies, jealous of their independence in matters such as finance, control of personnel, management methods, etc. It is a rare minister who can 'run' the agencies covered by his portfolio rather than be run by them. Not only has much of the responsibility for policy-making shifted from cabinet to the controllers of the large public corporations and the various regulatory commissions, but there is little in the way of an apparatus of control or co-ordination at the ministerial level to enable cabinet—and *a fortiori* the individual minister—to enforce changes in policy. In Davies' words, 'the relation of the central administration to the State utilities suggests the image of a dwarf in control of a troop of giants . . . in recent years, the main policy differences between passing cabinets have concerned the rank order of the corporations in the queue for funds'.[14] State politics, he adds, is 'taken up more and more with detailed problems in the running of a long-established machine, and less and less with adding new parts to this machine or thinking of new things for it to do'.

Co-ordination in the twentieth century has been largely a matter of finance, and the regular assumption by Premiers of the Treasury portfolio reflects this fact. Yet, even here, the necessity for policy decisions is largely removed by the dependence of all states on the financial policy of the Commonwealth government— firmly riveted by the establishment of the Loan Council in 1928, and the introduction of uniform income tax in 1942.

Traditional distinctions between policy and administration do not fit easily into this picture. Public corporations are, in theory, established to relieve ministers of the duty of day-to-day adminis-

13 *Australian Democracy*, p.117.
14 In G. W. Leeper (ed.), *Introducing Victoria*, p.295.

tration of complex enterprises. Yet, in the states, a minister who does not occupy himself with administrative detail has little else as a *raison d'être,* and in practice both ministers and the public regard ministerial responsibility for acts of administration as extending to the routine affairs of a business undertaking like the railway system.[15] The principle laid down by the Speaker of the House of Commons in 1948, that ministers may be asked to answer questions regarding the day-to-day administration of public corporations if the question is of sufficient public interest, has no relevance to the Australian situation.

The emergence of long-lived ministries and the long tenure of office by individual Premiers can lead to considerable centralization of authority in the hands of a strong Premier and a small group of permanent officials. In South Australia, the unparalleled tenure of Sir Thomas Playford since 1938 has led to a quite remarkable concentration of power in the hands of the Premier and a few senior officials, especially the head of the Chief Secretary's department (often described as *'The* Under-Secretary') and the Auditor-General. In New South Wales, it was well known for many years that the most powerful man in the government was the late chairman of the Public Service Board, Mr Wallace Wurth, who occupied the position from 1938 until his death in 1960.

Co-ordination

The apparatus of co-ordination at cabinet level is fairly rudimentary in character.[16] In New South Wales, a separate Premier's department was set up in 1907. W. A. Holman used the department to provide a cabinet secretariat, and employed one of his private secretaries (nicknamed 'The Boiler') to prepare briefs on important matters to come before cabinet. One of his successors, B. S. B. Stevens, appointed a senior official of the Premier's Department as cabinet officer, and the post has remained. Victoria set up a separate Premier's Department in 1936, whose head has become one of the most important officials of the government, but there is only a tiny staff responsible for cabinet affairs. A separate cabinet secretariat was also set up by the Queensland government

---

15 Confusion can result, as shown by repeated disputes in Western Australia over control of the railways. The Minister for Railways is incorporated (as a 'corporation sole') instead of the Railways Commissioners, as in other states. The Railways Act places responsibility for 'policy' on the minister. and for 'management' on the Commissioners. Disputes on what constitutes a matter of 'policy' are to be referred to the Governor-in-Council (i.e. cabinet).

16 S. Encel, 'Cabinet Machinery in Australia', *Public Administration,* 1956, vol. 15, no. 2.

in 1957, housed in the department of 'Premier and Chief Secretary'. In Western Australia, the Premier's office is relatively large and does attempt some co-ordination.

In none of these cases are minutes of cabinet meetings taken by a permanent official. In South Australia, decisions made at the weekly meeting are passed on immediately to 'The Under-Secretary'. In New South Wales, it is a well-established practice that one member of cabinet should act as secretary. Under Premier Stevens, it became the custom for this minister to write up the minutes before a cabinet meeting ended, so that they could be read and confirmed on the spot. To simplify the cabinet secretary's task, he is given blank decision sheets by the Premier's Department, which may afterwards produce copies of the minutes for circulation before the next cabinet meeting, and generally endeavour to do this four days before a meeting is due. In Victoria, the secretary to cabinet was, until 1947, the government whip in the Legislative Assembly. In the latter year, the constitution was amended to provide that one of the three honorary ministers should be secretary to cabinet, with an allowance. (The number of honorary ministers was reduced to two in 1950.) The duties of this functionary are somewhat vague, as it is also common for individual ministers and for the Premier to make their own notes of cabinet decisions. This can have confusing results. On one occasion, three different versions of what had been decided were firmly held by the cabinet secretary, the Premier, and the minister principally concerned, and a legal opinion on the constitutional status of a cabinet decision had to be sought from the Crown Solicitor before the controversy could be resolved!

In some ways the Treasury is more important as an agency of co-ordination even than cabinet. As so much of the work of policy-making is done outside cabinet, the problems of co-ordination depend more and more on the control of finance. The processes of Treasury control in the Australian states are modelled directly on the methods developed in Britain since the time of Gladstone.[17] As in Britain, the final veto of the Treasury over departmental estimates is the heart of the matter, and it is the annual 'cutting of the cake' which is the focus of Treasury authority. In addition, the Treasury shares with the Auditor-General the responsibility for scrutiny of expenditure within the estimates approved by parliament in the annual Appropriation Act.

[17] Described, e.g., by Jennings, *Cabinet Government,* ch. 7, or by S. H. Beer, *Treasury Control.* On Australia, see Jenks, *The Government of Victoria,* pp.18-21; W. J. Campbell, *Australian State Public Finance,* chs. 2-4.

Most state Treasury departments are organized on a fairly simple basis, and only the New South Wales Treasury has a separate Budget branch, with a staff of inspectors whose task is to review the estimates and expenditure of all departments and agencies. In Victoria, an attempt to strengthen Treasury control over departmental operations was made in 1932 when an unofficial body known as the 'Treasury committee' was set up at the instigation of the then head of the Treasury, the late H. A. Pitt.[18] The committee, whose membership was restricted to officials qualified in accountancy or economics, met weekly, and was given official status by the government when its usefulness was realized. During its lifetime, the committee recommended some important changes in the budgetary system. It lapsed on Pitt's retirement in 1938.

A fundamental difference between Treasury control in Australia and in Britain resides in the divorce of authority over finance from authority over staff and establishments. The control of personnel in the states is fragmented, in keeping with the character of state administration as a whole. The vice of departmentalism is apparent in the rarity of staff movements between various agencies, and in the strongly exclusive *esprit de corps* which results. In each state, the control of staffing in the 'traditional' departments is in the hands of a Public Service Board or Commissioner whose powers are laid down by statute, but these authorities have no say in the personnel management of the large corporations and statutory commissions which, between them, account for three-quarters of all state government employees, and jealously maintain their distinction from the 'public service'.

The establishment of independent statutory authorities to control personnel matters was the result of a long struggle to do away with patronage and 'spoils' by removing the powers of appointment and promotion from the hands of ministers. The first important attempt in this direction was the Victorian Public Service Act of 1883, but this was overshadowed by the New South Wales Act of 1895, which vested wide powers of control and inspection in a Board of three. Because of its staff of inspectors and its powers to make searching investigations into the work of departments, the Board has an unrivalled insight into the workings of the entire machine, and is in a position to give the government a great deal of advice on general policy. In recent years, as a result of the finan-

18 H. A. Pitt, 'Some Aspects of the System of Public Finance in Victoria', Papers and Proceedings of the Victorian Regional Group of the Institute of Public Administration, 1934, vol. 1, no. 5.

cial difficulties of the states, the Board's control has become even stronger. Economies in departmental expenditure, sometimes involving important changes of policy, are now made with the participation of representatives of the Board. Similarly, a check on the preparation of departmental estimates is made by Public Service Board inspectors and Budget inspectors from the Treasury, working in co-operation. New appointees to the Budget branch of the Treasury are now seconded to the Board's office for one year. In the case of statutory bodies whose staffs are not under the Board's supervision, a government decision in 1950 setting up a standing committee of the heads of all these authorities, presided over by the Chairman of the Board, has enabled a rationalization of policies on personnel administration, finance, supply and industrial relations.

In Victoria, public service control has had a more chequered history. Despite the recommendations of successive Royal Commissions that the Public Service Commissioner (replaced by a board in 1940) should be given authority to make decisions on personnel matters instead of merely recommending to cabinet, governments refused to relinquish their authority until 1946, when an amended Public Service Act gave the Board considerably enlarged powers.

Another factor detracting from the influence of state Treasury departments lies in the financial position of the large public corporations. In all states, some of these do not appear in the Budget. In Victoria, for example, one group of corporations, including the State Electricity Commission, do not appear in the public account and are subject to ministerial control only in regard to the fixation of charges, borrowing, and audit. Another group are not included in the Budget but do appear in the public account because they operate on trust funds. In New South Wales, some of the most important corporations do not appear in the Budget (e.g., the Electricity Commission and the Sydney Water Board), their capital being provided partly through loans. Their operating funds are held by the Treasury, but are available on simple requisition.

Finally, the dependence of the states on Commonwealth financial policy means that no state budget can be finally settled until it is clear what finance will be available from loans, Commonwealth tax reimbursements, and grants-in-aid. The Loan Council is effectively dominated by the Commonwealth and fixes the annual level of loan flotations. Although corporation borrowing was for a time outside the Council's authority, a 'gentlemen's agreement' in 1936 provided that corporation loans should be included in the round sum for each state. This has, to some extent, increased the influence of the state Treasuries over corporation policy.

Economic Policy

During the 1930s, several state governments made experiments with economic advisory bodies in an attempt to find ways of dealing with the acute economic situation following the world depression. The most notable of these was in New South Wales, where the Premier from 1932 to 1939, B. S. B. Stevens, had formerly been permanent head of the Treasury.[19] From 1933 to 1937 W. C. Wentworth[20] acted as economic adviser to the Treasury and Premier's Department, in which capacity he was responsible for some important changes in methods of preparing the Budget estimates. When he resigned, his place was taken by R. J. Randall, who was officially 'research officer' in the Premier's Department until 1940. In 1935, a Budget Bureau was established, which in 1938 became the Budget division of the Treasury, staffed by inspectors with training in economics or accountancy. Since its establishment, the Budget division has been the main source of recruitment for under-secretaries of the Treasury.

One of the main centres of economic research and policy formulation under Stevens was the Bureau of Statistics and Economics, whose assistant chief, S. R. Carver, functioned as Stevens' principal assistant on economic matters throughout his Premiership. Advice was also obtained from an economic research unit in the Rural Bank of New South Wales set up under the leadership of J. G. Crawford, economic adviser to the Bank, and from the economic department of the Bank of New South Wales whose establishment was due to the initiative of the general manager of the bank, the late Sir Alfred Davidson. In addition, considerable use was made of academic economists from the University of Sydney, who served as advisers on a part-time or *ad hoc* basis. They included Professor R. C. Mills, Dr E. R. Walker, H. D. Black, and S. J. Butlin. H. L. Harris, lecturer in economics at the Sydney Teachers' College, was attached to the Bureau of Statistics from 1935 to 1938.

The functions of this team of advisers were to prepare informa-

[19] Stevens resigned from the public service in 1925 after disagreements with J. T. Lang, who was Premier and Treasurer from 1925 to 1927. He entered politics and became Treasurer in the Bavin ministry, 1927-30.

[20] Great-grandson of the colonial politician of the same name; M.H.R. since 1949.

tion on local and international economic trends, to advise on budgetary policy, and to assist in preparing submissions to the Loan Council, where expansionist policies advocated by New South Wales were often in conflict with the deflationary orthodoxy of the Commonwealth and other states. Stevens and his successor as Treasurer, E. S. Spooner, placed stress on accurate information about economic conditions, and a weekly report on economic trends was prepared for members of cabinet under the editorship of Dr F. B. Horner, a staff member of the Bureau of Statistics, to which Harris and Professor Mills were the main contributors. In addition, a regular bulletin on international affairs was circulated to ministers, prepared largely by S. H. Roberts, then Professor of History at the University of Sydney.

Another state to make attempts in this direction was Queensland. In 1930 the Moore (Nationalist) government established a Bureau of Economics and Statistics under an Act of parliament. Its statutory function was 'to acquire and disseminate knowledge concerning the economic conditions of Queensland, including the income, production, and industrial efficiency of the community, and to collect statistical and other information relating thereto'. A director was appointed by the Governor-in-Council for a statutory term of seven years, the first incumbent being J. B. Brigden, previously Professor of Economics at the University of Tasmania.

The Bureau attracted great hostility from the trade unions as a result of its role in preparing evidence for the Queensland Arbitration Court to show why the state basic wage should be reduced following the decision of the Commonwealth court to reduce the federal wage in 1931. During the 1932 election campaign the Labour leader, Forgan Smith, promised to abolish the Bureau. On becoming Premier, however, he decided not to abolish but only to reorganize it, and the Act was amended, renaming it the Bureau of Industry. The Bureau was removed from the control of the Minister for Labour and Industry and became a branch of the Treasury, with fifteen members, eight appointed for terms of three years by the Governor-in-Council the other seven being permanent heads of departments appointed *ex officio*. Brigden remained as director, and was given the additional post of state statistician. The Bureau was deprived of its function of reporting on wages to the Arbitration Court, but given the added duty of advising on the expenditure of loan funds.

In 1938, the economist Colin Clark succeeded Brigden as director, and remained in that position until his resignation in 1952.

Since then the Bureau has virtually disappeared, and the duty of advising on loan expenditure has devolved upon the Co-ordinator-General of Works, who is responsible to the Premier.

Victoria also experimented briefly with an economic advisory committee at this period. In 1938, Premier Dunstan established a body of three members comprising a city businessman, the permanent head of the Treasury, and D. B. Copland, Professor of Commerce at the University of Melbourne, as chairman. This committee became less active when Copland was appointed Commonwealth Prices Commissioner at the outbreak of war, and lapsed entirely when he took up a diplomatic post in 1945.

With the assumption of general responsibility for economic policy by the Commonwealth during the war, the states lost most of their independent concern with such matters. It is of some interest, in conclusion, to note the continuity of personnel between the states and the Commonwealth.[21] From New South Wales, Carver became Commonwealth Statistician; Mills, Director of the Commonwealth Office of Education; Randall, deputy head of the Treasury; Walker, Deputy Director-General of War Organization of Industry and afterwards a diplomat; Crawford, head of the Department of Trade; W. A. McLaren, one of the original members of the Budget Bureau, head of the Department of the Interior; Horner, Assistant Commonwealth Statistician. From Queensland, Brigden became head of the Department of Supply and later economic adviser to the Australian Minister to the United States. From Victoria, Copland, after being Prices Commissioner, was successively Minister to China, Vice-Chancellor of the Australian National University, and High Commissioner to Canada.

21 The list is not exhaustive. In particular, it does not include members of the New South Wales Rural Bank's economic section, or of the economic department of the Bank of New South Wales, who were recruited *en bloc* to the Commonwealth service during the war.

22

THE ADMINISTRATIVE STRUCTURE
IN THE COMMONWEALTH

Ministerial Portfolios

SECTION 64 of the Commonwealth Constitution originally provided for seven Ministers of State, a number which could be increased by Act of Parliament. The first federal cabinet had nine members, including one who held the office of Vice-President of the Executive Council, and one honorary minister. This number gave each state a representative in cabinet. The seven departments established at federation were those of External Affairs, Attorney-General, Treasury, Trade and Customs, Defence, Home Affairs, and Posts and Telegraphs. No increase was made for ten years, until the establishment of the Prime Minister's Department in 1911.

The most important variation from state practice emerged when Deakin, in 1909, established the tradition that the Prime Minister should hold no other portfolio. The tradition has been broken by several Prime Ministers since then—especially Fisher (1910-13 and 1914-15), Lyons (1932-5) and Chifley (1945-9), each of whom was his own Treasurer. Barton, first Prime Minister, had already been urged not to burden himself with departmental administration by a colleague who wrote: 'May I urge on you to yourself take no portfolio, but start the Commonwealth with the proper precedent of leaving the Prime Minister free from the cares of an office?'[1] When Deakin did, however, take this step, its constitutional propriety was questioned in parliament by a member who pointed out that Deakin was not a Minister of State and therefore only an honorary member of the Executive Council.[2] This consideration probably influenced Deakin in his intention to set up a separate department for the Prime Minister, which was given effect to by his successor, Andrew Fisher, in 1911.

[1] Letter to Barton from B. R. Wise, 26 December 1900 (Barton Papers, National Library, Canberra).
[2] G. H. Wise, on 8 July 1909, *Parl. Deb.* (C. of A.), 49: 1008-10. It will be recalled that the constitution identifies members of the Executive Council with Ministers of State administering departments.

The size of federal cabinet grew slowly until 1939. On the outbreak of war there were eleven ministerial portfolios, responsible for fourteen departments and a number of public corporations and statutory commissions. In addition, cabinet included five ministers without portfolio. The war brought about an unexampled increase in government activity, so that by the end of hostilities there were twenty-six departments.[3] Although this number dropped as wartime activities were wound up, by the end of 1958 it had risen to twenty-four, together with a number of important sub-departments, bureaux, public corporations, and regulatory boards. To provide a 'political overhead' sufficient for this enormously enlarged administrative structure, the statutory number of ministers was increased to nineteen in 1941, twenty in 1951, and twenty-two in 1956.

Commonwealth Administration in December 1958

Department	Sub-departments, bureaux, corporations, and boards
1. Prime Minister	Public Service Board
	Audit Office
	Commonwealth Grants Commission
	Commonwealth Office of Education
	Australian Universities Commission
	C.S.I.R.O.
2. Treasury	Taxation Branch
	Bureau of Census and Statistics
	Government Printing Office
	National Debt Commission
	Australian Loan Council
	Commonwealth Bank
3. Attorney-General	Crown Solicitor
	Commonwealth Investigation Service
	Patent Office
4. External Affairs	Antarctic Division
5. Defence	Defence Committee and associated inter-service bodies
	Board of Business Administration
6. Navy	Naval Board
7. Army	Military Board
	Army Canteens Service Board

3 For a full analysis, see S. Encel, *et. al.,* 'Papers on Commonwealth Machinery of Government', *Public Administration,* 1958, vol. 17, no. 4; Spann (ed.), *Public Administration in Australia,* ch. 3. An official account is given in periodic issues of *The Federal Guide.*

8. Air   Air Board
9. Supply   Weapons Research Establishment
                             Contract Board
                             Munitions and Aircraft Production
                               Division
                             Stores and Transport Division
10. Customs and Excise   Film Censorship Board
                             Literature Censorship Board
11. Trade   Tariff Board
                             Export Payments Insurance
                               Corporation
                             Import Licensing Branch
                             Trade Commissioner Service
12. Primary Industry   Bureau of Agricultural Economics
                             War Service Land Settlement
                               Division
                             Australian Agricultural Council
                             Standing Committee on Agriculture
                             Commodity boards and
                               committees (19)
13. Postmaster-General   Overseas Telecommunications
                               Commission
                             Australian Broadcasting Control
                               Board
                             Australian Broadcasting Commission
14. Interior   News and Information Bureau
                             Australian War Memorial
                             Commonwealth Electoral Office
                             Forestry and Timber Bureau
                             Bureau of Meteorology
                             National Capital Development
                               Commission
15. Labour and   Conciliation and Arbitration
      National Service   Commission
                             Coal Industry Tribunal
                             Stevedoring Industry Authority
                             Commonwealth Hostels Ltd
16. Shipping and   Australian Coastal Shipping
      Transport   Commission
                             Australian Shipbuilding Board
                             Commonwealth Railways
                             Marine Branch
17. Works

18. Civil Aviation

Australian National Airlines Commission
Qantas Empire Airways
Tasman Empire Airways Ltd (with New Zealand)

19. Social Services
20. Repatriation
21. Immigration
22. Health

National Health and Medical Research Council
Commonwealth Serum Laboratories
School of Public Health and Tropical Medicine
Health Laboratories

23. Territories

British Phosphate Commissioners (with U.K. and N.Z.)
Christmas Island Phosphate Commission (with N.Z.)

24. National Development

Bureau of Mineral Resources
National Mapping Council
Snowy Mountains Hydro-Electric Authority
Joint Coal Board (with N.S.W.)
River Murray Commission (with N.S.W., Vic., and S.A.)
Australian Aluminium Production Commission (with Tas.)
War Service Homes Division
Australian Atomic Energy Commission

External Affairs

Foreign policy and defence, the two fields in which the executive power is virtually exclusive, are of special concern in the study of cabinet government. In Australia, the slow development of federal government as a decision-making body on international questions reflects the long-standing dependence of Australian government on the British connection, a dependence which is still emphasized in certain formal procedures. Australian diplomats and consular representatives are appointed not by the Governor-General, but by the British monarch on the advice of his/her Australian ministers—i.e., by the Minister for External Affairs. Letters of credence and letters of recall are signed by the Queen, and foreign envoys are accepted by her on the advice of the minister. In the latter case, credentials are transmitted unopened to London by the Governor-General, and then returned to Australia.

One practical result is that the English common-law rules concerning legation operate unchanged in Australia.[4] Another is that all treaties and international agreements are made on behalf of the Queen. Treaties between governments are signed either by the Governor-General-in-Council, or by the Minister for External Affairs, or by another minister with the authority of the Crown. The Governor-General-in-Council usually effects ratifications or accessions. The English law concerning treaties, which does not require parliamentary ratification except under certain conditions, operates in Australia, but for political reasons parliamentary ratification is common. This was, of course, significant in connection with the International Monetary Agreements Act of 1947, which expressly authorized the Commonwealth government to ratify the Bretton Woods agreement of 1944.[5]

The extension of Australian authority over neighbouring islands, especially New Guinea, which for the first time provoked an independent line in foreign affairs, is complicated by the existence of mandate and trusteeship arrangements. In the 1930s, uncertainty arose concerning the application of the executive power over external affairs to the League of Nations mandate over the northeastern part of New Guinea, formerly in German hands. The minority view of the High Court, expressed by Latham C. J. and Evatt J., was that the mandate power depended on the external affairs power, and in the post-war period this view was applied by the Chifley government (in which Evatt was Minister for External Affairs) when Australia subscribed independently to the United Nations Charter and thereby to its provisions regarding trusteeships.[6]

The slowness of Australia to assert a separate voice in foreign policy is reflected in the very gradual development of an administrative structure for the purpose.[7] Until 1935, in fact, the Prime Minister was usually responsible for external affairs in regard both to policy and administrative responsibility. Between

4 Wynes, *Legislative, Executive and Judicial Powers in Australia,* p.117.

5 The development of procedures for ratification and negotiation is examined in detail by H. J. Harvey, *Consultation and Co-operation in the Commonwealth,* pp.344-52.

6 Wynes, op. cit., pp.119-22.

7 'The Australian Diplomatic Service', *Current Notes,* 1951, vol. 22, no. 5; R. G. Casey, 'The Conduct of Australian Foreign Policy', *Current Notes,* 1952, vol. 23, no. 9.

1916 and 1921 the Department of External Affairs went out of existence entirely, its functions in relation to the Australian territory of Papua being taken over by the Department of Home and Territories, and its foreign policy activities by the Prime Minister's Department. In 1921 it was re-established as a division of the Prime Minister's Department, which also acquired a Pacific Branch. In 1928 External Affairs again became responsible for territorial affairs; in 1935 it became a fully separate department; in 1941 a separate department of External Territories was set up (renamed Territories in 1951).

For a number of years, the principal signs of concern with external relations were the attendance of successive Prime Ministers at successive Imperial Conferences. External relations meant, in effect, relations with Great Britain. In 1910, after long delays, a High Commissioner in London was appointed, responsible directly to the Prime Minister.[8] The incumbent has always been a former minister, and four were former Prime Ministers. At the Imperial Conference of 1923, S. M. Bruce pressed for closer consultation, and as a result a liaison officer was appointed between the U.K. cabinet office and Australia House. (The first occupant of this position, R. G. Casey, later became Minister for External Affairs.)

No further steps were taken until 1937, when an Australian diplomat of counsellor's status was attached to the British embassy in Washington; this was followed by the appointment of a Minister in 1940 (Casey, then Treasurer, was the first incumbent). In the same year, a High Commissioner to Canada was appointed, and since then the extension of separate diplomatic representation has been continuous.[9] The permanent place of diplomacy in Australian government was underlined by the introduction of a regular system of recruitment (through cadetships) in 1943.

The crux of foreign policy for Australian cabinets had been that the United Kingdom should recognize Australia's right to be consulted on matters to which she might be a party. Successive Prime Ministers have expressed their disquiet over the failure of the British government to inform Australia on critical occasions. W. M. Hughes wrote acidly in 1929 of the failure to consult or even inform Australia about negotiations between Lord Milner and the Egyptian nationalist leader Zaghlul Pasha: 'The Govern-

---

[8] A draft Bill establishing the post had been considered by cabinet as early as 1904. (Deakin's cabinet diary, 7 March 1904.) Various intrigues delayed the appointment, e.g. those of B. R. Wise; cf. letter to C. N. Jackson, 22 September 1904 (ML).

[9] At the end of 1958, Australia was represented abroad by ten High Commissioners, eleven Ambassadors, four Ministers, and various lesser fry.

ment was committed, and nothing remained for the representatives of the Empire but to register their formal acquiescence.'[10] The British attitude has, of course, been influenced by frequent utterances of politicians in the colonies and dominions which suggested that they regarded Britain's failure to do what they wanted as a betrayal.[11] Australian Prime Ministers have, on the whole, been cautious in their utterances, recognizing that Britain had to make its own decisions. Labour Prime Ministers have glossed this viewpoint by emphasizing Australia's right to do the same, ever since Andrew Fisher, at the Imperial Conference of 1911, supported the Canadian Prime Minister, Sir Wilfrid Laurier, in the contention that each dominion parliament must decide for itself what direct assistance would be given in the event of war.[12]

The stress on consultation has led to frequent proposals by Australian Prime Ministers, generally with the support of New Zealand, for the establishment of inter-governmental consultative machinery. At the Imperial Conference of 1907, Deakin supported a scheme put forward by the Colonial Secretary, Alfred Lyttelton, for an Imperial Council-cum-secretariat. In 1911 Fisher, together with Laurier and Botha, opposed a similar suggestion by Sir Joseph Ward of New Zealand, but supported an alternative proposal by Harcourt, the Colonial Secretary, for a standing committee of the Imperial Conference. The idea of an Imperial Council was revived in 1943 by Curtin, in a speech at Adelaide during the general election campaign. Curtin proposed that the High Commissioners of the dominions in London should be the permanent representatives, with cabinet ministers attending wherever possible. The Council would have an expert secretariat with staff drawn from all over the Commonwealth. The federal conference of the A.L.P. in December 1943 carried a resolution supporting Curtin's plan, with the rider that Commonwealth co-operation should be a step towards wider international co-operation. The Press was generally favourable to these moves, which were also supported by the Opposition in the Commonwealth parliament.

Curtin's views were recalled in 1948 by Bruce, now Viscount Bruce of Melbourne, who initiated a debate on this topic in the

---

[10] *The Splendid Adventure,* p.181. Milner had, in fact, kept the British cabinet in the dark as well.

[11] A. B. Keith, *Imperial Unity and the Dominions* (Oxford, 1916), pp.280-1. It is of interest that the Colonial Office, in 1883, unsuccessfully tried to persuade the Foreign Office to support the annexation of Papua by McIlwraith, Premier of Queensland. (Hall, *Australia and England,* pp.225-9.)   [12] Hall, op. cit., p.215.

House of Lords in 1948, during which he recalled his own support for an Imperial Secretariat in 1924. This latest attempt was received with the usual coolness both in Britain and other Commonwealth countries. In the South African parliament, Field-Marshal Smuts commented tersely that 'the more machinery we have, the more friction there will be'.[13]

The only concrete success registered by the policy of establishing Commonwealth consultative machinery came as a result of an agreement, reached at the Commonwealth Prime Ministers' Conference in 1948, for regular ministerial conferences on questions of foreign policy and economic relations. In pursuance of this agreement there came the Colombo conference of 1950, where the Australian Minister for External Affairs, P. C. Spender, put forward the scheme that came to be known as the Colombo Plan. The scheme provided for a consultative committee, which held its inaugural meeting in Sydney later in the same year. In addition, regional arrangements such as ANZUS, ANZAM, and SEATO, reflecting the changed perspective of world affairs, have removed a great deal of the original motive for concern.

Another means of consultation which has now been used on three occasions is the appointment of a member of cabinet as Resident Minister in London. Although the suggestion was first made in 1911, it was not until 1932 that Bruce, then Assistant Treasurer in the Lyons government, was appointed to such a post. In the following year he resigned from cabinet to become High Commissioner, a position he held until 1945. He was replaced by J. A. Beasley, whose appointment as Resident Minister lasted only a few months before he, in turn, was made High Commissioner. On Beasley's death in 1949, the High Commissionership remained vacant until 1951, but in the meantime E. J. Harrison had been Resident Minister from February 1950 until May 1951.[14]

The desirability of direct contact between dominion Prime Ministers and the British government has been urged with particular strength by Australia ever since World War I. In July 1918 the Imperial War Cabinet, on the initiative of Hughes, supported by Sir Robert Borden, Prime Minister of Canada, resolved that the various Prime Ministers should have the right to make contact directly on important cabinet matters. This was a step towards the eventual abandonment of communication through the medium of the Governor-General. In the Australian case, Sir Ronald Munro-

13 Harvey, op. cit., p.109.
14 In 1956 Harrison (now Sir Eric) returned to London as High Commissioner.

Ferguson expressed his opposition.[15] Henceforth, Hughes received a duplicate copy of the minutes of the British cabinet which had previously been sent only to the Governor-General.[16]

In practice, contact between Prime Ministers means contact between cabinets, although in the abdication crisis of 1936 Mr Baldwin consulted the dominion Prime Ministers direct, and three of them—Canadian, Australian, and South African—replied directly without prior cabinet consultation.[17] In common with the other Commonwealth countries, Australia's channel of communication is through the Commonwealth Relations Office (established to replace the Dominions Office and the India Office in 1947). The Foreign Office also has a Commonwealth Liaison Department, and the High Commissioners have a regular meeting with the Secretary of State for Commonwealth Relations and a minister from the Foreign Office. Since 1948, High Commissioners have had ambassadorial status and their diplomatic precedence throughout the Commonwealth has been assimilated to ordinary diplomatic protocol. The post of British High Commissioner to Australia was established in 1931, but not filled until 1935.

Defence

Defence Consultation

The problem of consultation with the United Kingdom government has always been most acute in connection with defence in wartime. It has often been suggested that the conscription crisis of 1916 arose at least partly from misleading figures on the manpower position supplied to Australia by the British cabinet. At any rate, Hughes' experiences in London left him with a poor opinion of the British service chiefs and of the ability of the British cabinet to impose its will on them. Writing after the war, he found a scathing explanation for the British failure to consult the dominions until the Imperial War Cabinet first met in 1917. 'The British government did not consult the Dominions about their plans . . . for the simple but sufficient reason that, except in a few instances, they had no plans.'[18] The Gallipoli campaign was a ghastly failure because of failure to co-ordinate plans, to carry them out

---

[15] Scott, *Australia During the War,* pp.184-8.

[16] Hughes' secretiveness led him to adopt a variety of subterfuges to prevent the Governor-General from knowing the details of his communications with Britain. He would, for instance, borrow Munro-Ferguson's copy of the minutes on the pretext of having mislaid his own, and then 'forget' to return them.   The Governor-General became so exasperated that he instructed his official secretary, Captain Steward, to abstract his copy from Hughes' office.   [17] Harvey, op. cit., p.166.   [18] Hughes, op. cit., p.72.

vigorously, or to take the dominions into Britain's confidence. 'When it was decided to evacuate the peninsula, the British government communicated with the Australian government and asked if it wished to make any comments. No doubt there were many comments that I could have made, that I felt strongly moved to make, but they were hardly suitable for telegraphic communication.'[19]

The need for consultation was first recognized in concrete form by the summoning of the Imperial War Cabinet in March 1917, which Hughes was unable to attend.[20] The second meeting, which opened in June 1918, set up an 'Inner Imperial War Cabinet', comprising the British and dominion Prime Ministers, and assisted by the Chief of the Imperial General Staff.[21] Between the two world wars, consultation took place through the machinery of the Committee of Imperial Defence, full meetings of which were attended by the High Commissioners after an invitation issued by Baldwin at the Imperial Conference of 1926. Dominion liaison officers were attached to the 'numerous progeny of committees and sub-committees'[22] to which the Committee of Imperial Defence gave birth. The experiences of World War II (of which more presently) underlined the need for more effective consultation, and in 1946 a British White Paper devoted a separate section to 'collective defence', in which it was proposed that liaison teams should be exchanged between Britain and the dominions.[23] At the 1946 conference of Prime Ministers, a number of schemes for co-operation were discussed, in connection with intelligence, scientific co-operation, and the joint long-range weapons project in Australia. On his return to Australia from the conference the Prime Minister, J. B. Chifley, outlined proposals made by Australia, including Commonwealth representation on United Kingdom committees, co-operation in defence planning, and special arrangements for Pacific security.[24]

World War II, involving as it did a direct attack on Australian territory, sharpened Australia's concern with the right to be consulted and also the right of independent decision. At the outset, dominion ministers were invited to attend meetings of the British War Cabinet whenever they were in London. In 1941, the Prime Minister, R. G. Menzies, visited Britain in response to an invitation from the War Cabinet. During A. W. Fadden's short term as

19 Ibid., pp.76-7.   20 Ibid., pp.46-9.
21 Report of War Cabinet for 1918, Cmd. 325, 1919.
22 Quoted, Jennings, Cabinet Government, p.285.
23 Central Organization for Defence, Cmd. 6923, 1946.
24 Current Notes, 1946, vol. 17, no. 6.

Prime Minister, he announced that Sir Earle Page, then Minister for Commerce, would go to London 'to inquire into many vital matters which closely affect the welfare of this country'.[25] Before leaving, Page had discussions with the Advisory War Council, at which Curtin emphasized the need for a minister to be in London to press the Australian viewpoint constantly.[26] As it happened, Page was *en route* to London when Curtin became Prime Minister, and the latter promptly announced that Page's mission would continue.

After the outbreak of war with Japan in December 1941, Curtin pressed for the establishment of an Allied war council, whose formation was announced in London in the following February. The Pacific War Council met in Washington for the first time on 20 March 1942, and continued to function during the war, meeting both in London and Washington. The original Australian representative was Page, who also sat with the British War Cabinet until S. M. Bruce, High Commissioner in London, was permanently appointed as Australia's War Cabinet representative. In June 1942, Bruce delegated his functions as High Commissioner to the Official Secretary at Australia House, and took up his quarters in the War Cabinet offices.

The early months of the Japanese war witnessed a great strain on this consultative machinery. Federal cabinet was anxious that the 1st Australian Corps, comprising the 6th, 7th and 9th Divisions A.I.F., then in the Middle East, should be transferred *en bloc* to Australia to meet the threat of a Japanese invasion. The Chief of the General Staff, Lt-General Sturdee, advised the Curtin government that this step was essential, and that no components of the corps should be detached to Burma or Indonesia, as the British government wished. On 17 February 1942, Curtin sent a cable to Mr Churchill asking for the return of the 1st Corps. At the same time the newly-formed Pacific War Council had before it a request from General Wavell, commanding in South-East Asia, that one Australian division should be sent to Burma, and Page cabled to Curtin asking for agreement to this request. The Advisory War Council considered this on the 19th, and although non-government members favoured compliance, War Cabinet rejected the request. As the military situation rapidly deteriorated, there developed 'a cabled controversy of a volume and intensity unprecedented in Australian experience'.[27] Curtin was under pressure

25 *Parl. Deb.* (C. of A.), 168: 293-4.
26 Hasluck, *The Government and the People*, pp.535-6.
27 L. G. Wigmore, *The Japanese Thrust*, p.449.

not only from Page and Bruce in London, but also from Casey in Washington, from Mr Churchill, and from President Roosevelt, reaching its peak in a lengthy message from Churchill on 20 February in which 'appeal, reproach, warning and exhortation were mingled'.[28]

Curtin won his point, although some Australian troops were landed in Java and could not be extricated in time, but he was then requested to allow the 7th Division to land in Ceylon pending the arrival of the British 70th Division. In reply to Page's cable of 24 February, containing this further request, Curtin rebuked him for not espousing Australia's case with sufficient determination. When Page stuck to his guns, Curtin finally agreed (on 2 March) to the landing of two brigades from the 6th Division in Ceylon.

Ministerial Responsibility

The problem of ministerial responsibility for the formulation and execution of decisions is nowhere more acute than in the sphere of defence, especially in time of war. World War I, with its succession of crises in Britain, France and Germany over the locus of ultimate responsibility for military decisions, produced Clemenceau's immortal remark that war was too serious a matter to be left to generals, as well as a spate of writings reviewing the tortuous history of civil-military relations.[29] In Australia, a cabinet sub-committee declared in 1918 that there had been at all times

> a prolonged struggle to determine whether the final authority with regard to the administration of both Army and Navy should be civil or military. Great Britain has resolutely upheld the principle that the civil authority should prevail, and it is unthinkable that any different policy should be adopted here.[30]

The principle of civilian control was incorporated in the Australian defence structure from an early stage. In 1904, the Minister for Defence, J. W. McCay, introduced an amendment to the Defence Act providing for a Council of Defence, a Naval Board and a Military Board, on grounds similar to those advanced in Britain by the Hartington Commission of 1890 and the Esher Committee of 1904, whose reports led to the establishment of the

---

[28] Ibid., p.450. Churchill's account of the exchange is given in *The History of the Second World War*, vol. 4, pp.136-45, where he describes it as 'a painful episode'.

[29] e.g. Winston Churchill, *The World Crisis* (4 vols., London, 1923-9), vol. 1, pp.240-2; Lloyd George, *War Memoirs* (London, 1938), vol. 3, pp.1171-2; Jennings, op. cit., ch. 10.

[30] *Report of the Royal Commission on Navy and Defence Administration*, 1917-18, Appendix, par. 8.

Committee of Imperial Defence. During his speech, McCay declared:

> We shall bring the Cabinet as a whole, which is responsible through the Minister at the head of the department, into more direct touch with the defence policy of Australia, and we shall also maintain a closer touch between the carrying out of that policy and the Parliament which, as the representative of the people, controls it.[31]

In 1918, the cabinet sub-committee restated the case for ultimate ministerial authority, after a Royal Commission had recommended that the Naval Board should have the final say on naval policy and administration. Both in naval and in military affairs, declared the sub-committee, no minister

> can fairly be expected to answer to Parliament regarding the administration of a department over which he exercises no authority . . . In the event of the Board over-riding the Minister, in a matter of administration to which exception is taken in Parliament, what attitude is the Minister to take up? He cannot be expected to defend an action with which he has disagreed. Is he then to join in a criticism of—or may be, an attack upon— the Board, or to remain silent? He could not be held responsible, and with the removal of Ministerial responsibility, it is difficult to see how Parliament could exercise any control over departments' administrative activities.[32]

The Council of Defence set up by the 1904 legislation comprised the Prime Minister, the Minister for Defence, an unspecified number of other ministers, the service chiefs, and the Secretary of the Defence Department. The Military and Naval Boards were established in 1905, and the Air Board in 1923. In 1926 the Defence Committee, comprising the Chiefs of Staff and a senior official of the Defence Department, was set up and its functions defined by regulation.[33] In 1946, its task was described as that of 'an advisory and consultative body to advise the Minister of State for Defence'. The 1946 regulation also empowered the minister to appoint a chairman (who is invariably the Secretary of the Defence Department), and to approve of the co-option of other members. In 1956, the heads of the Treasury, the Prime Minister's Department, and the Department of External Affairs were thus co-opted.

[31] *Parl. Deb.* (C. of A.), 23: 6383-4.
[32] *Report of the Royal Commission on Navy and Defence Administration,* 1917-18, Appendix, par. 8.
[33] Statutory Rules, 1929, no. 26; 1938, no. 81; 1946, no. 39.

In 1938, cabinet agreed that the Council of Defence should be replaced by a War Cabinet in the event of hostilities. When war broke out, this step was taken, the Prime Minister noting on the cabinet paper that War Cabinet would deal with 'all matters other than major matters of general policy'.[34] Summaries of War Cabinet decisions were circulated to other ministers. When War Cabinet met for the first time on 27 September 1939, it comprised the Prime Minister and Treasurer (both portfolios held by Menzies), the Attorney-General, and the Ministers for Supply and Development, Defence, External Affairs and Information, and Commerce. In conformity with plans in the War Book,[35] the Secretary of the Defence Department, F. G. (later Sir Frederick) Shedden, attended War Cabinet meetings to record decisions. In June 1941, following the British practice, War Cabinet agreed that one of Shedden's principal subordinates should also be admitted to its meetings, and that other ministers, the chiefs of staff, other experts, and representatives of the Allied governments should be invited as required. As its members became more familiar with the technique, a procedure was evolved for classifying agenda items as being of major or of specialized importance, with the approval of the Prime Minister. Specialized questions were sometimes submitted to *ad hoc* sub-committees which were authorized to decide them.

In 1946, the Council of Defence was reconstituted, and an elaborate network of joint committees was established to service it on the official level. Since 1952, its functions have been overshadowed by a standing committee of cabinet, the Defence Preparations Committee, which in 1956 comprised the Prime Minister as chairman, the Treasurer, the Minister for Defence, the three service ministers, and the Ministers for External Affairs, Supply, and Customs.[36] In 1957, a special committee of investigation into defence organization, under Lt-General Sir Leslie Morshead, was appointed following stringent criticisms of the control of defence by the Joint Parliamentary Committee of Public Accounts in its 29th report. The Morshead committee made several sweeping suggestions for reorganization, including the amalgamation of the three service departments with the Defence Department, and the appointment of 'associate' ministers on a functional rather than a 'service' basis to help the Minister for Defence. The Prime Minister, in announcing the government's rejection of this suggestion,

---

34 Hasluck, op. cit., p.440.
35 Prepared during the later 1930s on the lines of the British War Book. The 1930 Imperial Conference had agreed on a standard form of War Book to be adopted by the dominions.
36 *29th Report*, Public Accounts Committee, 1956.

pointed out that 'associate ministers' would be trying to operate 'without that clear vertical line of authority which exists when a Minister deals with a permanent head and the permanent head deals with those through whom authority devolves to the point of immediate action'.[37] He announced, as the government's alternative, that the authority of the Minister of Defence would be strengthened, and that an independent chairman of the Chiefs of Staff Committee would be appointed, who would sit on the Defence Committee and would act as adviser to the Australian representative on SEATO, ANZUS and ANZAM.[38]

The inherent stresses in the relation of civilian ministers and officials to the service chiefs were dramatically illustrated during the New Guinea campaign of 1942. In 1937 the Chief of the General Staff, Lt-General Lavarack, proposed to cabinet that a Commander-in-Chief should be appointed in wartime, and in 1941 the suggestion was revived by the Minister for the Army, P. C. Spender. In July 1941, War Cabinet finally agreed, and Lt-General Mackay was appointed G.O.C.-in-C. home forces, ranking equally with the Chief of the General Staff, General Sturdee. The arrangement did not succeed, partly because both generals had direct access to the minister, although Sturdee was senior in rank.[39] A few months later, the arrival of General Douglas MacArthur from the Philippines introduced a new complication. On 17 March 1942, Curtin was informed by General Brett, U.S. commander in Australia, that MacArthur had just landed at Darwin, and that he had been instructed by President Roosevelt to suggest that 'it would be highly acceptable to him and pleasing to the American people' if Australia would nominate MacArthur as supreme commander in the South-West Pacific area. War Cabinet agreed to the request, and the appointment was announced on the following day.[40]

Under the terms of a directive from the Pacific War Council, MacArthur was not directly to command any national force, while the national commanders were to treat orders from MacArthur as if they came from their own governments. Under pressure from Curtin, the Council agreed that each national commander could appeal to his own government, and each government could refuse the use of its forces if it considered the project inad-

[37] *Parl. Deb.* (C. of A.), 1958, 7 Eliz. II, H. of R., 18: 433-7.
[38] One consequence of these arrangements is that the Council of Defence is no longer formally constituted.
[39] D. McCarthy, *South-West Pacific Area, First Year,* pp.4-5; Hasluck, op. cit., pp.441-4.
[40] McCarthy, op. cit., pp.17-18.

visable. In the meantime, a fresh post of Commander-in-Chief, Australian Military Forces, had been created, which was filled in March by General Sir Thomas Blamey, previously Deputy G.O.C. in the Middle East. The Military Board was suspended at the same time, its members becoming staff officers to Blamey. Under pressure from Washington, MacArthur agreed to the appointment of Blamey as his deputy.

The division of authority between War Cabinet, sitting in Canberra, Blamey, with his headquarters in Melbourne, and MacArthur, who had set up his own establishment in Brisbane, was bound to lead to difficulties, especially as Curtin and MacArthur found a common bond in resisting the emphasis placed by Roosevelt and Churchill on the policy of 'beat Hitler first'. The most explosive incident occurred in September 1942, over the tactics of Lt-General Rowell, G.O.C. New Guinea forces.[41] The retreat of the A.I.F. before the Japanese led to repeated expressions of concern from MacArthur. On 17 September, Blamey addressed the Advisory War Council, expressing his confidence that Port Moresby would be held; but on the same day, MacArthur telephoned from Brisbane asking that Blamey should take personal command in New Guinea. Blamey, a politician as well as a soldier, did not hurry his arrangements, arriving in Port Moresby on the 23rd. In a letter to Rowell, he had already expressed his hope that the latter would not take Blamey's arrival as implying lack of confidence: 'I think it arises out of the fact that we have very inexperienced politicians who are inclined to panic on every possible occasion.'[42] Nevertheless, Rowell refused to serve under these conditions, and on the 28th Blamey relieved him of his command. On 1 October he wrote to Curtin accusing Rowell of 'personal animus', adding: 'It seemed to me that when I received your directions and those of the Commander-in-Chief, S.W.P.A., that it behoved me to carry out these instructions, and there can be no doubt that when the consequent instructions were given to General Rowell, it was his duty also to carry them out without question.'[43]

One of the most vexed aspects of the civil-military division of responsibility is in regard to finance. This problem had become sufficiently acute during World War I to require the appointment of a Royal Commission, and it flared up again as a result of Blamey's appointment as Commander-in-Chief. Disputes arose

[41] Rowell had previously been Deputy Chief of the General Staff and G.O.C. 1st Australian Corps.   [42] McCarthy, op. cit., p.236.
[43] Ibid., p.237. See also John Hetherington, *Blamey*, pp.160-70.

whether financial control should be vested in a staff officer responsible to Blamey, or in the Secretary of the Army Department, whose responsibility was to the Minister. A conference at the end of 1942 between Curtin, Chifley, Blamey, and the Minister for the Army, F. M. Forde, decided that control should be vested in the Secretary of the Army Department.[44] The principle was reaffirmed in 1954 in a directive issued by the Minister of Defence, Sir Philip McBride, which stated that the responsibility of the permanent head of a service department, as a member of a service Board, included 'financial administration and control of expenditure. This responsibility extends not only to the financial order and regularity of accounts but also to the correct and proper use of public funds in all fields of administration.' The directive went on to point out that although each member of a service Board could be required to act individually, where such action 'affects the responsibilities of the Permanent Head or other members of the Board, such action or advice should be co-ordinated'.[45]

In practice, such directives can do little to mitigate the inherent struggle between military and political considerations which has become a continuing feature of government in the democratic countries since World War I. It is rarely possible, as a former permanent head of the Army Department has complained, to achieve a harmonious synthesis between advice on strictly military aspects and advice on the related civilian and financial considerations.[46] The Joint Committee of Public Accounts had stringent criticisms to make of the results of this lack of co-ordination, which repeatedly leads to faulty estimation of financial needs and to evasions of crucial matters of policy concerning manpower and *matériel*.[47] Before the committee, the Secretary of the Defence Department admitted that, in effect, military expenditure was based on guesswork and that control was virtually impossible.[48] In the words of a contemporary American commentator, the government has been unable to draw 'a fair middle line between the demands of economy and preparedness', and successive attempts at reorganization have 'evaded rather than faced most of the basic issues of military policy'.[49]

[44] Hetherington, op. cit., pp.149-53.
[45] A. D. McKnight, 'The Role of the Public Servant in a Service Department' (unpublished lecture, 1956).
[46] Ibid.
[47] *29th Report,* Public Accounts Committee, 1956.
[48] Ibid., Minutes of Evidence, pp.12-16.
[49] Walter Millis, *et. al., Arms and the State* (New York, 1958), p.425.

Cabinet Secretariat

Until 1925, no regular procedure for recording decisions of federal cabinet had been instituted.[50] Each minister kept his own notes, and several Prime Ministers—Barton, Deakin, Fisher, and Hughes—had their own diaries. In 1906, the government Whip, J. N. H. Hume Cook, was made secretary to cabinet, and it was common practice thenceforth to appoint one minister as secretary.

In 1904, a Prime Minister's office was set up as part of the Department of External Affairs. In 1910 it became an entirely separate branch of the latter department under Fisher's private secretary, M. L. Shepherd, who became Secretary of the Prime Minister's Department when this was set up in the following year. During World War I, the Prime Minister's Department grew largely in importance, equally because of the growth of business and because of W. M. Hughes' impatience with routine and incapacity to devolve responsibility. The staff of the department had to be prepared for anything, including domestic errands. Records of cabinet meetings had to be pieced together from the scribbled notes on the Prime Minister's copy of the cabinet agenda. Only while Hughes was abroad did the methodical W. A. Watt, as acting Prime Minister, inject some order into proceedings.

Under Bruce, studies were made of the system developed in Britain under Sir Maurice Hankey,[51] first by an honorary minister, C. W. C. Marr, who was appointed cabinet secretary in 1925, and later by his successor, Sir Neville Howse. Some aspects of the British system were copied, but not its central feature, the appointment of a permanent official as secretary to cabinet. The Scullin government reverted to the practice of a private diary but under Lyons the principle of an official secretary to cabinet was again suggested by the Attorney-General, Sir John Latham, and by Lyons' private secretary, Martyn Threlfall. Lyons would not agree to this, but allowed Threlfall to institute a secretarial system similar to that which had operated under Bruce. In 1939, the proposal to appoint an official secretary was revived, but while the project was still being discussed Lyons died suddenly and nothing more was done. Until 1939, officials had only attended cabinet

50 For detailed accounts, see Encel, 'Cabinet Machinery in Australia', *Public Administration*, 1956, vol. 14, no. 2; K. Penny, 'The Origins of the Prime Minister's Department', *Public Administration*, 1956, vol. 15, no. 3; Crisp, *The Parliamentary Government of the Commonwealth*, pp.212-15; Encel, *et. al.,* 'Papers on Commonwealth Machinery of Government', *Public Administration*, 1958, vol. 16, no. 4.
51 Lord Hankey, *Diplomacy by Conference*, ch. 3.

meetings for short periods to give information on technical points, and the suggestion that an official secretary be appointed had been consistently rejected. Threlfall argued against this reluctance. The ministerial secretary, he remarked, 'is himself an exceedingly busy man with his own departmental work. Moreover, he may not be trained in the precise formulation of minutes.' Rebutting the suggestion that cabinet secrecy would be prejudiced by the admission of an outsider, he wrote:

It cannot be said that the absence of any such official has rendered inviolate the deliberations of Ministers. The leakage of Cabinet information over many years is notorious. Some matters before Cabinet have highly important party political implications . . . but the great majority of items on any Cabinet agenda are of a routine character.[52]

An unflattering description of the lack of effectiveness of the system before 1939 is given by an official war historian.

The practice had been simply for the Prime Minister, or sometimes another minister, to note on the memoranda submitted to the Cabinet what had been decided and hand the paper back to the minister who had brought it forward. Pre-war Cabinet decisions have consequently to be sought on departmental files, where sometimes will be found the original piece of paper with 'Approved' and a Prime Minister's initials, or a formal memorandum from the Secretary of the Prime Minister's Department to the Secretary of the Department concerned saying that, with reference to the memorandum of such and such a date on such and such a subject, Cabinet had decided so and so. The Secretary of the Prime Minister's Department, in order to start the administrative wheels moving in this fashion, relied chiefly on a word of mouth authority from one of the members of Cabinet who had been rather loosely designated as its secretary. He would wait outside the Cabinet room when ministers were dispersing, ask what had happened on this item or that, and try to collect any initialled submissions which had not been carried off by ministers. It was not unknown for some further informal conversation among departing ministers to be necessary to check each other's recollection of what exactly had happened on the less important items. Some of the so-called secretaries of Cabinet were methodical; others were inclined to trust to memory and scribbled scraps of notes. There were no Cabinet records as such, and the making of Cabinet records would have been regarded as contrary to the principles of Cabinet responsibility and the secrets of the Cabinet room. Under this system

[52] Martyn M. Threlfall, 'Work of the Cabinet', *S.M.H.*, 23 March 1939.

only the matters on which Cabinet agreed became known. The rest was silence.[53]

The formation of War Cabinet, with an elaborate secretariat located in the Defence Department, and the presence of Shedden, its Secretary, at War Cabinet meetings, was bound to produce some effect on the machinery of full cabinet. At the end of 1940, cabinet agreed that Strahan, Secretary of the Prime Minister's Department, should attend its meetings to record decisions. For a long time, however, there was no attempt to give the cabinet secretariat any centralizing function, and the records of each important cabinet committee were kept by the department of the minister chiefly concerned. This continued even after the war, when the Prime Minister's Department was not even concerned to keep copies of the memoranda dealt with by cabinet committees, except where a committee presented a submission to full cabinet. Apart from defence, the important staff work was done by the Treasury and the Department of Post-War Reconstruction.

By 1949, the transition from war to peace was largely complete, and the Prime Minister, J. B. Chifley, envisaged a new role for the cabinet secretariat. He decided that the Department of Post-War Reconstruction should be wound up and its Economic Policy Division transferred to the Prime Minister's Department, where it would become the basis of such a secretariat. In June 1949, A. S. Brown, head of the Department of Post-War Reconstruction, was appointed Secretary of the Prime Minister's Department. With the advent of a new government after the 1949 general election, the process of reorganization was carried through, after some hesitation, by the Menzies administration, which had inherited the greatly enlarged apparatus of administration with some suspicion of its personnel, practically all of whom had been appointed by the Chifley government. Under the Menzies régime, the secretariat developed further, in conscious emulation of the British pattern, aided by occasional exchanges of personnel with the Cabinet Office in London.

All meetings of cabinet and its committees are now handled by the secretariat, which circulates to ministers, in advance, copies of submissions for the next meeting. (In theory, submissions should be in the hands of the secretariat three working days before the next cabinet meeting.) It arranges meetings, submits agenda to the Prime Minister or the chairman of the committee in question, records decisions and dispatches copies of them as re-

53 Hasluck, op. cit., p.422.

quired. Ministers, however, remain responsible for the instructions needed to carry out such decisions. Minutes of meetings may comprise only a bare record of decision, or a more detailed summary of the problem and the main points leading to the conclusion. The latter is more commonly done in recording committee proceedings.

The recording of cabinet meetings is most commonly done by the Secretary to Cabinet—i.e., the head of the Prime Minister's Department—but sometimes also by his immediate subordinate in charge of the cabinet division. Cabinet committees are usually attended by a limited number of officials, though more may be standing by.

The Committee System

Before 1939, there was little in the way of standing committees of cabinet; since then, continuous experimentation has taken place. The establishment of War Cabinet was soon followed by an attempt to deal with economic problems on the same level as defence.[54] The attempt did not succeed, and the committee, the 'Economic Cabinet' lapsed after a few months. In July 1941, a further trial was made with an 'Economic and Industrial Committee', which lapsed when the Curtin government took office three months later. Instead, cabinet set up a 'Production Executive' in November 1941, to be an executive rather than a policy-making body. This body was headed by the Minister for War Organization of Industry, and his department (which had been established in July 1941, but had hardly functioned) provided the secretariat and expert staff. Despite some attempts on the part of the Production Executive to insist on its authority as the economic counterpart of War Cabinet, it remained a largely executive body, and in this capacity gradually became responsible for co-ordinating the great bulk of questions relating to the 'home front'. It did not, however, function as an 'inner cabinet' like the war cabinet.

Two other wartime committees of importance were the Allied Supply Council, chaired by the Minister for Supply, with a representative of the United States forces; and the Food Executive, a committee of three headed by the Minister for Commerce and Agriculture.

After the war, Production Executive was replaced by four committees—on trade, investment, secondary industries, and the dollar

[54] For detailed accounts, see Hasluck, op. cit., ch. 11; E. R. Walker, *The Australian Economy in War and Reconstruction,* ch. 5; S. J. Butlin, *War Economy 1939-42,* chs. 2-7.

budget. In practice, however, matters were dealt with by a large array of *ad hoc* sub-committees.[55] The Menzies government inherited the more important of these, and at the outset attempted to operate a system of nineteen more or less permanent ones. The attempt soon broke down, and in 1952 an experiment was made with four main standing committees dealing with economic policy, general administration, defence preparations, and the legislative programme.[56] The aim was to transfer a great deal of business from the agenda of full cabinet, which was left with politically controversial subjects and matters of basic policy. The next step was the formation, in July 1954, of two main parallel committees —the Prime Minister's Committee and the Vice-President's Committee. The latter was in fact the renamed general administrative committee; the former, according to the official statement, was to be concerned chiefly with policy questions, especially economic policy. In addition, the committees dealing with defence and legislation continued to function. The distinction in functions between the two main committees was, at least in part, a distinction of status as well. This was underlined by the fact that the Prime Minister's Committee consisted roughly of the first nine ministers in order of seniority, and the Vice-President's Committee of the eleven lower down the list (with the exception of its chairman, the Vice-President of the Executive Council). The general Press comment was that cabinet had been divided into 'first and second elevens', and on this occasion at least the implied forecast had some substance, for the change proved to be a transitional stage on the way to the final distinction between ministers 'above the line' and 'below the line'.

In January 1956, the Prime Minister announced that the ministry, now comprising twenty-two members, would be divided into a cabinet of twelve plus ten ministers not in cabinet. Although Press comment was occupied with speculation about the possibly sinister political significance of the step, it was in fact a belated response to the unwieldy size of the federal ministry.[57] It was probably also a consequence of the apparent failure of the 1954 experiment, which had in its turn been a reaction against the en-

[55] One estimate of the number of such transient bodies during the Chifley administration puts the figure at two hundred.

[56] The general administrative committee is understood to have comprised, in its first phase, the Vice-President of the Executive Council, the Treasurer, and the Ministers for Commerce and Agriculture, Social Services, and Territories.

[57] Cf. speech by W. C. Wentworth, *Parl. Deb.* (C. of A.), 1956, 5 Eliz. II, H. of R., 9: 63-5. Wentworth had already urged such a step in 1952.

demic tendency to refer everything to cabinet, which in its turn was obliged to refer matters continuously to *ad hoc* committees. Attempts to separate discussion of policy too rigidly from responsibility for its execution are usually self-defeating.[58] In official circles, the members of the two committees set up in 1954 were nicknamed 'gentlemen' and 'players'.

Since 1956, the three standing committees on defence preparations, general administration, and legislation have continued to operate. Practically all ministers belong to at least one of them. Committee membership ignores the distinction between cabinet and ministry, and ministers not in cabinet are invited to attend cabinet if they have a submission before it. On important questions of foreign policy and budgetary policy the Prime Minister has summoned the ministry to meet as a whole before a statement of government policy is made.

Interdepartmental Consultation

The control of policy at cabinet level depends on forms of control and co-ordination at the official level, operating partly through interdepartmental committees and partly through controlling agencies like the Treasury and the Public Service Board.[59]

Most interdepartmental consultation is informal, and various obstacles exist in the way of a more effective formal framework, the need for which has been recognized by a number of observers (e.g., Crawford remarks that 'despite the pressure of time, I think Commonwealth permanent heads do not meet enough on policy issues'). An important obstacle is the prevalence of a strongly competitive spirit throughout the Commonwealth public service, which when allied with the ambitions of ministers, may subordinate the requirements of co-operation to the drive for empire-building. The allocation of a single item of administrative responsibility may make a perceptible difference to the importance of a department and consequently to that of its responsible minister and his permanent head, and one result will be insistence that that department alone should deal with these questions. An added dimension of the problem is due to the absence of a firm hierarchy of senior officials such as that which exists in the old-established civil services of Britain and Europe. Because of the fragmentary

[58] The objections to a 'study group' of senior ministers are discussed, e.g., by Laski, *Reflections on the Constitution,* pt. 2.

[59] For detailed discussions, see J. G. Crawford, 'The Role of the Permanent Head', *Public Administration,* 1954, vol. 13, no. 4; Canberra Research Group, 'Commonwealth Policy Co-ordination', *Public Administration,* 1955, vol. 14, no. 4; Encel, *et. al.,* loc. cit.

system of classification of public service grades, there are few general categories which tend to equalize the status and salaries of officials engaged in comparable work. The system makes, instead, for narrow monetary assessments of the duties of the two or three hundred men who are concerned with 'policy formulation'.

The personal influence of the Prime Minister is of great importance in deciding the manner in which co-ordinating functions are exercised. The difference in the personal impact of Churchill and Attlee on the wartime coalition government in Britain has been aptly contrasted.

> When Mr Attlee is presiding in the absence of the Prime Minister the Cabinet meets on time, works systematically through the agenda, makes the necessary decisions and goes home after three or four hours' work. When Mr. Churchill presides we never reach the agenda and we decide nothing. But we go home to bed at midnight, conscious of having been present at an historic occasion.[60]

In Australia, this personal influence is probably even greater, as the structure of the official machine itself may be profoundly affected by political and personal differences. Under Chifley, there was a wide network of consultation which assumed the form of an 'official family':

> They knew each other well enough to put most of their cards on the table and to be critical of each others' notions in a reasonably good and constructive spirit . . . There was enough of the spirit of give and take, of mutual understanding and of zest for the game and of appreciation where final responsibility lay, to lubricate the machinery. Above all, each knew Chifley well and could usually gauge the practical limits of policy pretty well and plan accordingly . . . He was the co-ordinator and the machinery played its part by presenting him with the data upon which decisions could be made with reasonable consistency. The fact that he had a faculty for prompt, firm and generally consistent decision, enabled the sort of policy co-ordinating machinery here outlined to operate a good deal more successfully than would otherwise have been the case.[61]

This closely integrated group was the result of a unique constellation of circumstances arising out of the war and post-war periods, in which Chifley's personality was an indispensable component. Under the Menzies administration, the personality of the Prime Minister, allied with the conservatism of his government,

60 Ellen Wilkinson, quoted by Kingsley Martin, *Harold Laski* (London, 1952), p.158.   61 Canberra Research Group, loc. cit.

resulted in considerable changes in the character of the machine. A revealing contrast is shown in the methods adopted by the two governments for dealing with international negotiations which had begun while Chifley was still in office.

Under the Chifley procedures, this matter had been the subject of the three-tier discussion and co-ordination technique amongst actively interested Ministers and administrative departments along lines already described. When the negotiations were revived again under the Menzies Government the Cabinet determined on a different technique. Officers of three Departments *not administratively* concerned with the policy involved —Prime Minister's, Attorney-General's and External Affairs —were constituted a committee to hold hearings of the cases of the Departments which were administratively concerned with the policy content of the negotiations. The committee heard the Departments in turn separately, weighed their cases, consulted them at will from time to time on particular points, integrated and reconciled their proposals as far as possible and then submitted a draft brief to the appropriate Cabinet Committee. With Cabinet approval, the same officers were then instructed to carry on the negotiations with the officers of the other Government concerned.[62]

Nevertheless, a number of comparatively formal bodies do exist for the purpose of interdepartmental co-operation in the formulation and execution of policy. Four types may be distinguished: (a) *ad hoc* bodies commissioned by cabinet or a committee of cabinet to examine a policy question and report back; (b) standing bodies with administrative duties; (c) standing bodies with mixed duties of policy formulation and administration of decisions reached at ministerial level; (d) advisory bodies containing non-governmental members.[63] An important example of a body of the first type was the Sulphuric Acid Committee, set up in 1951 to examine the problems of using indigenous raw materials in the manufacture of sulphuric acid. The committee drew up a report and recommendations to the government, and a permanent body, the Sulphuric Acid Executive, was set up within the Department of Supply (later transferred to the Department of National Development) to administer government policy in the matter. A body of type (b) is the Overseas Visits Committee, set up at the instance of the Prime Minister, to regulate visits by officials to other countries. This committee, whose permanent members are

[62] Ibid.
[63] A full discussion and a chart are given in Encel, *et. al.,* loc. cit.

all of senior rank, has the power to make decisions, but a minister can appeal to the Prime Minister against an unfavourable one. The third type contains some of the most important bodies dealing with economic questions. One such is the Committee on Export Controls, established to review the need for controls and to consider requests for their removal; another pair are the Import Budget and Dollar Committees, set up to deal continuously with import licensing, currency restrictions, and the like. The most important instance of the fourth type is the Consultative Committee on Import Policy, established by the Prime Minister to give unofficial advice on this very delicate question; it is presided over by the chairman of the Tariff Board. Another was the National Security Resources Board, set up in 1950 in an unsuccessful attempt to establish priorities in the allocation of resources in the event of war.[64]

Treasury Control

The position of the Treasury as a co-ordinating department is based primarily on its responsibilities in the field of financial and economic policy. The extent of these responsibilities can be seen by examining the principal instrument of co-ordination in this field, namely the Budget, and the Treasury's role in framing it.

The Budget brings together the government's proposals for raising and spending revenues and even if it does not reconcile, it at least resolves the competing claims, not merely of the various departments whose annual votes are affected but of the numerous groups in the community who, on the one hand, may stand to benefit from particular measures or, on the other hand, may have to bear the cost of them.

The process of framing the Budget begins in the departments. There, the relative merits of various proposals which involve expenditure are first assessed and decisions are made as to the amounts to be sought in the estimates. It is then the Treasury's job to bring all of these separate estimates together and, through the Treasurer, to assist cabinet in making decisions that will determine not only the total amount to be provided but also how it will be distributed as between the many purposes that now come within the scope of the Commonwealth Budget.

The broader decisions and some of the details of budgetary policy are made by cabinet. Most of the details, however, are settled between the departments and the Treasury in accordance

64 R. S. Mendelsohn, 'The Allocation of Resources as an Administrative Problem', *Public Administration*, 1958, vol. 17, no. 3.

with the general directions laid down by cabinet. This process gives the Treasury not only an opportunity to carry out its 'watchdog' function in relation to public expenditure—it is expected to be on the look-out for possible savings—but it also affords an opportunity for a comprehensive review of the activities of the departments.

The Treasury's role as a co-ordinator does not, of course, begin and end with the Budget. In its day to day operations the Treasury examines particular proposals which have or may have a financial implication either directly with the department concerned by correspondence and/or discussion or in association with a number of departments or inter-departmental committees. Because so many matters contain financial implications at some point or other, the Treasury is in a unique position to influence in varying degrees the formation of consistent policy objectives over the range of Commonwealth activity.

The predominant role of the Treasury has developed only gradually since federation. During World War I, considerable acrimony was generated as a result of extravagant spending by the armed services. The Secretary of the Treasury, J. R. Collins, made repeated suggestions that the Treasury be given control over departmental paying officers, and that this should apply not only to the armed services but to all departments except the Post Office.[65] He reminded the Treasurer that a similar suggestion had been made after an investigation by Sir Robert Anderson in 1915. In reply to a letter from Pearce, the Minister for Defence, opposing these suggestions and offering an independent inquiry as an alternative, Collins wrote (22 May 1917): 'It cannot be admitted that a proposal, emanating from the Treasury, for the improvement of Departmental accounting, should be subject to independent inquiry . . . there is no higher authority, in matters of Government accounting, than the Treasury itself.'

The position of the Treasury was gradually strengthened, over a period, by amendments to the Audit Act and by regulations made under it. The steady growth of Commonwealth financial supremacy over the states, capped by the introduction of uniform income taxation in 1942, was perhaps the decisive factor, and the assumption of general responsibility by the Commonwealth for the economic welfare of Australia added a new and important dimension to its functions. In 1943, a special branch of the Treasury dealing with general financial and economic policy was established, and under the tender care of J. B. Chifley, first as

[65] *C.P.* 103, ser. 11 (c-a).

Treasurer and then as Prime Minister-cum-Treasurer, the pre-dominance of the Treasury in formulating economic and fiscal policy became increasingly marked.

The pre-eminent position of the Treasury is, in part, a function of the personnel structure of the Commonwealth public service. In the absence of a recognized 'administrative class' or its equivalent, competition between departments for the limited supply of able men is all the keener, and in this contest the Treasury is at a considerable advantage. It is also strengthened by the fact that, in contrast with the states, the public corporations set up by the Commonwealth have no independent borrowing powers and are correspondingly dependent for their finances on the Treasury.

The influence of the Treasury throughout the whole field of policy-making has, in consequence, gone beyond considerations which are simply financial. An interesting admission on this point was made by the Secretary of the Treasury, Sir Roland Wilson, in 1956. He admitted that:

> There can be a certain amount of difficulty in regard to the Treasury's instructing departments to do something in which it might not have jurisdiction to exercise the power of instruction, but, on the whole, our experience has been that departments can be convinced by logical arguments . . . I have not come across any cases where a department has said 'what has this to do with the Treasury?' In the rare case where that might happen, there is other machinery which could be followed.[66]

Although in the Commonwealth, as in the states, the control of establishments is in the hands of the Public Service Board, the predominant role of the Treasury has enabled it to exercise rather more influence than would theoretically be the case. Complaints are sometimes heard that Treasury officials make a second review of departmental personnel requirements which have been already vetted by the Public Service Board. Crawford speaks of 'the joyous struggles of a Permanent Head in organization, management and staffing matters which nowadays seem to involve him with Treasury hardly less than with the Public Service Board'.[67]

The exercise of the Treasury's influence is not, of course, without considerable resistance from the spending departments. Treasury attempts to impose conditions on expenditure will be resisted as a challenge to ministerial (and hence departmental) responsibility. One curious result appears in repeated requests for supplementary appropriations, noted by the Public Accounts Committee.

[66] *25th Report*, Public Accounts Committee, 1956, Minutes of Evidence, p.10.   [67] Crawford, loc. cit.

It was our impression that on some occasions a Department was instructed by the Treasury to reduce its expenditure on all or certain of its items; that the Department complied by submitting reduced estimates of expenditure; but nevertheless spent the amount originally sought. It was even suggested to us that, because a Department's Estimates had been 'cut', they were no longer the Estimates of the Department and therefore no longer the responsibility of that Department. Therefore, the applications for Supplementary Estimates implied no error in estimating by the Department: they simply vindicated the accuracy of their original estimate.[68]

Such incidents may be regarded as ripples on the surface; there is no doubt that the current has flowed continuously for a long time in the direction of greater and more effective influence by the Treasury throughout the whole governmental structure.

[68] *28th Report,* Public Accounts Committee, 1957, p.6.

23

CONCLUSION

THE DEVELOPMENT of cabinet government in Australia illustrates the tension between a constitutional structure, elaborated in one political system, and the expectations engendered by a rather different political system. The ability of the cabinet institution to survive under these circumstances has been due to the relative absence of acute social tensions. In the process of accommodation to a different context, there have evolved certain norms of behaviour and certain institutional devices that provide the framework within which any Australian cabinet must operate. It is these that constitute the novel and distinctive features of cabinet government in Australia; as far as the processes of political and administrative control are concerned, Australian governments have largely been content to go on borrowing from Britain. The nature of these norms and devices and the manner of their origin has, it is hoped, been made clear in the preceding chapters. It was argued in the preface that such an investigation made it necessary to study the federal and state levels of government as related parts of a single system, and this contention may now perhaps be regarded as valid.

In chapter 11, emphasis was laid on the importance of placing the frequent crises at the parliamentary and cabinet level in their proper perspective against the great stability and continuity of policy that has characterized Australian government in this century. Notable contributions to this stability have been made by the fact that decisions about the distribution of the national income are, to a large extent, the province of decisions by semi-judicial arbitration tribunals, and by the very considerable independence of the large public utilities that manage the policies of 'development' that are the central concern of all Australian governments. (Readers of J. D. B. Miller's *Australian Government and Politics* will recall Professor Miller's persuasive exposition of this point.) In many cases, the recurrent crises described in this book had little to do with policy. In Victoria, for example, the series of explosions that occurred periodically from 1913 to 1952 were mostly concerned with electoral reform, and in New South Wales the repeated struggles within the Labour movement were, as often as not, fights for the leadership. Only on rare occasions, as in the depression years, or in Queensland in the early 1920s, or the conscription schism of 1916, have substantial issues of policy been involved. The general tendency in the present century, in Australia as elsewhere, has been the steady extension of governmental action into fields of economic and social policy, and specific extensions can be credited to all parties. Only occasionally has it occurred that the Labour Party, which is naturally the most ready to use governmental action for social purposes, exercises this propensity in a spectacular way, as with the Curtin and Chifley administrations.

In state politics, the unceasing trend towards dependence on the Commonwealth accentuates this situation, and election platforms reflect this in terms of promises to administer existing policies better rather than to introduce alternative ones. Moreover, though the independent power of the states has shrunk, their administrative apparatus has continued to grow, and problems of coordination and control have more and more become the chief preoccupation of a state cabinet.

'Stability' in state government during the past generation has too often meant one-party rule and one-man rule. Whether it also means that the quality of government has declined is an inherently unanswerable question, requiring as it does comparisons with the past that are intrinsically unreliable. As the saying goes, things aren't what they used to be—but then, they never were. Nevertheless, certain clearly adverse consequences of one-party rule are apparent in the Australian states as they are, for instance, in the Canadian provinces. One is the decay of effective opposition, and with it the failure to recruit—nay, to be positively afraid of— vigorous and effective leadership. The recent history of the Liberal opposition in New South Wales, or of the A.L.P. opposition in South Australia, are striking instances. The effeteness of the constitutional opposition, matched by the decline of internal criticism within the government party, encourages the growth of a legend of the papal infallibility of the Premier. The danger that the Premier himself may come to believe in the legend is suggested by the petulance of reactions to criticism of government acts. The Queensland Premier, Mr Gair, found it impertinent that the academic community should oppose legislation interfering with the appointments system of the University of Queensland. Sir Thomas Playford, in South Australia, was convinced that Press and public attacks on the conduct of a Royal Commission into the Stuart murder trial were malicious and subversive. The Premier of Victoria, Mr Henry Bolte, was outraged by criticisms of his Minister for Transport, Sir Arthur Warner.

Not only do one-party states become pocket boroughs, but the excessive security of the government tends to remove the feeling of urgency required to make policy on such complex and difficult questions as urban planning, where the record of state governments in Australia is even more abysmal than that of their overseas counterparts. All in all, the average state cabinet has become little more than a moderately capable, moderately honest, and moderately unpopular greater municipal council.

The position of the Commonwealth government is influenced not only by its role in making decisions that will determine the course of state government, but also by the changes in Australia's internal economy and in its international position, especially in relation to Britain. On the one hand, the need for long-term economic policies leads to a situation where the rank-and-file, or even the extra-parliamentary machine, of the party in power, finds it difficult to contest effectively the decisions reached by the government on the advice of its officials and experts. The result is to strengthen the cabinet as against the party, and within cabinet, to strengthen the predominance of the Prime Minister. This was already evident during J. B. Chifley's term as Prime Minister, but under his successor R. G. Menzies it became far more pronounced, especially because of the longevity of the Menzies government. The adverse effects of this long term of office have been similar to those already noted in the states. The Labour Opposition has failed to exploit the most remarkable failures of both policy and administration, a task performed much more effectively on occasions by the Press. Some ministers have become so closely identified with detailed departmental administration that it is not always clear whether they are speaking as the political or the permanent heads of their departments. Above all, the predominance of the Prime Minister has become so marked that the ministry often appears as a one-man show, where the conventions of cabinet responsibility are replaced by the effective responsibility of ministers to the Prime Minister alone. Complaints about such a situation are, of course, familiar in other countries, but in Australia, whose political traditions have pointed so sharply in the other direction, they still have a certain charm of novelty.

A large part of the relative simplicity of Australian politics in the past has been due to the role of Britain in Australian affairs, especially in the three fields of defence, foreign policy, and international economic relations. In each of these spheres there has, since the war, been a steady advance in awareness that the interests of Britain and Australia do not completely coincide. Mr Curtin's now famous speech of December 1941 ('no pangs') may perhaps indicate a watershed, although its roots are to be found in the history of the 1930s. In defence and foreign affairs the status of Australia will never be other than that of a small power, but the growing problem of its relationship with its Asian neighbours adds a special dimension to the concerns of the Commonwealth government. In international trade and finance, reliance on Britain is rapidly ceasing to be a substitute for properly conceived policies. Moreover, these are all areas where the political parties are not notably effective in formulating such policies. The net result will be the same as that of the increased responsibility for internal economic policy.

All countries today find themselves in a situation where the institutions and traditions of the past are creaking loudly under the strain of new and intractable difficulties. In Australia, a long-established tradition of enforcing the responsibility of governments and ministers to their party must adjust itself to the palpably greater strength of the government. Whether it can survive in the process remains to be seen.

BIBLIOGRAPHY

1. OFFICIAL DOCUMENTS

Command Papers
Report of the War Cabinet for 1918, 325, 1919.
Imperial Conference, Summary of Proceedings, 2768, 1926.
Imperial Conference, Summary of Proceedings, 3717, 1930.
The Central Organization for Defence, 6923, 1946.
Commonwealth Joint Parliamentary Committee of Public Accounts, *25th, 28th* and *29th Reports.*
Commonwealth Parliamentary Debates, vols. 1-221, and 2 Eliz. II, H. of R., vols. 1-21.
Commonwealth Parliamentary Handbook, 1953, 1957, 1959.
Commonwealth Year Book, 1908-60.
Documents Relating to the Simultaneous Dissolution of the Senate and the House of Representatives on 19/3/51, Canberra, 1956.
Law Reports
R. v. *Davenport* (1874), 4 Q.S.R. 99.
Davenport v. *Reg.* (1877), 3 L.R.A.C. 115.
Toy v. *Musgrove* (1888), 14 V.L.R. 349.
Commonwealth Law Reports, vols. 1-65.
Commercial Cable Co. v. *Governor of Newfoundland* (1916), 2 L.R.A.C. 616
Mackay v. *Attorney-General for British Columbia* (1920), 1 L.R.A.C. 457.
Attorney-General v. *de Keyser's Royal Hotel* (1920), 1 L.R.A.C. 508.
Attorney-General v. *Wilts United Dairies* (1920), 91 L.J.K.B. 897.
Hogan v. *Cameron* (1934), V.L.R. 88.
New South Wales Parliamentary Record, 1935.
Official Record of the Proceedings and Debates of the National Australasian Convention, Sydney, 1891.
Proceedings of the Australasian Federal Convention, 1897-98.
Report of the Royal Commission on the Civil Service of Victoria. Melbourne, 1859.
Report of the Royal Commission on Postal Services. Melbourne, 1910.
Report of the Royal Commission on the Public Service of Victoria. Melbourne, 1916.

Report of the Royal Commission on Navy and Defence Adminis-
tration. Melbourne, 1917-18.
Report of the Royal Commission on the Victorian Public Service.
Melbourne, 1927.
Report of the Royal Commission on Greyhound Racing and Fruit
Machines, *P.P.* (N.S.W.), 2nd Session, 1932.
Report of the Royal Commission regarding the contract for the
erection of additions to the General Post Office, Sydney. Can-
berra, 1939.
Report of the Committee of Enquiry into the Salaries and Allow-
ances of Members of the National Parliament. Canberra, 1952.

2. PERIODICALS

Australian Worker (Sydney)
Australian Quarterly (Sydney)
Australian National Review (monthly, Sydney, 1913-42; from
1932-42, called the United Australia Review)
Australian Journal of Politics and History (Brisbane)
Australian Magazine (monthly, 1901-11)
Bulletin (Sydney)
Current Notes (Dept of External Affairs, Canberra)
Forum (fortnightly, Sydney, 1922-4)
Historical Studies of Australia and New Zealand (Melbourne)
Nation (Sydney)
Public Administration (Sydney)
Public Administration (London)
Round Table (London)
Stead's Review (Melbourne, monthly; 1892-1934; also called
Review of Reviews, Australasian edition)
Voice (monthly, Sydney, 1951-6)

3. UNPUBLISHED THESES AND PAPERS

Bryan, H., 'The Political Career of J. M. Macrossan'. M.A.,
Queensland, 1954.
Higgins, E. M., 'The Queensland Labor Governments, 1915-
1929'. M.A., Melbourne, 1954.
McKnight, A. D., 'The Role of the Public Servant in a Service
Department'. Lecture given to the Royal Institute of Public
Administration, Canberra, 1956.
Martin, A. W., 'Political Developments in N.S.W., 1894-96'.
M.A., Sydney, 1953.
Morrison, A. A., 'The Abandonment of Bicameralism in Queens-
land'. Section E, ANZAAS, 1951.

Rawson, D. W., 'The Organization of the Australian Labor Party 1916-1941'. Ph.D., Melbourne, 1954.

Rayner, S. A., 'The Evolution of the Queensland Labor Party to 1907'. M.A., Queensland, 1947.

Reid, R. L., 'South Australia and the First Decade of Federation'. M.A., Adelaide, 1954.

Robertson, J. H., 'The Scaddan Government and the Conscription Crisis 1911-1917'. M.A., Western Australia, 1958.

Sissons, D. C. S., 'Australian Attitudes to Japan and Defence 1890-1923'. M.A., Melbourne, 1956.

4. ARTICLES

Anonymous, 'The Prerogative of Dissolution', *Round Table,* vol. 20, no. 1, 1929.

—— 'The Governor-Generalship', *Stead's Review,* vol. 67, no. 6, 1930.

—— 'An Australian Governor-General', *Round Table,* vol. 21, no. 2, 1931.

—— 'The Australian Diplomatic Service', *Current Notes,* vol. 22, no. 5, 1951.

Alexander, F., 'The Governor-General and Dissolutions', *Australian Quarterly,* no. 7, 1930.

—— 'The State Governor and his Powers', *Australian Quarterly,* no. 10, 1931.

Barents, J., 'The Dutch Cabinet System', *Public Administration* (London), vol. 30, no. 1, 1952.

Bonnor, Jean, 'The Four Labor Cabinets', *Sociological Review,* vol. 6, no. 1, 1958.

Casey, R. G., 'The Conduct of Australian Foreign Policy', *Current Notes,* vol. 23, no. 9, 1952.

Canberra Research Group, 'Commonwealth Policy Co-ordination', *Public Administration,* vol. 14, no. 4, 1955.

Crawford, J. G., 'The Role of the Permanent Head', *Public Administration,* vol. 13, no. 4, 1954.

Edwards, J. E., 'The Double Dissolution as a Political Weapon', *Parliamentary Affairs,* vol. 4, no. 1, 1950.

Eggleston, F. W., 'Australian Politics', *Stead's Review,* vol. 66, no. 10, 1929.

Ellis, U. R., 'History of the Country Party', *New South Wales Countryman,* 1948-1955.

Encel, S., 'Political Novels in Australia', *Historical Studies,* no. 27, 1956.

—— 'Cabinet Machinery in Australia', *Public Administration,* vol. 15, no. 2, 1956.

—— 'The Concept of the State in Australian Politics', *Australian Journal of Politics and History,* vol. 5, no. 1, 1960.

—— 'The Political Elite in Australia', *Political Studies,* vol. 9, no. 1, 1961.

—— *et al.,* 'Papers on Commonwealth Machinery of Government', *Public Administration,* vol. 17, no. 4, 1958.

Evatt, H. V., 'The Discretionary Authority of Dominion Governors', *Canadian Bar Review,* vol. 18, no. 1, 1940.

Franck, Thomas, 'The Governor-General and the Head of State Functions', *Canadian Bar Review,* vol. 32, no. 3, 1954.

Graham, B. D., 'Finance Committees in Australian Non-Labour Politics 1910-30', *Australian Journal of Politics and History,* vol. 6, no. 1, 1960.

Guttsman, W. L., 'The Changing Social Structure of the British Political Elite', *British Journal of Sociology,* vol. 2, no. 2, 1951.

Hamilton, Celia, 'Catholic Interests and the Labor Party', *Historical Studies,* vol. 9, no. 33, 1959.

Holman, W. A., 'My Political Life', *Bulletin,* 1934-5.

—— 'The Rise and Fall of the Federal Ministries', *Red Funnel,* 1905-6.

Jenks, E., 'The Imperial Conference and the Constitution', *Cambridge Law Journal,* vol. 3, no. 1, 1927.

McHenry, D. E., 'The Origins of Caucus Selection of Cabinet', *Historical Studies,* vol. 7, no. 25, 1955.

—— 'Caucus over Cabinet', *University Studies in History and Economics,* Perth, 1955.

McKirdy, K. A., 'The Federalization of the Australian Cabinet 1901-1939', *Canadian Journal of Economics and Political Science,* vol. 23, no. 2, 1957.

Mallory, J. R., 'The Appointment of the Governor-General', *Canadian Journal of Economics and Political Science,* vol. 26, no. 1, 1960.

Mendelsohn, R. S., 'The Allocation of Resources as an Administrative Problem', *Public Administration,* vol. 17, no. 3, 1958.

Miller, J. D. B., 'The Bretton Woods Controversy', *Australian Outlook,* vol. 1, no. 3, 1947.

—— 'David Syme and Elective Ministries', *Historical Studies,* vol. 6, no. 21, 1953.

—— 'Party Discipline in Australia', *Political Science,* vol. 5, nos. 1-2, 1953.

—— 'Aspects of the Party System in Australia', *Parliamentary Affairs,* vol. 6, no. 4, 1953.

Molesworth, B. H., 'The Queensland Bureau of Industry', *Economic Record,* vol. 7, 1931; vol. 9, 1933.

Penny, K., 'The Origins of the Prime Minister's Department', *Public Administration,* vol. 15, no. 3, 1956.

Pitt, H. A., 'Some Aspects of the System of Public Finance in Victoria', *Papers and Proceedings* of the Victorian Regional Group, Institute of Public Administration, vol. 1, no. 5, 1934.

Sawer, G., 'Councils, Ministers, and Cabinets in Australia', *Public Law,* no. 1, 1956.

5. BOOKS AND PAMPHLETS

Attlee, C. R., *As It Happened.* London, 1954.

Bagehot, Walter, *The English Constitution.* World's Classics ed.

Baker, Sir Richard, *The Executive in a Federation.* Adelaide, 1897.

Bell, K. N., and Morrell, W. P., *Select Documents on British Colonial Policy 1830-60.* Oxford, 1928.

Bernays, C. A., *Queensland Politics During 60 Years.* Brisbane, 1919.

—— *Queensland—Our Seventh Political Decade.* Sydney, 1931.

Black, George, *A History of the N.S.W. Political Labor Party.* Sydney, 1927.

Blacket, J., *History of South Australia.* 2nd ed., Adelaide, 1911.

Brady, Alexander, *Democracy in the Dominions.* 2nd ed., Toronto, 1952.

Buchanan, Alfred, *The Real Australia.* London, 1907.

Butlin, S. J., *War Economy 1939-42* (Australia in the war of 1939-45, series 4, vol. 3). Canberra, 1957.

Cambridge History of the British Empire, vol. 7, pt 1—Australia. Cambridge, 1933.

Campbell, W. J., *Australian State Public Finance.* Sydney, 1954.

Carboch, D., and Wildavsky, A., *Studies in Australian Politics.* Melbourne, 1958.

Childe, V. G., *How Labor Governs.* London, 1923.

Chisholm, A. H. (ed.), *The Australian Encyclopaedia* (10 vols.), Sydney, 1958.

Churchill, Winston S., *History of the Second World War,* vol. 4. London, 1951.

Coghlan, T. A., *The Seven Colonies of Australasia.* Sydney, 1901.

—— *Labor and Industry in Australia.* Sydney, 1918.

Cramp, K. R., *State and Federal Constitutions of Australia*. Sydney, 1913.

Crisp, L. F., *The Parliamentary Government of the Commonwealth of Australia*. 2nd ed. London, 1954.

—— *The Australian Federal Labor Party, 1901-1951*. London, 1955.

—— and Bennett, S. P., *A.L.P. Federal Personnel 1901-1954*. Canberra, 1954 (processed).

Davies, A. F., 'Victorian Government and Politics' in G. W. Leeper (ed.), *Introducing Victoria*. Melbourne, 1955.

—— *Australian Democracy*. Melbourne, 1958.

Davis, S. R. (ed.), *The Government of the Australian States*. Melbourne, 1960.

Dawson, R. M., *The Government of Canada*. 2nd ed. Toronto, 1949.

Denning, Warren, *Caucus Crisis*. Sydney, 1937.

Duffy, C. Gavan, *My Life in Two Hemispheres*. London, 1898.

Duncan, W. G. K. (ed.), *Trends in Australian Politics*. Sydney, 1935.

Eggleston, Sir Frederic, *Reflections of an Australian Liberal*. Melbourne, 1953.

—— *State Socialism in Victoria*. London, 1932.

Ellis, U. R., *The Country Party*. Sydney, 1958.

Evatt, H. V., *The King and His Dominion Governors*. Oxford, 1935.

—— *Australian Labor Leader*. Sydney, 1940.

Fairfax, Warwick, *et al.*, *Men, Parties, and Politics*. Sydney, 1943.

Forsey, E. A., *The Royal Power of Dissolution in the British Commonwealth*. Toronto, 1943.

Fowler, J. M., *Statesman or Mountebank: An Australian Study*. Melbourne, 1919.

Fry, T. P., *The Crown, Cabinets and Parliaments in Australia*. Brisbane, 1946 (processed).

Garran, R. R., *The Coming Commonwealth*. An Australian Handbook of Federal Government. Sydney, 1897.

Green, F. C. (ed.), *A Century of Responsible Government*. Hobart, 1956.

Griffith, Sir Samuel, *Notes on Australian Federation*. Brisbane, 1896.

Groom, Lady, *et al.*, *Nation Building in Australia*. Sydney, 1941.

Hall, H. L., *Australia and England*. London, 1934.

Hancock, W. K., *Australia*. London, 1929.

—— *Politics in Pitcairn*. London, 1947.

Hankey, Lord, *Diplomacy by Conference*. London, 1946.

Harvey, H. J., *Consultation and Co-operation in the Commonwealth*. London, 1952.

Hasluck, Paul, *The Government and the People 1939-41*. (Australia in the War of 1939-45, series 4, vol. 1.) Canberra, 1953.

Hetherington, John, *Blamey*. Melbourne, 1954.

Hughes, W. M., *The Splendid Adventure*. London, 1929.

Jauncey, L. C., *Australia's Government Bank*. London, 1933.

—— *The Story of Conscription in Australia*. London, 1935.

Jenks, Edward, *The Government of Victoria*. London, 1891.

Jennings, W. Ivor, *Cabinet Government*. 3rd ed. Cambridge, 1959.

Jose, A. W., *Australia—Human and Economic*. London, 1932.

—— and Carter, H. J. (eds.), *The Australian Encyclopaedia* (2 vols). Sydney, 1927.

Keith, A. B., *Responsible Government in the Dominions*. 2nd ed. Oxford, 1928.

Knaplund, Paul, *James Stephen and the British Colonial System 1813-1847*. Wisconsin, 1953.

La Nauze, J. A., *The Hopetoun Blunder*. Melbourne, 1957.

Lane-Poole, S. (ed.), *Thirty Years of Colonial Government*. London, 1889.

Lang, J. T., *I Remember*. Sydney, 1956.

Larcombe, J., *Notes on the Political History of the Labor Movement in Queensland*. Brisbane, 1934.

Laski, H. J., *Parliamentary Government in England*. London, 1938.

McCarthy, Dudley, *South-West Pacific Area, First Year* (Australia in the War of 1939-45, series 1, vol. 5). Canberra, 1959.

McLachlan, A. J., *An F.A.Q. Australian*. Melbourne, 1948.

Maitland, F. W., *The Constitutional History of England*. New ed. Cambridge, 1946.

Marshall, A. J., *Australia Limited*. Sydney, 1942.

Matthews, D. R., *The Social Background of Political Decision-Makers*. New York, 1954.

Métin, Albert, *Le socialisme sans doctrines*. Paris, 1901.

Miller, J. D. B., *Australian Government and Politics*. London, 1955.

Moore, W. Harrison, *The Constitution of the Commonwealth of Australia*. 2nd ed. Melbourne, 1910.

—— 'Political Systems of Australia', in Meredith Atkinson (ed.), *Australia—Economic and Political Studies*. Melbourne, 1920.

Morris, E. E., *Memoir of George Higinbotham*. Melbourne, 1895.

Murdoch, Walter, *Alfred Deakin—A Sketch.* London, 1923.

Nicolson, Harold, *King George V.* London, 1952.

Overacker, Louise, *The Australian Party System.* New Haven, 1952.

Parkes, Sir Henry, *Fifty Years in the Making of Australian History.* London, 1892.

Perry, H. C., *Memoirs of Sir Robert Philp.* Brisbane, 1923.

Piddington, A. B., *Popular Government and Federation.* Sydney, 1898.

—— *Worshipful Masters.* Sydney, 1929.

Pratt, Ambrose, *David Syme.* London, 1908.

Quick, John, and Garran, Robert R., *The Annotated Constitution of the Australian Commonwealth.* Sydney, 1901.

Reeves, W. P., *State Experiments in Australia and New Zealand.* London, 1901.

Reid, Sir George, *My Reminiscences.* London, 1918.

Sawer, G., *Australian Federal Politics and Law 1901-1929.* Melbourne, 1956.

Scott, Ernest, *Australia During the War* (Australia in the War of 1914-18, vol. 11). Sydney, 1938.

Shann, E. O., and Copland, D. B., *The Crisis in Australian Finance.* Sydney, 1931.

Siegfried, André, *Democracy in New Zealand.* London, 1906.

Sladen, Douglas, *From Boundary Rider to Prime Minister.* London, 1916.

Smith, A. N., *Thirty Years.* Melbourne, 1933.

Socialism. Official Report of a Public Debate in the Centenary Hall, Sydney, between Rt Hon. G. H. Reid and Mr W. A. Holman. Sydney, 1906.

Spann, R. N. (ed.), *Public Administration in Australia.* Sydney, 1959.

Spence, W. G., *Australia's Awakening.* Sydney, 1909.

Sugden, E. H., and Eggleston, F. W., *George Swinburne.* Sydney, 1931.

Sweetman, E., *Australian Constitutional Development.* Melbourne. 1925.

Trotter, W. F., *The Government of Greater Britain.* Temple Primer Series. London, n.d.

Truman, T. C., *Catholic Action and Politics.* Melbourne, 1959.

Turner, H. G., *A History of the Colony of Victoria.* London, 1904.

——*The First Decade of the Australian Commonwealth,* Melbourne, 1911.

University of Melbourne, Department of Political Science, *The Government of Victoria*. Melbourne, 1958.

Walker, E. R., *The Australian Economy in War and Reconstruction*. New York, 1947.

Walker, H. de R., *Australasian Democracy*. London, 1897.

Wheare, K. C., *The Statute of Westminster and Dominion Status*. 4th ed., Oxford, 1949.

Whitington, Don, *The House Will Divide*. Melbourne, 1954.

Wigmore, Lionel, *The Japanese Thrust* (Australia in the War of 1939-45, series 1, vol. 4). Canberra, 1958.

Wise, B. R., *The Commonwealth of Australia*. 2nd ed. London, 1913.

Wynes, W. A., *Legislative, Executive and Judicial Powers in Australia*. 2nd ed. Sydney, 1956.

INDEX